The Sounds of English Around the World

Most introductions to English phonetics and phonology focus primarily on British or American English, which fails to account for the rich diversity of English varieties globally. This book addresses this gap, providing an overview of English phonetics and phonology through an exploration of the sounds of English around the world, including older varieties of English such as American, Canadian, British, and Australian Englishes, as well as new varieties of English such as Indian, Singapore, Hong Kong, and Kenyan English. It focuses on diversity in vowels and consonants, allophonic variation, and stress and intonation patterns across regional, ethnic, and social varieties of English in North America, the Caribbean, Asia, Africa, Europe, and Oceania. Listening exercises are incorporated throughout to facilitate the understanding of different concepts, and the book also has an accompanying website with a wide range of speech samples, allowing readers to hear the phonetics of the varieties under discussion.

Jette G. Hansen Edwards is Professor of Applied English Linguistics at The Chinese University of Hong Kong. She has published more than fifty articles, book chapters, and books, primarily in the area of the phonetics and phonology of World Englishes.

The Sounds of English Around the World

An Introduction to Phonetics and Phonology

Jette G. Hansen Edwards
The Chinese University of Hong Kong

CAMBRIDGE
UNIVERSITY PRESS

Shaftesbury Road, Cambridge CB2 8EA, United Kingdom

One Liberty Plaza, 20th Floor, New York, NY 10006, USA

477 Williamstown Road, Port Melbourne, VIC 3207, Australia

314–321, 3rd Floor, Plot 3, Splendor Forum, Jasola District Centre,
New Delhi – 110025, India

103 Penang Road, #05–06/07, Visioncrest Commercial, Singapore 238467

Cambridge University Press is part of Cambridge University Press & Assessment,
a department of the University of Cambridge.

We share the University's mission to contribute to society through the pursuit of
education, learning, and research at the highest international levels of excellence.

www.cambridge.org
Information on this title: www.cambridge.org/9781108841665

DOI: 10.1017/9781108894562

First published 2023

Printed in the United Kingdom by TJ Books Limited, Padstow Cornwall

Library of Congress Cataloging-in-Publication Data
Names: Edwards, Jette G. Hansen, author.
Title: The sounds of English around the world : an introduction to
    phonetics and phonology / Jette G. Hansen Edwards.
Description: Cambridge, United Kingdom ; New York, NY : Cambridge
    University Press, 2023.
Identifiers: LCCN 2023016924 | ISBN 9781108841665 (hardback) | ISBN
    9781108795029 (paperback) | ISBN 9781108894562 (ebook)
Subjects: LCSH: English language – Phonology. | English language – Phonetics.
    | English language – Variation.
Classification: LCC PE1133 .E38 2023 | DDC 421/.58–dc23/eng/20230628
LC record available at https://lccn.loc.gov/2023016924

ISBN 978-1-108-84166-5 Hardback
ISBN 978-1-108-79502-9 Paperback

Additional resources for this publication at www.cambridge.org/SoundsofEnglish

This book is dedicated to my husband, Scott, and my children, Marie and Jasper

Contents

Figures

Tables

Tasks

Preface

The purpose of this book and the accompanying website is to introduce students to the phonetics and phonology of English, with 'English' used as an umbrella term to refer to different ethnic, social, and regional varieties of English spoken around the world. It aims to provide students with an expansive and inclusive discussion of the sounds of English by presenting the phonetic and phonological features of a range of Englishes, including regional, ethnic, and social varieties of American, British, Irish, Australian, and New Zealand Englishes; African Englishes, including Kenyan, South African, Nigerian, and Zimbabwean Englishes; and Asian Englishes, including Singapore, Malaysian, Hong Kong, Indian, Pakistani, and Philippine Englishes, among others.

The book and website are necessarily expansive in the presentation of the phonetics and phonology of different varieties of English. While students are encouraged to read about and listen to a range of Englishes to further their understanding about World Englishes, guidance is given in each chapter to help students navigate the text and the listening tasks to focus on the varieties of English that are of interest to them.

Audio files for this publication can be found at www.cambridge.org/ SoundsofEnglish.

Acknowledgements

This book would not have been possible without help and inspiration from many wonderful people. Firstly, the thousands of students in Hong Kong that I have been privileged to teach over the past twenty years have been a rich source of inspiration – our discussions about and explorations of English accents, including our own, have provided the initial impetus for this project. Secondly, I am grateful to all the people who have allowed me to record their English accents; thank you for helping to bring alive the diversity and beauty of the sounds of English around the world to the readers of this book. I am also grateful to the members of the wonderful Shek O Book Gang for the insightful readings and discussions we have had over the years; a number of these discussions have inspired parts of this text. And, finally, I am deeply grateful to my family – my husband, Scott, and our children, Marie and Jasper – for their support. Our dinner discussions about language, and accents in particular, not only are entertaining but also highlight the incredible diversity in how English sounds (even within one family!).

Abbreviations

AAVE	African American Vernacular English
AM	Autosegmental Metrical
AmE	American English
Appal AmE	Appalachian American English
AusAborE	Australian Aboriginal English
AusE	Australian English
BrE	British English
BSAE	Black South African English
Calif AmE	California American English
CanE	Canadian English
CaribE	Caribbean Englishes
CCR	Consonant Cluster Reduction
ChiE	Chicano English
ChilE	Chilean English
CR	Cooperative Rise
EAfE	East African Englishes
ELF	English as a Lingua Franca
EMidBrE	East Midlands BrE
FijE	Fiji English
GAmE	General American English
HAR	Height, Advancement, Rounding
HausaE	Hausa English
HKE	Hong Kong English
HRT	High Rising Terminal
IndE	Indian English
IPA	International Phonetic Alphabet
IrE	Irish English
JamE	Jamaican English
KenE	Kenyan English
LonE	London English
MalE	Malaysian English
MāoriE	Māori English
MLE	Multicultural London English
Mod RP	Modern Received Pronunciation

MOP	Maximum Onset Principle
NAE	Native American English
NBrE	Northern British English
NDubE	New Dublin English
NE AmE	New England American English
NepE	Nepalese English
NigE	Nigerian English
NIrE	Northern Irish English
NiuE	Niuean English
NVE	New Varieties of English
NYC AmE	New York City American English
NZE	New Zealand English
OVE	Old Varieties of English
PakE	Pakistani English
PasE	Pasifika English
PCEs	Postcolonial Englishes
PhlE	Philippine English
PIE	Proto-Indo-European
PRE	Puerto Rican English
PVI	Pairwise-Variability Index
Qld AusE	Queensland Australian English
RP	Received Pronunciation; *see also* Mod RP, Trad RP
SA AusE	South Australia Australian English
SAE	South African English
SAfE	Southern African Englishes
SAmE	Southern American English
ScotE	Scottish English
SgE	Singapore English
SLE	Sri Lankan English
SNigE	Southern Nigerian English
SoCal AmE	Southern California American English
SSBE	Standard Southern British English
SSE	Standard Scottish English
SSP	Sonority Sequencing Principle
StAmE	Standard American English
TaiE	Taiwanese English
ToBI	Tone and Break Indices
Trad RP	Traditional Received Pronunciation
UNBE	Urban North British English
VOT	Voice Onset Time
WAfE	West African Englishes

WALS	*World Atlas of Language Structures Online*
WelE	Welsh English
WMidBrE	West Midlands BrE
WSAE	White South African English
ZimE	Zimbabwean English

1 Introduction

TASK 1.1 PRE-READING

Before reading Chapter 1, think about the following questions. You may wish to discuss your answers with your classmates and teacher.

- How do you define the word *accent*?
- What is the difference between a *dialect* and an *accent*?
- Who speaks with an accent?
- Does everyone who speaks English have an accent?
- What non-linguistic information do accents convey about people?

1.1 Introduction to the Chapter

How do you define the word 'accent'? We begin this book by looking at the word **accent** – what it means, and how it relates to other people and ourselves. A common definition of accent is that it refers to a speaker's pronunciation – the way a person *says* particular words. While the terms 'accent' and **dialect** are often used synonymously, 'accent' specifically refers to the **pronunciation** of speech sounds, words, and phrases, whereas dialect refers not only to pronunciation, but also to other linguistic features, including grammar, spelling, and vocabulary. An accent is a part of one's dialect; however, dialect is not *only* one's accent. The term **variety** also refers to other features than pronunciation alone and is often used synonymously with 'dialect' to refer to the different Englishes around the world. In this book, the term 'variety' is used to refer to the English spoken in a country or region, such as Singapore English in Singapore, Nigerian English in Nigeria, and Australian English in Australia. 'Accent' in this book is used to refer to the *pronunciation* of speakers of a given variety of English. Accents are by nature idiosyncratic, however, and therefore may be best interpreted as the types of features – vowel and consonant sounds and stress, intonation, and pitch patterns – that are associated with speakers of a particular variety of English. In this book, we focus primarily on *accent* – how individual speech sounds, words, and phrases are pronounced in varieties of English around the world.

1.2   Understanding and Describing Accents

Who speaks with an accent? Does everyone who speaks English have an accent? Everyone speaks with an accent! Our accents are the result of a range of factors: where we grew up, where we have lived and currently live, the age we learned different languages, other languages spoken, our friendship and peer group networks, our educational background – including educational models, the accents of our teachers and peers at school – among others. Accents are a tapestry of our lives, containing pieces of fabric representing our lived experiences, families, and friendships. They also display our identity – like clothing, hair, jewellery, and make-up, accents can reveal to others how we see ourselves and who we want to be. We reveal social characteristics about ourselves through the way we speak: accents are a powerful mechanism through which we can establish our identity to others and that others use to identify us, particularly in relation to different social groups.

Many different words are used to describe accents – standard vs non-standard; native vs non-native; foreign or second language, or multilingual, are just some of the terms that are used to describe a speaker. These terms can have negative connotations and can imply that one accent is better or more legitimate than another. This leads us to several key tenets of the book:

* *Everyone speaks with an accent.*
* *No accent – or variety of English – is inherently better than another accent or variety.*

As this book will show, there are many different varieties of English around the world, with significant differences in pronunciation, and thus difference in accents, across these Englishes; there are also differences in accents *within* varieties of English – speakers of British English may have a Mancunian accent if they grew up in Manchester, whereas other speakers may have a Southern English accent if they are from the south of England. Similarly, speakers of American English may have different regional or ethnic accents, including Southern American English, California American English, Appalachian American English, and African American Vernacular English. *Every* speaker of English – regardless of where they are from, where they grew up, whether they speak English as their only language or one of multiple languages – has an accent. This accent is based on the variety or mix of varieties of English the person speaks – Australian, Indian, or South African English – as well as the sub-variety the person may speak within that variety of English, for example Southern British or Manchester English within British English. Due to increased globalization and migration, many people may speak a mix of different Englishes and have a mixed English accent, with features from different varieties.

What non-linguistic information do accents convey about people? Accents carry social meaning. They can tell us whether the speaker speaks other languages – for example, is a multilingual speaker of English (this is often called having a foreign or second language accent if English is learned after childhood). They can also tell us where someone is from – which *variety* of English they speak. The variety can be based on a country of origin – a speaker of English from South Africa, for example, speaks a variety of South African English, while a speaker from Australia speaks Australian English – or it can be a region or even a city within a country, as in Edinburgh English, a variety of Scottish English spoken in the city of Edinburgh. Accents may also be able to tell us ethnic group membership, as in African American Vernacular English in the United States.

Aside from telling us where someone is from and possibly our ethnic group affiliation, the way we speak can also impart a range of social information:

- *Whether we speak other languages:* If you identify someone as being from Singapore or Kenya, for example, you might infer that they are likely to speak another language. In the case of Singapore and Kenya, the speaker may be a multilingual speaker of English, with English one of several languages learned in childhood. The Singapore English speaker may also speak one or more of Singapore's other languages – Mandarin Chinese, Cantonese, Hokkien, Tamil, or Malay, among others – while the Kenyan English speaker may also speak Kiswahili, as well as other local languages.
- *Gender:* You will likely be able to ascribe gender to the speaker based on vocal characteristics.
- *Age:* You may also be able to ascribe an age range to the speaker based on vocal characteristics – for example, whether this is a child, a teenager, young adult, middle-aged adult, or older adult.
- *Socio-economic status:* If you are familiar with a speaker's variety of English, and/or features of the speaker's accent, you may be able to ascribe a particular social class to the speaker based on accent – for example, working, middle, or upper class.

TASK 1.2 Listening for Varieties of English

🎧 Listen to the speech samples from fifteen speakers of English and try to answer the following questions for each speaker:

(1) Where is the speaker from?
(2) Which variety of English is the person speaking?
(3) Can you identify unique features for each variety of English?
(4) Can you give any other information about each speaker (for example, gender, approximate age)?

What did you notice or listen for in the speech samples? We may be able to identify the speaker's variety of English based on our experience and/or familiarity with particular varieties. If we are familiar with a given variety, we may be able to identify a speaker by listening for specific vowel and consonant sounds, speech rhythm, and pitch and tone associated with this variety. If you are familiar with Malaysian English, for example, you may easily be able to identify Speaker 4 as being a speaker of Malaysian English. If you are not familiar with this variety, however, it may be more difficult to identify which variety Speaker 4 speaks. We may know there are particular ways in which a Malaysian English speaker pronounces vowels, consonants, words, and phrases; if we hear a speaker exhibit those features, we may very likely be able to identify that speaker as a speaker of Malaysian English. We may also be able to identify the region within a country that a speaker is from if we are familiar with regional variation in different varieties: for example, we may identify Speaker 6 as being from the United States and a speaker of American English; if we are familiar with American English, we may also identify the speaker as a speaker of Midwestern American English, a variety spoken in the Midwestern region of the United States.

In addition to country and region, we may also be able to identify the speaker's gender and age. To identify age, we may rely on rate of speech: Skoog Waller, Eriksson, and Sorqvist (2015) have shown that speech rate decreases across time, meaning that older speakers have a slower rate than younger speakers. This speech cue has been found to be a reliable indicator of age. Usage of pronunciation features may also vary with age in particular varieties of English. In addition, we may assign gender to the speaker based on speech cues; how we ascribe gender is the result of physiological differences in the vocal tracts of men and women, which can result in a higher pitch for women and lower pitch for men, along with other differences (this will be discussed in more detail in subsequent chapters) (Pernet & Belin, 2012).

Let's go back to Task 1.2.

- What did you notice about each speaker's accent?
- Could you accurately identify gender and approximate age?
- Can you give any other information about each speaker based on their accent?
    (1) Speaker 1 is from Wellington, New Zealand. The speaker is a man aged 21–5. His native language is English. He speaks *New Zealand English.*
    (2) Speaker 2 is from Cape Town, South Africa. The speaker is a woman aged 18–20; her native language is English. She also speaks some Afrikaans. She speaks *White South African English.*
    (3) Speaker 3 is from the Aschaffenburg region in Bavaria, Germany. The speaker is a woman aged 21–5 and her native language is German. She speaks *German English.*
    (4) Speaker 4 is from Selangor, Malaysia. The speaker is a woman aged 21–5; her native languages are Malay and English. She also speaks Putonghua (Mandarin Chinese) and Cantonese. She speaks *Malaysian English.*
    (5) Speaker 5 is from Harare, Zimbabwe. The speaker is a woman aged 18–20. Her native languages are English and Shona. She speaks *Zimbabwean English.*
    (6) Speaker 6 is from Wyoming, a state in the Midwestern region of the USA. The speaker is a woman aged 21–5. Her native language is English. She speaks a Midwestern dialect of *American English.*
    (7) Speaker 7 is from Allahabad in Uttar Pradesh, India. The speaker is a man aged 26–30. His native languages are Hindi and English. He speaks *Indian English.*
    (8) Speaker 8 is from Queensland, Australia. The speaker is a woman aged 18–20. She is a native speaker of English. She speaks *Australian English.*
    (9) Speaker 9 is from Anhui, China. The speaker is a man aged 21–5. He is a native speaker of Putonghua. He speaks *China English.*
    (10) Speaker 10 is from Derby, East Midlands, England. The speaker is a woman aged 31–5. She is a native speaker of English. She speaks an East Midlands dialect of *British English.*
    (11) Speaker 11 is from Santiago, Chile. The speaker is a man aged 26–30. His native language is Spanish. He speaks *Chilean English.*

> (12) Speaker 12 is from Seoul, South Korea. The speaker is a man aged 21–5. He is a native speaker of Korean. He speaks *Korean English*.
>
> (13) Speaker 13 is from Hong Kong SAR. The speaker is a woman aged 18–20. She is a native speaker of Cantonese. She speaks *Hong Kong English*.
>
> (14) Speaker 14 is from Bishkek, Kyrgyzstan. The speaker is a man aged 18–20. He is a native speaker of Russian and the Kyrgyz language. He speaks *Kyrgyzstan English*.
>
> (15) Speaker 15 is from Islamabad, Pakistan. The speaker is a man aged 26–30. He is a native speaker of Urdu and Sindhi. He speaks *Pakistani English*.

In addition to country, region, ethnicity, age, and gender, speech cues – and particularly pronunciation features – may also indicate membership in social and peer group networks, socio-economic status and/or educational level, and possibly our profession. This leads to several other key tenets of the book:

- *The social meaning of different accent features varies across contexts.*
- *Accents can change across time.*
- *No linguistic feature is inherently better than another.*

The use of specific accent features may help identify us as a speaker of a particular variety of English. The use of postvocalic /r/ (this is the 'r' sound after the vowel in words such as *car* and *heard*; the term 'postvocalic' means that the 'r' is realized after – or post – the vowel) may indicate that a person is a speaker of a variety of American English, while not having postvocalic /r/ may indicate a speaker of a variety of British English (this will be discussed at length in Chapter 4). Within a particular variety of English, it may also indicate the region the speaker is from: in the US, for example, not having postvocalic /r/ may be one feature that indicates a person is from New England, the Southern US, or New York City. Not having postvocalic /r/ is also a feature of African American Vernacular English, and thus it may be one feature (of many) that may indicate ethnic group membership. Postvocalic /r/ may also indicate socio-economic status and educational background in some contexts, but the status of it varies. In Singapore, for example, not all speakers have postvocalic /r/; it is typically associated with a higher educational background as well as a higher socio-economic status (Tan, 2012). In India, however, not having postvocalic /r/ may be more prestigious to some speakers and associated with higher socio-economic status (Chand, 2010).

As this demonstrates, just as no accent is inherently better than another, no accent feature is better than another. However, social judgements about speakers often result from how our accents (and varieties of English, in general) are interpreted. Just as we use our accent as well as other linguistic and non-linguistic features to create and mark our identity, others use our speech to identify us.

Language is dynamic and changes across time, and our accent may change across our lifetime. This can be a result of moving to different countries and regions, our educational experiences, and peer and social group influences. In my own research on Hong Kong English, I have also found that exposure to mass media – and particularly American mass media – spreads American features of English, including increasing the use of post-vocalic /r/, for example, in contexts where this is less common (Hansen Edwards, 2016a). What we want to sound like – and in which social groups we want to aspire to gain or retain membership – may also impact our accent; in other words, we may be able to change our accent and/or dialect if we perceive that the social meaning of the linguistic features we use are at odds with how we identify ourselves and want to be identified by others. This, of course, requires awareness of the social meaning of different linguistic features as well as the ability to change them. As noted above, some people speak a mix of different varieties of English, particularly if they have moved from one region or country to another during their childhood or adolescence; other people may be multi-dialectal or multi-varietal, moving between two or more dialects (and accents) depending on the social setting and interactants. In my own case, I was a monolingual speaker of Danish until the age of 10, as I was born in Jutland, Denmark. My family immigrated to the state of Wisconsin, in the Midwestern region of the United States, when I was 10; I learned to speak American English with a General American English dialect, meaning that my English does not have any notable regional features. Sadly, most linguistic traces of my Danish childhood have disappeared from my English. Nearly twenty years ago, I moved to Hong Kong SAR, a former British colony where British English still has prestige. As a result of living in this former British colony, and marriage to an Australian, my English has changed. I have picked up British (and Australian) English vocabulary that is more commonly used in Hong Kong: I no longer stand in line, but rather queue; I add fuel to my car, not gas; and a friend is a mate. My pronunciation has shifted slightly too; once in a while, I find myself saying *water* with a mix of American and British sounds. I still speak American English but, through my experience in Hong Kong, I have acquired new pronunciation and vocabulary features, allowing me to change the way I sound (consciously or unconsciously) depending on the social situation and interactants.

TASK 1.3 Listening for English Accents

🎧 Listen to the eleven speakers of English talk about their accents.

(1) Where are they from?
(2) Where have they lived?
(3) Which other languages do they speak?
(4) Which variety of English do they state they speak?
(5) Why do they feel they speak this variety of English?
(6) What has influenced their accents the most?
(7) Have their accents changed?
(8) If so, which factors have influenced these changes?

1.3 Accents and Varieties of English

In this book, the term **varieties of English** is used as an umbrella term for the ways in which English is spoken around the world. While the current book focuses primarily on the *accents* of these Englishes, there are also differences across varieties in other linguistic aspects, including vocabulary, grammar, and discourse. 'Varieties of English' in this book references the pronunciation of English across and within different continents, countries, and regions – the sounds of English around the world. The term **English** is also used as an umbrella term for hundreds of Englishes that are spoken around the world due to social, geographic, sociopolitical, and linguistic factors. Just as there is no one accent, there is no *one* English. As we will discover in Chapter 2, when we learn about the history of the English language, English has never been one language, but rather arose from a mix of different languages, including Germanic, Scandinavian, and Romance languages, among others, and different English accents have always existed as the English language is continually in a state of change.

As an example, 'British English' is a term used for the varieties of English spoken in the United Kingdom, which comprises England, Wales, Northern Ireland, and Scotland. There are many different varieties of British English, including: 'English' English, spoken in England; Welsh English in Wales; and Scottish English in Scotland. Within each of these varieties, in turn, there many different varieties based on regional, ethnic, and social variation. 'English' English, for example, has significant regional variation, with differences between northern and southern varieties, and even between smaller regions and counties, such as Yorkshire English, and cities, including Manchester English. The standard (and most socially prestigious) form of this English is called Standard Southern British English (SSBE), as it is most closely associated with the speech features of southern England. In the past, this variety was called Traditional Received Pronunciation (Trad RP); the term 'BBC English' has also been used, as British newscasters traditionally had this accent, though that is no longer the case. The term 'Modern RP' ('Mod RP') represents a more current RP and is often used interchangeably with SSBE. 'Northern Irish English' is a general term used for varieties of English spoken in Northern Ireland, which includes several sub-varieties based on regional differences: Ulster English, Belfast English, Ulster Scots, and Hiberno English. Similarly, regional differences exist in Scottish English and Welsh English, as well as many other varieties of English around the world, including American English, which comprises a range of Northern, Southern, Midwestern, New England, and Western varieties.

'Varieties of English' also refers to any ethnic group varieties that exist within and across different regions, including both Pasifika and Māori Englishes in New Zealand, and African American Vernacular English, Native American English, and Asian American English in the United States, among others, due to immigration as well as geographic concentration of different ethnic groups in particular regions. Ethnic varieties of English are referred to as **ethnolects** – ethnic dialects. Different dialects – and therefore accents – also exist within ethnolects: as an example, 'Native American English' (also called American Indian English and/or Reservation Accent) is best viewed as an umbrella term for a range of Native American Englishes, due to the many Native American tribes in the United States, including the Cherokee, Lumbee, Lakhota People, Apache, Sioux, and Navajo, and the different languages spoken by these tribes.

1.4 The Purpose of This Book

Why does this book focus on varieties of English? The book and the accompanying website aim to inform you about the diversity in how English is spoken around the world to provide an expansive and inclusive discussion of English phonetics and phonology. The book seeks to broaden your understanding of what English *sounds* like, to demonstrate that English has many different ways of sounding and that this reflects both historical and geographical language influences. The book has been designed to provide you with training in English phonetics and phonology, to expose you to variation in the phonetics and phonologies of varieties of Englishes around the world, and to enable you to acknowledge and represent your own English accents. The book and website also aim to equip you with the tools – phonetic transcription, acoustic analysis, and exposure to different English varieties – to acknowledge, understand, and analyse similarities and differences across Englishes worldwide, and to analyse your own phonological features. Phonetic transcription practice is embedded into the tasks of many of the chapters, with a particular focus on your transcription of your own speech in order to investigate your own pronunciation and to avoid a prescriptive approach to English phonetics and phonology based on American or British English pronunciation norms.

The book draws on current research in English phonetics and phonology to provide a state-of-the art discussion of the sounds of English around the world. In aiming to be inclusive and expansive, the book draws on a wide range of available resources and research; if discussions of some varieties have been omitted or appear brief, it is primarily for two reasons: (1) there are few available resources or research on a given variety; and (2) there is a need to balance representation across different continents and countries where English is spoken.

1.5   The Features of This Book

The book focuses on both English **phonetics** and English **phonology** in varieties of English around the world. 'Phonetics' refers to the individual vowel and consonant sounds of a language – in our case, varieties of English – while 'phonology' refers to how these individual speech sounds pattern in a language, or a variety of English: where each speech sound occurs, in which combination the sounds can occur together, and how the nature of speech sounds may change based on where they occur in a syllable or word. The book has several notable features:

(1) acoustic descriptions of different speech sounds, with accompanying visuals displaying a range of information, including the acoustic characteristics of vowels and consonants, intonation, and pitch in different varieties of English, in order to demonstrate visually the concepts of the book.

(2) a website with speech samples from a wide range of Englishes around the world, including Englishes from Africa, such as Kenyan, Zimbabwean, and South African Englishes; Asia, for example Hong Kong, Singapore, Malaysian, Sri Lankan, Nepalese, Indian, and Pakistani Englishes; North America, including different varieties of American and Canadian English; the Caribbean, including Puerto Rican English; Europe, including several varieties of British English, as well as Irish English; and Oceania, including Australian and New Zealand Englishes. Reference to these speech samples is made in every chapter in the book. While speech samples are available for many of the varieties discussed, not

all varieties are represented. Table 9.1 in Chapter 9 provides a list of various websites that students and teachers can use to supplement the listening tasks in this volume.

(3) exercises to check and expand your understanding of the content discussed in the book. Listening exercises are incorporated into the book in every chapter to facilitate your understanding of different concepts and constructs, and to familiarize you with a range of varieties of English, and the vowel, consonant, stress, pitch, and intonation patterns within and across these varieties. For ease of use, these speech extracts are organized on the website by chapter, rather than variety. All the listening tasks are based on the speech data on the book's web page; they are marked with a headphone icon 🎧. Along with listening exercises, the book also features a range of exercises and discussion questions to help you check and expand your understanding of the content. The answers to some of the questions are in the text of the book. These discussion questions and exercises are marked with a book icon 📖.

(4) the analysis of your own data set; this is detailed below.

Throughout the volume, guidance is given on how to use the book and listening tasks, with particular reference to the detailed discussion of the vowel, consonant, stress, and intonation inventories and variation across varieties of English. This is marked with a text box and the symbol ☞. The book and website are necessarily expansive in the presentation of the phonetics and phonology of different varieties of English; while you are encouraged to read about and listen to a range of Englishes to further your understanding, you may also wish to focus only on the varieties that are of interest to you. These are clearly marked in tables in the text and in the listening tasks on the website.

1.6   Recording Your Own Data Set

You are encouraged to create a data set to analyse your own pronunciation to explore the topics discussed in this book more fully. Your recordings will also be used as the basis of transcription practice in this book. You will be guided in analysing your data in each chapter. Instructions for each recording task are placed at the ends of chapters and are denoted by a microphone icon. Recording the data can be done quickly and easily. The first step is to locate a device to use for the recording – this can be a computer, an iPad, or phone, or any other recording device.

In Appendix A, you will find a series of reading tasks: (1) a word-list task based on Wells' (1982) Lexical Sets, which has been developed to categorize vowels across varieties of English; (2) a word list to elicit different consonant sounds, syllable structures, and stress patterns; (3) sentences to elicit different suprasegmental features. These speech tasks have been designed to elicit pronunciation features discussed in this book; they also correspond to many of the speech samples available for the book on the website. Further instructions on how to record your speech sample for best results are given in Appendix A.

1.7 CHECK YOUR UNDERSTANDING

EXERCISES

(a) What do we mean by the term 'accent'? How is accent different from dialect?
(b) Why are terms like 'British English' or 'American English' best viewed as umbrella terms for a range of different dialects and accents?
(c) Name an example of each type of variety:
    1. a regional variety of English
    2. an ethnic variety of English

DISCUSSION QUESTIONS

(a) Why do some people speak a mixture of different varieties of English and have a mixed accent?
(b) Which variety/ies of English do people in your country speak? Are there regional or ethnic group differences in varieties of English in your country?
(c) What do you think are the main factors impacting how people speak English in your country?

EXPAND YOUR UNDERSTANDING

Go back to Task 1.2.

(a) Why do you think the speakers identify as speakers of a particular variety of English?
(b) How do you think this reflects their identity when speaking English?

ANALYSE YOUR OWN PRONUNCIATION

You will be guided in the analysis of your own English pronunciation to understand more about which variety or varieties you speak and why, in subsequent chapters. Before we commence this analysis, ask yourself the following questions. These are the same questions the speakers were asked in Task 1.2. We will return to these questions in our analysis of your speech data in the following chapters:

(a) Where are you from? What is your home town and country?
(b) Where else have you lived? How long have you lived in each place?
(c) What other languages (other than English) do you speak?
(d) Which variety/ies of English do you speak?
(e) What do you think has had the most influence on the way you speak English?
(f) What are some features of your variety of English that are different from other varieties of English?

2 The History and Spread of English Worldwide

TASK 2.1 PRE-READING

Before you read Chapter 2, think about the following questions. What do you already know about the emergence and spread of the English language? You may wish to compare your answers with your classmates or teacher.

- Where did English come from? Did it originate in England?
- How did it emerge and when?
- How – and why – did it spread to become a global language?
- Why do so many different varieties of English exist?

2.1 Introduction to the Chapter

In this chapter, we will examine the emergence and evolution of the language called English. One of the first questions we will seek to answer is: *Is English 'English'?* In other words, did English originate in the geographic area known today as England? To answer this question, we journey back to the roots of English, beginning with Indo-European. We then begin the story of English, with the emergence of Old English after 449 CE, after which we move into the era of Middle English, focusing on the impact of Anglo-Norman French on Middle English. The emergence of English literature, and particularly the work of Chaucer, during this period is also discussed. We will examine how British international trade and colonization of the Americas, Australia, and New Zealand, as well as parts of Asia, the Caribbean, and Africa, changed and spread the English language worldwide. The chapter concludes with an overview of the terminology used to describe the varieties of English that will be examined in this volume. The final section of the chapter has a series of exercises and tasks to guide you through a revision of the contents of the chapter.

2.2   Pre-English: Indo-European and the Germanic Language Family

Where did English come from? A common assumption is that English is 'English' – a language that originated in the geographical area known as England. In fact, the root language of what we know today as English is not native to England, but was brought to England through migration. The roots of English are Germanic, as English emerged from the West Germanic part of the Indo-European language family.

What do we mean by language family? And what is Indo-European? All known languages, including languages spoken today and languages that are now extinct, are categorized into language families. There are approximately 7,100 languages spoken around the world today with all of these languages categorized into one of approximately 142 different language families on the basis of a common ancestor language (Eberhard, Simons, & Fennig, 2020). Each of these 142 language families comprises minimally 1 language, as in the case of the Basque language family, which only consists of Basque, a language of France and Spain; the largest language family in the world is the Niger–Congo language family, which comprises 1,526 languages (Eberhard, Simons, & Fennig, 2020).

English belongs to the Indo-European language family, which consists of 444 languages, making it one of the largest language families in the world. Figure 2.1 shows an overview of the various branches and some of the languages of the Indo-European language family; some Indo-European languages spoken in the past, such as Gothic in the East Germanic branch, are now extinct. The term 'Indo-European' is used to describe a group of people living during the Neolithic age, from around 5000 BCE; the Indo-European language is believed to have emerged after 5000 BCE. The Indo-Europeans lived in Central Asia and Eastern Europe, spreading out across Europe and Asia between 3500 BCE and 2500 BCE, likely in search of food and land as

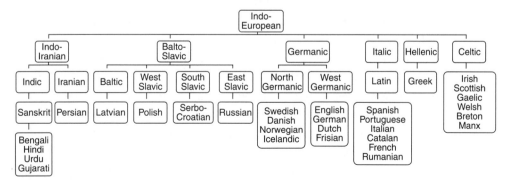

Figure 2.1 The Indo-European language family

they evolved from having a primarily hunter-gatherer lifestyle to a farming lifestyle. As the Indo-Europeans settled across Europe and Asia, new languages emerged as local norms arose. As a result, by around 1000 BCE, a number of different languages had emerged from Indo-European, including Germanic, Italic, Balto-Slavic, and Celtic languages, as seen in Figure 2.1. Other languages, now extinct, emerged as well, including Anatolian, which was believed to be spoken in areas that are now known as Turkey and Syria.

How do linguists know that Indo-European is the common ancestor language? The Indo-European family tree was first proposed by the linguist August Schleicher 150 years ago, and has since been developed and revised based on reconstruction of linguistic features, and particularly vocabulary and phonology, through a comparison of the languages that have evolved from Indo-European. This approach not only allows linguists to classify languages in various subbranches of the Indo-European and other language families, but also to reconstruct the ancestor language(s), including that of Indo-European, called Proto-Indo-European (PIE), as well as Proto-Germanic.

As Figure 2.1 shows, the Indo-European language family comprises some of the most widely spoken languages in the world today, including English, Spanish, and Hindi. Not surprisingly, the Indo-European language family has the largest number of speakers of all the language families, with 3.26 billion speakers (Lane, 2019). It is estimated that 50 per cent of the world's population speaks an Indo-European language as their first/native language. The second-largest language family by number of speakers is the Sino-Tibetan language family, which numbers 1.4 billion speakers; this language family includes Mandarin Chinese, the language with the most first (or native) language speakers globally, at 1.3 billion native speakers. Two Indo-European languages are ranked 2nd and 3rd, respectively, for number of native speakers: Spanish is 2nd, with 460 million speakers, and English is 3rd, at 379 million speakers.

Indo-European languages are spread across Europe, in Scandinavia (for example, Danish, Swedish), southern Europe (Spanish, Portuguese), western Europe (French, German, Dutch, Flemish, Frisian), the United Kingdom and Ireland (English, Irish, Welsh, Scottish Gaelic, Manx), and Eastern Europe (Polish, Russian). In fact, only a few of the languages spoken in Europe are not Indo-European; these include all sign languages as well as languages that are part of the Turkic (including Turkish) and Uralic language families (including Finnish, spoken in Finland and in parts of Sweden, and Sami, Hungarian, and Estonian). Basque, a language spoken in Basque regions of both France and Spain, is known as a **language isolate** – a language that does not appear to be related to any other language and is therefore not classified as part of a language family, but rather as a language family in its own right. Indo-European languages are also spread across all of the continents, with the exception of the Arctic and Antarctica: Africa (French, English), South America (Spanish, English, Portuguese), North America (French, English), Asia (Hindi, Urdu, Persian, English), and Oceania (English).

Turning back to English, if English developed from the same Germanic language ancestor as German (as did other languages, including Danish and Icelandic), how did it evolve to become the distinctive language that we now call English? Or, to put it another way, if English is a Germanic language, how and why did it evolve to become a different (and mutually unintelligible) language from German? As noted above, the Indo-European peoples began migrating across Europe and Asia around 3500–2500 BCE, settling in different parts of Europe and Asia; as a result of this settlement, local language norms began to emerge in different geographical areas, giving rise to various languages within the Indo-European language family, including the Germanic languages, which emerged in northern Europe in the areas now known as Scandinavia, Germany, and The Netherlands. In southern Europe, the Hellenic (Greek) and Italic (Spanish, Italian, Portuguese, French) languages began emerging from Indo-European. The Celtic subbranch of Indo-European (which includes Manx, Cornish, Irish, Welsh, Breton, and Scottish Gaelic) also emerged, as Indo-Europeans spread into western Europe, including the United Kingdom, Ireland, and the Isle of Man.

Germanic can be traced to the region between southern Sweden and the northern region of the Elbe river in Germany. As members of the Germanic tribe migrated and settled in different regions of Scandinavia and central Europe around 250 BCE, new tribes and languages began emerging, including West Germanic languages (see Figure 2.2). This includes the Anglo-Frisian languages, from which English descended. The North Germanic languages include Old Norse, which forms the basis of modern-day Danish, Swedish, Norwegian, and Icelandic, as well as Faroese.

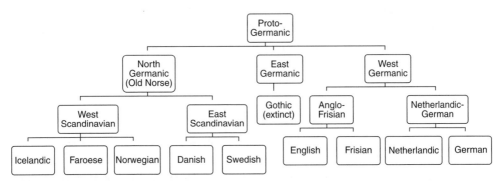

Figure 2.2 The Germanic language family

2.3   Old English: the Celts, Romans, Anglo-Saxons, Vikings, and Normans

By around 250 BCE, the Indo-Europeans had spread across Europe and Asia, with the result that different tribes, with distinctive cultures (including forms of food production, religion, and weaponry, among other things) and languages, had emerged. The Celts had settled in the United Kingdom, Ireland, and on the Isle of Man, as well as in other areas of central Europe, bringing with them the Celtic language, which eventually evolved into Scottish Gaelic (in Scotland), Welsh (in Wales), Irish (in Ireland and Northern Ireland), Breton (in Brittany, France), Cornish (in the Cornwall region of England), and Manx (on the Isle of Man). Celtic did not have a large influence on English; some Celtic words that remain in English are names such as Kent, York, Thames, Cornwall, and London. While the Celts were among the earliest settlers in the United Kingdom and Ireland, they were not the first: the Beaker people – named for a type of drinking vessel found in archaeological sites – probably migrated from central Europe to the United Kingdom and Ireland between 2800 and 1800 BCE, with the first *Homo sapiens* arriving over 40,000 years ago. *Homo sapiens*, from which modern-day humans are descended, were themselves preceded by the Neanderthals, who likely inhabited the United Kingdom and Ireland more than 300,000 years ago (Oxford University Museum of Natural History, n.d.).

Roman civilization had begun developing from the settlement of Italic tribes in southern Europe in the 700s BCE, eventually emerging as the Roman Republic in 509 BCE and the Roman Empire in 27 BCE. Around 55 BCE, the Romans invaded and began occupying England as well as Wales, which became part of the Roman Empire. The occupation lasted more than 400 years, until around 410 CE, when the Celtic tribes defeated the Romans in a series of battles. The Roman Occupation influenced British culture, religion, and architecture; Latin, the language of the Romans, was largely spoken by the Roman elite, and Celtic remained the most common language spoken in England during the Roman Occupation. A number of Latin words did remain in use in England; these words, including *plante* (plant), *candel* (candle), *cetel* (kettle), and *piper* (pepper), mostly originated from trade between the Celts and Romans (Mastin, 2011).

The story of English as we know it today begins in around 449 CE, after the Roman Occupation ended, when members of Germanic tribes began settling in England. This included the Angles, from the region of northern Germany and southern Denmark called Angel, and the Saxons, from the Saxony region of northwestern Germany. The Jutes, from the northern part of the Jutland peninsula of Denmark, also began settlement, as did the Frisians, from Holland and Germany. These settlers sowed the seeds of Modern English as they were all speakers of various varieties of Germanic; it is likely that these varieties were mutually intelligible. These settlements developed into major regions, and kingdoms, of England: Northumbria, Mercia, East Anglia, Wessex, Essex, Kent, and Sussex, and eventually into four main dialects of Old English: Northumbrian, Mercian, West Saxon, and Kentish (Crowley, 1986). As a result of these settlements, the Celts, and their languages, were pushed to remote parts of Wales, Scotland, England, Ireland, Northern Ireland, and the Isle of Man, as well as to Brittany, France. Celtic ceased to be the dominant language of England, with the lasting influence of Celtic on English primarily in place names such as Kent and Cornwall.

Of the different groups, the Saxons were the most dominant, and England became known as Anglaland/Englaland, and eventually England. The language that emerged from the Anglo-Saxons became known as English, which is rooted in the Germanic term *Angeln*, or *Angul*, named for the land shaped like a hook (*angle*) that they occupied in northern Germany / southern Denmark (Mastin, 2011). Old English most closely resembles Old Frisian; both English and Frisian are part of the Anglo-Frisian subbranch of the West Germanic language family. Frisian is still spoken in parts of Germany (North Frisian) and The Netherlands (West Frisian).

TASK 2.2 Proto-Germanic

📖 In the table below, you can find three different words in Proto-Germanic (a reconstructed language) as well as other Germanic languages (Danish, Icelandic, German, and Frisian) and Romance languages (Classical Latin, Spanish, and French) (based on Heggarty et al., 2019).

- Can you guess what the English word is for each of the three words?
- What enabled you to do this? What clues in the words in each row did you use?
- What differences exist between the Romance and Germanic languages for each word?
- Do the words provide evidence that the words evolved separately in Germanic and Romance languages or that they have a common Indo-European ancestor?

Proto-Germanic (* = reconstructed)	Danish	Icelandic	German	Frisian (West)	Classical Latin	Spanish	French
*mōdēr	moder	móðir	mutter	moer	māter	madre	mère
*fadēr	fader	faðir	vater	faar	pater	padre	père
*þrejez	tre	Þrjú	drei	trije	trēs	tres	trois

The settlement in 597 CE by the Roman Catholic bishop St Augustine, along with 40 of his missionaries, had a major impact on the development of English. They brought with them Latin and Christianity, the latter of which spread throughout England when King Ethelbert of Kent converted to Christianity shortly after St Augustine's arrival. St Augustine became the Archbishop of Canterbury in 601 CE. Importantly, St Augustine and his missionaries brought with them the Roman alphabet, and literacy. The Roman alphabet replaced the Runic alphabet, or Old Norse, which had been brought to England by the Anglo-Saxons. The Roman alphabet is believed to have first emerged in Italy beginning in 6–7 BCE; it has roots in earlier alphabets, including the Greek and the Etruscan, both of which in turn had emerged from the Phoenician alphabet and Egyptian hieroglyphics. The earliest known writing system was invented by the Sumerians, in around 3000 BCE.

The introduction of the Roman alphabet and the development of literacy among the elite and ruling classes, as well as monks and clerks of the Catholic church, fostered the emergence of literature, which was written primarily in the West Saxon dialect of Old English due in part to the influence of Alfred the Great, King of the West Saxons, who ruled from 871 to 899 CE, and was a patron of literature (Greenblatt & Abrams, 2006). One of the earliest examples of this is the poetry of Caedmon, a cowherder, written in the seventh century CE; his *Caedmon's Hymn* is considered the oldest surviving piece of literature written in Old English. *Caedmon's Hymn* was written down in Latin by the monk Bede, and later transcribed into Old English. One of the best-preserved manuscripts of the poem is in the Northumbrian dialect of Old English (Crowley, 1986). The epic poem *Beowulf* (author unknown) is the best-known piece of Old English literature, and in 3,000 lines recounts the heroic battles of Beowulf, a sixth-century Scandinavian hero, against the monster Grendel in Denmark. It is not known when it was first composed; it exists in a single manuscript that is believed to have been copied early in the eleventh century. It was written in the West Saxon dialect of Old English.

Around 786 CE, the Viking invasions of England commenced, and eventually created settlements in eastern regions of England, including in Northumbria, East Anglia, and Mercia. The most aggressive of the Vikings were from Denmark (the Danes), though Vikings also came from Norway and Sweden. To quell the invasions, Alfred the Great entered into a treaty with the Vikings in 878 CE, which established Danelaw, a region of England under Viking control. This included parts of Northumbria and East Anglia, and effectively gave the Vikings control of the north and the east of England. Such was the Danish influence on England that the Dane, Cnut the Great, reigned as King of England from 1016 until 1035, as well as the

King of Denmark (1018–35) and the King of Norway (1028–35), creating a North Sea Empire.

The Viking invasion had a significant effect on the English language. Vikings spoke a language that we now call Old Norse, the North Germanic branch of Indo-European (see Figure 2.2). Old Norse is not dissimilar to Old English and it is likely that Old Norse and Old English were mutually intelligible to some extent (Denison & Hogg, 2006). Approximately 1,000 words from Old Norse entered the English language during the Viking invasions; many were place names in areas within the Danelaw. Geographic names ending in *gate*, *by*, *stokc*, and *kirk*, among them, can trace their roots back to the Vikings; family names ending in -*son* (*Johnson*, *Harrison*) also stem from Old Norse. Everyday terms such as *happy*, *seat*, *die* also stem from Old Norse, in some cases replacing terms that already existed in Old English (Mastin, 2011). The days of the week – including *Thursday*, named after the Norse god Thor (Thor's day), and *Wednesday*, named after the Norse god Odin (*Wōdnesdæg* in Old English) – also came from Old Norse. The Viking invasions of England ended when they were no longer profitable; this occurred at around the same time as William the Conqueror of France won the Battle of Hastings, in 1066 CE. This event marked the beginning of the Norman Conquest of England, which continued from 1066 CE until 1154 CE, and begins the era of Middle English.

How similar is Old English to the English(es) we use today? An excerpt from *Beowulf* is given in the box, with the Modern English translation in italics. *Beowulf* is written in the West Saxon dialect of Old English.

Ic þæs wine Deniga,
I that the lord of the Danes,

frean Scyldinga frinan wille
the ruler of the Scyldings ask will

beaga bryttan swa þu bena eart
of rings the giver as thou petitioner art

þoeden mærne ymb þinne sið
the prince famous concerning thy travel (visit)

'I shall ask the lord of the Danes, the ruler of the Scyldings, giver of rings, as you make petition, ask the famous prince concerning your visit ...'

(*Beowulf;* cited from Kastovsky, 2006, p. 219)

As the extract from *Beowulf* shows, Old English differs significantly from Modern English in spelling; without training, it is not possible to read and understand the excerpted text. Crystal (2019, p. 17) states that the Old English alphabet comprised 24 letters: *a, æ, b, c, d, e, f, g, h, i, k, l, m, n, o, p, r, s, t, þ, ð, u, w, y*. You may have noticed the symbol *þ* in the excerpt; this was incorporated into the Old English alphabet from the Runic alphabet to represent the *th* sound. The symbol *ð* was also used to represent *th*. Both of these symbols are still in use in Icelandic today; for example, the word *three* in Icelandic is written as *þrjú*. The vowel letter *æ* also does not exist in Modern English, though it does exist in some Germanic languages, including Danish (for example, my middle name is *Gjaldbæk*). It is also important to note that, because literacy was not widespread and because the printing press, which helped foster the regularization of spelling, had not yet been invented, Old English spelling differed widely by scribe and thus across manuscripts. Later translations and editions of these manuscripts differed as well, due to different editorial and translation conventions employed. There were also dialectal, and therefore pronunciation, differences in regions of England, which also impacted how Old English was written by scribes (Crystal, 2019).

As Crystal (2019) notes, it is not possible to know exactly how Old English sounded, given that there are no written or spoken records of its pronunciation. Researchers have conducted analyses of written Old English and employed comparative reconstruction by examining different dialects of Modern English and analyses of the sound changes that have taken place in English (Crystal, 2019). Through these analyses, it is possible to come to conclusions about how Old English probably sounded: as with Modern English, Old English had a relatively large number of vowels and consonants (see Chapters 3 and 5) compared with other languages, some with roots in both West and North Germanic (the *th* sounds in words like *the* and *bath*, for instance, came from Old Norse during the Viking invasions). According to Lass (2006), Old English, like some varieties of Modern English today, had a series of short and long vowel sounds (see Chapter 3), with four long/short **front vowel** pairs (here the notation : is used to mark the long vowel; this is a convention of the International Phonetic Alphabet used throughout this book) – front vowels: /iː i yː y eː e æː æ/, back vowels: /uː u oː o ɑː ɑ/ – and two pairs of diphthongs (vowel sounds comprising a change from one vowel to another during articulation; see also Chapter 3): /eːo, eo, æːɑ, æɑ/. While wide differences exist in Modern English vowel inventories based on the variety of English, one difference between Old English and Modern English is that the high front rounded vowels /yː y/ no longer exist in English, though they are found in other Germanic languages including Danish and German. In addition, the Old English vowel inventory

Table 2.1 Vowels in Old English	
Old English word	Meaning
bītan	*bite*
hit	*it*
hȳdan	*hide*
fyllan	*fill*
mētan	*meet*
bed	*bed*
lǣdan	*lead*
rætt	*rat*
hūs	*house*
full	*full*
flōd	*flood*
God	*God*
bān	*bone*
catte	*cat*
bēon	*be*
lēaf	*leaf*

(From Lass, 2006)

is comprised of only front and back vowels; Modern English also has a number of central vowels, as will be seen in Chapter 3. These vowel sounds can be illustrated by sample words in Table 2.1. In these examples, a line is placed over a long vowel to denote its longer length.

The first of several vowel shifts that have occurred, and are still occurring, is the *i*-mutation in English; this refers to a phonological change that took place in the seventh century CE, after the Anglo-Saxons arrived in England but prior to the first texts written in Old English. This change explains why the plural form of *foot* became *feet*; in Old English, *foot* (likely *fōt*) was probably inflected as *fōtiz* in the plural (note: Modern English still employs this type of inflection for some nouns – e.g., *speech* to *speeches* – as well as in the genitive and third person singular). The second vowel, *i*, which is a high front vowel (see Chapter 3), appears to have created a shift in the first vowel, *o*, from a mid-back to a front vowel, the vowel *ē*, in a process known as vowel harmony. Eventually, the ending *iz* became redundant as the plural was already marked by a vowel change, and was lost (Crystal, 2019, p. 19).

The Old English consonant system is likely to have consisted of the following consonants: /p b t d k g m n l r f θ s ʃ h j w/, some of which may have alternative pronunciations in different word contexts (Cruttenden, 2014, p. 64). Lass (2006) also notes that there were length differences in consonant sounds in Old English, with longer consonants represented by

Table 2.2 Consonants in Old English

Old English word	Meaning
ǣppel	*apple*
pœþ	*path*
cribb	*crib*
bœþ	*bath*
sette	*set*
tellan	*tell*
bedd	*bed*
deorra	*dear*
brocces	*badger's*
cynn	*kin*
hogg	*hog*
gold	*gold*
wrecca	*wretch*
cinn	*chin*
ecg	*edge*
sengean	*singe*
pyffan	*puff*
fœder	*father*
cyssan	*kiss*
singan	*sing*
moþþe	*moth*
þēoh	*thigh*
scip	*ship*
hlœhhan	*laugh*
niht	*night*
ramm	*ram*
mann	*man*
cann	*can*
nosu	*nose*
eall	*all*
lufu	*love*
feorr	*far*
for	*for*
wœter	*water*
geoc	*yoke*

(From Lass, 2006, p. 54)

double spelling as in *sette* (set) for long *t* versus *tellan* (tell) for a short *t*. This length distinction for consonants does not exist in Modern English. Table 2.2 shows Lass's example consonant inventory for Old English, with individual consonants highlighted in bold.

The **stress** pattern of Old English was based on Germanic Stress Rules (Lass, 2006), with stress on the first syllable of the lexical root, with most prefixes unstressed except on some nouns. You may have noted the -*an* ending on many of the sample words given in Tables 2.1 and 2.2 – including *pyffan* (puff), *fyllan* (fill), and *cyssan* (kiss) – these endings do not exist in Modern English. They derive from PIE, which had a complex noun inflectional system, with eight inflections; Old English had fewer inflections but retained {-an}, among other noun inflections, for some nouns when marked for the dative, genitive, or accusative case.

2.4 From Middle to Modern English: The Norman Conquest, Chaucer, and the Great Vowel Shift

TASK 2.3 Shakespeare

An excerpt from *Romeo and Juliet*, one of Shakespeare's most famous plays, is given here in the original as written during Shakespeare's lifetime. In which English – Old English, Middle English, Early Modern English, Late Modern English – did Shakespeare write? Why do you think it was this English?

Enter Sampson and Gregorie, with Swords and Bucklers, of the house of Capulet

SAMPSON	Gregorie, on my word weele not carrie Coles.
GREGORIE	No, for then we should be Collyers.
SAMPSON	I meane, and we be in choller, weele draw.
GREGORIE	I while you liue, draw your necke out of choller.
SAMPSON	I strike quickly being moued.
GREGORIE	But thou art not quickly moued to strike.
SAMPSON	A dog of the house of Mountague moues me.
GREGORIE	To moue is to stirre, and to be valiant, is to stand: Therefore if thou art moued thou runst away.
SAMPSON	A dog of that house shall moue me to stand: I will take the wall of any man or maide of Mountagues.
GREGORIE	That shewes thee a weake slaue, for the weakest goes to the wall.

(Wells & Taylor, 1986, p. 379)

TRANSLATION

Enter SAMPSON and GREGORY, with swords and bucklers, of the house of Capulet

SAMPSON: Gregory, on my word we'll not carry coals.

GREGORY: No, for then we should be colliers.

SAMPSON: I mean, an we be in choler we'll draw.

GREGORY: Ay, while you live, draw your neck out of collar.

SAMPSON: I strike quickly, being moved.

GREGORY: But thou art not quickly moved to strike.

SAMPSON: A dog of the house of Montague moves me.

GREGORY: To move is to stir, and to be valiant is to stand: therefore if thou art moved thou runn'st away.

SAMPSON: A dog of that house shall move me to stand. I will take
the wall of any man or maid of Montague's.

GREGORY: That shows thee a weak slave, for the weakest goes to
the wall.

(Shakespeare, 2000, pp. 143–4)

The Middle English period began around 1100–50 CE, lasting until around 1500 CE. After the Norman Conquest in 1066, William the Conqueror – now William I of England – settled in England, bringing with him the French language, an Italic (Romance) language. The Normans were themselves descendants of Vikings and the term 'Norman' is the short-form name for the Norsemen who had settled in the French region of Europe and had adopted the French language (Greenblatt & Abrams, 2006). The Normans spoke a dialect of French that was influenced by Germanic; this dialect is called Anglo-Norman or Norman French (Mastin, 2011) and was different from the French spoken in Paris, the capital of France. Although Anglo-Norman French did influence English, it did not replace English, which the majority of the population continued to speak; French was spoken primarily by the nobility and elite. The use of French in the English courts was to last 300 years; Latin, brought to England during the Roman Conquest, was also in use in England, primarily in the Roman Catholic church. Marriage between the Norman ruling class and landowning classes in England resulted in some bilingualism emerging in England (Denison & Hogg, 2006); Celtic languages were also still spoken in regions of Scotland, Northern Ireland, Ireland, Wales, Cornwall, the Isle of Man, and Brittany, France. During the Norman rule of England, literature and literacy were predominantly in Latin or French, resulting in few works written in early Middle English. It was not until 1362 that English was used in Parliament and began being used as the primary spoken and written language in England – consequently, more works were written in Middle English. Henry IV (1399–1413) was the first king of England from the time of the Norman Conquest in 1066 to take the oath in English. Anglo-Norman

French impacted the development of English through the introduction of more than 10,000 words, particularly in relation to the court and law (*duke*, *judge*), art and literature (*colour*, *poet*), government and control (*city*, *servant*), war (*armour*), and upper-class life (*money*, *gown*) (Mastin, 2011).

Middle English comprised five major dialects: Northumbrian, East Midland (also called East Anglian), West Midland (also called West Anglian), Southern (also called West Saxon), and Kentish. A notable work of literature written during this time was *Sir Gawain and the Green Knight*, an anonymous poem based on Arthurian legend written in the late fourteenth century. It was written in a West Midlands dialect. Geoffrey Chaucer (1343–1400), considered one of the greatest English writers of all time, wrote his best-known work, *The Canterbury Tales*, between 1387 and 1400. It is worth noting that Chaucer wrote in the East Midlands dialect of Middle English, though some of the characters in his writing – including characters in *The Canterbury Tales* – use a northern dialect. The East Midlands (which includes London) dialect gained in prestige during the Middle English era as London acquired greater political and economic influence in England due in part to its port, which was a European hub. It is the East Midlands dialect that forms the basis of Modern English, rather than the West Saxon dialect which, as noted above, held prestige during the Old English period. In the Middle English period, English literature flourished as education was spreading among the English population, though still primarily among the wealthy, in part because of wider availability of printed books after the introduction of the printing press into England by William Caxton in 1476, after its invention by Johan Gutenberg in Germany in 1450. The invention of the printing press had a significant effect on regularization of English spelling: Caxton lived in London and employed the East Midlands dialect when printing, principally because it had become the most widely accepted written variety of English and Caxton wanted to be able to sell as many books as possible (Nevalainen & Tieken-Boon van Ostade, 2006, p. 279). As Nevalainen and Tieken-Boon van Ostade note, Caxton was also considered to be a linguistic innovator because of the new vocabulary that entered the English language after first being recorded in Caxton's works. Caxton, and later printers from the fifteenth to the seventeenth centuries, also influenced Modern English spelling by favouring particular spellings of words, which eventually became the accepted norms for those words (Howard-Hill, 2006, p. 17). The chancery, the office responsible for writing official documents, had also adopted the East Midlands dialect in their written documents in the early 1420s (Nevalainen & Tieken-Boon van Ostade, 2006, p. 279).

How similar was Middle English to Modern English? Excerpts from *Sir Gawain and the Green Knight*, written in a West Midlands dialect, and the Prologue of *The Canterbury Tales*, written in an East Midlands dialect, are given in the boxes. As these excerpts illustrate, by the time these two poems were written, Middle English had evolved significantly from Old English, and is to some extent readable to those familiar with Modern English, though it does require some guesswork and interpretation: the line *The hooly blisful martir for to seke*, from *The Canterbury Tales*, is partly recognizable as *The holy blissful martyr for to seek*, or *To seek the holy blessed martyr*. It should be noted that there is variation in how words are spelled in different manuscripts, as illustrated by the same excerpt from *Sir Gawain and the Green Knight* from an edition of the poem edited by J. R. R. Tolkien and E. V. Gordon.

Sir Gawain and the Green Knight

Sithen the sege and the assaut was sesed at Troye,
After the siege and the assault was ceased at Troy,

The foorgh fcrittened and brent to fcrondes and askes,
The city crumbled and burned to brands and ashes,

The iulk that the frammes of iresoun ther wroght
The man who the plots of treason there wrought

Was tried for his tricherie, the trewest on erthe.
Was tried for his treachery, the truest on earth.

(From Greenblatt & Abrams, 2006, p. 161)

Sir Gawain and the Green Knight

SIÞEN þe sege and þe assaut watz sesed at Troye,
After the siege and the assault was ceased at Troy,

Þe borȝ brittened and brent to brondeȝ and askez,
The city crumbled and burned to brands and ashes,

Þe tulk þat þe trammes of tresoun þer wroȝt
The man who the plots of treason there wrought

Watz tried for his tricherie, þe trewest on erthe:
Was tried for his treachery, the truest on earth.

(From Tolkien & Gordon, 1967)

From *The Canterbury Tales*: Prologue

1 Whan that Aprill with his shoures soote
   When April with its sweet-smelling showers

2 The droghte of March hath perced to the roote,
   Has pierced the drought of March to the root,

3 And bathed every veyne in swich licour
   And bathed every vein (of the plants) in such liquid

4 Of which vertu engendred is the flour;
   By which power the flower is created;

5 Whan Zephirus eek with his sweete breeth
   When the West Wind also with its sweet breath,

6 Inspired hath in every holt and heeth
   In every wood and field has breathed life into

7 The tendre croppes, and the yonge sonne
   The tender new leaves, and the young sun

8 Hath in the Ram his half cours yronne,
   Has run half its course in Aries,

9 And smale foweles maken melodye,
   And small fowls make melody,

10 That slepen al the nyght with open ye
    Those that sleep all the night with open eyes

11 (So priketh hem Nature in hir corages),
    (So Nature incites them in their hearts),

12 Thanne longen folk to goon on pilgrimages,
    Then folk long to go on pilgrimages,

(Benson, 2008)

A number of pronunciation features were also adopted into English from Anglo-Norman French, including the *kw* pronunciation in words like *quit* and *question*, and *k* for *ch* so that *charrier* became *carry* and *chaudron* became *cauldron*. Other changes from Old to Middle English include the change of the spelling of *hw* to *wh*, and *c* to *k* in some words (Mastin, 2011). The unstressed vowel sound emerged in words such as *brittened* (crumbled) and *slepen* (sleep). To some extent, Middle English orthography more accurately indicates pronunciation than that of Modern English (see Chapters 3 and 5, for Modern English orthography and pronunciation patterns): long vowels, for example, were indicated by the use of double vowel letters as in *ee* or *aa*, or when followed by a consonant and then a final *e* in spelling as in *seke* (*seek*); unlike Modern English, the final *e* was not silent in early Middle English, though it had become silent by the end of the Middle English period (Greenblatt & Abrams, 2006). Short vowels were indicated by a double consonant after the vowel as in *Aprill*. The writing of the *th* sound changed from the use of the Old Norse ð and þ to *th* as in *Thanne* and *bathed*. The *ou* spelling also emerged, as did a differentiation between *v* and *f*, *s* and *z* and *ng* and *n* (Greenblatt & Abrams, 2006). The low front /æ/ had been raised to /ɛː/. A major grammatical and morphological change was the loss of many of the inflections from Indo-European, and the replacement of the {-en, -an} inflection with the French {-s}. As a result of the simplification of the English inflectional system, Middle English (and subsequently Modern English) became more dependent on word order for grammatical meaning.

Why is Middle English so different from Modern English? The Great Vowel Shift, which fostered the change from Middle into Early Modern English, occurred over a period of more than 200 years in the fifteenth–seventeenth centuries, and primarily affected the vowels we have been describing as long. According to Lass (2006), during the Great Vowel Shift, the high front vowel /iː/ changed to the diphthong /ai/, as in *bite* (Table 2.3). A detailed depiction of vowel changes from the sixteenth to the nineteenth century is provided by Lass (2006, p. 83). As this shows, /iː/ and /uː/ become diphthongs, though the quality of the vowel sounds in the diphthongs undergoes further changes between 1569 and the nineteenth century. The vowel /eː/ is raised to /iː/, /aː/ to /eː/, /oː/ to /uː/ and /ɔː/ to /oː/; /ɛː/ undergoes a split; and there is a merger between /iː/ and /eː/.

Table 2.3 The Great Vowel Shift

	ME	1569	1653	1687	19th c.	
bite	iː	ɛi	əi	ʌi	aiː	bite
meet	eː	iː	iː	iː	iː	meet, meat
break, meat	ɛː	ɛː	eː	eː		
name	aː	aː	ɛː	eː	eː	name, break
house	uː	ɔuː	əu	ʌu	auː	house
food	oː	uː	uː	uː	uː	food
bone	ɔː	ɔː	oː	oː	oː	bone

TASK 2.4 Germanic Languages

📖 The table below shows the Proto-Germanic, Icelandic, Danish, German, and Frisian equivalents for four words. The pronunciation of each word is given in square brackets: [ ].

- Using the descriptions of the Great Vowel Shift provided, can you guess what the Modern English word is for each of the four words?

Example	Proto-Germanic	Icelandic	Danish	German	Frisian (West)
1	*bīt	bíta	bid	beiß	byt
	*[biːt]	[ˈbiːtʰä]	[bɪð]	[bäɪs]	[bit]
2	*namōn	nafn	navn	name	namme
	*[namoːn]	[ˈnäpm̩]	[naʊʔn]	[ˈnäːmə]	[ˈnämə]
3	*xūsan	hús	hus	haus	hûs
	*[xuːsan]	[hy̞ːs]	[hy̞ˑs]	[häʊs]	[hy̞ːʂ]
4	*bainan	bein	ben	bein	bien
	*[bainan]	[be̞ˑɪn]	[biʔn]	[bäɪn]	[biˑən]

* = reconstructed (based on Heggarty et al., 2019)

When does the Modern English period begin? The Early Modern English period runs from around 1450–1500 CE until 1650 CE, the period of time when the Great Vowel Shift was in progress. The period of the fifteenth to seventeenth centuries is also known as the English Renaissance, which was a time of significant cultural and artistic development. The reign of Elizabeth I of England, from 1558 until 1603, was known as the Golden Age because of Elizabeth's support of literature, theatre, and education. Literature flourished during the period; William Shakespeare (1564–1616), considered the greatest writer in English literature, published his first poem, *Venus and Adonis*, in 1593. Shakespeare wrote in Early Modern English (see Task 2.3) and is credited for adding more than 1,700 words to the English language by recording new words and phrases in his plays and poems, including: *It's Greek to me, The be-all and the end-all, Something wicked this way comes, All that glitters isn't gold, The world is my oyster, Break the ice, Too much of a good thing, critic, bedroom, gossip, skim milk, undress* (Shakespeare Birthplace Trust, 2021). The English Renaissance was also a period of scientific discovery; as a result, many words entered the English language from Greek and Latin, particularly in relation to science and classification, including *genius, species, anatomy, skeleton, orbit, atmosphere, invention, technique, temperature* (Mastin, 2011).

The fifteenth to nineteenth centuries also saw the expansion of international trade; British naval power enabled England to establish several trade routes across the Indian, Pacific, and Atlantic Oceans. European colonial expansion had already begun by the 1500s, with Spanish, French, Portuguese, Dutch, and British colonization of parts of the Americas, Africa, the Caribbean, and Asia. This European expansion and subsequent colonization had devastating consequences for many peoples, cultures, and languages, with subjugation and extinction of indigenous peoples often a result of colonization. The voyages of Christopher Columbus to the Americas began in 1492; prior to his voyages, the Americas were largely unknown to Europeans, though evidence suggests that Leif Erikson, a Viking, landed on the North American continent in the tenth century. The trade industry, and the import of new foods and objects, led to a wide range of vocabulary entering English; this includes borrowings from Japanese (*tycoon*, *geisha*), Chinese (*tea*, *typhoon*), Arabic (*coffee*, *saffron*), French (*croissant*), Italian (*umbrella*, *piano*), German (*noodle*), Norwegian (*iceberg*, *ski*), Persian (*lemon*, *bazaar*), Malay (*bamboo*), Native American languages (*tomato*, *moose*), Indian languages (from Hindi and Urdu, and other Indian languages – *ginger*, *shampoo*, *shawl*) (Mastin, 2011).

The Late Modern English period began in the 1800s CE and continues to the present day, beginning at a time of significant scientific and industrial advancement, including the period known as the Industrial Revolution. One of the most significant changes between Early and Late Modern English is in the influx of vocabulary borrowings, as well as coinage to refer to previously unknown processes, objects, and concepts. These new words included *rain, engine, camera, telegraph, oxygen, nuclear, vaccine.*

The process of standardization of written and, later, spoken English that had begun in the 1400s continued throughout this period. One of the earliest and most influential English dictionaries, Samuel Johnson's *Dictionary of the English Language*, was published in 1755; Johnson's dictionary further helped to standardize the English language. The dictionary was also necessary to help people understand the meaning of all the new words that were rapidly entering the language; Johnson's dictionary became a highly regarded reference work (Nevalainen & Tieken-Boon van Ostade, 2006). In 1762, Lowth published the grammar book *A Short Introduction to the English Language*, which illustrated norms of what he considered to be good usage of English (Nevalainen & Tieken-Boon van Ostade, 2006). The first pronunciation dictionary of English was published in 1917 by Daniel Jones, a British phonetician: *English Pronouncing Dictionary*. The dictionary is now published by Cambridge University Press; the eighteenth edition was published in 2011 and includes over 215,000 pronunciations. Noah Webster Jr, an American linguist, educator, and lexicographer, published his first dictionary, entitled *An American Dictionary of the English Language*, in 1828; today, the influential dictionary is still published as *Merriam-Webster's Dictionary*. Webster wrote the dictionary in order to help codify and establish American English as a separate variety in its own right, as Americans were using and spelling words differently from the British; as an example, he added *skunk* and *squash* to the dictionary, words that had entered American English from Native American languages and were not in use in British English; he also used the common American spellings of words like *color* rather than the British English *colour* (Noah Webster House, 2021).

As Mastin (2011) notes, World War I (1914–18) and World War II (1939–45) also led to an influx of military terminology, including *camouflage, radar, shell-shocked*. In the past few decades, technological transformations have fostered the creation of many new words, including *telephone, phone, byte, laptop, software, mobile phone, email* (electronic mail), and, most recently, *zoom*.

2.5   Colonialism and the Spread of English Worldwide

TASK 2.5 Official Languages

📖 In which of the following countries or regions is English an official language?

Africa
- Kenya
- Nigeria
- South Africa

The Americas
- Belize
- Canada
- Guyana
- United States

Asia
- Hong Kong SAR
- India
- Singapore

The Caribbean
- Antigua and Barbuda
- Jamaica

Europe
- England
- Ireland
- Northern Ireland
- Scotland
- Wales

Oceania
- Australia
- Fiji
- New Zealand

It may be surprising to learn that, while English is a *de jure* (legal) official language in many countries and regions in Africa (including Kenya, Nigeria, and South Africa), Asia (including Singapore, Hong Kong SAR, and India), the Americas (including Belize, Canada, and Guyana), the Caribbean (including Antigua and Barbuda), Europe (including Ireland, Scotland), and Oceania (including Fiji and New Zealand), English is *not* a *de jure* official language in England, Australia, the United States, and Northern Ireland. In fact, England, Australia, the United States, and Northern Ireland do not have legal official languages, though English is the de facto (widely accepted but without legal status) official language due to common usage. In places with a legal official language, English is often one of several official languages, in recognition of the indigenous languages and multicultural heritage of each region, as well as to preserve indigenous languages that are at risk due to the increasing usage of English in society and globally. These include New Zealand, which has English, Māori, and New Zealand Sign Language as its official languages, while Ireland has both Irish and English; Scotland has English, Gaelic, Scots, and British Sign Language; Singapore has English, Malay, Mandarin Chinese, and Tamil; and Kenya has Kiswahili and English.

Many of the countries/regions that have English as an official language are former British or American colonies. British colonial expansion began in the late 1500s. The British successfully established settlements in North America, founding Jamestown in 1607 and Plymouth in 1620; there were also settlements in Nova Scotia, Canada, by 1670 and, by 1763, Britain had gained control of the lower part of Canada down to Mississippi and Florida. Colonization of Central and South America occurred in the 1700s, with Guyana colonized in 1796 and Belize (formerly British Honduras) colonized in 1862. Settlement in the Caribbean started in St Kitts (1624), expanding later to Barbados, Nevis, Antigua, Honduras, Jamaica, and the Bahamas.

Many of these countries and territories had previously been colonized by the Spanish, Dutch, French, and Portuguese, among others, with the British acquiring the territories through trade or war.

Colonization in Africa commenced after The Royal African Company was established in 1660, with the first British settlement occurring on James Island, now Kunta Kinteh Island, in the Gambia River (*Encyclopedia Britannica*, 2021). Nearly two centuries later, in 1821, British West Africa was formed, encompassing Sierra Leone, Gambia, and the Gold Coast. In 1884–5, Britain obtained territory stretching from South Africa to Egypt, the most African territory of any European nation.

Colonization of Asia began with the founding of The East India Company in 1600, with settlements in parts of India beginning in the 1630s, including in Bengal and Madras. In 1819, Singapore was founded by Sir Stamford Raffles; British colonization of Hong Kong began in 1841 after Britain's defeat of China in the First Opium War, with Hong Kong formally ceded to the British in 1842.

Nearly 100 years earlier, Captain James Cook had arrived in New Zealand (1769) and Australia (1770), which began what became the colonization of nearly all of Oceania in the eighteenth and nineteenth centuries. American colonization included the Philippines (1898–1946); islands in the Caribbean, including the US Virgin Islands (1917–present) and Puerto Rico (1899–present); Micronesia, including the Northern Mariana Islands (1986–present) and Guam (1899–present); and Polynesia: American Samoa (1900–present).

Today, there are only 14 British overseas territories, including the Cayman Islands and the British Virgin Islands. Decolonization began in 1776, in the War of Independence between the United States, then comprising 13 American colonies, and England. By 1783, the American colonies had gained independence from Britain; Canada gained independence in 1867. In 1901, Australia gained independence; New Zealand in 1931. In 1947, India and Pakistan achieved independence; African nations began gaining independence in the 1920s. In 1997, Hong Kong ceased to be a British territory.

The spread of English through globalization – through colonialism as well as migration, the Internet, and mass media – has led to English becoming the most widely spoken language in the world. English is also the number one language on the Internet, used by nearly 2 billion people worldwide (Internet World Statistics, 2020); approximately 55 per cent of all content on the Internet is in English (Wood, 2015). The emergence of the Internet and social media has also led to new terms entering English, including *vlog, podcast, emoji, meme*, and *emoticon*.

2.6   World Englishes: New and Old Varieties of English, and Postcolonial Englishes

As this chapter has shown, there has always been more than one variety of English, and Old English, Middle English, Early Modern English, and Late Modern English should each be viewed as umbrella terms for a range of English dialects and accents. Late Modern English, the English we speak today, comprises a myriad of varieties of English which have emerged due to colonial expansion and globalization of English to territories and countries with existing cultures and languages, as well as due to geographic, ethnic, and social influences and differences within regions and countries. The different varieties of English spoken around the world are referred to as **World Englishes**. In the remainder of this chapter, we will look at some of the terminology that has been used to classify and describe the Englishes that have emerged due to colonial expansion, migration, and globalization.

One approach to classifying Englishes is to view the spread of English in four waves of migration and colonization, from the first spread, or diaspora (dispersion across a geographical area), from England to Ireland, Scotland, and Wales in the Middle English period, to the fourth diaspora, with the continued spread of English globally today (Kachru, Kachru, and Nelson, 2009). This is depicted in Figure 2.3. The Englishes that emerged in the first and second diasporas are often called **Old Varieties of English** (OVEs), while the Englishes that emerged in later diasporas are referred to as **New Varieties of English** (NVEs).

Kachru's (1985) Concentric Circles Model is another model of World Englishes. Kachru's model consists of three categories of English, beginning with Englishes that emerged in the first and second diasporas as English spread in the United Kingdom (including England, Northern Ireland, Wales, and Scotland) and Ireland, as well as to North America and Australia and New Zealand. English is either a *de jure* or **de facto official language** in each of these countries, and the primary language spoken by the majority of the population. These Englishes, also known

First diaspora

(12th century – 16th century): From England to Ireland, Scotland, and Wales

Second diaspora

(17th century – 19th century):

North America, New Zealand, and Australia

Third diaspora

(17th century – 20th century):

Asia, South America, Africa, the Caribbean, Europe

Fourth diaspora

20th century – present

Figure 2.3 Diasporas of English

as OVEs, are categorized as **Inner Circle Englishes**, and are often considered the standard-bearers or norm-providing varieties against which other varieties – and speakers – are measured, with speakers of these Englishes often considered to be native (depending on age of learning and proficiency), in comparison to speakers of other varieties. The terms '*native*' and '*non-native*' have been widely used to distinguish between speakers of a language who learned the language as their mother tongue or first language, and speakers of a language who learned the language in later childhood or adulthood. This dichotomy has increasingly been viewed as problematic, however, as it fails to recognize the language experiences and proficiencies of speakers in multilingual, and often postcolonial, settings. Inner Circle Englishes comprise a range of ethnic, social, and regional varieties; one of these sub-varieties is usually considered the standard and employed as the educational norm. Australian English, for example, comprises Australian Aboriginal English and ethnocultural varieties (which in themselves comprise a range of dialects) as well as sociocultural dialects, including Cultivated, General, and Broad Australian English, which can be viewed as a continuum from Cultivated (closer to RP/SSBE) to Broad (most local Australian features). In England, Standard Southern British English or Modern RP is the standard, while in the US, the terms 'General' or 'Standard American English' refer to the standard.

Outer Circle Englishes have largely developed in former colonies of England and the United States, in Central and South America, Asia, Africa, and the Caribbean during the third diaspora; these NVEs have developed during the colonial and postcolonial periods and have distinctive vocabulary, grammar, discourse, and pronunciation features influenced by local languages and cultures. Due to their colonial history, they are also referred to as **Postcolonial Englishes**. Edgar Schneider's (2007) dynamic model of Postcolonial Englishes identifies five stages in their development – from stage 1: foundation (dialect mixing); to stage 2: exonormative stabilization (emerging bilingualism but reliance on external norms of the colonial variety of English); stage 3: nativization (colonized lands gain independence; incorporation of features of local languages into the new variety of English; external norms still held in prestige); stage 4: endonormative stabilization (legitimation and recognition of new variety of English with local norms); stage 5: differentiation (regional and ethnic variation may emerge). Schneider's model has been widely used in research on Postcolonial Englishes to classify the new Englishes and to understand their role and status in the language ecology of postcolonial societies. Malaysian and Hong Kong English, for example, have been classified by Schneider as being in stage 3, Singapore English in stage 4, while Australian and New Zealand English are classified as having reached stage 5.

Postcolonial Englishes have emerged due to contact between the colonial variety of English and local languages. As examples, Singapore English is influenced by Malay, Tamil, Cantonese, Hokkien, Mandarin Chinese, and other Chinese varieties, while Kenyan English is influenced by Kiswahili as well as other African languages. English is often a *de jure* official language in these countries/territories. The local languages that influence the Englishes are called **substrates** while the English variety (usually British or American English) that has been brought to the region is called the **superstrate**. While speakers of these Englishes have been described as second language speakers – meaning that English is not the first language acquired – this is an oversimplified characterization of the status and usage of English in many of these locations. Speakers of these varieties are often multilingual and may speak English as well as one or more native/first languages; in fact, many speakers of English in Outer Circle countries consider themselves to be native speakers of English, often multilingually with other languages (see Hansen Edwards, 2016b). English is typically a language of education in these countries and territories and may also be used in government and media. There exists a great deal of variation within these Englishes, with social differences (including educational and economic) often giving rise to different lects within the postcolonial varieties. Some speakers may speak a variety of English that is close to the superstrate, with the majority of features the same as in that language. This is called the **acrolectal variety** and is usually spoken by highly educated speakers. The **mesolectal variety** has significant influences from the substrates and therefore differs from the superstrate; in our discussion, we recognize these features as being the unique phonological features of that variety of English. Mesolectal speakers may be highly educated. The **basilectal variety** is heavily influenced by the substrate language(s); it is often less prestigious and may imply a speaker is less educated. It is the most distinctive from the superstrate and the acrolect.

Expanding Circle countries are placed in the fourth diaspora, where English has spread in education, trade, and finance, among other fields, through globalization. These countries, including Japan, China, Russia, and South Korea, were not colonized by the British or the United States and therefore English is not an official language in these countries, though it is often a required language in the education system. English is often characterized as a foreign language in these countries and is typically not the primary language or widely spoken among the population within the country.

As noted above, Inner Circle Englishes – and specifically General American English or Received Pronunciation – have historically been considered the standard-bearers in English education globally. Increasingly, however, speakers of English in the Outer Circle, as well as in the Expanding Circle, are laying claim to English as their own language due to the local norms – unique and distinctive vocabulary, grammar, pronunciation, and discourse features – that have developed, through the influence of local languages and cultures. As the discussion of the history of the English language has shown, English was never *just* English – it emerged from West Germanic and became the language we know today by absorbing linguistic features – including pronunciation, grammar, and vocabulary – from hundreds of other languages, such as Latin, French, Danish, Persian, Hindi, Urdu, Arabic, Spanish, Portuguese, Japanese, Malay, and Cantonese. In addition, there was never just one English dialect or accent, with Old, Middle, and Modern English best viewed as umbrella terms for a range of features spoken in different regions in the United Kingdom and Ireland, and, later, around the world. The NVEs that have emerged due to colonial expansion and globalization continue the process of language evolution and change that began our story of English with the migration of Indo-European peoples across Europe, and the spread of West Germanic languages to England. Just as West Germanic tribes spread across England, displacing the Celts and their languages, the fifteenth to twentieth centuries saw the colonization of Asia, Africa, and the Caribbean, and the subsequent addition of English into the language ecology in these countries. English is a living and dynamic language and when it spread – whether in the Old, Middle or Modern English period – it absorbed cultural and linguistic features from other languages and cultures with which it made contact, to express new ideas, concepts, and items that were imported into the culture of English speakers. It is precisely this contact that has made English one of the most vocabulary-rich languages in the world. We could argue that English is *owned by none and owned by all* as the language we call English is continually evolving and changing, with new varieties emerging and more established varieties changing as new features emerge. This view of English is in line with the English as a Lingua Franca (ELF) paradigm, which defines ELF as 'English as it is used as a contact language among speakers from different first languages' (Jenkins, 2009, p. 142). In this paradigm, all users of English – whether they are from Inner, Outer, or Expanding Circle countries, or speakers of OVEs or NVEs – develop English linguistic resources based on their own background, but also their communication with other users of English (Jenkins, 2017). As Jenkins (2017) notes, ELF should be viewed as a complementary paradigm to the World Englishes paradigm; whereas ELF focuses on how users make use of their linguistic resources in communication with speakers of English from different backgrounds, the World Englishes paradigm focuses on the characteristics within unique varieties of English – a focus on English across (ELF) or within (World Englishes) varieties.

NVEs are gaining recognition among their speakers for expressing a unique sociocultural and linguistic history and present; a significant body of research has sought to describe the unique features of NVEs; as noted in Chapter 1, while this book aims to present an inclusive and expansive approach to the discussion of English phonetics and phonology, with variation across Englishes at the heart of this discussion, it necessarily focuses primarily, though not exclusively, on World Englishes that have a longer history of development and are receiving greater recognition and legitimization among their speakers. More research has subsequently been available on the systematicity of their phonetics and phonology; this book draws upon the available research, as well as my own research on World Englishes, to illustrate the sounds of English worldwide.

As we conclude this chapter, it is important to highlight the impact that the spread of English has had on other languages and cultures. The spread of English into Celtic-speaking areas, commencing with Anglo-Saxon settlements in 449 CE, began the process of marginalization and subsequent endangerment of the Celtic languages. The United Nations Educational, Scientific and Cultural Organization (UNESCO) categorizes endangered languages on a continuum of least to most endangered, as follows:

- Safe: Language is spoken by all generations.
- Vulnerable: Most children speak the language, but it may be restricted to certain domains (e.g., home).
- Definitely endangered: Children no longer learn the language as a mother tongue in the home.
- Severely endangered: Language is spoken by grandparents and older generations; while the parent generation may understand it, they do not speak it to children or among themselves.
- Critically endangered: The youngest speakers are grandparents and older, and they speak the language partially and infrequently.
- Extinct: There are no speakers left.

(UNESCO, 2011, p. 6)

All the Celtic languages are listed on this index: Welsh as vulnerable, Irish and Scottish Gaelic as definitely endangered, Breton as severely endangered, and Cornish and Manx as critically endangered. Manx, a Celtic language historically spoken on the Isle of Man, became extinct as a first language in 1974 when the last native speaker of Manx died. In North America, over 200 Native American languages are endangered or already extinct, while in Australia, 109 Aboriginal languages are listed as endangered, from vulnerable to extinct. Te Reo Māori, an indigenous Polynesian language in New Zealand, is listed as vulnerable (from Moseley, 2010).

There is a multitude of reasons that languages (and dialects/varieties of languages) become endangered, and English is also not the only language that has impacted the existence of other languages and varieties. One reason why some languages, and specific varieties or dialects of a given language, spread and become powerful in education, media, and government is the speakers of that language, dialect, or variety gaining power. In our story of English, we saw how the prestige dialect of English changed from the West Saxon dialect in the Old English period to the East Midlands dialect in the Middle English period as the seat of power shifted from West Saxony to the East Midlands. As English spread globally, it had inherent power as the language of the colonizers, which has been retained even during postcolonial times, as English became a *de jure* or de facto official language in many postcolonial societies. Both during colonial and postcolonial times, use of local languages – including, but not exclusively, the languages of the First Nations Peoples in Canada, Native Americans in the United States, Aboriginal Peoples of Australia, and the Māori Peoples of New Zealand – was often suppressed, or even forbidden, by the colonial and postcolonial governments, with devastating results.

While there are now concerted efforts by many governments to protect and revitalize endangered languages – including giving them official language status, as we saw above with Irish in Ireland, Scottish Gaelic in Scotland, and Māori in New Zealand, or through mandatory or supplementary language education in schools – the road is uphill. In the United States, the Cherokee Nation has worked to protect and promote the Cherokee language, particularly after a 2002 survey found no fluent speakers of Cherokee under the age of 40; this has led to a large-scale effort to rejuvenate the language through research-driven development of language immersion classes, satellite classes, a youth choir, online classes, radio shows, and a Cherokee Education degree programme (Honoring Nations, 2006). In New Zealand, Māori language revitalization efforts by the government, in collaboration with the Māori community, have led to a range of bilingual education programmes, including immersion programmes for both young children and their family members. Language revitalization requires significant financial and government investment and support, which is not always affordable for many endangered language speakers or governments. While the cost of language revitalization programmes is high, the cost of losing more languages is by far greater, as language loss leads to a loss of culture, history, knowledge, and identity for both indigenous peoples and for the world.

2.7   CHECK YOUR UNDERSTANDING

EXERCISES

(a) Can you guess the Modern English word for the words in each row? If you guessed correctly, what linguistic information helped you find the correct answer?

Example	Proto-Germanic (* = reconstructed)	Danish	Icelandic	German	Modern English
1	*xunda-radan	hundrede	hundrað	hundert	
2	*mēnon	måne	máni	mond	
3	*baþan	bad	bað	bad	
4	*þunraz	torden	þora	donner	
5	*wullō	uld	ull	wolle	
6	*rextaz	ret	rétt|ur	recht	

(Based on data from Heggarty et al., 2019)

(b) Here are four versions of the first lines of The Lord's Prayer (based on Pressley & the Shakespeare Resource Center, 2021). Arrange the versions in order by the period of English – Old English, Middle English, Early Modern English, and Late Modern English. What linguistic features in the versions did you use to help you to order them chronologically? What time periods correspond to each period of English?

(1) Our father which art in heauen, hallowed be thy name. Thy king-dome come. Thy will be done, in earth, as it is in heauen.

(2) Fæder ure þu þe eart on heofonum; Si þin nama gehalgod to becume þin rice gewurþe ðin willa on eorðan swa swa on heofonum.

(3) Our Father, who art in heaven, Hallowed be thy Name. Thy kingdom come. Thy will be done, On earth as it is in heaven.

(4) Oure fadir that art in heuenes, halewid be thi name; thi kyndoom come to; be thi wille don in erthe as in heuene.

(c) What is the *i*-mutation? When did it occur? What impact did it have on the English language?

(d) What is the Great Vowel Shift? When did it occur? What impact did it have on the English language?

DISCUSSION QUESTIONS

(a) What are some of the consequences of English having become a global language?

(b) I write that we could say that *English is owned by none and owned by all*. How do you interpret this statement? Do you agree or disagree with it? Why or why not?

(c) If the Angles, Saxons, and Jutes had not settled in England, would English have become English? What might be the language spoken in England today?

(d) How is the diaspora of English similar to the spread of Indo-European?

(e) What is the future of English? How will globalization, the Internet, and social media change English?

EXPAND YOUR UNDERSTANDING

In Chapter 1, you were asked to listen to speech extracts from the following fifteen speakers to try to identify their variety, age, and gender. Go to Task 1.2 to listen to them again; you can also refer to the information given below for each speaker. Answer the following questions:

(a) Which speakers are speakers of Inner Circle, Outer Circle, or Expanding Circle Englishes?

(b) Which speakers speak a Postcolonial English?

(c) Which speakers speak an Old Variety of English (OVE) or a New Variety of English (NVE)?

(d) Which speakers identify themselves as native speakers of English, either monolingually or multilingually with another language(s)? Why do you think these speakers identify as native speakers of English?

(e) Which speakers do not identify themselves as native speakers of English? Why do you think they do not consider themselves as native speakers of English?

(f) Do all speakers of Outer Circle Englishes and Postcolonial Englishes identify as native speakers of English? Why do you think this is the case?

---

(1) Speaker 1 is from Wellington, New Zealand. The speaker is a man aged 21–5. His native language is English. He speaks *New Zealand English*.

(2) Speaker 2 is from Cape Town, South Africa. The speaker is a woman aged 18–20; her native language is English. She also speaks some Afrikaans. She speaks *White South African English*.

(3) Speaker 3 is from the Aschaffenburg region in Bavaria, Germany. The speaker is a woman aged 21–5 and her native language is German. She speaks *German English*.

(4) Speaker 4 is from Selangor, Malaysia. The speaker is a woman aged 21–5; her native languages are Malay and English. She

also speaks Putonghua (Mandarin Chinese) and Cantonese. She speaks *Malaysian English*.

(5) Speaker 5 is from Harare, Zimbabwe. The speaker is a woman aged 18–20. Her native languages are English and Shona. She speaks *Zimbabwean English*.

(6) Speaker 6 is from Wyoming, a state in the Midwestern region of the USA. The speaker is a woman aged 21–5. Her native language is English. She speaks a Midwestern dialect of *American English*.

(7) Speaker 7 is from Allahabad in Uttar Pradesh, India. The speaker is a man aged 26–30. His native languages are Hindi and English. He speaks *Indian English*.

(8) Speaker 8 is from Queensland, Australia. The speaker is a woman aged 18–20. She is a native speaker of English. She speaks *Australian English*.

(9) Speaker 9 is from Anhui, China. The speaker is a man aged 21–5. He is a native speaker of Putonghua. He speaks *China English*.

(10) Speaker 10 is from Derby, East Midlands, England. The speaker is a woman aged 31–5. She is a native speaker of English. She speaks an East Midlands dialect of *British English*.

(11) Speaker 11 is from Santiago, Chile. The speaker is a man aged 26–30. His native language is Spanish. He speaks *Chilean English*.

(12) Speaker 12 is from Seoul, South Korea. The speaker is a man aged 21–5. He is a native speaker of Korean. He speaks *Korean English*.

(13) Speaker 13 is from Hong Kong SAR. The speaker is a woman aged 18–20. She is a native speaker of Cantonese. She speaks *Hong Kong English*.

(14) Speaker 14 is from Bishkek, Kyrgyzstan. The speaker is a man aged 18–20. He is a native speaker of Russian and the Kyrgyz language. He speaks *Kyrgyzstan English*.

(15) Speaker 15 is from Islamabad, Pakistan. The speaker is a man aged 26–30. He is a native speaker of Urdu and Sindhi. He speaks *Pakistani English*.

ANALYSE YOUR OWN PRONUNCIATION

(a) What is the status of English in your country? Is it a de facto or *de jure* official language? Is/are the variety/ies spoken in your country New or Old? Postcolonial English?

(b) How do you define the term 'native speaker'? What are your native languages?

3 | The Vowels of English

TASK 3.1 PRE-READING

Before you read Chapter 3, think about the following questions. What do you already know about vowels? You may wish to compare your answers with your classmates or teacher.

- How many vowels are there in the English language?
- What are the English vowels?
- What is the difference between a vowel and a consonant?
- Do all English words need vowels?
- Do all English words need consonants? (The sentence given below may help you answer this question.)

I felt a pain in my left eye.

3.1 Introduction to the Chapter

The chapter introduces you to English vowels and variation in vowel inventories across varieties of English. The discussion will first focus on English phonetics – the production of individual speech sounds. We will begin by examining the articulatory features used to classify and describe vowels, namely tongue **height**, front/backness of tongue articulation (also called **advancement**), and degree of lip rounding/spreading, known together as **HAR** (Height, Advancement, Rounding). In this overview, we will also examine vowel inventories across a range of languages to understand which vowels are most common cross-linguistically, and why. This discussion will also look at the vowel inventories of several languages that influence varieties of English, including Kiswahili, Spanish, and Cantonese, which influence Kenyan English, Puerto Rican English, and Hong Kong English, among others.

In the next sections of the chapter, we will focus on English vowels by first introducing the types of vowels that exist in different varieties of English. We will then examine the vowel inventories in a range of Englishes, including OVEs (see Chapter 2) such as American, British, Australian, and

New Zealand Englishes, and NVEs including African, Asian, and Caribbean Englishes. We will also discuss the concepts of phoneme, phone, and allophone in this chapter, which sets the stage for exploring the concept of phonology through vowel variation within varieties of English and phonological rules that govern this variation.

In the final section of the chapter, you will be guided through exercises designed to check your understanding of the content in the chapter. You will also be guided through an analysis of your own pronunciation based on your recorded speech samples and the discussion of the vowel inventories and phonological rules of different varieties of English.

3.2   What Are Vowels?

What are vowels? How are vowels different from consonants? To answer these questions, we first have to differentiate between vowel *letters* and vowel *sounds*. You may have answered the first two questions in Task 3.1 with 'five' or sometimes 'six', and listed *a, e, i, o, u*, and *y* as the English vowels. These are all vowel *letters*, representing a range of vowel sounds in spelling, either alone or in combination, as in *meat* and *meet* and *mete*, all of which have the same vowel sound though with three different spellings (these words are **homophones** – they have the same pronunciation but different meanings; homo = same, and phone = speech sound). Many varieties of English have between 11 and 15 individual vowel sounds; to represent these vowel sounds, we use the International Phonetic Alphabet, known as the IPA. The IPA is used to represent the sounds of all the world's known languages. We will use the IPA throughout this volume to represent the vowels, consonants, stress, pitch and tone patterns of varieties of English.

The IPA was developed in the late 1800s by the International Phonetic Association to standardize how all known speech sounds were represented, regardless of language. Daniel Jones, who, as we noted in Chapter 2, published the *English Pronouncing Dictionary* in 1917, was a member of the International Phonetic Association and helped create the IPA along with other linguists including Henry Sweet, A. J. Ellis, and Paul Passy. The IPA is based on the Latin alphabet, with additional symbols from other languages, including Greek. Many of these letters are modified to create a unique symbol for each speech sound; each of these speech sounds is called a **phoneme**.

How do we produce speech sounds? The IPA classifies speech sounds using a number of descriptors based on how the sounds are physically articulated. To produce many speech sounds, we first breathe air into our lungs. This air is then expelled through our larynx, the part of the throat where our vocal cords are, as shown in Figure 3.1; our vocal cords, often called vocal folds, are folds of tissue: as the air passes through the larynx, these vocal folds can be wide open, or opening and closing at a rapid pace; they can also be closed or only slightly open. These are called different types of **phonation**: when the vocal folds are open, the phonation is called **voiceless**, while a vibration or movement of the vocal folds as the air passes through the larynx is called **voicing**. This air pressure is converted to sound waves, which are altered as the air passes into our mouth and nose; different lip shapes and tongue and mouth positions alter the sound waves to produce different speech sounds. The pathway of airflow from the vocal folds to the edge of the lips is called the vocal tract; the organs we use to create different speech sounds – including our tongue, lips, and teeth – are called **articulators** or **articulatory organs**.

It might be helpful to think of the vocal tract as a long tube, or a wind instrument like a recorder or flute (see Figure 3.2). To play a wind instrument, you first breathe air into your lungs, which you then blow into the opening of the tube or instrument. You can change the notes or sounds of the instrument by changing the shape of the tube; on a recorder, for example, you use the pads of your fingertips to cover one or more of the holes; as the air passes through the tube, it changes to different sound waves based on the shape of the tube or instrument. This is what happens in your vocal tract: you breathe air in, and as you expel it from the lungs into your vocal tract, the shape of the vocal tract – including whether your vocal folds are open or vibrating – alters the sound waves, producing different speech sounds. We use a range of articulatory organs to produce different sounds.

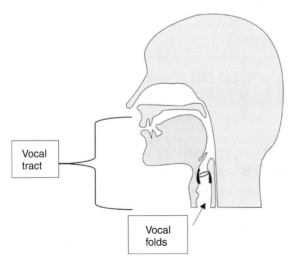

Figure 3.1 The vocal tract

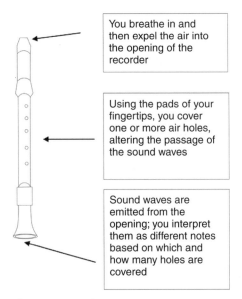

You breathe in and then expel the air into the opening of the recorder

Using the pads of your fingertips, you cover one or more air holes, altering the passage of the sound waves

Sound waves are emitted from the opening; you interpret them as different notes based on which and how many holes are covered

Figure 3.2 Recorder

A subtle change such as touching our tongue tip on the roof of our mouth versus between our teeth alters the vocal tract, and thus the sound.

The length of the vocal tract differs between adults and children, and between males and females. (This book uses the terms 'women' and 'men' when discussing gender differences in speech, except when the cited research uses the terms 'female' and 'male' to discuss biological differences in speech characteristics). Males usually have a longer vocal tract than females, and children have shorter vocal tracts than adults. Males also usually have longer and thicker vocal folds than females; both this, and the longer vocal tract length, results in male voices usually having a lower pitch than those of females, and children's voices having a higher pitch than those of adults (Simpson, 2001).

While both vowels and consonants are produced by pushing air from the lungs through the vocal cords into the mouth and/or nose, vowel and consonant articulation differs in several ways: vowels are produced with a relatively open vocal tract, meaning that the mouth is open during articulation. In addition, vowels use varying lip shapes and the mouth and tongue for articulation; in contrast, consonants use a wider range of articulators, including different parts of the roof of the mouth, the glottis, teeth, nose, lips, and tongue. For some consonants, these articulators touch or are brought close together, either stopping the airflow entirely or leaving a small space for the air to pass through, which creates friction, like white noise. This is not the case for vowels, which, as noted above, have a relatively open vocal tract during articulation. Finally, vowels are usually voiced, meaning that they are articulated with the vocal folds moving quickly, resulting in vibration as the air is pushed through the moving folds. You can feel this yourself by saying *aaaaa* and placing your hand on your vocal folds (the middle part of your throat). You should be able to feel some vibration while you say *aaaaa*. This is voicing. While some consonant sounds are produced by voicing, others are produced while the vocal folds are open, and are therefore labelled as voiceless.

These are the *phonetic differences* between vowels and consonants; there is also a *phonological difference*. If you look at the example sentence in Task 3.1, you may have noted a difference between vowels and consonants: every word in the sentence *I felt a pain in my eye* has a vowel sound, but not every word has a consonant sound. The words *I*, *a*, and *eye* do not have consonant sounds. This is a *phonological difference* between vowels and consonants: all words and all syllables within multisyllabic words must have a vowel or vowel-like sound; vowels (or a vowel-like sound, see Chapter 6) are at the centre or *nucleus* of a syllable. In English, consonants are not obligatory in a word or syllable, as we can see in the words *I*, *a*, and *eye*, which only have a vowel sound in each. All languages have vowels and consonants, but vary in the number and quality of vowels and consonants.

3.3   Characteristics of Vowels

How do we describe individual vowel sounds? In Figure 3.3, you will find a vowel diagram or chart often used to show vowel sounds in different languages and varieties. The vowel chart presented here is in the shape of a trapezoid, which may seem an unusual shape to categorize vowels. Importantly, however, the shape represents the way vowel sounds are physically articulated. Can you guess what the shape might represent?

The vowel chart is shaped like the inside of your mouth cavity, as shown in Figure 3.4. The chart represents the way in which each vowel is pronounced in terms of HAR: (1) height of the tongue; (2) front/backness of the tongue (also referred to as advancement); and (3) rounding of the lips.

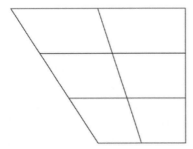

Figure 3.3 Vowel trapezoid

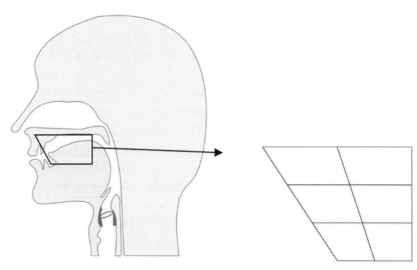

Figure 3.4 Vocal tract shape

☞ Throughout the volume, acronyms will be used for the varieties discussed in this book and as labels for the corresponding speech files.

A full list of acronyms can be found in the List of Abbreviations. When regional, social, or ethnic differences exist within a variety of English, such as Northern British English and Modern RP, these are marked with a separate acronym (e.g., BrE stands for British English, NBrE for Northern British English, and Mod RP for Modern Received Pronunciation).

A similar labelling system is employed for speech extracts from speakers from different regions of the same country, if notable regional differences exist – such as SA AusE for a speaker of Australian English from South Australia.

TASK 3.2   Listening for Height and Advancement

🎧 Listen to the speaker of General American English (GAmE) say *iiiii*, *uuuuu*, and *aaaaa*.

Let's try an experiment. If you have a mirror and/or a small hard candy or lollipop on hand, you can use them to help you feel and see how you articulate vowels. We will first compare the pronunciation of the vowel /i/ in *beat* with the vowel /æ/, which some speakers have in the word *bat*. First say *iiii* as in *beat*. Now change to *aaaaa* as in *bat* or *bad*. You may also wish to listen to Task 3.2 to hear the speaker of General American English (GAmE) say *iiiii* and *aaaaa*. What do you notice? If you have a mirror, you might see that your mouth is nearly closed when you say *iiiii* but it is relatively open when you say *aaaaa*. You might be able to feel that the tongue is lifted higher in the mouth for *iiiii* – if you insert the lollipop in the front of the mouth, you will feel that your tongue pushes the lollipop into the roof of the mouth. In contrast, if you say *aaaaa*, the lollipop rests on the tongue and does not touch the roof of your mouth. This difference is called tongue *height* and refers to whether the part of the tongue that is used to articulate the vowel is raised up high in the mouth, as with /i/, or is low in the mouth, as in /æ/. We can also refer to this as jaw openness. For /i/, your mouth is almost closed, meaning this vowel is pronounced with jaw closeness; in contrast, for /æ/, the mouth is open, so the vowel is pronounced with jaw openness. If a vowel is pronounced with a tongue height or jaw openness between /i/ and /æ/, it is considered a **mid vowel**. These labels are placed on the vowel chart as shown in Figure 3.5. All the vowels in the first row of the trapezoid – whether the back or the front of the chart – are **high** or **close vowels**, as they are pronounced with a nearly closed mouth and a high tongue height. Conversely, vowels in the lowest row are **open** or **low**, while vowels in the middle row are *mid* vowels.

The second vowel descriptor is front/backness or *advancement*. Let us do another experiment by comparing the articulation of /i/ or *iiiii* as in *beat* or *bee* with /u/ or *uuuuu* as in *boot* or *boo*. You can also refer to Task 3.2 to hear a speaker of GAmE say these two sounds. If you place the lollipop in the front part of your mouth, you may feel that when you say /u/, or *uuuuu*, the tip of your tongue does not press the lollipop high into the mouth; however, if you place the lollipop farther back in the mouth and then say /u/, the back part of the tongue pushes the lollipop into the roof of the mouth. Both /i/ and /u/ are high vowels. One difference between /i/ and /u/ is front/backness – whether the tongue is pushed forwards to the front of the mouth or pulled back in the mouth. For /i/, the tongue is raised up and pushed forwards in the mouth; conversely, for /u/, the tongue is pulled

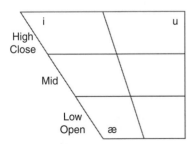

Figure 3.5 Vowel chart showing tongue height

back and high in the mouth. Therefore, /i/ is called a high **front** vowel, while /u/ is a high **back** vowel. The high back vowel /u/ is also a **rounded** vowel, with a rounded lip shape, while /i/ has a spread or neutral lip shape. /æ/ is a low front **unrounded** vowel. Vowels that are articulated with a relatively neutral tongue placement – neither pushed forwards nor pulled back – are **central** vowels.

Figure 3.6 shows the vowel chart of the IPA. The IPA vowel chart uses the terms 'close' and 'open' – rather than mentioning tongue height – which refers to the position of the jaw. 'Open' refers to an open jaw position, while 'close' refers to a nearly closed jaw position. This chart illustrates all the possible vowel sounds in the world's languages; every language has some of the vowel sounds given here though their actual pronunciation may be slightly different from how they are presented on the chart. As the IPA chart shows, it may be necessary to describe vowels as rounded or unrounded if, for example, a language has both /i/ and /y/ in its inventory, as both are high or close front vowels. As the lips are relatively spread when we say /i/, this is categorized as a high front unrounded vowel. If you say /i/ and round your lips (similar to the lip position for /u/), you have /y/, which is a high front rounded vowel. In many varieties of English as well as in most languages, front vowels tend to have a spread or neutral lip shape while back vowels tend to be rounded. Vowel duration, or length, is another characteristic used to define vowels; we will examine this below when we look at the vowels of English.

As you can see on the IPA chart, many of the symbols used to represent the vowel sounds are drawn from the Latin alphabet. However, as the Latin alphabet only has six letters to represent vowels, the IPA necessarily has modified vowel letters to represent the full range of vowel sounds – we

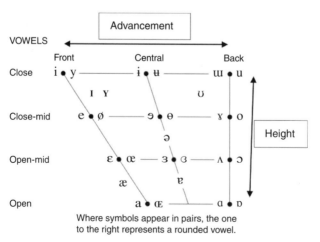

Where symbols appear in pairs, the one to the right represents a rounded vowel.

Figure 3.6 Full International Phonetic Alphabet vowel chart

therefore have *i* and *ɪ* as well as *y* and *ʏ*. Some symbols are upside down, as in *ɐ*. It is important to remember that even a slight difference in the way we write a symbol can change the vowel; for example, if we want to indicate that a vowel is a high central unrounded vowel, we must use *ɨ* – if we write *i*, we have (perhaps unintentionally) written the vowel as a high front unrounded vowel, which is a different vowel sound.

TASK 3.3 IPA Exercise

📖 Refer to the IPA chart in Figure 3.6 to answer the following questions.

(1) What are the IPA symbols for the following vowel sounds?
   (a) open back unrounded vowel
   (b) close central rounded vowel
   (c) close-mid front unrounded vowel
   (d) open-mid back rounded vowel
   (e) close-mid back rounded vowel
(2) How would you describe each of the following vowels using jaw open/closedness and/or height, rounding, and front/backness?
   (a) ʌ
   (b) œ
   (c) ɪ
   (d) ɯ
   (e) a

How many vowels do languages have? All languages have vowels. According to Maddieson (2013b), the smallest vowel inventory is 2 vowels, with the largest having 14 single vowel sounds. Of the 564 languages surveyed for vowel inventories in WALS (Dryer & Haspelmath, 2013), 93 (16%) have a small vowel inventory of 2 to 4 vowels, whereas 184 (33%) have a large vowel inventory of 7 to 14 sounds. The majority – 287 of the languages, or 51% – have a medium (or average) vowel inventory of 5 to 6 vowels. As Maddieson (2013b) notes, there are geographic differences in the number of vowels languages have: indigenous languages in Australia and North America typically have a smaller inventory of 2–4 vowels. Navajo and Aleut in the United States, Tiwi and Pitjantjatjara in Australia, Berber in northern Africa, and Greenlandic in Greenland are all languages with smaller vowel inventories. Average vowel inventories of 5 to 6 vowels are dispersed geographically across the world: in Europe, these languages include Spanish, Irish, and Modern Greek; in Africa, they include Zulu, Hausa, and Kiswahili; in Asia, they include Japanese, Hindi, Tagalog, and Mandarin Chinese; in Oceania, they include Māori and Fijian; in the Americas and the Caribbean, they include Hopi, Cherokee, and Jamaican Creole. The languages of the Niger–Congo, Nilo-Saharan, and Afro-Asiatic language families, which predominate between the Equator and the Sahara, have large vowel inventories, between 7 and 14. Larger vowel inventories also exist in many European languages, including Germanic languages such as English and German, as well as languages in Asia, including Korean and Cantonese (Maddieson, 2013c).

Which vowels are most common across languages? While languages differ in the number of vowels, which impacts the vowel inventories in different varieties of English, as we will see below, there are some commonalities in vowel inventories across languages. In Figures 3.7 and 3.8, you will see vowel charts for two languages that are average in the number of vowels: Spanish and Kiswahili; these languages influence Puerto Rican English (PRE) and Kenyan English (KenE), respectively, as well as other varieties of English. What can you notice about the vowels? Why do you think both languages have similar vowel inventories?

We can note a few things from the two vowel charts: both languages have 5 vowels; these 5 vowels are spread across the entire vowel space – there is one high/close front vowel, one mid front vowel, one low central or back vowel, one high back vowel, and one mid back vowel. Why do you think this is the case? These vowels are *maximally distinct* articulatorily and thus acoustically. In other words, the vowel inventory of both Spanish and Kiswahili utilize the entire vowel space in order to create the most distinctive types of vowels that can exist, which likely aids in intelligibility of these languages. Table 3.1 provides the most common vowels across languages, based on 451 languages analysed in the UCLA Phonological Segment Inventory Database (UPSID). As Table 3.1 shows, the most common vowels across the world's languages are /i a u/; languages with 5 vowels, like Spanish and Kiswahili, are most likely to have /i e a o u/, the most maximally distinct vowels by HAR, and therefore by acoustics (sound). In other words, if a language only has 3 vowels, these vowels are likely to

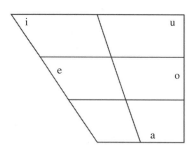

Figure 3.7 Spanish vowel chart

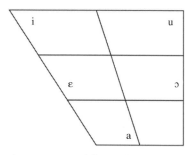

Figure 3.8 Kiswahili vowel chart

be the most distinctive articulatorily and thus acoustically – a high front vowel, a high back vowel, and low (often central) vowel. Languages with 5 vowels may have a mid front vowel as well as a mid back vowel in addition to the high front, high back and low vowels.

Figure 3.9 shows the vowel inventory for Cantonese, a Chinese language that influences Hong Kong English (HKE), among other varieties of English. Cantonese has a large vowel inventory, with 11 vowels, with some vowels differentiated by rounding (/i/ vs /y/) or a slightly higher or lower tongue height (e.g., /u/ vs /o/, and /e/ vs /ɛ/). As this vowel chart suggests, the more vowels a language has in its inventory, the closer in articulation some of the vowels are to each other, with in some cases only a slight change in mouth openness or tongue height and/or lip rounding differentiating the vowel phonemes.

How can you tell which vowels exist in a language and/or variety of English? One way to establish the vowel inventories in different languages and varieties is to analyse vowel sounds acoustically for a precise measurement of each vowel's height and front/backness in the same linguistic environment – meaning that the sounds preceding and following the vowel are the same. To do this, it is best to have a high-quality recording (see Appendix A) of vowels in the same linguistic environment to compare

Table 3.1 The most common vowels cross-linguistically

Vowel	Description	# of languages in UPSID	% of languages in UPSID
/i/	High front unrounded vowel	393	87.10
/a/	Low central unrounded vowel	392	86.90
/u/	High back rounded vowel	369	81.80
/ɛ/	Lower mid front unrounded vowel	186	41.20
/o/	Mid back rounded vowel	181	40.10
/e/	Mid front unrounded vowel	169	37.47
/ɔ/	Lower mid back rounded vowel	162	35.92

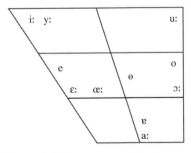

Figure 3.9 Cantonese vowel chart

vowel articulation. In English, many researchers have adopted the approach first used by Peterson and Barney (1952) of placing vowels in the linguistic environment of [hVd], where V denotes the vowel. The production of a vowel after the consonant [h] and preceding the consonant [d] creates a steady state for the vowel, a stable articulation, and therefore stable sound waves for analysis. Peterson and Barney created the following list of eleven words for the single vowel sounds of GAmE: *heed, hid, head, had, hod, hawed, hood, who'd, hud, hayed,* and *heard*. These words are often said in a carrier sentence to neutralize the linguistic environment: *I say [hVd] again.* Other linguistic environments are also commonly used, including [bVt], as in *beat, bit, bet, bat,* etc. We have already examined the vowel inventory of Kiswahili, which influences KenE. In Figure 3.10, you can find the vowel chart of a speaker of KenE. KenE has five single vowel sounds, /i e a o u/, due to influence from Kiswahili. The vowel chart was created by measuring individual vowel sounds in the same linguistic environment using the free software program Praat (Boersma & Weenink, 2021). The vowel chart resembles the articulatory chart we discussed above; in the vowel chart generated through an acoustic analysis, however, a series of numbers are used to represent tongue height and front/backness. There are two ranges shown on this chart – the first, representing height, is from 200 to 1200 hertz, while front/backness is from 3500 to 500 hertz. Hertz (Hz), named after Heinrich Rudolf Hertz, is a unit of frequency and measures cycles per second. Formant values represent bands of energy that can be measured acoustically; **formants** refers to the bands of frequency. You can listen to the KenE speaker say the individual vowel sounds in Task 3.4.

TASK 3.4 Listening for Vowels

🎧 Listen to the speaker of KenE say each single vowel sound: /i e a o u/.

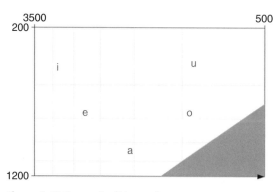

Figure 3.10 Kenyan English vowels

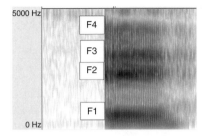

Figure 3.11 Formants for Kenyan English /e/

Four bands of energy can be seen and measured on a spectrogram, which is the visual image generated in an acoustic analysis; this is shown in Figure 3.11. Formants are labelled from F1 to F4: F1, the lowest band of energy, corresponds to tongue height; these are labelled in Figure 3.11. The lower the number for the F1, the higher the vowel; the **F2** formant represents front/backness – the higher the number, the more fronted the articulation; lip rounding lowers the F2 – as noted above, in English (as in many other languages), back vowels tend to be rounded while front vowels tend to have a neutral or spread lip shape. Measuring both the F1 and F2 is usually sufficient to identify and categorize vowels; movement of the **F3** can indicate rhoticity and will be discussed at length in Chapter 4. F4 is usually not measured in research on vowels as this formant does not provide acoustic cues to the identification of vowels, unlike F1 and F2. Something else that can be measured is labelled **F0**; this is the rate of vocal fold opening and closings (oscillations) per second and called **fundamental frequency**. We hear F0 as pitch; we will discuss this in more detail in Chapter 8.

Male and female voices have different formant values because of the difference in size and shape of the vocal tract: as noted above, males have longer vocal tracts as well as thicker vocal folds. Table 3.2 presents the average F1 and F2 values for female, male, and child speakers of American English (AmE), based on research by Hillenbrand, Getty, Clark, and Wheeler (1995). We can convert the F1 and F2 values to a Bark Scale (Zwicker & Terhardt, 1980; see Appendix A), which allows us to see the actual position of the vowels in the mouth. This is shown in Figure 3.12 for four of the vowels in Table 3.2.

Figure 3.12 shows a vowel chart created for four of the vowels based on Hillenbrand et al.'s values. Previous research (Simpson, 2001) has found that females' F1xF2 vowel space is larger than that of males, with a number of reasons posited to explain this difference, including socio-phonetic factors and anatomical (the size/shape of the vocal tract) differences. What is clear – and as both Table 3.2 and Figure 3.12 illustrate – is that we need to analyse vowels separately by gender and age due to different

Vowel	Children	Female	Male
/i/	F1: 452	F1: 437	F1: 342
	F2: 3081	F2: 2761	F2: 2322
/ɪ/	F1: 511	F1: 482	F1: 427
	F2: 2552	F2: 2365	F2: 2034
/e/	F1: 564	F1: 536	F1: 476
	F2: 2656	F2: 2530	F2: 2089
/ɛ/	F1: 749	F1: 731	F1: 580
	F2: 2267	F2: 2058	F2: 1799
/æ/	F1: 717	F1: 669	F1: 588
	F2: 2501	F2: 2349	F2: 1952
/ɑ/	F1: 1002	F1: 936	F1: 768
	F2: 1688	F2: 1551	F2: 1333
/ɔ/	F1: 803	F1: 781	F1: 652
	F2: 1210	F2: 1136	F2: 997
/o/	F1: 597	F1: 555	F1: 497
	F2: 1137	F2: 1035	F2: 910
/u/	F1: 568	F1: 519	F1: 469
	F2: 1490	F2: 1225	F2: 1122
/ʊ/	F1: 494	F1: 459	F1: 378
	F2: 1345	F2: 1105	F2: 997
/ʌ/	F1: 749	F1: 753	F1: 623
	F2: 1546	F2: 1426	F2: 1200
/ɚ/	F1: 586	F1: 523	F1: 474
	F2: 1719	F2: 1588	F2: 1379

Table 3.2 Average F1–F2 values for American English vowels for children and adults

(*Source:* Hillenbrand et al., 1995)

acoustic properties. To find the F1 and F2 values, we can use an acoustic software program such as Praat (Boersma & Weenink, 2021); as discussed above, Figure 3.11 shows a spectrogram of a KenE speaker's articulation of the vowel /e/ based on an acoustic analysis using Praat. In the spectrogram, four dark bands of energy are visible; each of these four bands represents a formant, with the lowest band in the picture representing tongue height – it is labelled F1; the second band represents front/backness and is labelled F2. To measure the F1 and F2, the midpoint of the F1 and F2 is used.

We can also compare the formant values visually on spectrograms to see whether a vowel is high or low (the lower the F1, the higher the vowel) or front or back (the higher the F2, the fronter the vowel). Figures 3.13, 3.14, and 3.15 show the same KenE speaker's production of /i/

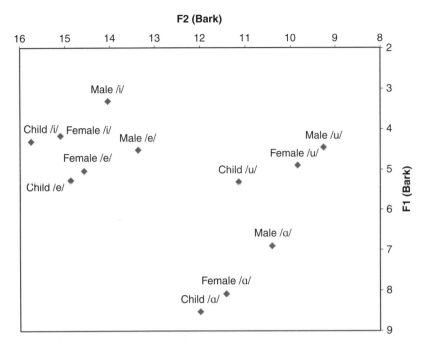

Figure 3.12 American English vowels

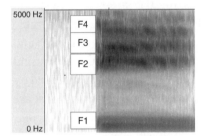

Figure 3.13 Formants for Kenyan English /i/

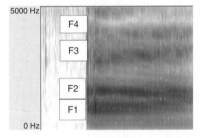

Figure 3.14 Formants for Kenyan English /ɑ/

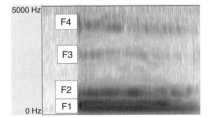

Figure 3.15 Formants for Kenyan English /u/

(Figure 3.13), /a/ (Figure 3.14), and /u/ (Figure 3.15). If we compare these four spectrograms, we can see that the F1 of /i/ and /u/ are both lower than the F1 of /e/ and /a/, as both /i/ and /u/ are high vowels. We can also see that the F2 of /i/ and /e/ are both higher than the F2 of /u/ and /a/, as both /i/ and /e/ are front vowels. To summarize, /i/ is a high front vowel and has a low F1 and high F2. /u/ is a high back vowel and has a low F1 and a low F2. As a mid vowel, /e/ has a lower F1 than /a/, a low vowel, which has a high F1; /e/ has a higher F2 than /u/ as a fronted vowel. /a/ has a higher F1 than the other vowels, and an F2 between /i/ and /u/, as a central vowel. These values are shown in the vowel space on the vowel chart in Figure 3.10.

3.4   Categorizing Vowel Inventories across Varieties of English

Which vowels sounds exist in the English language and how do vowels differ across varieties of English? The phonetician John Wells developed Lexical Sets to identify and categorize vowels systematically across different varieties of English; these are known as Wells' Lexical Sets (Wells, 1982). They are based on the vowel inventories of GAmE and Traditional Received Pronunciation (Trad RP) and categorize words into sets that share the same vowel, with a keyword to represent each distinctive vowel. It includes twenty-four different Lexical Sets for the stressed vowels and three additional sets for the weak vowels (happY, commA, lettER – see Chapter 6). The Lexical Sets and representative vowels in Trad RP and GAmE are given in Table 3.3, based on Wells (1982). The corresponding word in the [hVd] set is given, when relevant. It has been supplemented by nonsense words to represent vowels in other varieties of English. Nonsense words do not have any meaning but have been created to test a particular sound or feature. As Wells' Lexical Sets are widely used in research on World Englishes, we will refer to them throughout this book. The word list for analysing your own pronunciation in this book is also drawn in part from the Lexical Sets (see Appendix A.) It is important to note that the Lexical Sets may not represent all possible vowel sounds in varieties of English, necessitating the creation of subsets and splits/mergers within the different vowel sets. You can listen to Task 3.5 to hear speakers of GAmE and Modern RP (Mod RP) say the keywords in Wells' Lexical Sets (while a number of differences do exist between Trad and Mod RP, as will be discussed below, this exercise is designed to highlight differences between GAmE and RP). Key differences between the two varieties are bolded in Table 3.3. In words of more than one syllable, the relevant vowel or syllable is underlined.

Table 3.3 Vowels and keywords

Lexical Sets	[hVd]	Trad RP	GAmE	Typical spelling	Example words
KIT	hid	ɪ	ɪ	iC[a]	bit, sick, milk, wish, sing
DRESS	head	e	ɛ	eC	bet, pen, neck, edge, friend
TRAP	had	æ	æ	aC	tap, cat, back, hand, badge
LOT	hod	ɒ	ɑ	oC	stop, pot, sock, dodge, romp
STRUT	hud	ʌ	ʌ	uC	cup, cut, trunk, blood, pulse
FOOT	hood	ʊ	ʊ	uC, ooC, ouC	put, full, good, look, should
BATH		ɑː	æ	aCC (ff, th, ft, sp, st, sk ...)	path, dance, ask, staff, brass
CLOTH		ɒ	ɔ	o, au + fricative, ou	soft, long, cough
NURSE	herd heard	ɜː	ɜr	ur, ir, er, earC	hurt, lurk, urge, girl, shirt
FLEECE	heed	iː	i	e, ee, eCe, ea, oeC, i	teeth, meat, ski, chic, tea
FACE	hade hayed	eɪ	eɪ	aCe, aiC, ay, ey, eiC, aig, ea	cake, wait, rein, they, steak
PALM		ɑː	ɑ	a#,[b] ah	spa, calm, father, Bach, ma
THOUGHT		ɔː	ɔ	auC, ough, aw, al, alk, alC	taught, salt, saw, fought, talk
GOAT	hoed	əʊ	o	o, oC, oa, ow, ol	soap, home, toe, bowl, roll
GOOSE	who'd	uː	u	o, oo, oCe, ou, uCe, euC, ew, uiC, iew#, eaut	tooth, mute, fruit, view, shoe
PRICE	hide	aɪ	aɪ	iCe, i, y	write, time, fight, high, die
CHOICE	hoid	ɔɪ	ɔɪ	oy, oiC	boy, oil, noise, moist, toy
MOUTH	howd	aʊ	aʊ	ouC, ow	house, noun, cow, mouth
NEAR	heered	ɪə	ɪr	eer, ere, ier, ear, erV, ierC, eirC	beer, here, pier, weird, eerie
SQUARE	hared	ɛə	ɛr	are#, air#, ear#, eir#, ere#, ary, arC	care, air, area, fair, pear
START	hard	ɑː	ɑr	ar#, arC	far, part, farm, sari, sharp

Table 3.3 (Cont.)

Lexical Sets	[hVd]	Trad RP	GAmE	Typical spelling	Example words
NORTH		ɔː	ɔr	or#, ar#, orC, uar, aur	or, for, fork, born
FORCE	hoard	ɔː	or	ore, oar#, oor#, our#, ourC, oarC	hoarse, floor, four, sport
CURE	hured	ʊə	ʊr	oor#, our#, ourC, oori, ouri, ure, orV, eur	poor, tour, <u>jury</u>, sure, gourd
happY		ɪ	ɪ, i	y#, i#, ie#, ee#, ey#, ea#	city, vall<u>ey</u>, tax<u>i</u>, cop<u>y</u>, bab<u>y</u>
lettER		ə	ər	er#, or#, o(u)r#, yr#, ure#,	pap<u>er</u>, maj<u>or</u>, err<u>or</u>, leath<u>er</u>, tig<u>er</u>
commA		ə	ə	a#, ia#	pand<u>a</u>, sof<u>a</u>, vis<u>a</u>

^a C = consonant

^b # indicates previous sound is the final segment in a word or syllable

(*Source:* Based on Wells' (1982) Lexical Sets)

TASK 3.5 Listening for Wells' Lexical Sets

🎧 Listen to the speaker of GAmE and the speaker of Mod RP, a modern variety of Trad RP, say the keywords in the Lexical Sets in Table 3.3. Key differences between American and British English vowel pronunciations are highlighted in the table in bold.

- What do you notice about the pronunciation of the vowels by the GAmE and the Mod RP speaker in the following words: SQUARE, NEAR, CURE?
- Can you also hear differences in the pronunciation of FORCE, NORTH, NURSE, START, and lettER? What do these eight words have in common in spelling?
- What is the difference between BATH and TRAP for the GAmE and the Mod RP speaker?
- What is the difference between LOT and CLOTH for the GAmE and the Mod RP speaker?

As Table 3.3 shows, GAmE and Trad RP have similar (though not necessarily identical) vowels in the following Lexical Sets: KIT, DRESS, TRAP, STRUT, FOOT, FLEECE, FACE, PALM, THOUGHT, GOOSE, PRICE, CHOICE, MOUTH, COMMA, and HAPPY. The other Lexical Sets represent key differences in GAmE and Trad RP. LOT in Trad RP is merged with CLOTH (both [ɒ]), whereas in GAmE, LOT is merged with PALM (both [ɑ]). BATH in Trad RP is merged with PALM, whereas in GAmE it is merged with TRAP. Whereas CLOTH is merged with LOT in Trad RP, CLOTH in GAmE is merged with THOUGHT. Another key difference is the pronunciation of the vowel and /r/ in words in what are called the *r* Lexical Sets, words with an 'r' in spelling after the vowel: NURSE, SQUARE, NORTH, FORCE, START, CURE, NEAR, and lettER. As you can note from the examples of Trad RP and GAmE shown in Table 3.3, this is a major difference between these two Englishes – whether *r* is articulated after the vowel or not. For Trad RP, a **diphthong** (a series of two different vowel sounds, with movement from the first to the second vowel; see also below) exists in SQUARE, NEAR and CURE while GAmE has a single vowel sound followed by an *r* sound; GAmE also has an 'r' sound in other *r* Lexical Sets while Trad (and Mod) RP does not. This feature is called *rhoticity* and is a major difference among varieties of English worldwide. Rhoticity will be discussed in detail in Chapter 4.

Why do some vowels have one letter and other vowels have two? We need to distinguish among different types of vowel sounds; thus far, we have been discussing single vowel sounds, with a stable articulation that can be plotted on a vowel chart. These types of vowels are called **monophthongs**, with *mono* representing the single, or pure, nature of the sound. The vowel /i/ is a monophthong, as are /u/ and /æ/. In Wells' Lexical Sets (1982; see above in Table 3.3), all the vowels represented by single vowel letters are monophthongs: for GAmE and Trad RP, this includes KIT, DRESS, FLEECE, GOOSE, TRAP, and LOT, among others. English also has vowels that are produced by moving from one vowel sound to another, with a change of articulation from one vowel to the next. This includes /aʊ/ in MOUTH, as in *how* or *cow*, which moves from low central or back to a high back vowel, or /ei/ in FACE, as in *say* or *may*, which moves from mid front to a high front. These vowels comprise two different vowel sounds and are called *diphthongs*, as discussed above. As Table 3.3 shows, GAmE and Trad RP share diphthongs, as represented by PRICE, CHOICE, MOUTH, and FACE; Trad and Mod RP (as well as many other BrE and other English varieties) have several more diphthongs in CURE, NEAR, and SQUARE, which as you may have noted in Task 3.5 have an *r* in spelling after the vowel. Many AmE varieties have monophthong vowels in these words. **Triphthongs** can also occur when there is a movement from one vowel to a second and then a third. This occurs in some varieties of English, including some BrE varieties; these are not included in Wells' Lexical Sets, however, but will be discussed in more detail below.

We also need to distinguish between vowels that are **tense** and those that are **lax**, and vowels that are considered **long** vs **short**. These terms are sometimes used synonymously, with 'tense' and 'long' used to refer to the same category of vowels, as are 'lax' and 'short'. One definition of the tense/lax dichotomy is based on articulation, with vowels that are categorized as tense articulated with a tightening (or tensing) of the tongue muscles (try saying *iiii* as in the FLEECE Lexical Set and see if you feel that your tongue, and possibly jaw, feel tense or tight). Lax vowels, in contrast, do not have this tensing but instead are articulated with relaxed tongue muscles (you may notice a difference in jaw tightness when you say FLEECE vs KIT; KIT has a lax vowel). In some varieties of English, including GAmE and Trad RP, the vowels in the FLEECE, GOOSE, and NURSE Lexical Sets, among others, are tense, while the vowels in the KIT, DRESS, TRAP, FOOT Lexical Sets are lax. The vowels that are called tense may also be labelled as *long* in some varieties of English, while the lax vowels may be *short* if there is a length distinction in that variety of English. Not all varieties of English have a length distinction, as we will see below. If a length distinction does exist, the tense vowel should be longer than the lax vowel of the same height if the vowels are in the same linguistic environment – for example, the vowel in *beat* should sound longer than the vowel in *bit*, and the vowel in *pool* should sound longer than the vowel in *pull*. The symbol (called a diacritic) used to signify a longer length is : as in /uː/ in GOOSE. The diacritic : is often used to mark a tense/long vowel while singleton vowels (monophthongs) without the length mark are lax/short.

TASK 3.6 Listening for Vowel Length

🎧 Listen to the speakers of different varieties of English.

- Can you hear a length difference in *bead* and *bid* for some speakers?
- Which speakers and varieties have a length difference in *bead* and *bid* and which ones do not?
  Speaker 1   Modern RP
  Speaker 2   Singapore English (SgE)
  Speaker 3   Irish English (IrE)
  Speaker 4   Kenyan English (KenE)
  Speaker 5   White South African English (WSAE)
  Speaker 6   Australian English (AusE)

There is also a distributional difference in tense and lax vowels in some varieties, with tense vowels able to occur in what are called **open syllables** (see Chapter 6), without a consonant following the vowel in the same syllable, as in the word *bee* (FLEECE). In contrast, lax vowels can only occur in closed syllables in these varieties – with a consonant following the vowel in the same syllable, as in *bit* or *bid* (KIT), unless it is a weak vowel (see Chapter 6); for this reason, these vowels are often called **checked vowels**. Tense vowels can also occur in closed syllables but, unlike lax vowels, they also occur in open syllables and therefore are called **free vowels** as they can occur in both open and closed syllables. Diphthongs can also occur in both open and closed syllables and are therefore categorized as free vowels too. In Table 3.3, you can see the spelling patterns and sample words for each vowel in the Lexical Sets; as Table 3.3 shows, words in the Lexical Sets of the lax vowels in some varieties of English (including AmE and BrE), such as KIT, DRESS, TRAP, and LOT, are all spelled with a vowel plus C, with C representing a consonant sound after the vowel in the same syllable. In contrast, both tense vowels and diphthongs have spellings ending in the vowel, or with a vowel after the consonant (e.g., as in uCe in *mute* in the GOOSE Lexical Set). This *silent e* spelling for tense vowels and diphthongs is a historical spelling for long vowels from the Middle English period (see Chapter 2).

3.5　The Vowels of English Around the World

> ### TASK 3.7 Listening for Lexical Sets across Varieties of English
>
> 🎧 Listen to the following speakers say the keywords in Wells' Lexical Sets. What differences can you hear in the pronunciation of the keywords across the different varieties of English?
>
> Speaker 1　AmE speaker from California (Calif AmE)
> Speaker 2　AusE speaker from South Australia (SA AusE)
> Speaker 3　Mod RP
> Speaker 4　HKE
> Speaker 5　IrE
> Speaker 6　KenE
> Speaker 7　SgE
> Speaker 8　PRE

How and why do vowels differ across varieties of English? Vowel inventories vary significantly across varieties of English; in fact, there are greater vowel than consonant differences across Englishes around the world. These differences include regional features arising from historical and geographical factors; they also include linguistic influences from languages shared among members of a particular ethnic group, as in Chicano English (ChiE) in the US, and Māori English (MāoriE) in New Zealand. NVEs, including PCEs such as HKE, PRE, SgE, KenE, and Indian English (IndE), are influenced by local languages, among them Cantonese (HKE, SgE), Malay (SgE, as well as Malaysian English – MalE), Hindi (IndE), Kiswahili (KenE), and Spanish (PRE). As English spread among the local population through education, features of the substrate language entered into English, creating unique varieties of English.

Finally, it is important to note that there exists variation within varieties of English, so the vowel inventories and other phonetic and phonological features discussed throughout this book are to some extent a generalized description of each variety. The substrate and superstrate influences on varieties of English may also change across time; while BrE may have had more influence historically in postcolonial contexts such as Hong Kong and Singapore, American as well as other varieties of English, including African American Vernacular English (AAVE) and Multicultural London English (MLE), may exert a growing influence due to the spread of these varieties through education, music, and other media. As noted in Chapter 2, in some varieties of English, including AusE and NZE, we can distinguish among Cultivated (closest to RP), General (the more standard pronunciation, with a few regional and sociocultural features), and Broad (most local features) varieties, whereas PCE and other NVEs may have acrolectal (most prestigious and closest to the superstrate variety), mesolectal (unique linguistic features due to the influence of substrate languages), and basilectal (least prestigious and with the most substratum influences) varieties.

We will now look at the vowel systems of a range of varieties of English. These are arranged geographically, grouped by continent bodies. We will first examine the Englishes of the UK and Ireland, followed by the Americas and the Caribbean, and then Oceania, Africa, and Asia. Throughout our discussion, we will refer to Wells' Lexical Sets (see Table 3.3). Speech samples are provided for many of the varieties discussed to illustrate the key features of each variety.

☞ The following discussion is intended to provide a comprehensive overview of vowels across a wide range of Englishes to be inclusive in the presentation of English vowels.

Although you are encouraged to listen to examples of several different varieties of English to expand your understanding of vowels as well as World Englishes, you may wish to focus your attention on the varieties of English that are of interest to you. An index of the varieties and the relevant page numbers is given below:

- UK and Ireland: 67–72
- North America and the Caribbean: 72–6
- Oceania: 76–82
- Africa: 82–7
- Asia: 88–95

3.5.1   The Vowels of Varieties of English in the UK and Ireland

We begin by examining the vowel inventories of three varieties of English in England: Mod RP, London English (LonE), and Northern BrE (NBrE). Vowels differ significantly across England; these three varieties will form the basis of our discussion as they illustrate differences in BrE. Mod RP is a non-regional, non-class accent of BrE, which has changed to some extent from an older form of RP, which is now referred to as Trad RP (Upton, 2015). It is sometimes referred to as General British English or SSBE (Cruttenden, 2014). LonE is the innovator for BrE, with features spreading into LonE from Cockney English, and diffusing outside of London to other parts of Southeast England, and from the working into the higher classes (Altendorf & Watt, 2004). It has also been called Estuary English. NBrE is an umbrella term for varieties of English spoken in the northern counties of England (Beal, 2004). Northern varieties of BrE differ from Southern varieties of BrE, which will be highlighted below; as discussed in Chapter 2, regional differences existed in Old and Middle Englishes as well, with some of these differences still in existence today. The Northern dialects have greater influence from Scandinavian languages due to Danelaw (see Chapter 2); many of these historical differences remain in these varieties today. Table 3.4 presents vowels found in Mod RP, NBrE, and LonE.

BrE varieties have a tense/lax distinction and length difference. According to Upton (2015), the vowels of Mod RP consist of 12 monophthong vowels and 7 diphthongs. A major difference between Mod and Trad RP (see Table 3.3) is the lowering of the TRAP vowel from /æ/ to /a/; DRESS is also in the process of lowering from /e/ to /ɛ/, and BATH is becoming more centralized from /ɑː/ to /a/, while SQUARE and CURE are becoming or have become monophthongal (Upton, 2015). In CHOICE, for example, the movement is from a mid back /ɔ/ towards a high front /ɪ/. Some descriptions of RP also include 5 triphthongs, vowels with movement from one to a second to a third member, as in *fire* or *hour*. Other descriptions treat the vowels in words such as *fire* and *hour* as comprising two vowel sequences – a diphthong

Table 3.4 Vowels in British English

	Front	Central	Back
High	/iː/ FLEECE (R, N) /ɪ/ KIT	/ʉː/ GOOSE (L, N) /ø ʏ/ FOOT (L, N) – also /ʊ/	/uː/ GOOSE (R, N) /ʊ/ FOOT – also /ø ʏ/ (L, N); STRUT (N)
Mid	/ɛ/ (or /e/) DRESS (R, N) /e/ DRESS (L) /ɛː/ SQUARE (R, N) /eː/ FACE (N)	/ə: ɜː/ NURSE	/oː/ THOUGHT/ NORTH/FORCE – also /ɔə/ (L); GOAT (N) /ɔː/ THOUGHT/ FORCE/NORTH (R, N)
Low	/æ/ TRAP (L) /a/ TRAP (R, N) – also /æ/ (R); BATH (N) /aː/ PALM/START (N)	/ʌ/ STRUT (R, L)	/ɒ/ LOT/CLOTH /ɑː/ PALM/BATH/ START (L, R)
Diphthongs (starting vowel)	/ii/ FLEECE (L) /ɪə iə/ NEAR /eɪ/ FACE (R, N) /eə/ SQUARE (L) /ɛə/ SQUARE (N) /æʊ/ MOUTH (L) /aʊ/ MOUTH (R, N)	/əʊ/ – GOAT (R) /ʌɪ/ or /aɪ/ – PRICE (R) /aɪ/ PRICE (N) /ʌɪ/ FACE (L) /ʌʊ/ GOAT (L)	/jʊə/ but becoming /ɔː/ CURE (R, N) /uə/ CURE (L) /ɔɪ/ CHOICE /ɑɪ/ PRICE (L) /ɒʊ/ GOAL (L)

When differences exist in vowel inventories, they are marked as: R = Mod RP, L = LonE, N = NBrE

(/ʌɪ/ or /aɪ/ in *fire* and /aʊ/ in *hour*), with the second vowel a weak vowel, the /ə/. This is the approach adopted in this book.

LonE (and Southeast BrE more generally) has similar vowels to Mod RP for all the lax/short vowels (KIT, DRESS, TRAP, LOT, STRUT, and FOOT) as well as for several long vowels (BATH/PALM/START). Several diphthongs are shifting in the vowel quality of the first member of the diphthong, with the onset of MOUTH and GOAT becoming more fronted. Several long vowels are becoming diphthongal (FLEECE as /ii/, THOUGHT as /ɔə/) in LonE; these shifts are part of the Southern Vowel Shift, which will be discussed in more detail below. LonE also retains the diphthong in SQUARE as /eə/, which has become monophthongal in Mod RP. In LonE, GOOSE is a mid central vowel (/ʉ/), having undergone a process called GOOSE-fronting (Altendorf & Watt, 2004); FOOT is also undergoing fronting in LonE. Both fronting processes are part of the Southern Vowel Shift (see below). GOOSE-fronting and FOOT-fronting, to some extent, are also common in Southwest English, West Midlands English, and Multicultural London English (MLE), an ethnolect influenced by London Jamaican (Cheshire, Kerswill, Fox, &

Torgersen, 2011). They are also spreading into Northern varieties of English (Baranowski, 2017).

There is a major dialect boundary in England between Southern and Northern dialects, each of which have their own regional differences. A major difference between Northern and Southern dialects is the split between the FOOT and STRUT Lexical Sets: Southern BrE varieties differentiate FOOT and STRUT while NBrE varieties have a merger between FOOT and STRUT, which are both /ʊ/. Northern varieties of BrE also lack a TRAP/BATH distinction, which exists in Southern English, including RP and LonE (Altendorf & Watt, 2004). Northern varieties may also have a merger between NURSE and SQUARE (Beal, 2004).

TASK 3.8 Listening for British English

🎧 Listen to two speakers of different varieties of BrE read aloud words to represent the vowels of each variety. You may notice the following features:

Speaker 1   Mod RP from London: GOOSE-fronting, SQUARE as monophthong, TRAP and BATH as separate Lexical Sets, lowered DRESS

Speaker 2   Northern British English (NBrE) from Northwest England: TRAP/BATH merger, FOOT/STRUT merger, GOOSE-fronting

• You can also listen to the NBrE and a speaker of East Midlands British English (EMidBrE) talk about BrE accents.

The variety of IrE in Table 3.5 is based on New Dublin English (NDubE) (previously called *Fashionable Dublin English*) and adapted from Hickey (2004); it is a non-local urban variety of IrE spoken in Ireland by people born in the 1960s and later. As Hickey (2004) notes, it 'acts as a de facto standard for the rest of the south when speakers, outside of Dublin, are seeking a non-local, generally acceptable form of Irish English' (p. 86). Like other IrE varieties, it is influenced by Irish, a Celtic language. In Northern Ireland, varieties of IrE are referred to as either Ulster English or Northern IrE; these varieties are influenced by Ulster Irish and Scots, both Celtic languages. NDubE has similar short vowels to both Mod RP and LonE – /ɪ/ in KIT, /ɛ/ in DRESS, /æ/ in TRAP (LonE only), /ʌ/ in STRUT, and /ʊ/ in FOOT – as well as similar long vowels to Mod RP in FLEECE and GOOSE (not fronted), and THOUGHT, though the latter may be slightly raised for some speakers of NDubE. It also has the same diphthongs in PRICE (as LonE), CHOICE, GOAT (as Mod RP). Unlike Mod RP and LonE, NDubE has /ɔ/ in LOT and CLOTH. It also has a more centralized vowel in BATH/PALM /aː/ and a monophthongal (loss of one vowel in a diphthong to create a single vowel sound; typically the 2nd target is weakened and eventually lost) vowel in FACE (/eː/). The first vowel in the diphthong MOUTH is also notably fronted for the 1st target, /ɛʊ/. IrE also differs significantly in its number of diphthongs from many varieties of BrE, with monophthong vowels in the *r* Lexical Sets.

TASK 3.9 Listening for Irish English

🎧 Listen to a speaker of IrE from Dublin. His accent is NDubE. A few features you may notice in his speech:

- PALM/BATH have merged into a low central vowel
- MOUTH has a raised 1st target
- /r/ is produced after vowels in words in the 'r' Lexical Sets
- FACE is monophthongal

The vowel inventory of Welsh English (WelE) presented in Table 3.6 is Rural WelE, based on Penhallurick (2004). Similar to Mod RP and LonE, Rural WelE has a tense/lax vowel distinction, and has similar vowel sounds

Table 3.5 Vowels in Irish English

	Front	Central	Back
High	/iː/ FLEECE /ɪ/ KIT		/uː/ GOOSE /ʊ/ FOOT
Mid	/eː/ FACE /ɛ/ DRESS		/ɔː oː/ THOUGHT /ɔ/ LOT, CLOTH
Low	/æ/ TRAP	/ʌ/ STRUT /aː/ PALM/BATH	
'r' Lexical Sets	/iːɹ/ NEAR /eːɹ, øːɹ/ SQUARE	/ɚɹ, øːɹ/ NURSE	/juːɹ/ CURE – also /jəɹ/ /ɔːɹ, oːɹ/ FORCE /ɒːɹ, ɔːɹ/ NORTH /aːɹ/ START
Diphthongs	/ɛʊ/ MOUTH	/əʊ/ GOAT – also /oː/	/ɔɪ, oɪ/ CHOICE /aɪ/ PRICE

Table 3.6 Vowels in Welsh English

	Front	Central	Back
High	/i:/ FLEECE /ɪ/ KIT		/u:/ GOOSE /ʊ/ FOOT
Mid	/e:/ FACE /ɛ/ DRESS /ɛ:/ SQUARE /œ/ NURSE		/o:/ GOAT /ɔ/ LOT/CLOTH/ CHOICE /ɔ:/ THOUGHT/ NORTH/ FORCE
Low		/ʌ/ STRUT /a:/ PALM/BATH – also /a/; START /a/ TRAP/BATH – also /a:/	
Diphthongs	/iə/ NEAR /(ɪ)uwe/ CURE	/ai/ PRICE /au/ MOUTH	

in KIT, DRESS, TRAP (to Mod RP), STRUT, FOOT, THOUGHT, GOOSE (non-fronted), FLEECE (to Mod RP), NORTH and FORCE (to Mod RP), PRICE (Trad RP), and NEAR. Like NDubE, it has a mid back vowel in LOT and CLOTH, a centralized vowel in BATH/PALM, and a monophthong in FACE. Unlike the varieties discussed so far, Rural WelE has monophthongs in GOAT (/o:/) and CHOICE /ɔ/. It also has a more fronted articulation of the vowel in NURSE: /œ/. Vowels followed by *r* in SQUARE, START are produced as monophthongs, while CURE has a disyllabic (2-syllable) pronunciation with a consonant sound /w/ separating the vowels.

Table 3.7 shows the vowel inventory of Standard Scottish English (SSE), based on Stuart-Smith (2004). Stuart-Smith defines SSE as 'Standard English spoken with a Scottish accent' (p. 47). Key differences between SSE and the other varieties of English in the UK and Ireland that have been discussed above are that SSE speakers may have a lowered and more open vowel in KIT (as /ë/), and some speakers may have a low central vowel for BATH/TRAP/PALM. SSE also has a merger between FOOT/GOOSE, which are both realized as a central or fronted /ʉ/. Like NDubE, SSE also tends to monophthongize the vowels in GOAT and FACE, and realizes vowels before *r* as monophthongs as in SQUARE and NEAR, unlike Mod RP and LonE. The first and second members of the diphthongs in PRICE, CHOICE, and MOUTH also differ from other varieties of English, with a low central start in PRICE (similar to Mod RP), and MOUTH, and a mid front rather than high front end in CHOICE (/ɔe/).

Table 3.7 Vowels in Scottish English

	Front	Central	Back
High	/i/ FLEECE /ɪ ë/ KIT	/ʉ/ GOOSE, FOOT	
Mid	/e/ FACE /ɛ/ DRESS		/o/ GOAT /ɔ̈/ LOT/THOUGHT/CLOTH
Low		/ʌ/ STRUT /a/ TRAP/BATH/ PALM	
'r' Lexical Sets	/iɹ/ NEAR /eɹ/ SQUARE	/ʌɹ/ NURSE /aɹ/ START /jʉɹ/ CURE	/oɹ/ FORCE /ɔ̈ɹ/ NORTH
Diphthongs		/ʌʉ/ MOUTH /ʌi/ PRICE	/ɔe/ CHOICE

3.5.2   The Vowels of Varieties of English in North America and the Caribbean

Table 3.8 features the vowel inventories of both GAmE and Canadian English (CanE); unless otherwise indicated, the vowels are similar in the two varieties. The non-regional variety of AmE considered the standard is often labelled GAmE (see Wells, 1982, and Table 3.3 above). Kretzschmar (2004) refers to this variety as Standard American English (StAmE), a variety spoken by educated speakers in formal environments that does not have marked regional features. Midwestern AmE is also often considered representative of the GAmE accent, as many speakers of Midwestern AmE lack noticeable regional features. According to Wells (1982) and Kretzschmar (2004), GAmE has five diphthongs, which is fewer than many varieties of BrE, including LonE and both Trad and Mod RP. Like the English of the UK and Ireland, GAmE has both long and short vowels; although they are not marked by length marks in the description above, FLEECE, GOOSE, GOAT, NURSE, PALM/LOT, and THOUGHT/CLOTH are long vowels. Like IrE and SSE, it has monophthong vowels in the *r* Lexical Sets as in NEAR and SQUARE, which is a key difference between GAmE and many varieties of BrE, along with the merger of TRAP/BATH to /æ/, and the lack of a low back rounded /ɒ/ for LOT in GAmE, which is /ɑ/ in many varieties of AmE.

As in other varieties of English, there is a great deal of regional variation in varieties of AmE: one key difference is the LOT/THOUGHT merger (often called COT/CAUGHT merger in North America). For some speakers, there is no distinction between /ɑ/ (PALM/LOT) and /ɔ/ CLOTH/THOUGHT.

Table 3.8 Vowels in American and Canadian English

	Front	Central	Back
High	/i/ FLEECE (A) /ɪ/ KIT	/ʉ/ GOOSE (C)	/u/ GOOSE (A) – also /ʉ/ /ʊ/ FOOT
Mid	/ɛ/ DRESS		/o/ GOAT – also /oʊ/ (A) /ɔ/ CLOTH/ THOUGHT/ LOT – also /ɑ/ (A)
Low	/æ/ TRAP/BATH – also /a/ (C)	/ʌ/ STRUT /ɑ/ PALM/LOT (A); LOT – also /ɔ/	/ɒ/ THOUGHT/ LOT/CLOTH (C) /ɒ:/ PALM (C)
'r' Lexical Sets	/ʊɹ/ NEAR /ɛɹ/ SQUARE	/ɜɹ/ NURSE /ɑr/ START (A) /ʌɹ, ɐɹ/ START (C) /jər, jʊɹ, jəɹ/ CURE (C)	/jʊɹ/ CURE (A) – also /jəɹ/ /oɹ/ FORCE (A) /ɔɹ, oɹ/ NORTH (A) /ɔɹ/ FORCE, NORTH (C)
Diphthongs	/ɪi/ FLEECE (C) /eɪ/ FACE /aɪ/ PRICE (A) /aʊ/ MOUTH /ɵʊ/ GOAT (C)	/ʌɪ, ɜɪ, ɐɪ, aɪ/ PRICE (C) /ʌʊ, ɜʊ/ MOUTH (C)	/ɔɪ/ CHOICE

Differences in vowel inventories are noted with A = AmE, C = CanE

The merger occurs predominantly in the Midwestern, Western (including in California), and New England dialects of AmE, as well as in ChiE, an ethnic variety of English influenced by Spanish.

Southern AmE (SAmE), like LonE and other varieties of Southern BrE, is undergoing a Southern Vowel Shift (see more on this below), and has some features in common with Southern BrE varieties as well as other varieties of English in the UK and Ireland (Thomas, 2004). One reason for this is that contact between the Southern states in the US and England was maintained longer than with other American colonies and England, and there was later settlement by immigrants from Northern England, Ireland, and Scotland. SAmE has a number of features that differ from GAmE, including both GOOSE- and FOOT-fronting, no /r/ after vowels (this also occurs in other varieties of AmE), and realization of many GAmE monophthongs as diphthongs (DRESS as /eə/ and KIT as /iə/ as examples). Another feature of SAmE is the merger of the vowels in KIT and DRESS before /n/ in words, making *pin* and *pen* homophones; this is called the PIN/

PEN merger (Gordon, 2004). This merger is also found among speakers of Lumbee Native American English as well as Appalachian English (Appal AmE), which is spoken in the Appalachian mountain region, as well as in AAVE, a variety of English spoken by African Americans that is influenced by SAmE and various African languages (see Hazen, 2018; Thomas, 2007; Wolfram & Dannenberg, 1999). GOOSE-fronting has also been found in Eastern Cherokee English, a variety of Native American English (NAE) spoken by members of the Eastern Cherokee tribes, as well as in Western and Midwestern AmE, California AmE (Calif AmE), as well as ChiE, and Asian AmE (see Coggshall, 2015; Gordon, 2004; Hall-Lew, 2009; Santa Ana & Bayley, 2004).

GOAT-fronting has also been found in some varieties of AmE, including Western and Midwestern AmE, SAmE, Appal AmE, New England AmE (NE AmE), and Asian AmE (Gordon, 2004; Hall-Lew, 2009; Hazen, 2018; Nagy & Roberts, 2004; Thomas, 2004). GOOSE- and GOAT-fronting are part of a Southern Vowel Shift as well as Canadian and Northern California Vowel shifts, which will be discussed below. A merger also exists in the vowels of MERRY/MARY/MARRY in SAmE; this is a loss of a distinction among /ɛ e æ/ before /r/.

TASK 3.10 Listening for American English

🎧 Listen to the five speakers of AmE read aloud words for each vowel sound.

- Which speakers have a TRAP/BATH merger, /r/ after vowels in the *r* Lexical Set words, a LOT/THOUGHT merger, GOOSE-fronting?
- What other differences exist among the speakers of AmE?
- Why do you think these differences/similarities exist (are there any regional and/or ethnic differences?)?
   Speaker 1   GAmE
   Speaker 2   Calif AmE
   Speaker 3   Midwestern AmE
   Speaker 4   Midwestern AmE, also speaks Gujarati, an Indo-Aryan language
   Speaker 5   Appal AmE
- You can listen to Speaker 2 talk about the features of a Calif AmE accent. What does she say about the Valley Girl accent (an accent from California) and the NYC accent?
- You can also listen to Speaker 3 talk about a Midwestern AmE accent. What does she say about US media and the Midwestern dialect? How does she pronounce *roof* and *creek*? How does her pronunciation of

those words differ from other varieties of AmE (*roof* as GOOSE vs FOOT, *creek* as FLEECE vs KIT)?

- You can also hear Speaker 5 talk about the features of the Appal AmE accent. Which vowel may replace the KIT vowel in *think* in Appal AmE?

Canadian English (CanE) is considered relatively homogeneous and bears greater similarity to AmE than to BrE, with a few notable exceptions: the LOT/THOUGHT merger exists throughout Canada; in fact, PALM/THOUGHT/LOT/CLOTH and START is a low back vowel and considered a defining feature of CanE (Wells, 1982). GOOSE-fronting may occur for some speakers of CanE; a merger for MERRY/MARY/MARRY also exists in CanE. There are a number of diphthong differences between GAmE and CanE: FLEECE has become diphthongal in CanE; PRICE and MOUTH have a centralized 1st target while the 1st target in GOAT is fronted. Another notable feature of CanE is Canadian Raising: the 1st target of the diphthongs in PRICE and MOUTH is centralized when the diphthong occurs before a voiceless consonant – for example, *ride* is [raid] while *write* is [rəit] and *loud* is [laʊd] while *out* is [lʌʊt], though, as Boberg (2004, pp. 359–60) notes, while it continues to be a 'reliable and distinctive identifier of Canadian speech', it does not occur for all speakers of CanE.

TASK 3.11 Listening for Canadian English

🎧 Listen to the speaker of CanE read aloud words for each vowel sound. The speaker has /r/ after the vowel in the *r* Lexical Sets, a TRAP/BATH merger, PALM/LOT/CLOTH/THOUGHT as a low back vowel, and MOUTH with a low central 1st target.

Puerto Rico was a Spanish colony from 1493 until 1898, after which it became an American colony. Today, Puerto Rico is a territory of the United States. PRE is influenced by Puerto Rican Spanish, which is influenced by other languages of the Caribbean, including the indigenous Puerto Rican language Taíno, and various African languages. Little research has been published in English on the phonetics and phonology of PRE; the discussion here is based on my own data and research on an educated speaker of PRE. As Table 3.9 shows, PRE differentiates between FLEECE and KIT but has mergers of GOOSE and FOOT, TRAP and BATH, and LOT/THOUGHT/CLOTH. It has similar diphthongs to GAmE.

Table 3.9 Vowels in Puerto Rican English

	Front	Central	Back
High	/i/ FLEECE /ɪ/ KIT		/u/ GOOSE/FOOT
Mid	/ɛ/ DRESS		/o/ GOAT /ɔ/ LOT/ THOUGHT/CLOTH
Low	/æ/ TRAP/BATH	/ʌ/ STRUT /ɑ/ PALM	
'r' Lexical Sets	/ɪɹ/ NEAR /ɛɹ/ SQUARE	/ɜɹ/ NURSE /ɑr/ START	/jʊɹ/ CURE /oɹ/ FORCE/ NORTH
Diphthongs	/eɪ/ FACE /aɪ/ PRICE /aʊ/ MOUTH		/ɔɪ/ CHOICE

TASK 3.12 Listening for Puerto Rican English

🎧 Listen to the speaker of PRE. Can you hear the following:

- GOOSE/FOOT merger
- TRAP/BATH merger
- LOT/THOUGHT/CLOTH merger
- /r/ after vowels

Jamaican English (JamE) is a postcolonial variety of Caribbean English influenced by BrE (the main superstrate) and Jamaican Creole (the substrate; it is also called Jamaican Patois), which is an English-based creole influenced by West African languages (Devonish & Harry, 2004). According to Devonish and Harry (2004), and as illustrated in Table 3.10, JamE has a system of fifteen vowels, with six simple (monophthong) vowels /i e a u o ɔ/ and nine complex (longer, and in some cases diphthongal) vowels: /ii ee aa uu oo ɔɔ ai au ɔi/. The non-low long vowels /ii uu ee oo/ are long and tense in contrast to the non-low short vowels /i u e o/.

3.5.3 The Vowels of Varieties of English in Oceania

We begin our discussion of varieties of English in Oceania by examining two varieties of English in Australia, Australian English (AusE) and Australian Aboriginal English (AusAborE). English was brought to Australia in 1788. As Burridge (2010) states, the roots of AusE are primarily London or Southern British English, although different dialects of the British Isles

Table 3.10 Vowels in Jamaican English

	-Back	+Back
High	/ii/ FLEECE /i/ KIT	/uu/ GOOSE /u/ FOOT
Mid	/ee/ FACE/NEAR/SQUARE /e/ DRESS	/oo/ GOAT/FORCE /o/ NURSE/STRUT
Low	/aa/ BATH/PALM/START /a/ TRAP	/ɔɔ/ CLOTH/THOUGHT/NORTH /ɔ/ LOT
Diphthongs	/ai/ PRICE /au/ MOUTH	/ɔi/ CHOICE

Table 3.11 Vowels in Australian English

	Front	Central	Back
High	/i:/ FLEECE /ɪ/ KIT	/ʉ:/ GOOSE	/ʊ/ FOOT /o:/ CLOTH/THOUGHT/ FORCE/NORTH
Mid	/e/ DRESS /e:/ SQUARE	/ɜ:/ NURSE	
Low	/æ/ TRAP	/ɐ/ STRUT /ɐ:/ BATH/PALM/ START	/ɔ/ LOT
Diphthongs	/ɪə/ NEAR /æɪ/ FACE /æɔ/ MOUTH	/əʉ/ GOAT	/ʊə/ CURE /oɪ/ CHOICE /ɑe/ PRICE

mixed and blended to form a unique variety (a process called *koineization*). In this discussion, we are focusing on General AusE, also called Standard AusE (see Cox and Palenthorpe, 2007), the variety of AusE with the most speakers, falling between the more RP-like AusE referred to as Cultivated AusE and the more local Broad AusE. The discussion is based on work by Burridge (2010), Horvath (2004), and Cox and Palenthorpe (2007). AusE is generally considered to be uniform with little regional variation, though more recent research suggests that there are regional differences for some phonological features, as we will see below. As shown in Table 3.11, the most distinctive characteristic of AusE in comparison to the other varieties discussed so far is the vowel system; this is also the case for New Zealand English (NZE), which differs not only from AusE but also from American and British varieties of English. AusE is similar to both American and British varieties discussed in terms of vowels in KIT, FLEECE, FOOT,

DRESS, TRAP (to AmE), NURSE, and has similar diphthongs in CURE and NEAR to Mod RP, and diphthongs in many vowels in the *r* Lexical Sets, similarly to many varieties of BrE. Differences can also be noted: SQUARE is monophthongized, the vowel in BATH/PALM/START is a low central long vowel /ɐ:/, and STRUT has /ɐ/, a slightly lowered articulation than in many other varieties of English. An additional difference is that the BATH vowel may be merged with the TRAP vowel in words with a nasal after the vowel, or a nasal plus another consonant; this context is sometimes called the DANCE Lexical Set (Wells, 1982). AusE (and NZE, see below), like other varieties of Southern English (SAmE, Southern BrE) is part of the Southern Vowel Shift: the 1st target of MOUTH is fronted (/æɔ/) while the 1st target of FACE is lowered (/æɪ/); AusE also has GOOSE-fronting; the 2nd target of GOAT is fronted as well. AusE also has /o:/ for CLOTH/THOUGHT/FORCE/NORTH, a slightly more raised articulation than in other varieties of English. One regional feature of AusE is the merger of DRESS and TRAP before postvocalic (after vowels in the same syllable) /l/, rendering *salary* and *celery* homophones; this occurs primarily in the territory of Victoria, and is considered a marker of Melbourne AusE (Cox, 2006). This also occurs in NZE. South Australians may have a more retracted (back pronunciation) of GOAT for the 1st target, as well as more GOOSE-fronting than speakers from other Australian territories, including Victoria and New South Wales (Cox & Palenthorpe, 2019).

TASK 3.13 Listening for Australian English

🎧 Listen to the speakers of AusE read aloud words for each vowel sound. Both speakers have GOOSE-fronting, STRUT and BATH/PALM/START as low central vowels, no /r/ after vowels, a fronted 2nd target for GOAT, lowered 2nd target for PRICE, fronted 1st target for MOUTH, and lowered 1st target for FACE. SQUARE is realized as a long vowel.

Speaker 1   AusE speaker from South Australia (SA AusE)
Speaker 2   AusE speaker from Queensland (Qld AusE)

- You can also listen to Speaker 2 talk about AusE. What does she say about regional differences in AusE in contrast to AmE and BrE?

Hundreds of Aboriginal languages are spoken in Australia; as these languages vary in the number and quality of vowels, there is a great deal of variation in the vowel inventory of AusAborE. Many Aboriginal languages have a series of five vowels /i e o u a/, which may reduce the number of vowels in AusAborE. Table 3.12, based on Malcolm (2004), shows the range

Table 3.12 Vowels in Australian Aboriginal English	
Keyword	*Australian Aboriginal English*
KIT	ɪ, i, ɛ
DRESS	ɛ, æ
TRAP	æ, ɛ
LOT/THOUGHT	ɒ, ɔ
STRUT	ʌ, æ, ɒ, ɪ
FOOT	ʊ
PALM/START/BATH	a
CLOTH	ɒ
NURSE	ɜ, e, ɜə
FLEECE	ɪ, i
FACE	eɪ, e, ʌɪ
GOAT	oʊ, ʊ, ɔ, ʌʊ
GOOSE	u
PRICE	aɪ, a, ɒɪ
CHOICE	ɔɪ
MOUTH	aʊ, æ, a(ʊ)
NEAR	i
SQUARE	ɛ
NORTH/FORCE	ɔ
CURE	jʊə

of vowels possible within the different words of Wells' Lexical Sets. As the table shows, there may be some mergers and/or interchangeable use for some speakers of the vowels in the FLEECE/KIT, DRESS/TRAP, LOT/ THOUGHT/CLOTH Lexical Sets; /a/, a low central vowel, may occur more frequently across Lexical Sets than in other varieties of English (Malcolm, 2004), including in PALM/START/BATH/PRICE/MOUTH/LETTER/COMMA. GOOSE-fronting occurs in some environments.

Like AusE, NZE developed from a koine emerging from the mixing and blending of different varieties of English, including IrE and BrE. It also has three main varieties that differ by social class: Cultivated (closer to RP), General, and Broad (most local features). As illustrated in Table 3.13, it is more similar to AusE than to other varieties of English, though there are a number of notable vowel differences between these two Southern Hemisphere Englishes (Hay, Maclagan, & Gordon, 2008). In our discussion, we focus on General NZE and the English of members of the Māori ethnic group, called Māori English (MāoriE). The discussion is based on Hay, Maclagan, and Gordon, (2008). Like AusE, NZE has a more central or front articulation of the vowel in STRUT, a key difference between these two

Table 3.13 Vowels in New Zealand English and Māori English

	Front	Central	Back
High	/i:/ FLEECE /i/ KIT (M)	/ʉ:/ GOOSE – also /y/ (M) /i/ FOOT (N)	/ʊ/ FOOT – also /i/ (N) /o:/ NORTH (N, M) FORCE/THOUGHT (N) /o/ THOUGHT/ FORCE (M)
Mid	/e/ DRESS or /ẹ/ /ɛ/ TRAP	/ə/ KIT (N) – also /ɪ/ /ɵ:/ NURSE	/ɔ/ LOT (M)
Low		/ɐ/ STRUT /ɐ:/ PALM/BATH/ START	/ɒ/ LOT (N), CLOTH
Diphthongs	/æe/ FACE /æʉ/ MOUTH /iə/ NEAR /eə/ SQUARE	/ɐʉ/ GOAT /ʉə/ CURE	/oe/ CHOICE /ae/ PRICE

N = NZE, M = Māori E

Englishes and varieties of AmE and BrE. A key feature of NZE is the lowering and retraction of KIT vowels to a mid central realization, as shown in Table 3.13. In AusE, KIT is a high front vowel and the realization of KIT in AusE and NZE is a key difference between these two varieties (Hay, Maclagan, & Gordon, 2008). Like AusE and many varieties of BrE, including Mod RP and LonE, NZE has diphthongs in a number of words in the *r* Lexical Sets, including NEAR and SQUARE; it also has GOOSE-fronting and BATH/PALM/START as a low central vowel. Some speakers may also have FOOT-fronting. Both DRESS and TRAP are higher than in other varieties of English, including varieties of AusE, so that *pet cat* can sound like *pit ket* (Hay, Maclagan, & Gordon, 2008). NURSE is a rounded vowel, unlike in other varieties of English. NZE also has little lip rounding; while NURSE has gained lip rounding in NZE, FOOT is losing rounding (THOUGHT and GOOSE have retained rounding); in NZE, START/STRUT form a long/short pair, while FLEECE/KIT and GOOSE/FOOT do not, unlike in many other varieties of English (Hay, Maclagan, & Gordon, 2008). Like AusE, NZE is also undergoing the Southern Vowel Shift; the diphthongs also have different 1st and 2nd targets from AmE and BrE varieties, with fronting for the 1st target in MOUTH, a lowering of the 1st target in FACE, and fronting of the 1st target in CURE and 2nd in GOAT. The 1st target of PRICE is also retracted.

TASK 3.14 Listening for New Zealand English

🎧 Listen to the speaker of NZE read aloud words for each vowel sound. You may notice the following in his pronunciation:

- Lowered and retracted KIT
- Fronted GOOSE
- Rounded NURSE
- Raised DRESS
- A long/short pair in STRUT/STΛRT
- No /r/ after vowels
- 1st target in CURE and MOUTH and 2nd target in GOAT are fronted
- 1st target in FACE is lowered
- You can also listen to the speaker talk about his accent. What do you notice about his pronunciation of the second vowel in the word _accent_? Does he pronounce it as a DRESS or a KIT vowel? What feature of NZE does his pronunciation of _accent_ illustrate? What does he say about Māori?

Te Reo Māori is the language of the indigenous Polynesians who settled in New Zealand in the mid 1300s. Although Te Reo Māori has five vowels (/i e a o u/), MāoriE is generally similar to NZE, though with a few notable differences: it has a high front vowel /i/ in KIT, instead of the mid central NZE KIT; this is also the case for Pasifika English (PasE), the English of the Pacific Islanders of New Zealand (including Samoans, Tongans, Niueans, and Cook Islanders). GOOSE may also be fronted to a high front rounded vowel /y/ in MāoriE; GOOSE-fronting also occurs in PasE (Starks, Gibson, & Bell, 2015).

Fiji English (FijE) developed in the more than 300 islands of Fiji after colonization by the British in 1874; it is influenced by BrE (a superstrate) and both Fijian and Fiji Hindi (the substrates). As Table 3.14 shows, FijE has an inventory of five monophthong vowels due to the influence of Fijian (Tent, 2001); as noted in our discussion of vowel inventories cross-linguistically, languages with smaller vowel inventories tend to distribute vowels maximally across the vowel space, with no length distinction. This can be seen in FijE, which has a high front vowel /i/ for both FLEECE/KIT; a mid front vowel /ɛ/ for DRESS/TRAP/NURSE; a low central vowel /a/ for STRUT/BATH, PALM/START; a high back vowel /u/ for both GOOSE/FOOT; and a mid back vowel /ɔ/ for LOT/CLOTH/NORTH/FORCE. Most of these monophthongs are tense but short. FijE also has eight diphthongs; though FACE and GOAT may be realized as single vowels (e.g., /ei/ as /e/) by some speakers (Tent & Mugler, 2004). FijE has diphthongs in a number of _r_ Lexical Sets, including NEAR and SQUARE.

Table 3.14 Vowels in Fiji English

	Front	Central	Back
High	/i/ FLEECE/KIT		/u/ GOOSE/FOOT
Mid	/ɛ/ DRESS/TRAP/ NURSE		/ɔ/ LOT/CLOTH/ NORTH/FORCE/ THOUGHT
Low		/a/ STRUT/BATH/ PALM/START	
Diphthongs	/ei/ FACE (or /e/) /ɪɐ/ NEAR /ɛɐ/ SQUARE	/ai/ PRICE /au/ MOUTH /ʉɐ/ CURE	/oi/ CHOICE /ou/ GOAT (or /o:/)

3.5.4   The Vowels of Englishes in Africa

Table 3.15 shows the vowel inventories in varieties of English classified as East African Englishes (EAfE); this includes the Englishes that have developed in Kenya, Uganda, and Tanzania, starting in the late nineteenth century when English arrived in East Africa (Schmied, 2004). These varieties have BrE as the main superstrate and Kiswahili as one of the substrates. The variety of EAfE reported on here is the mesolectal variety, based on Schmied (2004). As we saw in Figure 3.8, Kiswahili, as well as other Bantu languages, has an inventory of five vowels: /i ɛ a u ɔ/. Due to the influence of the Kiswahili and other African language vowel systems, EAfE have a series of five monophthong vowels: one high front vowel /i/ for FLEECE/KIT, a mid front vowel /e/ for DRESS/FACE, a low central vowel /a/ for TRAP/BATH/STRUT/NURSE/PALM/START, a high back vowel /u/ in GOOSE/FOOT, and mid back vowel /o/ in LOT/CLOTH/GOAT/THOUGHT/ NORTH/FORCE (Schmied, 2004). EAfrE have diphthongs in SQUARE, CURE, and NEAR words in the *r* Lexical Sets.

TASK 3.15 Listening for Kenyan English

🎧 Listen to the speaker of KenE. She also speaks Kiswahili. You may notice the following in her pronunciation of the words:

- FLEECE/KIT merger
- GOOSE/FOOT merger
- TRAP/BATH/STRUT/NURSE/PALM/START merger
- No /r/ after vowels
- /a/ as the 2nd target in NEAR, SQUARE, and CURE

Table 3.15 Vowels in East African Englishes

	Front	Central	Back
High	/i/ FLEECE/KIT		/u/ GOOSE/FOOT
Mid	/e/ DRESS/FACE – also /eɪ/		/o/ LOT/CLOTH/GOAT/ THOUGHT/NORTH/ FORCE
Low		/a/ TRAP/BATH/ STRUT/NURSE/ PALM/START	
Diphthongs	/ɪa/ NEAR /eɪ/ FACE – also /e/ /ea/ SQUARE	/aɪ/ PRICE /aʊ/ MOUTH	/oɪ/ CHOICE /ʊa/ CURE

Table 3.16 shows the vowels of Nigerian English (NigE), a West African variety of English. There are two main varieties of NigE: Hausa English (HausaE), which is influenced by BrE and Hausa; and Southern NigE (SNigE), which is influenced by BrE and encompasses Yoruba English (influenced by Yoruba) and Igbo English (influenced by Igbo) (Gut, 2004). Both the Hausa English and SNigE reported here are for educated speakers of these varieties (Gut, 2004). As Table 3.16 shows, SNigE has a smaller vowel inventory than HausaE, with seven monophthong vowels and six diphthongs /i e ɛ a u o ɔ ia ea ai au ua ɔi/; in contrast, HausaE has twelve monophthongs (with a tense/lax distinction) and six diphthongs. As Gut notes, a key difference between the two varieties is the lack of length difference in vowels in SNigE (e.g., FLEECE/KIT and GOOSE/FOOT are merged in SNigE) as well as the lack of centralized vowels in SNigE. Both varieties have diphthongs in NEAR, CURE, and SQUARE, words in the *r* Lexical Sets.

TASK 3.16 Listening for Southern Nigerian English

🎧 Listen to the speaker of SNigE. She speaks some Igbo. You may notice the following in her pronunciation of the words:

- FLEECE/KIT merger
- GOOSE/FOOT/STRUT merger
- TRAP/PALM/START/BATH merger
- No /r/ after vowels
- /a/ as the 2nd target in NEAR, SQUARE
- GOAT as monophthong

Table 3.16 Vowels in Nigerian English

	Front	Central	Back
High	/i/ FLEECE/KIT (S) /i:/ FLEECE (H) /ɪ/ KIT (H)		/u/ GOOSE/FOOT (S) /u:/ GOOSE (H) /ʊ/ FOOT (H)
Mid	/e/ DRESS (S) – also /ɛ/ (S) /e/ FACE – also /a/ (S) /ɛ/ NURSE (S) – also /ɔ, a/ (S)	/ə/ DRESS (H) – also /a/	/o/ GOAT (S) – also /ɔ/ (S); FORCE (H) – also /oa/ (H) /o:/ THOUGHT/GOAT (H) /ɔ/ CLOTH/NORTH – also STRUT/LOT/THOUGHT/FORCE in (S)
Low	/a/ TRAP/START – also BATH/PALM (S); LOT (H) /a:/ BATH/NURSE/PALM (H)		/ɑ/ STRUT (H)– also /ʊ/; also /u/ (S)
Diphthongs	/ia/ NEAR – also /ija/ (S) /ea/ SQUARE – also /ia/ (S)	/ai/ PRICE – also /əi/ (H) /au/ MOUTH – also /əu/ (H)	/ɔi/ CHOICE /ua/ CURE – also /uo/ (S)

H = HausaE, S = SNigE

South Africa is a country in southern Africa; it has a long history of colonialism, first under the Dutch in the seventeenth century, and later the British in 1910 after the Anglo-Boer War; while it became an independent nation in 1960, it had a nearly 50-year period of apartheid (from 1948 to 1994), which was a policy of white minority rule and racial segregation. As van Rooy (2014) notes, this racial segregation has led to several main varieties of South African English (SAE) emerging, including Black SAE (BSAE), which is influenced by African languages including Xhosa, Zulu, Sepedi, Sesotho, Southern Ndebele, Swazi, Tsonga, Tswana, and Venda. These languages are typically spoken in specific regions of South Africa. White SAE (WSAE) is spoken by White South Africans; this has three varieties: Cultivated, which is closer to RP (like Cultivated AusE), General WSAE, and Broad WSAE, which refers to working-class speakers, or speakers of Afrikaans descent (Bowerman, 2004). Afrikaans is a variety of Dutch that has developed in South Africa (South African Dutch) which, along with English, was dominant in education and government until the end of apartheid. Afrikaans English is also used to refer to the English of Afrikaans

Table 3.17 Vowels in Black South African English

	Front	Central	Back
High	/i/ FLEECE/KIT		/u/ GOOSE/FOOT
Mid	/ɛ/ DRESS/TRAP/ NURSE/SQUARE /e/ NEAR		/o/ CURE /ɔ/ LOT/CLOTH/THOUGHT/ FORCE/NORTH and GOAT – also/ɔʊ/
Low			/ä/ STRUT/BATH/PALM/ START
Diphthongs	/ɛɪ, eɪ, ɛ/ FACE	/ʌɪ/ PRICE	/ɔɪ/ CHOICE /ɔʊ/ MOUTH – also/o/

speakers of SAE. Another variety of SAE is called Coloured SAE and is spoken by people of mixed or Asian background. A further variety of SAE is South African Indian English, which emerged from immigration from India to South Africa in the late 1900s. Our discussion of SAE vowels focuses on BSAE and WSAE, with mention of features of Afrikaans SAE.

A shown in Table 3.17, BSAE does not have tense/lax distinction, with mergers for DRESS/TRAP/NURSE/SQUARE/NEAR, FLEECE/KIT, STRUT/ BATH/PALM/START, and GOOSE/FOOT (van Rooy, 2004). There are no central monophthong vowels in BSAE. There is a tendency for diphthongs to be monophthongized, as in NEAR, SQUARE, GOAT, CURE, and FACE. The 1st target of PRICE is centralized (/ʌɪ/) while the 1st target of MOUTH is raised to a mid back vowel (/ɔʊ/).

Table 3.18 shows the vowel inventory for WSAE, as well as some of the differences among the three social varieties: Cultivated (near RP), General, and Broad (Afrikaans influence and/or working-class) based on Bowerman (2004). As the table shows, all varieties have a tense/lax distinction. Both General and Broad WSAE have a more fronted articulation for NURSE, as well as a fronted 1st target for GOAT. WSAE does not realize the 'r' after vowels for both General and Cultivated varieties; speakers of Afrikaans SAE may have 'r' after vowels, however, due to the influence of Afrikaans (Wells, 1982); GOOSE-fronting occurs in both General and Broad WSAE. There is also a tendency to monophthongize diphthongs in both General and Broad WSAE; another key marker of these two varieties of WSAE is the split of KIT to [ɪ] and [ï] in General WSAE and [ɪ ~ ï] or [ə] in Broad WSAE, with a fronted articulation appearing in front of consonants that are articulated in the mid or back of the mouth (**palatals** or **velars**, see Chapter 5); this will be discussed in more detail below. This split also occurs in Coloured SAE; Toefy (2017) notes that this split is relatively rare in other varieties of English. WSAE is also part of the Southern Vowel Shift, as seen

Table 3.18 Vowels in White South African English

	Front	Central	Back
High	/i:/ FLEECE /ɪ/ KIT	/ʉ:, y:/ GOOSE (G, B)	/u:/ GOOSE (C) /ʊ/ FOOT – also /ʊ̈/ (B)
Mid	/e/ DRESS – sometimes /ɛ/ (B) /ø/ NURSE (G, B)	/ɜ:/ NURSE (C)	/o:/ CLOTH/ THOUGHT/ NORTH/FORCE (G, B), /ɔ/ (C)
Low	/æ/ TRAP; /ɛ/ (B)	/ä/ STRUT	/ö/ LOT/CLOTH /ɑ:/ PALM/BATH/ START
Diphthongs	/eɪ/ FACE (C, G) /ɪə/ NEAR /ɛə/ SQUARE (C) – also /ɛ:/ (G), /e:/ (B) /œʉ, œ̈ŭ/ GOAT	/aɪ/ PRICE (C); /a:/ (B, G) /aʊ/ MOUTH (C); /a:/ (G), /æʊ/ (B) /ʌɪ/ FACE (B)	/uə/ CURE /ɔɪ/ CHOICE

B = Broad and/or Afrikaans, C = Cultivated, G = General

by the fronting of GOOSE, and the fronting of the 1st targets of GOAT, MOUTH, among others. FOOT may also have more rounding, particularly for Afrikaans speakers.

TASK 3.17 Listening for White South African English

🎧 Listen to the speaker of White South African English (WSAE). She also speaks some Afrikaans. Her pronunciation features some General and some Broad WSAE vowels. You may notice the following:

- GOOSE and NURSE fronting
- Fronting of 1st target for GOAT
- More rounding for FOOT
- TRAP and BATH split
- THOUGHT and LOT split
- 1st target of FACE retracted
- /r/ in NURSE
- You can also listen to the speaker talk about her accent and SAE.

Zimbabwe was a British colony from 1888 until 1980; prior to independence, Zimbabwe was known variously as Rhodesia, Southern Rhodesia, and Zimbabwe. The most widely spoken language in Zimbabwe

Table 3.19 Vowels in Zimbabwean English

	Front	Central	Back
High	/i/ FLEECE /ɪ/ KIT		/u/ GOOSE . /ʊ/ FOOT
Mid	/e/ DRESS	/ɜ/ NURSE	/o/ GOAT/THOUGHT/ NORTH/FORCE /ɔ/ LOT/CLOTH
Low	/æ/ TRAP	/ʌ/ STRUT /a/ BATH/START/PALM	
Diphthongs	/ɪa/ NEAR /eɪ/ FACE /ea/ SQUARE	/aɪ/ PRICE /aʊ/ MOUTH	/ɔɪ/ CHOICE /ʊa/ CURE – also /ʊr/

is Shona, a Bantu language, which is one of the sixteen official languages of Zimbabwe, along with English, Xhosa, Ndau, Tonga, Tswana, Ndebele, Shangani, Kalanga, Khoisan, Chibarwe, Chewa, Venda, Nambya, Sotho, and sign language. English is an important language in Zimbabwe and the main language of education from Grade Three in primary school through to tertiary (Kadenge, 2009).

Zimbabwean English (ZimE) is under-researched, with only a few studies (Kadenge, 2009; Mutonya, 2008) examining the phonological features of this variety of English; this research has focused on Shona speakers of ZimE, with the finding that ZimE has a five-vowel system due to the influence of Shona, which has five vowels: /i e a o u/. My own research, however, as illustrated in Table 3.19, shows that some speakers may have a larger vowel inventory, with tense/lax differences for FLEECE and KIT, as well as GOOSE and FOOT. Speakers of ZimE may have mergers for BATH/START/PALM, LOT/CLOTH, and GOAT/THOUGHT/NORTH/FORCE.

TASK 3.18 Listening for Zimbabwean English

🎧 Listen to the speaker of Zimbabwean English (ZimE). She also speaks Shona. You may notice the following in her pronunciation of the words:

- LOT/CLOTH merger
- GOAT/THOUGHT/NORTH/FORCE merger
- BATH/START/PALM merger
- /a/ as the 2nd target in NEAR and SQUARE
- /r/ after the vowel in CURE
- You can also listen to the speaker talk about her accent.

3.5.5   The Vowels of Englishes in Asia

The vowel inventories of Singapore English (SgE) and Malaysian English (MalE) are similar and therefore are considered together, as shown in Table 3.20. English arrived in Singapore in 1819, and Malaysia in 1824, after colonization by the British. The superstrate for both SgE and MalE has historically been BrE; a range of languages are spoken in Singapore and Malaysia and are substrate influences on these varieties of English: Tamil, a Dravidian language; Bahasa Malaysia, an Austronesian language; and three Sinitic languages: Cantonese, Hokkien, and Mandarin Chinese (Lim & Gisborne, 2009).

Due to the influence of the substrate languages, both SgE (Colloquial SgE is shown here, based on Wee, 2004) and MalE (the mesolectal variety of MalE is shown here, based on Baskaran, 2004) have a smaller vowel inventory than BrE, with no long/short vowel distinction and no GOOSE-fronting. According to Baskaran (2004) and Wee (2004), FLEECE/KIT is realized as the high front vowel /i/, GOOSE/FOOT as the high back vowel /u/, GOAT, FACE, SQUARE, and CURE are monophthongized to /o/, /e/, /æ/, and /ɔ/ respectively, while NURSE is a short mid central /ə/. TRAP is raised to /ɛ/ for some speakers of MalE, while DRESS is lowered to /æ/. LOT/THOUGHT/CLOTH/NORTH/FORCE/CURE are merged into one mid back vowel, /ɔ/, while PALM/BATH/START/STRUT are merged and realized as the low back vowel /ɑ/. There is no length contrast in vowels in SgE; there is also no tense/lax contrast, with all vowels equally tense (Wee, 2004). There is a tendency to produce all the long (i.e., long in other varieties of

Table 3.20 Vowels in Singapore and Malaysian English

	Front	Central	Back
High	/i/ FLEECE/KIT		/u/ GOOSE/FOOT
Mid	/e/ FACE – also /eɪ/ /ɛ/ TRAP – also /æ/ (M)	/ə, ɜː/ NURSE	/o/ GOAT /ɔ/ LOT/THOUGHT/ CLOTH/NORTH/ FORCE/CURE – also /jə/
Low	/æ/ DRESS – also /ɛ, e/; SQUARE – also /eə, ɛ/		/ɑ/ PALM/BATH/ START/STRUT – also /ʌ/
Diphthongs	/iə/ NEAR – also /iː/ (M) /eɪ/ FACE	/ai/ PRICE /au/ MOUTH	/ɔi/ CHOICE

S = SgE, M = MalE

English) vowels as short in MalE, due to the influence of Bahasa Malaysia. MalE also has a tendency to lengthen short vowels before /n l r s ʃ/, so that *fish* is pronounced [fiːʃ] and *pin* as [piːn] (Baskaran, 2004). There is a great deal of variability in the pronunciation of /r/ after vowels in both SgE and MalE.

TASK 3.19 Listening for Singapore and Malaysian English

🎧 Listen to the speakers of SgE and MalE.
Speaker 1   SgE, she also speaks Cantonese and Mandarin Chinese
Speaker 2   SgE, he also speaks Mandarin Chinese

- Both SgE speakers have mergers for DRESS/SQUARE, FLEECE/KIT, CLOTH/LOT/THOUGHT/NORTH/FORCE/CURE and GOOSE/FOOT. Neither pronounces /r/ after vowels.

Speaker 3   MalE, she also speaks Mandarin Chinese
Speaker 4   MalE, she also speaks Malay and Mandarin Chinese

- Both MalE speakers have FLEECE/KIT, LOT/THOUGHT/CLOTH mergers, and GOOSE/FOOT mergers. DRESS has a raised pronunciation (close to KIT). Both have /r/ after vowels.
- You can also hear Speaker 4 talk about her accent. What does she say about the MalE pronunciation of the GOOSE and FOOT vowels?
- You can also listen to Speaker 3 talk about her accent.

Hong Kong English (HKE) is spoken in the Hong Kong Special Administrative Region of the People's Republic of China (PRC). Cantonese is the Chinese language spoken by the majority of the population in Hong Kong; Cantonese, along with Mandarin Chinese to a lesser extent, is the substrate influence on HKE, whereas BrE has historically been the superstrate, as Hong Kong was a British colony for 150 years, until 1997. AmE may be becoming more popular in Hong Kong, as in other former British colonies, and therefore some features of AmE may be emerging in HKE. HKE is quite similar to both SgE and MalE in terms of the vowel inventory, which is shown in Table 3.21; the following discussion of HKE is based on educated speakers of English, and should be considered the mesolectal variety, as acrolectal HKE is quite similar to RP. Hung (2012) states that HKE has seven or eight monophthongs, with mergers for FLEECE/KIT (as /i/) and GOOSE/FOOT (as /u/), which is similar to both SgE and MalE. HKE also has a DRESS/TRAP merger (as /ɛ/) for some speakers, and LOT/THOUGHT/ CLOTH/NORTH/FORCE are merged and articulated as a mid back /ɔ/ while

Table 3.21 Vowels in Hong Kong English

	Front	Central	Back
High	/i/ FLEECE/KIT		/u/ GOOSE/FOOT
Mid	/ɛ/ DRESS/TRAP – also /æ/	/ɜ/ NURSE	/ɔ/ LOT/THOUGHT/ CLOTH – also /o/ NORTH/FORCE – also /or/
Low	/æ/ TRAP – also /ɛ/	/ʌ/ STRUT	/ɑ/ BATH/PALM – also START – also /ɑr/
Diphthongs	/ɪə/ NEAR – also /ir/ /eɪ/ FACE /eə/ SQUARE – also /er/		/ɔi/ CHOICE /oʊ/ GOAT – also /o/ /ɑɪ/ PRICE /aʊ/ MOUTH /jʊə/ CURE – also /jʊr/

BATH/START/PALM are /ɑ/. Similarly to many varieties of BrE, HKE has a series of eight diphthongs; it does not have GOOSE-fronting or a long/short vowel distinction.

TASK 3.20 Listening for Hong Kong English

🎧 Listen to the speaker of HKE. He also speaks Cantonese. You may notice:

- TRAP/BATH differentiation
- /r/ in NEAR, CURE, NORTH, FORCE
- FLEECE/KIT, GOOSE/FOOT, LOT/THOUGHT, PALM/BATH mergers

As Gargesh (2004) notes, Indian English (IndE) is a cover term for a range of varieties of Englishes that have developed in India as a result of British colonization. While the superstrate of IndE is BrE, different Indian languages are substrate influences in different regions of India, including Hindi, the most widely spoken Indian language in India, as well as Bengali, Marathi, Telugu, Tamil, Gujarati, and Punjabi, among others. The description of IndE here is based on Gargesh (2004) and Pandey (2015) and focuses on the characteristics that may occur more widely across the different types of IndE. As shown in Table 3.22, IndE has both long and short vowels and a contrast between GOOSE and FOOT, and FLEECE and KIT, for most varieties; it may monophthongize some diphthongs such as FACE, SQUARE,

Table 3.22 Vowels in Indian and Pakistani English

	Front	Central	Back
High	/iː/ FLEECE /ɪ/ KIT – also /iː/ (I)		/uː/ GOOSE /ʊ/ FOOT – also /uː/ (I, P)
Mid	/e/ DRESS – also /ɛ/ (I) /eː/ FACE – also /eɪ/ /ɛː/ SQUARE (I)	/ɜː/ NURSE; also /ɜr/	/oː/ GOAT – also /əʊ/ (P); CLOTH (I) /ɔ/ LOT/THOUGHT (I) /ɔː/ NORTH/ FORCE/CLOTH – also LOT/ THOUGHT (P); also /ɔr/
Low	/æ/ TRAP – also SQUARE (I), BATH (P) – also /ɑː/ (P)	/ʌ/ STRUT	/ɑː/ PALM/BATH; BATH – also /æ/ (P); START – also /ɑr/
Diphthongs	/aɪ/ PRICE /aʊ/ MOUTH /ɪə/ NEAR – also /eə/ (P); also /ir/ /eə/ SQUARE (P) – also /er/		/ɔɪ/ CHOICE /ɪjoː, jʊə, jʊr/ CURE (I) /jʊə/ CURE (P) – also /jeɔː/, /jʊr/

I = IndE, P = PakE

GOAT. While IndE is generally considered to realize 'r' after vowels, there exists a variation due to substrate influences as well as social factors. It does not have GOOSE-fronting.

Pakistani English (PakE) is similar to IndE, as can be seen in Table 3.22. PakE also has BrE as the superstrate, and, like IndE, has a number of different substrates depending on the region; these include Punjabi (the language with the most speakers in Pakistan), Sindhi, Pashtu, and Urdu (the official language of Pakistan, along with English) (Mahboob & Ahmar, 2004). The description of PakE in Table 3.22 focuses on the characteristics that may be found across varieties of PakE and is based on Mahboob and Ahmar (2004). PakE also has a short/long vowel contrast, lacks GOOSE-fronting, and has diphthongs similar to RP, though GOAT and FACE may be monophthongized in PakE. As in IndE, many speakers of PakE have r-coloured vowels, though there is variability across speakers and varieties of PakE (Mahboob & Ahmar, 2004).

TASK 3.21 Listening for Pakistani and Indian English

🎧 Listen to the speakers of PakE and IndE. You may notice the following features:

Speaker 1 PakE – speaks Urdu and Sindhi; GOOSE/FOOT merger; LOT/
           THOUGHT merger; TRAP/BATH merger; /r/ after vowels.
Speaker 2 IndE – speaks Hindi and Awadhi; GOOSE/FOOT merger;
           THOUGHT/NORTH/LOT merger; CLOTH/GOAT merger;
           BATH/FACE merger; /r/ in FORCE.

• You can also listen to the IndE and the PakE speakers talk about their
  accents.

While Nepal was never colonized by the British, the British have a long history of settlement in Nepal, giving Nepal – and Nepalese English (NepE) – a unique status as a non-postcolonial World English. In 1801, Nepal signed an agreement with the East India Company, allowing the British to set up residence in Kathmandu, thus leading to the importation and use of English in Nepal. In 1815, the Sugauli Treaty was signed between the then prime minister of Nepal and the East India Company; this treaty allowed the recruitment of Nepalese Gurkhas to the British Army, a tradition that still exists today, with thousands of Nepalese Gurkha soldiers still serving in the British Army (Pandey, 2020). Nepal has hundreds of indigenous languages; Nepali, the most widely spoken language in Nepal, is the official language (Khatiwada, 2009); English is widely used in Nepal in education and tourism.

Little research has focused on the features of NepE; the following overview is based on research on Nepali by Khatiwada (2009), research on the vowels of NepE by Koffi (2019), as well as my own analysis of data from a Nepalese speaker of English. As Table 3.23, shows, NepE has mergers between GOOSE and FOOT, PALM and BATH, and LOT/CLOTH/THOUGHT. Nepali is a rhotic language, and NepE has 'r' after the vowels in the *r* Lexical Sets.

TASK 3.22 Listening for Nepalese English

🎧 Listen to the speaker of NepE; she is also a speaker of Nepali and Hindi. You may note the following:

• LOT/THOUGHT merger
• /r/ after vowels
• GOOSE/FOOT merger
• You can also listen to the NepE speaker talk about her accent.

Table 3.23 Vowels in Nepalese English

	Front	Central	Back
High	/i/ FLEECE /ɪ/ KIT		/u/ GOOSE/FOOT
Mid	/e/ DRESS	/ʌ/ STRUT	/o/ GOAT
Low	/æ/ TRAP	/a/ PALM/BATH	/ɔ/ LOT/CLOTH/THOUGHT
'r' Lexical Sets	/ɪr/ NEAR /er/ SQUARE	/ɜr/ NURSE /ar/ START	/jʊr/ CURE /or/ NORTH/FORCE
Diphthongs	/aɪ/ PRICE /aʊ/ MOUTH /eɪ/ FACE		/oɪ/ CHOICE

Sri Lanka became a British colony in 1815, gaining independence in 1948 after over 120 years of British rule. The official languages of Sri Lanka are Sinhala and Tamil; English is considered a link language, with *de jure* official status in education and government (Gunesekera, 2005). There are only a few studies of the linguistic features of Sri Lankan English (SLE), with more known about its consonantal than its vowel features; while some researchers argue that SLE is similar to IndE, others note 'how close Sri Lankan English is to the British standard, when compared with other varieties' (Meyler, 2012, p. 542). The account of the vowels of SLE is based on my own research as well as work by Gunesekera (2005) and Widyalankara (2015).

As Table 3.24 shows, speakers of SLE may have a FLEECE/KIT distinction and a GOOSE/FOOT merger. Speakers may also have a merger of LOT/CLOTH/FORCE/THOUGHT/NORTH, as well as of PALM/BATH/START. While FACE and GOAT may be monophthongized, the diphthongs in PRICE, MOUTH, CHOICE, CURE, and NEAR are similar to those of many varieties of BrE; SQUARE may have a longer 2nd target: /eʌ/. SLE does not have a TRAP/BATH merger. Rhoticity varies in SLE.

TASK 3.23 Listening for Sri Lankan English

🎧 Listen to the speaker of SLE; he is also a speaker of Tamil and Sinhala. You may note the following:

- LOT/THOUGHT merger
- No /r/ after vowels
- GOOSE/FOOT merger
- You can also listen to the speaker of SLE talk about his accent.

Table 3.24 Vowels in Sri Lankan English

	Front	Central	Back
High	/i/ FLEECE /ɪ/ KIT		/u/ GOOSE/FOOT
Mid	/e/ DRESS	/ɜ/ NURSE	/o/ GOAT
Low	/æ/ TRAP	/ɑ:/ PALM/BATH/ START /ɑ/ STRUT	/ɔ/ LOT/CLOTH/ FORCE/THOUGHT/ NORTH
Diphthongs	/aɪ/ PRICE /aʊ/ MOUTH /eʌ/ SQUARE /ɪə/ NEAR /eɪ/ FACE – also /e:/		/ɔɪ/ CHOICE /jʊə/ CURE

Table 3.25 Vowels in Philippine English

	Front	Central	Back
High	/i: ɪ/ FLEECE/KIT		/u: ʊ/ GOOSE/ FOOT
Mid	/ɛ/ DRESS		/o/ CLOTH/ THOUGHT/GOAT
Low		/ʌ/ STRUT /ɑ/ PALM/BATH/ TRAP/LOT	
'r' Lexical Sets	/ɛr/ NURSE /ir/ NEAR /er/ SQUARE	/ɑr/ START	/or/ NORTH/ FORCE/CURE
Diphthongs	/eɪ/ FACE	/ɑɪ/ PRICE /aʊ/ MOUTH	/oɪ/ CHOICE

The Philippines is home to over 87 ethnic languages; a former Spanish colony, it became an American colony in the early 1900s. Philippine English (PhlE) comprises three lects – an acrolect, which is close to GAmE (the superstrate for all varieties of PhlE); a mesolect with influences from Filipino, the official language of the Philippines along with English, as well as other languages spoken in the Philippines; and a basilect with significant influences from various languages (Tayao, 2004). The presentation of PhlE in this chapter focuses on the mesolectal variety, based on Tayao (2004) and my own data. As Table 3.25 shows, PhlE has a smaller vowel system than GAmE: the long/short vowels in GOOSE/FOOT and FLEECE/KIT are in free variation (used interchangeably) for some speakers, and it generally does not have a long/short vowel or tense/lax vowel distinction.

TASK 3.24 Listening for Philippine English

🎧 Listen to the speaker of PhlE; she is also a speaker of Filipino, Itawis – a northern Philippine language spoken in the town of Tuao – and Ilocano, spoken by the Ilocano people. You may note the following:

- GOOSE/FOOT merger
- KIT in free variation with FLEECE (also listen to her pronunciation of *beat, bead, bit, bid*)
- /r/ after vowels
- PALM/BATH/TRAP/LOT merger
- CLOTH/THOUGHT/GOAT merger
- You can also listen to the speaker of PhlE talk about PhlE.

There is no GOOSE-fronting; PhlE has similar diphthongs to GAmE. As Tayao notes, there is no length difference between monophthongs and diphthongs in the basilectal and mesolectal varieties of PhlE. It has 'r' after vowels, due to the influence of AmE.

3.6 A Summary of Vowels in Varieties of English Around the World

Table 3.26, below, provides a brief summary of the vowel mergers in the varieties of English discussed in this chapter. As the chapter has shown, substratum influences have a significant impact on the vowel inventory of varieties of English, with smaller vowel inventories in many ethnic and Postcolonial Englishes such as FijE, KenE, ZimE, SgE, MalE, and BSAE, due to smaller vowel inventories in the substrate languages that influence these Englishes. The largest vowel inventories can be found in many OVEs that have diphthongs in the *r* Lexical Set words (e.g., SQUARE, NEAR – see Chapter 4). This includes varieties of BrE, AusE, and NZE. Despite these differences, there are some commonalities across varieties:

- All the varieties have the high front vowel FLEECE.
- Many varieties that have a tense/lax and/or durational difference in vowels also have the high front short vowel KIT.

- Many ethnic or postcolonial varieties, including Englishes in Africa and Asia, have only one high front vowel, with a merger between FLEECE and KIT.
- All varieties have a high or centralized back vowel GOOSE; this vowel tends to be centralized or fronted in varieties undergoing the Southern Vowel Shift (see below).
- Varieties that have tense/lax distinction may also have the high back short vowel FOOT, which may also be centralized or fronted in some varieties, similarly to GOOSE.
- Many ethnic or postcolonial varieties, including Englishes in Africa and Asia, have one high back vowel, with a merger between GOOSE and FOOT. A merger of GOOSE and FOOT before /l/ in the same syllable may also occur in NZE, AusE, and SAmE.
- While there is a great deal of variation across varieties with regards to number and quality (1st and 2nd targets) of diphthongs, the diphthong in CHOICE shows the least variation across varieties, followed by PRICE and MOUTH.
- FACE and GOAT are frequently realized as monophthongs, where the 2nd target is weakened and lost. This occurs across varieties of English in the UK and Ireland, Oceania, Africa, and Asia.
- There are frequent mergers between the DRESS/KIT Lexical Sets, particularly before /n/ in the same syllable as in the PIN/PEN merger, or before /l/ as in *till/tell*. This occurs in many varieties of AmE, as well as in some varieties of English in the UK and Ireland.
- DRESS is also often merged with TRAP in varieties of English in Asia and Africa. An 'el'–'al' merger (merger of the vowels of DRESS and TRAP before /l/) also exists in some Southern Hemisphere Englishes, including WSAE, AusE, and NZE.
- BATH is often merged with:
  ◦ TRAP: This occurs in varieties of AmE, including GAmE, and some varieties of BrE, and African and Asian Englishes.
  ◦ START/PALM: This occurs in many varieties of African and Asian Englishes, as well as in varieties of English in the Americas, the Caribbean, the UK and Ireland. In many of these varieties, particularly in PCEs, this merger may include other Lexical Sets such as STRUT and NURSE.
- LOT is commonly merged with THOUGHT in varieties of English in the Americas, the Caribbean, Africa, Asia, Oceania, and the UK and Ireland. In some varieties of English, particularly in the UK, the merger includes CLOTH, while in Africa and Asia, it may include CLOTH as well as FORCE and NORTH.

- THOUGHT/FORCE/NORTH is also a common merger; it exists in varieties of English in Africa, America, the Caribbean, Asia, Oceania, and the UK and Ireland.
- Less common is the merger of two of more of the CLOTH/THOUGHT/NORTH Lexical Sets, as well as the LOT/CLOTH (as opposed to LOT/THOUGHT) merger, though either or both of these mergers exist in varieties of English in Africa, Asia, America, the Caribbean, the UK and Ireland.
- Some varieties also have mergers with STRUT and NURSE (PakE) or FOOT (NBrE).

These mergers, as well as other features of vowels in varieties of English around the world, are summarized in Table 3.26. Listening tasks from our discussion of vowels that illustrate these mergers are also listed.

Table 3.26 Mergers in varieties of English

Merger	Varieties of English	Task
FLEECE/KIT 'beat' 'bit' are homophones	Africa: BSAE, EAfE, SNigE Americas and the Caribbean: ChiE Asia: HKE, SgE, MalE, some varieties of IndE, PhlE Oceania: AusAborE, FijE, MāoriE	3.15 KenE 3.16 SNigE 3.19 SgE, MalE 3.20 HKE 3.24 PhlE
GOOSE/FOOT 'pool' 'pull' are homophones	Africa: BSAE, EAfE, SNigE Americas and the Caribbean: PRE Asia: HKE, SgE, MalE, PhlE, some varieties of PakE and IndE, NepE, SLE Oceania: FijE UK and Ireland: SSE, NIrE, NBrE, EMidBrE, West Midlands BrE (WMidBrE)	3.12 PRE 3.15 KenE 3.16 SNigE 3.19 SgE, MalE 3.20 HKE 3.21 IndE 3.22 NepE 3.23 SLE 3.24 PhlE
DRESS/TRAP 'bet' 'bat' are homophones	Africa: BSAE (& BATH/NURSE/SQUARE) Americas and the Caribbean: Calif AmE Asia: HKE, MalE, IndE, PakE, SgE Oceania: FijE	3.19 SgE
TRAP/BATH	Africa: BSAE (& DRESS/ NURSE/ SQUARE), EAfE (& STRUT/NURSE/ START/COMMA/LETTER/PALM), SNigE (& START/PALM/LETTER/COMMA) Americas and the Caribbean: GAmE, AAVE, ChiE, CanE, PRE Asia: PakE, PhlE UK and Ireland: SSE, NBrE, WMidBrE	3.8 NBrE 3.10 GAmE, Calif AmE 3.11 CanE 3.12 PRE 3.15 KenE 3.16 SNigE 3.21 PakE 3.24 PhlE

Table 3.26 (Cont.)

Merger	Varieties of English	Task
BATH/START/ PALM	**Africa:** EAfE (& TRAP/BATH/STRUT/ NURSE/COMMA/LETTER), SNigE (& TRAP/LETTER/COMMA), WSAE, BSAE (& STRUT), HausaE (BATH/NURSE/ PALM), ZimE **Americas and the Caribbean:** JamE, NYC AmE (START/PALM only) **Asia:** HKE, SgE (& STRUT), MalE (& STRUT), IndE, PakE, NepE, SLE **Oceania:** FijE, AusE, AusAborE, NZE, MāoriE **UK and Ireland:** WelE, SSE, RP, LonE, WMidBrE (only PALM/START), NBrE, IrE (BATH/PALM)	3.8 NBrE, Mod RP 3.9 IrE 3.13 AusE 3.14 NZE 3.15 KenE 3.16 SNigE 3.17 WSAE 3.18 ZimE 3.19 SgE, MalE 3.20 HKE 3.21 IndE 3.22 NepE 3.23 SLE
LOT/THOUGHT	**Africa:** BSAE (& NORTH/FORCE/CLOTH), EAfE (& FORCE, NORTH), SNigE (& NORTH/FORCE/CLOTH/STRUT/GOAT) **Americas and the Caribbean:** Midwestern AmE, Western AmE, SAmE, NE AmE, Appal AmE, GAmE, ChiE, CanE, PRE **Asia:** HKE (& NORTH, FORCE, CLOTH), SgE (& NORTH, FORCE, CLOTH, CURE), MalE (& NORTH, FORCE, CLOTH, CURE), IndE (& NORTH/FORCE/CLOTH), PakE (& NORTH/FORCE/CLOTH), NepE (& CLOTH), SLE (& CLOTH/FORCE/NORTH) **Oceania:** FijE (& NORTH/FORCE/CLOTH), AusAborE (& NORTH/FORCE/CLOTH) **UK and Ireland:** ScotE (& CLOTH), Rural IrE (& CLOTH)	3.10 GAmE, Calif AmE 3.11 CanE 3.12 PRE 3.15 KenE 3.16 SNigE 3.19 SgE, MalE 3.20 HKE 3.21 PakE, IndE 3.22 NepE 3.23 SLE
THOUGHT/FORCE/ NORTH	**Africa:** WSAE, BSAE (& LOT/CLOTH), SNigE (& LOT/CLOTH/STRUT/GOAT), ZimE **Americas and the Caribbean:** NORTH/ FORCE ONLY: GAmE, AAVE, ChiE, SAmE, PRE, CanE **Asia:** HKE (& LOT/CLOTH), SgE and MalE (& LOT/CLOTH/CURE), IndE, PakE, SLE (& LOT/CLOTH), PhlE (NORTH/ FORCE) **Oceania:** FijE (& LOT/CLOTH), AusE, AusAborE (& LOT/CLOTH), NZE **UK and Ireland:** Rural WelE, RP, Southeast BrE, WMidBrE, NBrE	3.8 NBrE, Mod RP 3.10 GAmE, Calif AmE 3.11 CanE 3.13 AusE 3.14 NZE 3.16 SNigE 3.17 WSAE 3.18 ZimE 3.19 SgE 3.20 HKE 3.21 PakE, IndE 3.23 SLE

Merger	Varieties of English	Task
CLOTH/THOUGHT/ NORTH	Africa: EAfE (CLOTH/NORTH/GOAT), SNigE (CLOTH/THOUGHT/NORTH/LOT/ FORCE) Americas and the Caribbean: JamE, AmE (CLOTH/THOUGHT) Asia: PhlE (CLOTH/THOUGHT/GOAT), SgE (& THOUGHT/FORCE/CURE), SLE (& LOT/THOUGHT)	3.10 GAmE 3.15 KenE 3.16 SNigE 3.19 SgE 3.23 SLE 3.24 PhlE
LOT/CLOTH	Africa: WSAE, SNigE Americas and the Caribbean: NYC AmE, AAVE, ChiE (& THOUGHT, PALM) Asia: SgE (& CURE/CLOTH/THOUGHT/ NORTH), MalE, PakE, NepE, SLE (& THOUGHT/FORCE/NORTH) UK and Ireland: Rural WelE, RP, Southeast BrE, Southwest BrE, WMidBrE, NBrE, IrE	3.8 NBrE, Mod RP 3.9 IrE 3.16 SNigE 3.17 WSAE 3.19 SgE, MalE 3.21 PakE 3.22 NepE 3.23 SLE
STRUT	Africa: KenE (& START/PALM/TRAP/ BATH/NURSE) Asia: PakE (& NURSE, LETTER, COMMA), MalE (& PALM/BATH), SgE (& START) UK and Ireland: Rural WelE, SSE (& NURSE), WMidBrE, NBrE (& FOOT)	3.8 NBrE 3.15 KenE 3.19 SgE, MalE
NURSE	Africa: KenE (& START/PALM/TRAP/ BATH/NURSE), SNigE (GOOSE/FOOT/ NURSE) Asia: SgE (& LETTER/COMMA), MalE (& LETTER/COMMA), PakE (& LETTER, COMMA, STRUT) UK and Ireland: NBrE (NURSE/SQUARE)	3.15 KenE 3.16 SNigE

☞ The summary of vowel mergers above is intended to provide a comprehensive overview of vowels in varieties of English worldwide.

Although you are encouraged to listen to different types of vowel mergers, you may wish to focus your attention on the mergers that occur in the Englishes that are of interest to you.

In Table 3.26, you can find a list of varieties in which the mergers have been found. It may be useful to refer to this list to help guide your listening.

As we saw in Chapter 2, English has always been in a state of change; it is a dynamic language continually adding new vocabulary and changing phonological features due to contact with other varieties or languages, or historical changes that are still in progress. In Chapter 2, we discussed the Great Vowel Shift (GVS), which occurred in the fifteenth to seventeenth centuries, and helped to transition Middle English into Modern English. The GVS, and the *i*-mutation (see Chapter 2), which occurred prior to the GVS in the seventh century, are two of the vowel shifts that have occurred in English. There are a number of vowel shifts that are currently in progress, including the Southern Vowel Shift (SVS), the Northern Cities Vowel Shift (NCVS), the Northern California Vowel Shift, and the Canadian Vowel Shift. These are all examples of chain shifts, in which the change in the position of one vowel – through fronting, or retracting, rising or falling – is linked to or causes a change in the position of another vowel which, in turn, causes a change in a third vowel, and so on. When chain shifts occur:

I.   Long vowels rise.
II. Short vowels and nuclei of upgliding diphthongs fall.
III. Back vowels move to the front (Labov, Ash, & Boberg, 2006).

Chain shifts are language internal and natural processes; some of these shifts are occurring simultaneously across geographically separated varieties of English, suggesting that the shifts are a continuation of a process of language change that began centuries ago, before and during the spread of English worldwide (Kerswill, Torgersen, & Fox, 2008, p. 456). One such shift is the Southern Vowel Shift, which has been found to occur in Southern varieties of English, including in the United States in SAmE and AAVE, the latter of which is influenced by SAmE; Southern BrE, and, in particular, LonE; and in the Southern Hemisphere in WSAE, AusE, and NZE. The Southern Vowel Shift consists of:

- fronting of GOOSE (and FOOT, in some varieties)
- glide weakening in PRICE
- fronting/lowering of first member of GOAT
- lowering and retraction (backing) of FACE
- lowering and retraction of FLEECE
- raising of KIT and DRESS
- LOT/THOUGHT (raised or diphthongized (Thomas, 2004))

TASK 3.25 Listening for the Southern Vowel Shift

🎧 The pronunciation of the speaker of NZE illustrates some of the features of the Southern Vowel Shift. You may note the fronting of GOAT and GOOSE, the raising of DRESS, and the lowering of FACE.

Table 3.27 Diphthong Shift in varieties of English					
	RP		LonE	AusE	NZE	WSAE
MOUTH:	aʊ	→	æʊ	æɔ	æ̈	æʊ (B), aː (G)
PRICE:	aɪ	→	ɑɪ	ɑe	ɑe	aː (B, G)
GOAT:	əʊ	→	ʌʊ	əʉ	ɐʉ	œʉ, œɤ̈ (B, G)
FACE:	eɪ	→	ʌɪ	æɪ	æe	ʌɪ (B), eɪ (G)
GOOSE:	uː	→	ʉː	ʉː	ʉː	ʉː, yː (B, G)
FLEECE:	iː	→	ɪi	iː	iː	iː (B, G)

B = Broad, and G = General

The Diphthong Shift is part of the Southern Vowel Shift; it is assumed to have originated in LonE and is an inherited process (or continuation of an ongoing process) in other Southern Englishes worldwide. Table 3.27 shows how this is changing LonE in comparison to RP. The table also shows the corresponding diphthongs in NZE, which has a more shifted diphthong system than LonE (Kerswill, Torgersen, & Fox, 2008), as well as AusE, and both Broad and General WSAE, which also have the Diphthong Shift. Trudgill (2004) states that the Diphthong Shift follows a fixed route, first for MOUTH, then PRICE, GOAT, FACE, GOOSE, FLEECE, in that respective order. As Table 3.27 shows, the 1st target of MOUTH is fronted; the 2nd target may also be centralized (NZE) or lowered (AusE). The 1st target of PRICE is retracted (backed) while the 2nd target may be lowered (NZE, AusE) or weakened (WSAE). The 1st target of GOAT may be lowered (LonE, NZE) or fronted (WSAE) while the 2nd target may be centralized or fronted (AusE, NZE, WSAE). The 1st target of FACE is lowered and often retracted (LonE, AusE, NZE, Broad WSAE); GOOSE is fronted to a central or front vowel (LonE, AusE, NZE, WSAE) while FLEECE may become diphthongal (LonE).

TASK 3.26 Listening for the Diphthong Shift

🎧 Listen to the speakers of AusE, NZE, Mod RP, and WSAE say: MOUTH, PRICE, GOAT, FACE, GOOSE, and FLEECE. Which features of the Southern Vowel Shift can you find for each speaker/variety?

As we saw in our discussion of vowels in varieties of English, above, GOOSE-fronting (and FOOT- and GOAT-fronting to a lesser extent) is also a feature of the Southern Vowel Shift, and is prevalent across a range of Englishes, including in the Americas and the Caribbean, where both GOOSE- and FOOT-fronting have been found in Western AmE (including Calif AmE), Midwestern AmE, and SAmE (and FOOT-fronting); GOOSE-fronting also occurs in Eastern Cherokee English (a NAE), Appal AmE, and CanE, as well as in Southern Hemisphere Englishes, including in AusE,

AusAborE, NZE, MāoriE, and WSAE. In the UK and Ireland, it has been found in Southeast BrE, Southwest BrE, LonE (which also has FOOT-fronting), MLE (also FOOT), SSE (also FOOT), and NIrE (see Cheshire, Kerswill, Fox & Torgersen, 2011). It appears to be rare in varieties of African English (aside from WSAE) and Asian Englishes. Figure 3.16 shows a vowel chart for a speaker of Mod RP. His vowel chart demonstrates that he has a fronted GOOSE; his articulation of the vowel in GOOSE is nearly as fronted as the vowel in KIT; FOOT is also fronted.

Another vowel shift that is occurring is the Northern Cities Vowel Shift, also called the Northern Chain Shift or NCS, which occurs in Inland North varieties of AmE, including the English of regions of New York, Ohio, Michigan, Wisconsin, Indiana, Pennsylvania, and Illinois (Labov, 2010). According to Labov (2010), in the Northern Cities Vowel Shift:

(1) /æ/ is fronted and raised in TRAP.
(2) /ɑ/ is fronted in PALM.
(3) /ɔ/ is lowered and fronted in LOT/THOUGHT.
(4) /ɛ/ is backed and lowered in DRESS.
(5) /ʌ/ is backed in STRUT.
(6) /ɪ/ is backed and lowered in KIT.

Another shift that is occurring in AmE is the Northern California Vowel Shift; as the name implies, this is a shift that began in California (Eckert, 2008). It is spreading across the United States into Western and Midwestern

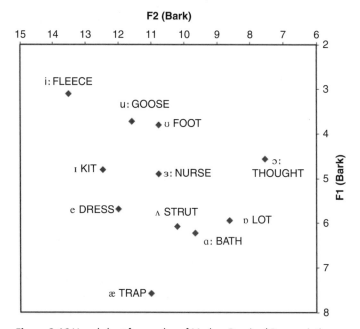

Figure 3.16 Vowel chart for speaker of Modern Received Pronunciation

AmE, as well as part of the South. The Northern California Vowel Shift has features of both the Northern and Southern Vowel Shifts. The elements are:

- GOOSE- and GOAT-fronting
- Lowering of KIT and DRESS
- Backing of TRAP
- Lowering of THOUGHT
- Backing of LOT

Another vowel shift that is occurring in North America is the Canadian Vowel Shift; this occurs across Canada and is also found in some varieties of AmE in the Northwest and Midwest (Boberg, 2004). It is similar to the Northern California Vowel Shift: it has lowering and retraction of both DRESS and TRAP; in addition, it has further retraction (backing) of PALM/LOT/THOUGHT.

3.7   English Vowel Variation

Is there also variation in vowel sounds within varieties of English? It is important to make a distinction between the vowels that exist in a variety of English, and how these vowels are actually pronounced in each variety. In our discussion above, we have primarily focused on the vowel inventories of each variety of English, though some mention has been made of how vowel sounds may differ in various environments, as in the 'el'–'al' merger in AusE. We use the terms 'phoneme' and **phone** to describe this difference. The term 'phoneme' refers to the individual vowel sounds, described by HAR – height, advancement, and lip rounding/spreading – as discussed above, that exist in a language or variety; this is English phonetics. The term 'phone', in contrast, refers to the actual physical realization of a vowel or consonant, which is dependent on the linguistic environment in which it occurs – for example, whether it occurs before a consonant or not, or at the beginning or end of a word – this is part of the phonology of English. In English, as in many other languages, vowels may change in pronunciation depending on the linguistic environment they are in – for example, they may be pronounced with slightly shorter length or with a nasal pronunciation.

TASK 3.27 Listening for Vowel Length

🎧 Listen to the speakers of Calif AmE and IrE say the words in the table below. For both speakers, which words are longer – the words in Column A or Column B? What is the difference between the words in

Column A versus Column B, for all four vowels, that may explain the difference in length? (The spelling of the words may help you answer these questions.)

Vowel	Column A	Column B
/iː/	*beat*	*bead*
/e ɛ/	*bet*	*bed*
/æ/	*bat*	*bad*

You may have noticed that both speakers in Task 3.27 have a length difference for vowels and that, for both speakers, the vowel pronunciation in words in Column B is longer than for those in Column A for each word pair. The vowel /iː/, for example, is pronounced longer in *bead* than in *beat* by both speakers. It is the same vowel – the same phoneme – but it has two different pronunciations, or physical realizations, for these speakers. The reason the pronunciation is different is because the linguistic environment is different – all the vowels in Column A are followed by the letter 't', which represents the consonant sound /t/, a *voiceless* **alveolar** stop; vowels in the words in Column B, in contrast, are followed by the letter 'd', which represents the consonant /d/, a *voiced* alveolar stop. In short, the following linguistic environment for vowels in words in Columns A and B differ, and it is this difference that creates a slightly different pronunciation – in this case, length difference – for some speakers and varieties of English. 'Voiced' refers to vibration in the vocal folds (or cords) when the air passes through from the lungs into the mouth/nose, whereas 'voiceless' means the vocal folds are open and therefore do not vibrate as the air passes through the vocal tract. We can also measure the length of the vowels through an acoustic analysis; Figures 3.17 and 3.18 shows spectrograms and waveforms (the upper visual) for the IrE speaker's production of *bat* and *bad*. The upper visual is called a waveform and shows the waveform generated by the opening and closing of the vocal folds. As Figures 3.17 and 3.18 show, the waveform for the vowel in *bat* is shorter than for *bad*.

How do we know whether a sound is a phoneme? We have already discussed the acoustic analysis of vowel sounds to determine which vowels exist in a variety of English (or any other language). Another test of whether a sound is a phoneme is the **minimal pair test**; this is used by linguists to classify speech sounds. As we noted in Task 3.27, for each vowel sound, the words in Column A and Column B have one difference – the final consonant sound is /t/ or /d/. When there is only one sound difference in either the consonant or the vowel or in the tone between

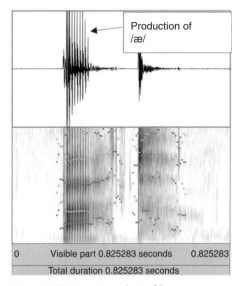

Figure 3.17 Acoustic analysis of *bat*

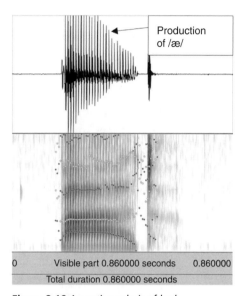

Figure 3.18 Acoustic analysis of *bad*

a pair of words, the words are a minimal pair. There are two important points to note: (1) the difference must be in sound (vowel or consonant or tone) and not in spelling; the words *meat, meet,* and *mete* are not minimal pairs: while they have a different spelling, the actual vowel and consonant sounds are exactly the same in both words; (2) the two words must have the exact same number of sounds – the difference cannot be in the number of consonants/vowels in each word. As an example, the words *bee* and *beat* do not form a minimal pair as the two words do not have the same number of speech sounds – *bee* has one consonant and one vowel, while *beat* has two consonants and one vowel sound. Likewise, *stop* and *top* do not form a minimal pair. The words *beat* and *bead* form a minimal pair; this minimal pair, however, does not demonstrate that /iː/ is a vowel phoneme as the vowel in both words is /iː/; rather, as will be shown in Chapter 5 in more detail, it shows that /t/ and /d/ are two different consonant phonemes. In contrast, each pair of words selected from Column A constitute a minimal pair as the linguistic environment is the same: [bVt] (where V stands for a vowel; the same is true for the words in Column B: [bVd]; the use of square and slant brackets will be clarified below). We can replace the V in [bVt] with one of the four vowel sounds listed in the table: /iː/ as in /biːt/, which creates *beat*, while /bæt/ creates *bat*, and /bet/ *bet*. The [hVd] word list is also a list of words which contrast with each of the other words to constitute a minimal pair. A critical component of the minimal pair test is that the words have different meanings – by replacing the /iː/ sound with /æ/, we change the meaning of the word from *beat* to *bat*, for example. This demonstrates that /iː/ and /æ/ are separate vowel phonemes as, when we put them in a minimal pair, the words have **contrastive meaning** – the meaning is different. In short, the vowels are in **contrastive distribution**: when placed into the same linguistic environment, as in [bVt], they have different – contrastive – meanings.

In contrast, a *phone* is the way a phoneme is actually physically realized or pronounced in a given environment. A phoneme may have different phones, or actual physical realizations, in different environments. These phones may be in **complementary distribution**. This means that the phones, or different pronunciations of one phoneme, have a specific environment where they appear. For instance, in some varieties of English, the phones of /iː/ can be described as regular length, as in *bead* – marked as [iː] as in [biːd] – or slightly shortened, as in *beat*, marked as [i·], with only one length mark, as in [bi·t]. These two pronunciations of /iː/ – [iː] or [i·] – do not exist in the same environment; the slightly shorter pronunciation appears only when it is directly followed by a voiceless consonant in the same syllable, as in *beat*. The regular long pronunciation occurs everywhere else. To show how the vowels are physically pronounced, we use square brackets [ ] – this indicates that the sounds are phones, while slant brackets / / indicate that a sound is a phoneme. All the phones of a given phoneme are called *allophones*. For some varieties of English, as shown above, the phoneme /iː/ is shortened before a voiceless consonant and not shortened anywhere else. We use [iː] to show the non-shortened phone and [i·], with one length mark only, to show the shortened phone. We can write phonological rules to express the sound change, and to show the allophones of a given phoneme and how these allophones have complementary distribution. Our phonological rules can be written as follows: vowels are shortened in the environment preceding a voiceless consonant in the same syllable. In many varieties of English, this vowel shortening rule applies to all vowels, not just the vowels given in the examples above; other rules may apply as well. Phones of a phoneme can also exist in free variation, which means they are interchangeable without set rules for when each phone occurs. We saw this for vowels in FLEECE/KIT in PhlE (see also Task 3.24). In this case, we cannot write a phonological rule, given that we cannot predict when each phone will occur.

We will now look at some of the phonological rules that exist for vowels in English, with examples drawn from varieties of English in which these rules exist. Many of these allophones exist because of natural phonological processes of **assimilation** – the influence preceding or following sounds have on a given sound. In the word *ban*, for example, the nasal may influence the articulation of the vowel; this is called *regressive (backward) assimilation*, when the influence is backwards to the preceding sound or sounds. When assimilation occurs for the following sound/sounds, this is called *progressive (forward) assimilation*. A summary of the rules is given in Table 3.28; listening tasks for some of the allophones are provided in Task 3.28.

Task 3.28 Listening for Vowel Allophones

☞ The following discussion of allophonic variation of vowels is intended to provide a comprehensive overview of vowel allophones in varieties of English worldwide.

Although you are encouraged to listen to different types of allophonic variation, you may wish to focus your attention on the variation that occurs in the Englishes that are of interest to you.

In Table 3.28, you can find a list of varieties in which the allophonic variation has been found. It may be useful to refer to this list to help guide your reading and listening. You can listen to examples of the allophones in Task 3.28.

Table 3.28 Allophones of vowels in varieties of English

Rule	Diacritic symbol/ examples:	Varieties of English	🎧 Listening Task 3.28
Vowel shortening: vowels are shortened preceding voiceless consonants in the same syllable	[ˇ] [ˑ] *bead* vs *beat* [biːd] vs [biˑt] *bid* vs *bit* [bɪd] vs. [bɪ̆t]	AmE, CanE, NZE, AusE, Educated NigE, KenE, WSAE, WelE, IrE, BrE	(A) IrE, Mod RP, SA AusE, GAmE, KenE
Vowel length: (a) All else being equal, vowels are longest in an open syllable, next longest before a voiced consonant and shortest before a voiceless consonant. (b) All else being equal, vowels are longest in a stressed syllable. (c) All else being equal, vowels are longest in monosyllabic words, next longest in words with 2 syllables, and shortest in words with more than 2 syllables.	*bee* *bead* *beat* *depreciate*	AmE, CanE, NZE, AusE, Educated NigE, KenE, WSAE, WelE, IrE, BrE	(B) IrE, Mod RP, SA AusE, GAmE, KenE

Table 3.28 (Cont.)

Rule	Diacritic symbol/ examples:	Varieties of English	🎧 Listening Task 3.28
MalE Vowel Lengthening: short vowels are lengthened before /n l r s ʃ/: /i/→[iː]; /ʌ/→[aː]; /ɔ/ →[ɔː]; /u/→[uː]	*bean* [biːn] vs *bead* [bid]	MalE	(C) MalE
SVLR (Scottish Vowel Length Rule): vowels are lengthened before /r/, before voiced fricatives, before a boundary (including morpheme boundary)	Longer vowels in *beer*, *breathe*, *bee* than in *brief*, *bead*, and *greed*	SSE	
Vowel nasalization: vowels become nasalized preceding nasals in the same syllable	[˜] *bee* vs *bean* [biː] vs [bĩːn] *boo* vs *boon* [buː] vs [bũːn]	AmE, NZE AusE, BrE, IrE, WelE, CanE, Educated NigE, JamE, KenE, WSAE *Exception:* AusAborE	(D) IrE, CanE, KenE, SA AusE, Mod RP, GAmE
TRAP raising before nasals in the same syllable	AAVE: *hand* [hɛ̃nd] (to DRESS); AusE: [̞] *hand* [hæ̞̃nd]	AusE, Midwestern/ Western AmE, AAVE	(E) SA AusE
BATH raising: retention of [æ] before voiceless plosive or affricate or /l/; raising and lengthening before final voiced stop, voiceless fricative, or /m/ or /n/	*cap, hat, back, pal* [æ] vs [ɛː] in *man*, *bath, laugh*	NYC AmE	
Vowels raising in the presence of palatal consonants	*cat* [kæt] vs *catch* [kɛʧ]	AusAborE	
Canadian Raising: PRICE/ MOUTH raised before voiceless consonants in the same syllable	*write* [rʌɪt] vs *ride* [raid]	CanE	(F) CanE
Vowel neutralization: DRESS/KIT merger before nasals in the same syllable (PIN/PEN merger)	*pin* and *pen* as homophones	AmE: Southern (also before /l/), AAVE, Lumbee NAE, Appalachian, Midwestern, Western Urban ScotE; IrE; Northern, West, Southern, Midland BrE	

Rule	Diacritic symbol/ examples:	Varieties of English	🎧 Listening Task 3.28
/r/ neutralization: phonemic distinction between vowels disappears before 'r'	NZE: NEAR & SQUARE FLEECE & NEAR neutralized to /i:/ NZE, AusE: DRESS & SQUARE to /e/ GOOSE & CURE to /ʉ:/ AmE, CanE: MERRY/MARY/MARRY /æ ɛ e/ to [ɛ]		(G) SA, Qld, Qld NSW AusE
/l/ neutralization: vowels are neutralized (phonemic distinction disappears) before /l/ and the words become homophones	NZE: FLEECE/NEAR: *reel & real* DRESS/TRAP: *Allan & Ellen, salary & celery* FOOT/GOOSE: *pull & pool* KIT/FOOT: *pill & pull* KIT/GOOSE: *pill & pool, skill & school* LOT/GOAT/THOUGHT, GOAT/FOOT THOUGHT: *poll & pole, pull & Paul* Melbourne, Victoria AusE: DRESS/TRAP Midwestern and Western AmE: *feel/fill, pill/pull, fail/fell* SAmE, WSAE: DRESS/TRAP		(H) SA, Qld AusE, NZE
GOOSE-fronting: GOOSE is fronted to a front or centralized articulation	Aus AborE: In the presence of palatals *food* [fud] vs *shoot* [ʃʉt] (or [sʉt]). When allophonic: After coronals > before coronals; retracted before /l/: *too* vs *pool*	Calif AmE, Appal AmE, SAmE, Western AmE, Midwestern AmE, AusE, NZE, SAE, Southern BrE	(I) Calif AmE, Appal AmE, CanE
KIT split: fronter [ɪ] articulation in velar/palatal environments, after /h/, word-initially; central [ɨ] elsewhere	*trip, ship, dip, tip, fill* [ɪ] vs *things, kitten, hid, sing* [ɨ]	WSAE, Coloured SAE	(J) WSAE
PRICE glide reduction: PRICE reduced to monophthong before nasals, pauses and voiced obstruents (extending to voiceless obstruent)	/aɪ/ to [aː] –*mine* [maːn] *hi* [haː], *slide* [slaːd], *white* [waːt]	AAVE	

Sources for allophonic variation are drawn from the references cited in Section 3.5.

Vowel shortening and vowel length: Vowel length differences occur in many varieties of English; one vowel length difference is phonetic – dependent on the linguistic environment – as we saw above, when we discussed phones and allophones. In some varieties of English, vowels are shortened when they occur before a voiceless consonant (such as /t/ as in *beat* or *bit*) in the same syllable. You can hear the difference in vowel length in *beat* vs *bead*, and *bit* vs *bid*, for speakers of SA AusE, GAmE, IrE, KenE, and Mod RP in Task 3.28A. Vowels are also longer when they occur in an open syllable (e.g., *bee*) than in a closed syllable, and longer in monosyllabic (one syllable) over polysyllabic words in some varieties of English; you can hear this for *bee* > *bead* > *beat* > *depreciate* (the underlined syllable has the FLEECE vowel) for speakers of GAmE, SA AusE, IrE, KenE, and Mod RP in Task 3.28B. Both MalE and SSE have vowel lengthening rules: in MalE, short vowels become longer when they precede /n l r s ʃ/; you can hear this for the MalE speakers in *bead* vs *bean* in Task 3.28C; in SSE, vowels are lengthened before /r/, before voiced **fricatives**, before a boundary including a morpheme boundary.

Vowel nasalization and raising: A common phonological process across many varieties of English is the nasalization of vowels that occur before a nasal consonant (see Chapter 5) in the same syllable, as in *bean* and *boon*, where the 'n' represents the nasal consonant /n/. Nasals are sounds where the airflow is pushed through the nasal cavity (the nose); most consonants and vowels are oral sounds, where the airflow exits the vocal tract through the mouth. In some circumstances, however, oral speech sounds can become nasalized; this occurs for vowels when they precede nasal consonants in the same syllable due to assimilation in manner of articulation (airflow) of the vowel to the nasal. In short, as we produce the vowel, we anticipate the nasal airflow of the following consonant and, in doing so, begin pushing air through the nose as we move from the vowel into the nasal. You can hear nasal assimilation in *boon* vs *boo*, and *bean* vs *bee*, for speakers of SA AusE, GAmE, CanE, IrE, KenE, and Mod RP in Task 3.28D. In some varieties of English, including AusE, TRAP vowels may be raised (have a higher tongue articulation) when they precede nasals. TRAP raising is illustrated for a speaker of SA AusE in Figure 3.19: as Figure 3.19 shows, the speaker's articulation of the TRAP vowels in a pre-nasal environment in *tan, can,* and *pan* is as high as his articulation of DRESS vowels in *bed* and *den*. In contrast, his articulation of the TRAP vowel is much lower in a non-pre-nasal environment in *bat* and *bag*. You can also listen to his pronunciation of these words in Task 3.28E.

Vowel raising also occurs for BATH vowels when they precede a final voiced stop, voiceless fricative, /m/ or /n/ in NYC AmE; it may also occur for all vowels in the presence of a palatal consonant for AusAborE; palatal consonants are consonants articulated with the body of the tongue raised close to the hard palate in the roof of the mouth (see also Chapter 5).

Raising of vowels also occurs in CanE: the process called *Canadian Raising* refers to the well-documented raising of the 1st target of the diphthongs of PRICE and MOUTH before a voiceless consonant. This is illustrated for a speaker of CanE for MOUTH in Figure 3.20. As Figure 3.20 shows, the articulation of the 1st target in *lout* is higher than it is in the 1st target of *loud*. You can also listen to a speaker of CanE say *lout* and *loud* in Task 3.28F.

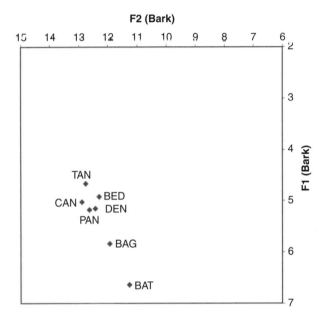

Figure 3.19 TRAP raising in Australian English

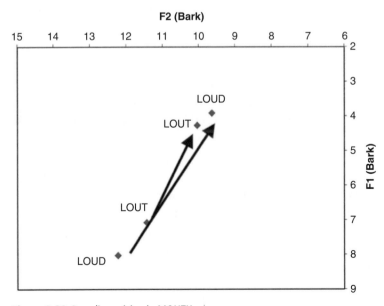

Figure 3.20 Canadian raising in MOUTH

Vowel neutralization: A following nasal may also neutralize height differences between KIT and DRESS vowels, leading to what is called a PIN/PEN merger, where these two words, as well as other words with the DRESS and KIT vowels preceding a nasal, become homophones. Vowel neutralization also occurs in AusE and NZE, as well as CanE and some varieties of AmE, before 'r', so that DRESS and SQUARE become homophones; you can listen to the AusE speakers from SA and Qld, as well as Queensland and New South Wales, labelled as Qld NSW, say *dress*, *head*, and *square* in Task 3.28G. Vowel neutralization before /l/ for *pool* and *pull* (GOOSE/FOOT) and *feel* and *fill* (FLEECE/KIT) as well as *fail* and *fell* (FACE/DRESS) also occurs in some varieties of English, including AusE and NZE. You can listen to speech samples from AusE and NZE speakers illustrating this in Task 3.28H.

GOOSE-fronting: We have discussed GOOSE-fronting as a phonemic change in some varieties of English, where the vowel in GOOSE is articulated as a central or front vowel; as noted above, this is a part of the Southern Vowel Shift and occurs widely in Southern Englishes, including AusE, Southern BrE, and SAmE. In these Englishes, a fronted GOOSE is in many cases phonemic. It is a feature that is spreading into other Englishes, including NBrE, and Midwestern and Western AmE; as it spreads into these Englishes, it may be allophonic, occurring in a more fronted articulation in specific environments before spreading across all phonetic environments. When allophonic variation in GOOSE-fronting does occur, it occurs more often after a coronal consonant (coronal consonants are articulated with the front part of the tongue) than before, such as /t/ as in *too*, /s/ as in *Sue*, and /z/ as in *zoo*, and less frequently before an /l/ and after non-coronal consonants such as /k/ as in *cooed* (see Chapter 5 for a discussion of coronals). Figure 3.21 shows an example of variable GOOSE-fronting for a speaker of Appal AmE. As the figure shows, the speaker has a more fronted articulation of the GOOSE vowel in *zoo* and *Sue* than in *cooed* and *who'd*, with the most retracted (back) articulation in *pool*. You can listen to the Appal AmE speaker say these words, as well as speakers of CanE and Calif AmE illustrating GOOSE-fronting in *boo*, in Task 3.28I.

KIT split: As noted above, in our discussion of SAE, the KIT split is a key feature of WSAE and Coloured SAE: vowels in the KIT Lexical Set are articulated with a fronter articulation in velar (e.g., /k g/) and palatal environments, after /h/, and word-initially. They are centralized as [ï] everywhere else, with the two dots over the vowel sound a diacritic to show centralization. Figure 3.22 shows the KIT split for a speaker of WSAE. As the figure shows, KIT is fronter in *hid*, *kitten*, *sing*, and *things* and more centralized in *trip*, *fill*, *ship*, *dip*, and *tip*. You can listen to the WSAE speaker's pronunciation of these words in Task 3.28J.

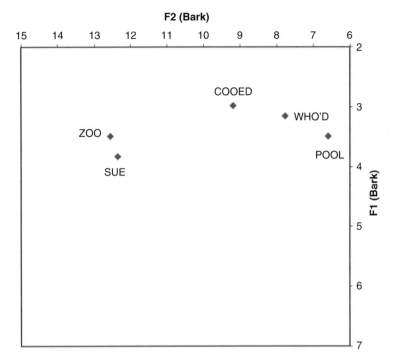

Figure 3.21 GOOSE-fronting in Appalachian American English

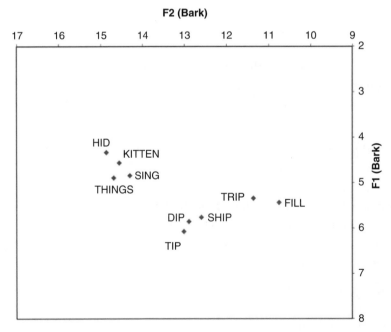

Figure 3.22 White South African English KIT split

PRICE glide reduction: The reduction of the glide in PRICE exists in AAVE: in this process, vowels in the PRICE Lexical Set are reduced to a monophthong vowel when they occur before nasals, pauses, and voiced – and in some cases voiceless – obstruents (see Chapter 5).

3.8   CHECK YOUR UNDERSTANDING

EXERCISES

(a) Draw a vowel trapezoid and label the chart with the following names:
High, Mid, Low
Open, Mid, Close
Front, Central, Back
(b) What do each of the terms mean?
(c) Which types of vowels tend to be rounded? Which types of vowels tend to be spread?
(d) What is the three-part description for each of these vowels?
/æ/
/ɛ/
/ɪ/
/ʉ/
/ɜ/
/ʊ/
/ɔ/
(e) What do F1 and F2 mean? How do F1 and F2 correlate with HAR?
(f) Find at least five minimal pairs from the list of words below. Are there any words in the list that do not form a minimal pair with another word?

sleep   *slip*   *pal*   *pill*   *feel*   *fill*   *ship*   *sheep*   *steep*
stop   *lit*   *let*   *latte* *man*   *moon*   *many*   *map*   *tea*

In your own words, define what a minimal pair is.
(g) Which of the following words show a vowel allophone? What is the allophone and when does it occur (which phonological rule in Table 3.28 does it illustrate)?

Sam [sæ̃m] vs *sad* [sæd]
sat [sæt] vs *sad* [sæd]
hike [hʌɪk] vs *hide* [haɪd]
too [tʉː] vs *coo* [kuː]

DISCUSSION QUESTIONS

(a) If a language only has three vowels, what are these vowels? Five vowels? Why are these vowels most common among the world's languages?

(b) What do we mean by Cultivated, General, and Broad, and acrolect, mesolect, and basilect, with regard to varieties of English?

(c) What is a superstrate? What is a substrate?

EXPAND YOUR UNDERSTANDING

(a) In Task 3.29, you can find a speech sample from a woman from Derbyshire, East Midlands, UK. This region is often categorized as part of the Northern dialect region of England. Can you find any features similar to the NBrE speaker in Task 3.8 above? You can also listen to the speaker talk about her EMidBrE dialect. Table 3.29 shows the vowel inventory of speakers of EMidBrE.

TASK 3.29 Listening for East Midlands British English and Chilean English

🎧 In Task 3.29, you can listen to a speaker of East Midlands English. The vowel inventory of this speaker is shown in Table 3.29.

Table 3.29 Vowels in East Midlands English

	Front	Central	Back
High	/iː/ FLEECE – also /ɪi, iːɪ/ /ɪ/ KIT	/ʉː/ GOOSE – also /ʉː/	/uː/ GOOSE – also /ʉː/ /ʊ/ FOOT/STRUT
Mid	/ɛ/ DRESS /ɛː/ SQUARE – also /eː/	/əː/ NURSE – also /ɪː/	/ɔː/ THOUGHT/FORCE/NORTH
Low	/a/ TRAP/BATH		/ɒ/ LOT/CLOTH /ɑː/ PALM/START – also /ɒː, aː/
Diphthongs (starting vowel)	/ɪə/ NEAR – also /ɪː/ /ɛɪ/ FACE /aʊ/ MOUTH – also /aː/	/əʊ/ GOAT – also /ɔʊ, əʉ/ /aɪ/ PRICE – also /ɑɪ, ɑː/	/jʊə/ CURE – also /ɔː/ /ɔɪ/ CHOICE

(b) We have focused on Inner and Outer Circle Englishes in Chapter 3, as these Englishes have been established as unique and independent varieties of English due to their long history and the status of English as a *de jure* or de facto official language in these contexts. There is also increasing recognition of Expanding Circle Englishes as unique varieties of English. We now turn our attention to one of these emerging varieties of English – Chilean English (ChilE). In Figure 3.7, you can find a picture of a Spanish vowel chart, based on Ladefoged and Johnson (2014).

(1) Based on the Spanish vowel chart, which of the following mergers would you expect in ChilE?
FLEECE/KIT
DRESS/TRAP
GOOSE/FOOT

(2) Listen to the speech samples in Task 3.29 for a speaker of ChilE who speaks Spanish as his native language. Can you hear a difference between HEED (FLEECE) and HID (KIT), HEAD (DRESS) and HAD (TRAP), WHO'D (GOOSE) and HOOD (FOOT)?

(3) Formant values were taken for each word in the [hVd] environment, with the F1 and F2 values taken from the same midpoint of each vowel. Additional measures for GOOSE and FOOT were taken in a preceding-/l/ environment in PULL and POOL for supplementary data. The formant values are given below in Table 3.30 and shown in Figure 3.23.

Table 3.30 Chilean English vowel formant values		
	F1	F2
FLEECE (HEED)	330.84	1974.85
KIT (HID)	344.02	2000.63
HEAD (DRESS)	533.56	1704.69
HAD (TRAP)	678.43	1456.33
WHO'D (GOOSE)	361.97	1504.30
HOOD (FOOT)	399.15	1389.13
POOL (GOOSE)	347.06	779.62
PULL (FOOT)	364.13	798.51

(4) These values have then been converted using a Bark Scale and plotted on a vowel chart, as seen in Figure 3.23. Are FLEECE and KIT merged for this speaker? Are DRESS/TRAP merged? What is the difference in the articulation of the GOOSE/FOOT vowels in WHO'D/HOOD and POOL/PULL? What does this indicate? Do you believe this speaker has a GOOSE/FOOT merger?

ANALYSE YOUR OWN PRONUNCIATION

(a) What other language/s do you speak? What is the vowel inventory of this/these language/s? You may need to do some online research to access this information.

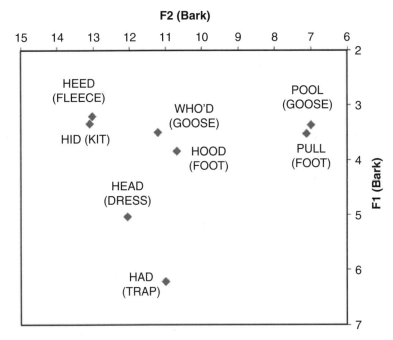

F2 (Bark)

Figure 3.23 Chilean English vowel mergers

(b) What variety of English do you think you speak? What are the vowels of this variety?

(c) What predictions can you make about your own vowel inventory?

(d) In Appendix A, you will find the instructions on how to record your own word list and short conversational sample. In this chapter, we have focused on the vowels in the [hVd] word list. You will also find instructions on how to create a vowel chart based on your F1 and F2 values.

(e) In Figure 3.24, you will find the vowel chart I created for my own pronunciation, using the Bark Scale for my F1 and F2 values (the template is available online for your own use; see Appendix A).

I speak Midwestern/GAmE, with some Danish influence as Danish was my sole language until the age of 10, when I learned English. Based on the description of GAmE in Table 3.8, above, I note that I have:

• a TRAP/BATH merger
• some fronting in GOAT, GOOSE, and FOOT
• a merger between LOT/THOUGHT (COT/CAUGHT) and CLOTH

We will examine the vowels in the 'r' Lexical Set in Chapter 4. For diphthongs, we will simply look at the spectrograms to see whether we can see a change from one vowel to another, a transition from a 1st target to a 2nd target. Instructions on how to do this are given in Appendix A. Using this plus our auditory abilities, we should be able to categorize each of our diphthongs.

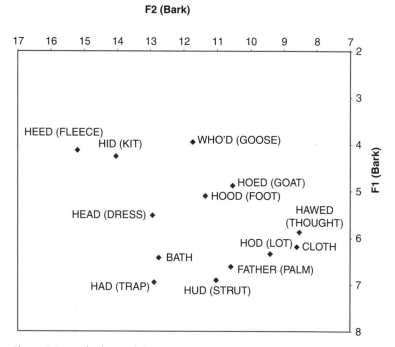

Figure 3.24 Author's vowel chart

On the basis of these analyses, I can now determine that my vowel inventory consists of 10 monophthongs and 4 diphthongs, for a total of 14 vowel phonemes.

/i/ FLEECE
/ɪ/ KIT
/ɛ/ DRESS
/æ/ TRAP/BATH
/ʉ/ GOOSE
/ʊ/ FOOT
/ʌ/ STRUT
/ɑ/ PALM
/o/ GOAT
/ɔ/ CLOTH/LOT/THOUGHT
/eɪ/ FACE
/aɪ/ PRICE
/aʊ/ MOUTH
/ɔɪ/ CHOICE

(f) How many vowel phonemes can you identify in your own English? Transcribe the vowel in each of the [hVd] words.

(g) Why do you think you have this number of vowel phonemes?

(h) What do you think are the main influences on your English vowels?

4 | Rhoticity in Varieties of English

4.1 Introduction to the Chapter

In the previous chapters, we examined the vowel inventories across varieties of English, noting that historical changes in English as well as the influence of different languages have resulted in substantial differences in how English is spoken around the world. We also mentioned that rhoticity – the production of the 'r' sound after a vowel in words such as *car* and *hear* – impacts the number of vowels in different varieties of English. Rhoticity is one of the main phonological features distinguishing different varieties of English; therefore, in this chapter, we will discuss rhoticity in more depth, and examine the historical patterns of rhoticity across Englishes worldwide.

4.2 Defining Rhoticity

What is rhoticity? Before we examine rhoticity across varieties of English, it is important first to define what we mean by rhoticity, and how we produce and measure rhoticity. Can you identify rhoticity when you hear someone speak English? Let us start by listening to a few speech samples to see whether we can identify whether speakers have rhoticity in their pronunciation.

TASK 4.2 Listening for Rhoticity

🎧 Listen to the recording of the sentence *Bother, father caught hot coffee in the car park* for the speakers of AmE and BrE.

Pay attention to the final 'r' sound in the words: *Bother, father, car, park.*

What differences can you hear between the AmE and the BrE speakers?

Speaker 1   Midwestern AmE
Speaker 2   Calif AmE
Speaker 3   New England AmE (NE AmE)
Speaker 4   Mod RP
Speaker 5   Mod RP

In the case of the speakers of AmE, you may be able to hear a noticeable sound like 'err' at the end of the word where there is an 'r' in spelling after the vowel. For the speakers of BrE, there is no 'err' sound at the end of the word. When a speaker produces the final 'r' sound as 'err', the speaker is said to be **rhotic**. A speaker who does not produce the 'r' sound after the vowel is **non-rhotic**. We can classify varieties of English as rhotic, meaning that the 'r' after the vowel is produced, or non-rhotic, meaning that the 'r' after the vowel is not produced. There are also some varieties of English that are **variably semi-rhotic**, such as JamE, which means the 'r' is produced in some, but not all, environments after the vowel (for example, only when the final 'r' sound is in a stressed syllable: in *ap'pear* but not *'wa.ter*). BrE is a good example of a non-rhotic variety of English, while AmE is a good example of a rhotic variety; rhoticity is a key feature that differentiates varieties of English around the world.

The pronunciation of the 'r' sound *after* a vowel in the same syllable is defined as rhoticity, as in the 'r' in *car*; rhoticity does not refer to the pronunciation of the 'r' *before* the vowel, as in the 'r' in *red* or *tree*. In other words, rhoticity only refers to contexts with the 'r' in **postvocalic** (after the vowel) position in the same syllable, as in *water, paper,* and *heard*. This is also called a non-prevocalic position, or absolute final (as in *car*) or preconsonantal (as in *card* or *cards*) position. Most Englishes have an 'r' sound in **prevocalic** (before the vowel) position, as in *ray* [reɪ], *tray* [treɪ], and *stray* [streɪ], although it may be omitted or replaced by another sound in some varieties of English.

4.3   The Articulation and Measurement of Rhoticity

How do we produce and measure rhoticity? Rhoticity may be articulated differently across varieties of English; this will be reflected in the use of different IPA symbols for rhoticity. In this book, the symbol /r/ is used as an umbrella term to refer to all articulations of 'r'. There are a number of articulations of rhoticity across varieties of English; as these will be referred to in the discussion on rhoticity, a brief overview of the most common articulations is given here:

- *Bunched /r/:* This is a very common articulation of /r/. The tongue is pulled back with the sides touching or nearly touching the upper teeth. The tip of the tongue is resting and not touching anything. This is also called a *molar* or *dorsal* /r/. There currently is no IPA symbol to denote this articulation of 'r'.
- */r/ – Alveolar trill:* This is also known as the 'rolled r'; the tongue is close to the alveolar ridge, with air pushed over the tongue during one or more (usually two or three) quick contacts with the roof of the mouth; this creates a vibration, or trill.
- */ɹ/ – Postalveolar approximant:* This 'r' has a **retroflex** articulation, with a curved tongue that is pulled back towards the back of the mouth, with the body and the tip of the tongue curved backwards. The sides of the tongue may be near or touching the upper teeth, and the tip of the tongue is close to but not touching the roof of the mouth.
- */ɾ/ – Alveolar tap or flap:* The name refers to the quick contact between the tongue and the roof of the mouth or back of the teeth. It may involve a quick forward movement of the tongue.
- */ʁ/ – Uvular fricative:* In this articulation, the back of the tongue (the dorsal area) is pulled back towards the uvula region, creating a narrow opening for the airflow that results in turbulence (frication).
- */ɻ/ – Retroflex approximant:* The right tail is used to denote a retroflexed articulation, which means that the tip or entire tongue is either slightly or fully curved back in the mouth, usually between the alveolar or palatal regions of the mouth. There are varying degrees of actual curvature.

How do we know whether someone is rhotic or not? As Task 4.2 demonstrated, it is often possible to rely on the human ear to determine rhoticity. Another way of determining whether a speaker's articulation of a word is rhotic or non-rhotic is through an acoustic analysis of formant values. As we saw in Chapter 3, we can use software such as Praat to create a spectrogram, or acoustic picture, of a speaker's pronunciation. For both vowels and rhoticity, we are interested in formant values, which represent bands or concentrations of energy at different levels of the sound spectrum. Although four formant values (F1, F2, F3, F4) are visible in a spectrogram, we typically only need to measure the F1 and F2 values to differentiate and describe different vowels. As we noted in Chapter 3, F1, the formant with the lowest frequency, is associated with tongue height, while F2, which has the second-lowest frequency, is associated with front/backness of tongue articulation. A third formant, F3, is associated with lip rounding as well as rhoticity; in particular, a lowered F3 frequency may indicate the presence of rhoticity, particularly in varieties of AmE. This lowering of the F3 is due to a co-articulation effect with the preceding vowel; rounding of the lips can also cause a lowering of the F3. Lowering of the F3 begins on the preceding vowel for some vowels, most typically for the mid central vowels /ɜ, ə/, which is referred to as **r-colouring** of the vowel and continues through the articulation of the 'r'. Some research suggests that F3 values for rhoticity are between 1,300 and 1,950 hertz, regardless of speaker sex or word position (Espy-Wilson, Boyce, Jackson, Narayanan, & Alwan, 2000, p. 344); Hagiwara (1995) suggests a more reliable measure of rhoticity is to calculate the overall F3 for vowels for a given speaker and then subtract the F3 value of the /r/ articulation in a word with final 'r'. For AmE speakers, the result may indicate that the /r/ token is between 60 and 80 per cent of the value of the speaker's overall vowel F3 values (Thomas, 2010).

Due to the variation across speakers as well as varieties of English with regard to rhoticity, one way of determining its existence is to examine differences within one speaker in F3 values for words with or without an 'r' in spelling after the vowel. As discussed above, we can measure the F3 values of the 'r' token as well as calculate the F3 values of the 'r' token in view of the speaker's vowel F3 values. In some cases, we can also determine whether a speaker's articulation of a word is rhotic through a visual examination of the spectrogram: if there is a noticeable lowering of the F3, then that speaker may have a rhotic articulation of that word. In many instances, the lowering of the F3 may be accompanied with a raising of the F2 value. Both can be seen in an acoustic analysis; as such, we can measure rhoticity in three ways: (1) auditorily, by listening (human ear) for an 'err' sound; (2) acoustically, by measuring F3 values; and (3) visually, by looking at the F3 (and F2) values across the articulation of a word to see whether the F3 is lowered.

In the examples below, we will examine rhoticity by first comparing the pronunciation of a word with final 'r' and one without final 'r' for an AmE speaker who is rhotic, to examine whether the speaker has a lower F3 in the articulation of the word with 'r' (*car*) than in the word without 'r' (*caught*). For this activity, we will look for lowered F3 values at the end of the word with the 'r' in its spelling. The words are extracted from the speech sample in Task 4.2.

In Figure 4.1, a spectrogram of a speaker of Midwestern AmE (Speaker 1) saying *caught* [kʰɑ·t], we can mark the four formants on the spectrogram, starting from the bottom with F1.

As you can see, the F3 formant stays relatively stable throughout the articulation of *caught*, with no F3 lowering. Figure 4.2 shows the same speaker saying *car*.

As this spectrogram shows, there is a noticeable lowering in the F3 value, starting from the vowel to when the speaker is articulating the 'r'. This suggests that this speaker is rhotic and pronounces *car* as [kʰɑːɹ]. Let us now look at the spectrograms of a speaker of Mod RP (Speaker 4 in Task 4.2) for these same two words. We can predict this speaker will likely be non-rhotic given that he is a speaker of Mod RP.

As Figure 4.4 demonstrates, the speaker of Mod RP is non-rhotic as his articulation of *car* does not have F3 lowering. He pronounces *car* as [kʰɑː].

Which varieties of English are rhotic? Which are non-rhotic? And why? As Speaker 1 (AmE) and Speaker 4 (BrE) illustrate, AmE is generally rhotic and BrE is generally non-rhotic, although there is regional variation within both varieties. A key question one could ask with regard to the differences in rhoticity across varieties of English is whether English was originally rhotic or non-rhotic. To put it another way, did BrE lose rhoticity or did AmE gain rhoticity? To answer these questions, we need to re-examine the

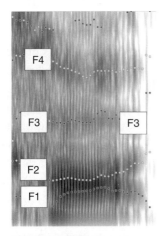

Figure 4.1 Midwestern American English *caught*

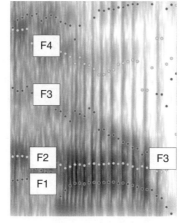

Figure 4.2 Midwestern American English *car*

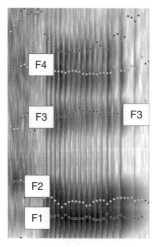

Figure 4.3 Modern Received Pronunciation *caught*

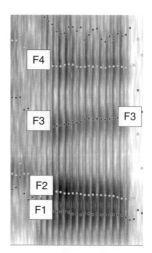

Figure 4.4 Modern Received Pronunciation *car*

historical evolution and colonial spread of English worldwide, with a specific focus on rhoticity. This is the topic of the next section.

4.4   Rhoticity and the History of English

Was English originally rhotic or non-rhotic? Did BrE lose rhoticity or did AmE gain rhoticity? Rhoticity was, in fact, a feature of the Germanic languages brought to England in the fifth century, which became Old English (fifth to eleventh centuries CE); Crystal (2005) states that BrE varieties were rhotic from the period of the Anglo-Saxons, from around 449 CE until around the seventeenth century, with rhoticity a feature of both Old and Middle English. In the fifteenth century, at the beginnings of the Early Modern English period, a non-rhotic pronunciation entered BrE, emerging first in the London area and surrounding regions (Lass, 1999); this **r-dropping** (also called *r-loss*) gained popularity as a marker of upper-class speech. As such, it spread across London and southern England in the seventeenth and eighteenth centuries (Lass, 1999). In 1774, for example, the well-known Walker's *Pronouncing Dictionary of English* stated that 'r' was disappearing from London English speech (Crystal, 2005, p. 467). As the r-less pronunciation became popularized, it gradually spread to other parts of England, eventually becoming the elite pronunciation and the norm for RP. By the early nineteenth century, in the Late Modern English period, Southern BrE was essentially non-rhotic. Rhoticity still prevails in a few

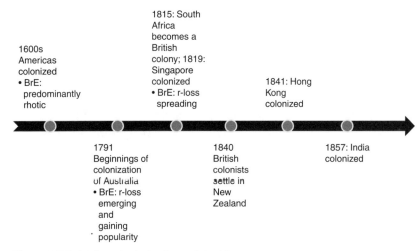

Figure 4.5 A timeline of colonization and rhoticity

regions of England, most notably the northern regions of Lancashire and Northumbria and in Southwest England in Dorset, although there is some indication that these dialects are losing rhoticity.

Why did AmE retain rhoticity – and why did other varieties of English such as AusE and NZE not retain rhoticity? As discussed above, BrE was originally rhotic, losing rhoticity in the Early Modern English period. Why AmE retained rhoticity while AusE and NZE did not is best explained by looking at the various colonializations against a timeline of the evolution of BrE. This is presented in Figure 4.5.

As Figure 4.5 demonstrates, a major factor explaining why some varieties of English are rhotic and others are non-rhotic is the time of colonization and whether BrE was largely rhotic or non-rhotic when colonization took place. Colonization of the Americas began in the early 1600s, at a time when BrE was still predominantly rhotic. As such, the original settlers in regions in the Americas brought the rhotic pronunciation with them. In contrast, the colonization of Australia, New Zealand, Hong Kong, Singapore, India, and South Africa, among others, took place after BrE began losing rhoticity.

Of course, many other factors, including levelling of dialects and mixing with other languages, also impacted the development of different varieties of English in the various British colonies. Another factor is key as well: whether settlers in different colonies in the Americas, Asia, and Australia/New Zealand came from rhotic or non-rhotic regions of the UK and Ireland. This will be examined in more detail in the following section.

4.5   Rhoticity and Varieties of English

☞ The following discussion is intended to provide an overview of rhoticity across a wide range of Englishes.

Although you are encouraged to listen to examples of several different varieties of English to expand your understanding of rhoticity as well as of World Englishes, you may wish to focus your attention on the varieties of English that are of interest to you. An index of the varieties and the relevant page numbers is given below:

- UK and Ireland: 126–9
- North America and the Caribbean: 129–31
- Oceania: 131–3
- Africa: 133–4
- Asia: 134–7

4.5.1   The UK and Ireland

TASK 4.3 Listening for British English

🎧 Listen to the speakers of varieties of BrE pronouncing words in the 'r' Lexical Set or other 'r' words. You may wish to refer back to our discussion of vowels in Chapter 3 for each variety. Are the speakers rhotic, non-rhotic, or variably semi-rhotic?

Speaker 1   Mod RP
Speaker 2   NBrE
Speaker 3   EMidBrE

Are all varieties of BrE non-rhotic? Although BrE, and particularly RP as well as Standard Southern BrE (SSBE), is considered non-rhotic, as illustrated by the three speakers of BrE in Task 4.3, Northern England and the southwest of England have traditionally been rhotic (Hughes & Trudgill, 1996). As Wells (1982) states, 'The preservation of historical /r/ in all environments is the best-known phonetic characteristic of the west of England' (p. 341). In this part of England, 'r' is produced as a retroflex approximant /ɻ/.

Recent research (Piercy, 2012) indicates that r-loss is occurring in some regions of England that have retained historical 'r'. In Dorset, in the Southwest region of England, younger speakers aged 30 or below have been found to have noticeably less rhoticity, and in some cases to be non-rhotic, in contrast to other age groups, indicating that r-dropping is an age-stratified sound change in progress in this region (Piercy, 2012). In Lancashire, in Northwest England, which has also traditionally been rhotic, there is again a great deal of non-rhoticity (Wells, 1982). R-loss is also occurring in the Black Country, in the West Midlands, an area that has historically been rhotic (Asprey, 2007). R-loss appears to be phonologically conditioned, meaning that the linguistic environment of the 'r' influences whether r-loss is occurring. In the case of the Black Country, rhoticity was found most often on words in the NURSE (ɜ:/ɜrC) Lexical Set, and then on unstressed 'r' as in the letterER Lexical Set. The least amount of rhoticity was found on words in the NEAR, SQUARE, START, NORTH, and CURE Lexical Sets (see Wells, 1982 and Chapter 3). In summary, while BrE is predominantly non-rhotic, there are regional varieties of BrE that have some degree of rhoticity, although recent research suggests that the speech of younger individuals in these regions is merging towards RP/SSBE and becoming non-rhotic. This is illustrated by Speaker 2 in Task 4.3, a young speaker of NBrE, who is non-rhotic.

What about Ireland and Northern Ireland? Is Irish English rhotic or non-rhotic? Let us examine the English pronunciation of a speaker of IrE to determine whether IrE is rhotic or non-rhotic. We will first listen to Task 4.4 and do an auditory (human ear) analysis.

TASK 4.4 Listening for Irish English

🎧 Listen to the speaker of IrE say the sentence and the words in the 'r' Lexical Set:

Bother, father caught hot coffee in the car park.

Can you hear the 'err' or not on words with an 'r' in the spelling after the vowel?

Second, we can examine spectrograms of the speaker saying *caught* and *car*, as shown in Figures 4.6 and 4.7. Can you see F3 lowering for the 'r' in *car*?

Is the speaker rhotic or non-rhotic? In the listening task, you may have heard a noticeable 'err' at the end of *bother, father, car, park*, indicating that this speaker is rhotic. If we do an acoustic analysis of the speaker's production of two words, one without final 'r' (*caught*) and one with final 'r' (*car*), we can also note that there is a lowering of the F3 in *car*. This demonstrates that this speaker is rhotic; in fact, rhoticity is a known feature of IrE and is one feature that distinguishes it from BrE. Rhoticity is realized variously in different parts of Ireland and Northern Ireland. In Ireland, rhoticity is

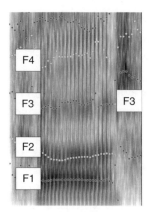

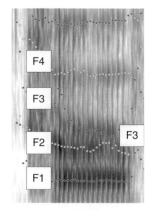

Figure 4.6 Irish English *caught*   **Figure 4.7** Irish English *car*

commonly realized as a retroflex approximant, symbolized with /ɻ/. It may be articulated with velarization (backing) in the southern part of Northern Ireland (as /ɻˠ/), whereas in the northern region of Northern Ireland it is typically produced with a retroflex articulation: /ɻ/ (Hickey, 2007).

In Ireland and Northern Ireland, however, the prestige variety/ies is/ are based on local norms: Dublin English, and particularly NDubE, as we saw in Chapter 3, is the prestige variety in Ireland; this is spreading to Northern Ireland as well (Hickey, 2007). BrE, and particularly RP, is generally not considered a prestige variety in Ireland for historical political reasons (Hickey, 2007). IrE has historically represented an Irish identity in contrast to Englishness; this continues to the current day and, as Hickey (2007, p. 21) notes, individuals who emulate an RP or BrE pronunciation are viewed as 'un-Irish'.

If Irish English is rhotic, is Scottish English also rhotic? English entered Scotland around the Old English period (500–1100 CE); this variety of English, named Scots, developed independently from other varieties of English. It still retains many features of Old English, including rhoticity. Scottish English (ScotE) is used here as an umbrella term for varieties of English in Scotland, with Scots on one end of the continuum and SSE on the other. ScotE began emerging in Scotland after the seventeenth century due to contact between Scots, as well as Gaelic, another language in Scotland, and BrE. Even though ScotE is influenced by BrE, Scots is rhotic, and ScotE is considered to be rhotic. Rhoticity in ScotE is typically realized as the alveolar approximant /ɹ/, although it may also be an alveolar tap /ɾ/ or alveolar trill /r/ or uvular fricative /ʁ/ for some speakers.

Like the r-loss patterns occurring in historically rhotic areas of England, there are some indications that age-stratified r-dropping is occurring in parts of Scotland, particularly among younger people. Several decades ago, Romaine (1978) found this was happening in Edinburgh, and current research (Stuart-Smith, Timmins, & Tweedie, 2007) indicates this is occurring in other urban areas of Scotland as well, including Glasgow, particularly among younger working-class men.

What about Welsh English? Although it shares a border with England, Wales was not heavily influenced by English until quite recently. It has only been in the past two centuries that English has begun being widely used in Wales; it is now the most widely spoken language. Welsh, the second most widely spoken language, is still a first language for some people, with English a second (school) language. WelE is heavily influenced by Welsh. Welsh is a rhotic language, and speakers who often use Welsh may also have rhoticity in WelE, usually as a tap /ɾ/ or trill /r/ (Wells, 1982). Due to the influence of BrE, most speakers of WelE are non-rhotic, however, and therefore WelE is considered a non-rhotic variety of English (Wells, 1982).

4.5.2   North America and the Caribbean

TASK 4.5 Listening for American and Canadian English

🎧 Listen to the AmE and CanE speech samples. Are the speakers rhotic, non-rhotic, or variably semi-rhotic?

Speaker 1   Calif AmE
Speaker 2   Appal AmE
Speaker 3   Midwestern AmE
Speaker 4   CanE
Speaker 5   CanE

Are all North American Englishes rhotic? Although both AmE and CanE are predominantly rhotic, there is some variation within these two varieties of English, due to where the settlers in different parts of the US and Canada originally came from, as well as whether the settlements took place before or after r-loss began in BrE. In the US, the first English settlements in 1607 were to the Chesapeake Bay area in the state of Maryland, and then later to Massachusetts and Virginia. The settlers in the northern parts of the US came from London and surrounding regions such as Suffolk, Essex, and Norfolk, regions of the British Isles which had begun losing the 'r' and therefore the English that developed in the Northern US and New England was originally non-rhotic; port cities along the eastern coast, including New York City, Boston, Savannah, Philadelphia, Alexandria, and Charleston, have historically remained non-rhotic, originally due to trade and close ties with Britain.

Settlers in inland regions of the Americas came from northern and western parts of England, as well as Wales, Scotland, and Ireland. It was also primarily settlers from rhotic regions of both the early American colonies and England who eventually moved westwards across the United States, spreading a rhotic pronunciation of English across the US. After the end of the Civil War, there was a shift in the centre of power away from the cities with ties to Britain, including New York City, Boston, and Philadelphia, and, as a result, rhotic accents gained prestige in the US. Rhoticity is a feature of GAmE. The AmE 'r' sound following vowels is often described as a (voiced) postalveolar approximant, which is represented with the symbol /ɹ/. This symbol will be used throughout this book to reflect an AmE pronunciation of postvocalic 'r'.

Research indicates (Becker, 2009, 2014) that, while many speakers in the northern areas of the US continue to be non-rhotic, rhoticity is becoming more common, particularly in formal speech. Recent research (Becker, 2009, 2014) on NYC AmE confirms that rhoticity is rapidly emerging in the speech of New Yorkers, particularly among the middle and upper classes. There is also a shift towards rhoticity in eastern New England, including in New Hampshire and Boston (Nagy & Irwin, 2010), particularly among younger age groups. It appears that speakers who have regional features such as a lack of rhoticity are merging towards GAmE norms. Rhoticity also appears to be phonologically conditioned in New England, appearing first on the NURSE Lexical Set and last on words in the lettER (unstressed 'r') Lexical Set.

The southern parts of the US have historically been non-rhotic though, as Wells (1982) notes, except for upper-class and more highly educated speakers. However, many speakers – particularly the younger generation – are also becoming rhotic (Labov, Ash, & Boberg, 2006). Feagin (1990), for example, found variable semi-rhoticity in the southern state of Alabama, with the most rhoticity on NURSE, followed by the NEAR, SQUARE, START, NORTH, FORCE Lexical Sets, and the least on unstressed /r/ (lettER). A recent study (Schoux Casey, 2016) of the English of New Orleans in the southern state of Louisiana also found that southern varieties of English have become rhoticized over the past sixty years, with rhoticity most common on the NURSE Lexical Set and in stressed rather than unstressed syllables. In this study, greater use of rhoticity was also correlated with higher education levels. AAVE, a non-regional variety of English spoken predominantly by urban working-class African Americans, is also non-rhotic, possibly due to its origins in the southern varieties of AmE as well as African languages. All three speakers of AmE in Task 4.5 are rhotic, regardless of the region of the United States in which they grew up. This is likely due to the spread of rhoticity into historically non-rhotic Englishes.

CanE is also rhotic, although parts of Nova Scotia (Lunenburg) and Newfoundland are non-rhotic (Trudgill & Gordon, 2006), probably due to the early settlers in these regions, who may have come from New England and Southeastern England and were largely non-rhotic at the time of the settlements (Chambers, 2010). Both speakers of CanE in Task 4.5 are rhotic.

Most Caribbean Englishes (CaribE) are non-rhotic, except the Englishes of Barbados, Guyana, and Jamaica (Aceto, 2009). While Jamaica is a former British colony, JamE is variably semi-rhotic, likely due to the influence of AmE norms, with rhoticity primarily on words in the NURSE Lexical Set, and some rhoticity on words in the NEAR, SQUARE, FORCE, and CURE Lexical Sets (Rosenfelder, 2009).

TASK 4.6 Listening for Puerto Rican English

🎧 Listen to the speaker of PRE. Is the speaker rhotic, non-rhotic, or variably semi-rhotic?

Puerto Rico is still an American territory and, as such, as well as due to geographical proximity, is strongly influenced by AmE. PRE is also influenced by Spanish, the most commonly spoken language in Puerto Rico, and an official language along with English. Due to the influence of AmE, we would expect this variety of English to be rhotic. You may be able to hear a noticeable 'err' at the end of the words with 'r' for the speaker of PRE, indicating that, as we predicted, PRE is rhotic.

4.5.3 Oceania

TASK 4.7 Listening for Australian and New Zealand English

🎧 Listen to the speakers of NZE and AusE. Are they rhotic, non-rhotic, or variably semi-rhotic?

Speaker 1   NZE
Speaker 2   NZE
Speaker 3   AusE speaker from Queensland (Qld AusE)
Speaker 4   AusE speaker from Queensland and New South Wales (Qld NSW)
Speaker 5   AusE speaker from South Australia (SA AusE)

NZE is non-rhotic, as illustrated by both NZE speakers in Task 4.7. Colonization of New Zealand began in the mid 1800s, at a time of an ongoing r-loss process in BrE. Most settlers in New Zealand came from Southeast England and thus were non-rhotic speakers of English, leading to the likely conclusion that early NZE was in fact non-rhotic (Hay, Maclagan, & Gordon, 2008). Interestingly, recent research (Trudgill & Gordon, 2006) on the historical development of NZE indicates that early NZE was rhotic as the r-loss in the southeast of England was an ongoing phonological change when the settlements of New Zealand occurred. As Trudgill and Gordon (2006, p. 244) state, 'New Zealand English did not inherit non-rhoticity from English English as such, but rather inherited an ongoing process involving loss of rhoticity.' NZE appears to have completed the r-loss process in the last twenty years of the nineteenth century, becoming fully non-rhotic only in the early twentieth century (Hay & Sudbury, 2005).

As English has only been spoken in New Zealand for a short duration of time, in comparison to the US or Canada, very little regional variation exists within NZE (Hay, Maclagan, & Gordon, 2008). One exception is the Southland province in the south of New Zealand, which has retained the rhoticity brought by early settlers from Scotland who were speakers of Scots, which, as noted above, is rhotic (Hay, Maclagan, & Gordon, 2008, p. 98). Speakers of the Southland dialect are not 100 per cent rhotic, however, having retained rhoticity primarily after the mid central vowels [ɜː, ə], in the NURSE and lettER Lexical Sets (Hay, Maclagan, & Gordon, 2008). This has led to a bidialectal situation between the Southland region and the rest of New Zealand, with plus or minus rhoticity a key feature of this bidialectal divide (Marsden, 2017). Recent research (Marsden, 2017), however, suggests that rhoticity is also present on the North Island of New Zealand, though it is highly variable in use, with rhoticity favoured for words in the NURSE Lexical Set, followed by SQUARE.

Another distinctive variety of English in New Zealand is MāoriE, which is influenced by Māori, an indigenous language of New Zealand. Speakers of MāoriE may also have rhoticity, primarily on words from the NURSE Lexical Set, and it is best considered to be variably semi-rhotic (Hay, Maclagan, & Gordon, 2008).

Colonization of Australia began in the late 1700s, earlier than in New Zealand. The early settlers in Australia came from the southeast of England, similarly to the settlers in New Zealand. Trudgill and Gordon (2006) also suggest that a similar pattern of phonological change may have occurred in early AusE, with early AusE likely to have been rhotic as the English the early settlers brought with them was undergoing the phonological r-loss process, which continued into the earlier forms of AusE. Modern-day AusE is non-rhotic, as illustrated by the three speakers of AusE in

Task 4.7. Very little research exists on rhoticity in the Aboriginal English varieties in Australia, though there is some suggestion that rhoticity exists in the Aboriginal English spoken in the region of Adelaide, South Australia (Sutton, 1989).

4.5.4 Africa

TASK 4.8 Listening for Kenyan, Zimbabwean, White South African, and Southern Nigerian English

🎧 Listen to the following speakers. Are they rhotic, non-rhotic, or variably semi-rhotic?

Speaker 1   KenE
Speaker 2   ZimE
Speaker 3   WSAE
Speaker 4   SNigE

When we speak of African Englishes, we speak of a wide range of Englishes due to the vast number of indigenous and colonial languages that have influenced these varieties of English. More than 1,300 languages are spoken in Africa today (Kirkpatrick, 2007). As with the discussion of CaribE, the complex colonial and linguistic history of Africa makes it difficult to provide more than a brief overview of the current understanding of rhoticity that has emerged in different African Englishes.

African Englishes can be divided into three major groups: East African Englishes (EAfE), including Kenyan, Tanzanian, and Ugandan English; Southern African Englishes (SAfE), including South African, Zimbabwean, and Botswanan Englishes; and West African Englishes (WAfE), including Cameroon, Ghanaian, Nigerian, and Liberian Englishes (Wolf, 2010). Most varieties of African English are non-rhotic (Bobda, 2001; Trudgill & Gordon, 2006). Speaker 1 is a speaker of KenE, an EAfE, and is non-rhotic. Speaker 2 is a speaker of ZimE, a SAfE; she is semi-rhotic, with rhoticity on CURE and lettER but not on START, SQUARE, NEAR, NURSE, FORCE, or NORTH.

More data is available about SAE, which is considered non-rhotic, as colonization by England occurred in 1909, after r-loss occurred in many regions of England. As we noted in Chapter 3, there are multiple varieties of English that can be classified as SAE, including WSAE, Afrikaans English, Coloured SAE, SA Indian English, and BSAE (Hartmann & Zerbian, 2009). Afrikaans English is rhotic as it is influenced by Afrikaans, a rhotic West Germanic language of Africa (Hartmann & Zerbian, 2009). Rhoticity is also emerging in BSAE, particularly among more affluent women, possibly due to the influence of AmE. Research on WSAE-speaking women from the middle class also found that rhoticity is spreading within this social group, and that rhoticity may be becoming a marker of a young, non-racial elite identity in SAE (du Plessis & Bekker, 2014, p. 34). Speaker 3 is a speaker of WSAE and also speaks some Afrikaans. She is semi-rhotic and has rhoticity on NURSE and lettER but not on START, SQUARE, NEAR, CURE, FORCE, or NORTH. Speaker 4 is a speaker of SNigE, which is non-rhotic.

4.5.5   Asia

TASK 4.9 Listening for Singapore and Malaysian English

🎧 Listen to the following speakers. Are they rhotic, non-rhotic, or variably semi-rhotic?
Speaker 1   SgE
Speaker 2   SgE
Speaker 3   MalE
Speaker 4   MalE

One may expect that varieties of English in British postcolonial contexts in Asia, such as Hong Kong, Singapore, Malaysia, and India, are largely non-rhotic, since the English that had the earliest influence on the development of the local variety was BrE at a time when r-loss had already occurred in many regions of England. English in the Philippines – in contrast – is largely influenced by AmE as the Philippines is a former American colony, and therefore PhlE could be expected to be rhotic. The situation with these Englishes is, of course, much more complicated, as these varieties have substrate and superstrate influences from multiple languages, which also may affect whether they are rhotic or non-rhotic. In addition, these varieties have themselves changed since the end of colonial times. Two factors appear to impact rhoticity: education models, and exposure to American media and, thus, AmE accents. We will explore each of these varieties of English in turn.

English was brought to Singapore in the late eighteenth / early nineteenth century after Singapore became a British colony in late 1819. Due to its British colonial past, Singapore adopted BrE – in this case SSBE – as the model of English (Tan, 2012). SgE is influenced not only by SSBE but also by a variety of indigenous (and official) languages, including Standard Malay, Tamil, Hokkien, Cantonese, and Mandarin Chinese. Standard Malay is non-rhotic; some varieties of Mandarin Chinese, such as Northern Mandarin Chinese and the influential Beijing dialect, are rhotic. Tamil is also rhotic. Most speakers of SgE, both Standard Singapore English and colloquial SgE – also called **Singlish** – are believed to be non-rhotic (Low & Brown, 2005). This is illustrated by Speaker 1 and Speaker 2 in Task 4.8. Recent research on SgE (Poedjosoedarmo, 2000; Tan, 2012, 2016), however, suggests that rhoticity is becoming a prestige variant among younger, typically Chinese, speakers of SgE, as well as those from higher socio-economic backgrounds, indicating that rhoticity may be stratified by age, ethnicity, and socio-economic status. It is possible, as researchers (Poedjosoedarmo, 2000; Tan, 2012, 2016) suggest, that exposure to AmE media is impacting the way English is developing in Singapore.

English arrived in Malaysia in the late eighteenth century, after r-dropping had begun spreading across England. MalE is influenced by both BrE, which was also adopted as an educational model and norm in Malaysia, and Standard Malay, which is non-rhotic. MalE is generally believed to be non-rhotic (Baskaran, 2004) although recent research (Rajadurai, 2006) suggests some features associated with AmE are emerging in MalE, indicating that this variety of English may also be influenced by AmE through the media. This suggests that rhoticity may in fact eventually emerge in MalE; this is evidenced by Speakers 3 and 4, who are both rhotic.

TASK 4.10 Listening for Hong Kong English

🎧 Listen to the speaker of HKE. Is he rhotic, non-rhotic, or semi-rhotic?

Hong Kong was colonized by the British in the 1800s; Hong Kong has also traditionally adopted BrE norms in education. HKE is influenced by Cantonese, which is the most widely spoken variety of Chinese in Hong Kong. Cantonese is non-rhotic. Research (Bolton & Kwok, 1990) suggests that, while there has always been a great deal of variation within HKE, a growing number of HKE speakers are becoming rhotic, or variably semi-rhotic. For example, while early research on HKE (Bolton & Kwok, 1990) found that none of their HKE-speaking participants were rhotic, research almost two decades later (Deterding, Wong, & Kirkpatrick, 2008) found that 40 per cent of the participants had some degree of rhoticity in their speech. My own research (Hansen Edwards, 2016a) suggests this may be increasing: in a recent study on phonological features of HKE, I found that 88 per cent of my research participants, all university students, had some rhoticity in their speech. I suggest that the growing influence of AmE, largely through unparalleled access to American media, has impacted how English is learned and used in Hong Kong. In Task 4.10, the HKE speaker is semi-rhotic, with rhoticity on the SQUARE, CURE, NORTH, FORCE, NEAR, and lettER Lexical Sets.

TASK 4.11 Listening for Indian, Pakistani, Nepalese, and Sri Lankan English

🎧 Listen to the speakers of IndE, PakE, NepE, and SLE. Are they rhotic, non-rhotic, or variably semi-rhotic?
Speaker 1   IndE
Speaker 2   PakE
Speaker 3   NepE
Speaker 4   SLE

Due to the large number of languages spoken in India (there are over 1,000 mother tongues there), it is not possible to have a definitive answer as to whether IndE is rhotic. However, many of the languages of India, including the Dravidian Indian as well as Indo-Aryan languages, are rhotic. Because of the rhoticity in many substrate languages for IndE, this variety is often considered to be rhotic (Wells, 1982). Speaker 1 speaks Hindi, which has rhoticity; he is semi-rhotic, with rhoticity in the lettER and FORCE Lexical Sets.

Rhoticity may not occur for all speakers of IndE, as research (Chand, 2010; Gargesh, 2004) and the data from Speaker 1 suggest: it may be more prevalent among bilingual Hindu–English men than women. In Delhi, at least, it appears that rhoticity is stigmatized, and that a non-rhotic pronunciation is the prestige form. Gender may also play a role: women may have less rhoticity – and more prestige variants – than men; ethno-linguistic identity also appears to impact rhoticity in IndE, with Hindi speakers from the Punjab and Upper Pradesh / Haryana exhibiting the most rhoticity, followed by Bengalis, with, finally, individuals from Delhi being the least rhotic. Age may also impact rhoticity in IndE, with older generations being the most rhotic, likely due to sociopolitical as well as educational factors.

Like many other Indian languages, Urdu is rhotic, and PakE is also considered to be rhotic (Mahboob & Ahmar, 2004); this is evidenced by Speaker 2, who is rhotic. Nepali is a rhotic language (Khatiwada, 2009), and NepE is rhotic, as illustrated by Speaker 3. While both languages that influence SLE, Sinhala and Tamil, are rhotic, the superstrate language, BrE, is non-rhotic. As a result, some speakers of SLE may be rhotic while others may be non-rhotic. Speaker 4 is non-rhotic.

> **TASK 4.12 Listening for Philippine English**
>
> 🎧 Listen to the speaker of PhlE. Is she rhotic, non-rhotic, or variably semi-rhotic?

PhlE is largely influenced by AmE as it was an American colony from 1895 until 1946. English is one of the two official languages of the Philippines, along with Filipino, which is one of the hundreds of languages spoken in the Philippines. Filipino is rhotic. PhlE is rhotic, and rhoticity is realized as either a retroflex approximant /ɻ/ or a flap/tap /ɾ/ in PhlE. This is evidenced by the speaker of PhlE in Task 4.12, who is rhotic.

4.6 /r/-Sandhi

There are two other phenomena that are important to talk about in our discussion of rhoticity: linking-/r/ and intrusive-/r/, which together are referred to as **/r/-sandhi**. **Linking-/r/** refers to the production of the final /r/ in a word or syllable as the beginning of the next word or syllable if the next word or syllable begins with a vowel. For example, a speaker may pronounce *here I am* as [hɪə.raɪ.æm], with [.] denoting a syllable boundary if the speaker links the end of the word *here* with the word *I*. This results in a process of resyllabification, where the 'r' is produced at the beginning of the following syllable or word. This only occurs when the following syllable or word begins with a vowel. Linking-/r/ can occur word-internally, as in the word *hearing* as [hɪə.rɪŋ]. It can also occur word-finally, as the example of *here I am* illustrates. Both of these contrast with contexts where the following syllable or word begins with a consonant, such as *here my*, which do not favour linking-/r/: [hɪə.maɪ]. Linking-/r/ is a common speech phenomenon in varieties which are non-rhotic.

Intrusive-/r/ is considered an overgeneralization of linking-/r/ and occurs when there is no actual 'r' in the spelling (or sound) in the word. The general rule is that it occurs most frequently after a non-high vowel or diphthong with a non-high off glide (commonly /ɔː ə ɑː/) and before another vowel in the next syllable or word, as in *data(r) analysis*; it can be both word-internal and word-final.

Both linking-/r/ and intrusive-/r/ are considered part of the historical r-loss process, and use of both is inversely proportional with rhoticity: as r-loss increases, /r/-sandhi increases. While linking-/r/ appears to be more common overall than intrusive-/r/, both are typically present in non-rhotic varieties of English, even in RP for some speakers. /r/-sandhi began emerging in BrE in the eighteenth century in regions where English was becoming derhoticized (Crystal, 2005).

TASK 4.13 /r/-Sandhi

Which of the varieties given below would you expect to have /r/-sandhi?

AusE

NZE

WSAE

MāoriE

NYC AmE

LonE

Mod RP

Although it is generally believed that most non-rhotic dialects have /r/-sandhi (Sudbury & Hay, 2002), some varieties – like some dialects in the southern US – may have neither rhoticity nor /r/-sandhi (Wells, 1982). As Hay and Sudbury (2005, p. 801) note, /r/-sandhi has been found in most varieties of English that are non-rhotic, including in non-rhotic varieties of BrE such as Mod and Trad RP, and LonE; it is also pervasive in EMidBrE (Braber & Robinson, 2018). It has been found in northeastern non-rhotic varieties of English in the US, including NYC and NE AmE, and in non-rhotic varieties of English in the Southern Hemisphere, including SAE, NZE, and AusE. In some varieties, including NZE and RP, intrusive-/r/ may be associated with lower socio-economic status and thus socially stigmatized (Hay & Sudbury, 2005; Hay, Maclagan, & Gordon, 2010). MāoriE is semi-rhotic, and therefore has very little /r/-sandhi.

Though there has been little research on /r/-sandhi in NVEs, research (Tan, 2012) indicates that the rules for /r/-sandhi may differ in NVEs from in OVEs such as NZE and AusE. Research on SgE (Tan, 2012) found that, while intrusive-/r/ was largely inversely correlated with rhoticity in SgE – the more a speaker used postvocalic-/r/, the less they used intrusive-/r/, as in other varieties of English – there were surprisingly very few instances of linking-/r/ in the data. In addition, some speakers who had rhoticity also had intrusive-/r/, indicating that phonological rules for /r/-sandhi in SgE differ from those in other varieties of English.

Figure 4.8 illustrates rhoticity as a continuum, rather than as a strictly binary (+/-) phenomenon. As Figure 4.8 shows, non-rhotic speakers or varieties generally (though not always) have /r/-sandhi, both linking-/r/ and intrusive-/r/.

Table 4.1 gives a continuum of environments for rhoticity, from those that favour rhoticity the most to the least favourable. It features an additional environment, illustrated by FUR: in most varieties of English, the NURSE Lexical Set is the result of a merger among several vowels in words such as *fern*, *fir*, and *fur*. In some varieties of English, as shown in Table 4.1, the FUR vowel still exists as distinctive from the NURSE Lexical Set.

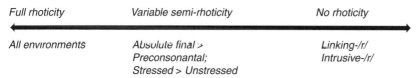

Full rhoticity	Variable semi-rhoticity		No rhoticity
All environments	Absolute final > Preconsonantal; Stressed > Unstressed		Linking-/r/ Intrusive-/r/

Figure 4.8 A continuum of rhoticity

Table 4.1 A continuum of rhoticity across Lexical Sets

Variety of English	Spread of rhoticity from most to least			
West Midlands BrE (Asprey, 2007)	NURSE ⟶	FUR ⟶	lettER ⟶	NEAR, START, SQUARE, NORTH, CURE
NE AmE (Nagy & Irwin, 2010)	NURSE ⟶	NEAR, START, SQUARE, NORTH, CURE, FUR ⟶		lettER
SAmE – Alabama (Feagin, 1990)	NURSE ⟶	FUR ⟶	NEAR, START, SQUARE, NORTH, CURE ⟶	lettER
SAmE – Louisiana (Schoux Casey, 2016)	NURSE ⟶	NEAR, START, SQUARE, NORTH, CURE, FUR ⟶		lettER
Southland NZE (Hay, Maclagan, & Gordon, 2008)	NURSE, ⟶ lettER			
North Island, NZE (Marsden, 2017)	NURSE ⟶	SQUARE ⟶ FUR, NEAR, START, NORTH, CURE, lettER		
MāoriE (Hay, Maclagan & Gordon, 2008)	NURSE ⟶	NEAR, START, SQUARE, NORTH, CURE, lettER		
WSAE (du Plessis & Bekker, 2014)	NURSE ⟶	FUR ⟶	NEAR, START, SQUARE, NORTH, CURE ⟶	lettER
WSAE (my data)	NURSE, lettER ⟶	START, SQUARE, NEAR, NURSE, NORTH		
ZimE (my data)	CURE, lettER ⟶	START, SQUARE, NEAR, NURSE, NORTH		
JamE (Rosenfelder, 2009)	NURSE ⟶	NEAR, SQUARE, FORCE, CURE	⟶	START, lettER

While there are differences among varieties of English, as demonstrated in the discussion in this chapter, generally words in the NURSE Lexical Set favour rhoticity – it is usually the first environment in which rhoticity emerges and the last environment for r-loss in varieties with ongoing derhoticization. The least likely environment for rhoticity – the first environment to lose rhoticity and the last to gain it – appears in unstressed syllables, such as the lettER Lexical Set, though this does vary among varieties.

4.7 CHECK YOUR UNDERSTANDING

EXERCISES

(a) In this chapter, the following IPA symbols were used to denote the realizations of 'r' across different varieties of English: /ɹ ʁ ɾ ɻ/. Go back over the text and find the description for each symbol as well as at least one variety of English in which this realization of 'r' occurs:

/ɹ/

/ʁ/

/ɾ/

/ɻ/

(b) Figures 4.9 and 4.10 show spectrograms of different speakers saying *car* from the sentence *Bother, father caught hot coffee in the car park.* Locate and mark the F1, F2, F3, and F4 for each speaker. Which speaker is rhotic?

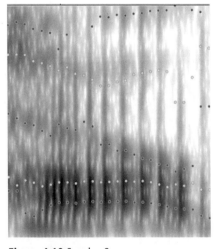

Figure 4.9 Speaker 1   **Figure 4.10** Speaker 2

DISCUSSION QUESTIONS

(a) What are the main factors impacting whether a variety of English is rhotic or non-rhotic? In particular, why is AmE rhotic while AusE is non-rhotic, if both varieties of English evolved from BrE?

(b) Why do you think speakers of traditionally non-rhotic varieties of English in the US (such as speakers of English from Boston or NYC) are merging towards a rhotic pronunciation? How is this similar to or different from the factors influencing the r-loss – and merging towards an SSBE pronunciation – in the varieties of BrE and ScotE which have traditionally been rhotic?

(c) Which social (non-linguistic) factors seem to impact on these shifts the most?

EXPAND YOUR UNDERSTANDING

In this task, we will examine another Expanding Circle English – China English. The speaker of China English is from Beijing and speaks Mandarin Chinese with a Beijing dialect. This variety of Mandarin Chinese is rhotic. Does the speaker of China English have rhoticity?

(a) In Task 4.14, you can listen to the China English speaker read aloud the 'r' Lexical Sets keywords. Can you hear a rhotic pronunciation on any of the keywords?

(b) Figure 4.11 shows a spectrogram of the China English speaker's pronunciation of NURSE. What information does the spectrogram show you about rhoticity for this speaker?

TASK 4.14 Listening for China English

🎧 In Task 4.14, you can listen to a speaker of China English.

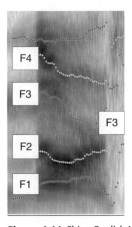

Figure 4.11 China English NURSE

(c) Based on your answers to (a) and (b), would you categorize this speaker as rhotic, non-rhotic, or variably semi-rhotic?

ANALYSE YOUR OWN PRONUNCIATION

(a) Following the instructions in Appendix A, record yourself reading aloud the Word List and Sentence for Rhoticity. You may find that you are non-rhotic, rhotic, or variably semi-rhotic (some words have rhoticity while others do not).

(b) Listen to your own pronunciation of the words in the sentence *Bother, father caught hot coffee in the car park.* Can you hear an 'err' sound in any of the words with final 'r' in the spelling? If so, these words are produced with rhoticity. If not, you may be non-rhotic. If some words have rhoticity and others do not, you are variably semi-rhotic.

(c) Using Praat, open your speech file for *Bother, father caught hot coffee in the car park.* For each word with a final 'r' in the spelling, see if you can verify your auditory analysis of plus or minus rhoticity. Do the words you heard with an 'err' sound (if any) have F3 lowering? Does the visual acoustic analysis match your auditory analysis? If not, go back and listen to the words again.

(d) At this point, you may have found that, based on the analysis of your pronunciation of *Bother, father caught hot coffee in the car park*, you are fully rhotic, fully non-rhotic, or have rhoticity on some words, but not others, indicating that you are variably semi-rhotic. To verify your conclusions, go back over your production of the 'r' words in Wells' (1982) Lexical Sets or the [hVd] or [bVt]/[bVd] words, as listed in Appendix A. You may also wish to transcribe each of the 'r' Lexical Sets keywords phonemically and phonetically in order to examine whether you are semi-rhotic.

(e) You could also do an acoustic analysis of your reading of these words following the directions for using Praat in Appendix A. What can you conclude about your own rhoticity? If you are variably semi-rhotic, in which Lexical Sets do the words that have rhoticity in your speech belong? How does this compare with the other varieties discussed in this chapter?

(f) Why do you think you are rhotic, non-rhotic, or variably semi-rhotic? Think about different types of influences on your speech, such as education (models, norms in your schooling), peer/parent/teacher influences, accent preference(s), other languages you speak, and media influences.

5 The Consonants of English

TASK 5.1 LISTENING FOR CONSONANTS

🎧 Listen to the six speakers pronounce the following words, paying attention to the underlined sound in each word.

pat bat tip dip cot got fine vine Sue zoo three these
she Asia hot church judge man note sing red light yellow white

Speaker 1	NZE
Speaker 2	WSAE
Speaker 3	Midwestern AmE
Speaker 4	NBrE
Speaker 5	MalE
Speaker 6	SLE

- What differences can you hear in the pronunciation of the underlined consonants?
- Why do you think these differences exist? Which part of the mouth/nose are used to create these differences?
- Are there differences across speakers in the pronunciation of certain words?

Your turn: pronounce the words given above, paying attention to the underlined sound in each word.

- Which parts of the mouth do you use for each underlined sound? Think about how you use your nose, teeth, lips, tongue, and the roof of your mouth.
- What other differences can you find in how you pronounce the underlined sounds?
- What are some of the differences between the articulation of vowels (seen in Chapter 3) and that of consonants?

5.1 Introduction to the Chapter

Following our discussion of English vowels in Chapter 3 and rhoticity in Chapter 4, this chapter introduces you to English consonants, as well as variation in consonant inventories across varieties of English. We begin the chapter with a discussion of the characteristics of consonants, focusing on the classification of consonant sounds by place of articulation, manner of articulation, and voicing. This overview also examines consonant inventories cross-linguistically, to help you understand which consonants – and consonant features – are the most common across languages, and why.

The next two sections of the chapter provide an overview of English consonants by introducing the consonant phonemes common to many varieties of English, with variation in these inventories discussed as relevant. A brief overview of modern-day spelling of English consonants is also given. Consonant variation within varieties of English and phonological rules that govern this variation are then discussed. In the final section of the chapter, you will be guided through exercises designed to check your understanding of the content of the chapter and an analysis of your own English consonant inventory.

5.2   What Are Consonants?

What are consonants? And how do they differ from vowels? In Chapter 3, we learned that vowels differ from consonants both articulatorily and phonologically. Vowels are articulated through movement of the mouth and tongue, resulting in differences in HAR – height, advancement of the tongue, and lip rounding. Consonants, in contrast, use a wider range of articulators, including teeth, nose, tongue, and mouth; in addition, the airflow of consonants may differ, as may voicing (see Chapter 3).

TASK 5.2 Articulation

- Do you have a difference in the position and movement of your lips and teeth for the first sound in _these_ and _fine_? How would you describe your articulation of the _th_ in _these_ and the _f_ in _fine_?
- What is the difference between the articulation of _t_ in _tip_ and _s_ in _Sue_? Which sound – the _t_ or the _s_ – can you hold the longest?
- What is the difference in the airflow of _t_ in _tip_ and _n_ in _note_?
- Do you have a difference in _s_ in _Sue_ and _z_ in _zoo_? Does one sound have voicing (and is therefore a voiced consonant) and one not have voicing (therefore a voiceless consonant)?

To describe the articulation of consonants, we use three classifications: **place of articulation,** which refers to which articulatory organs are involved in the production of the consonant. This could be the tip of the tongue and teeth for some speakers for *th* for *these*, or the teeth and lower lip as in *f* in *fine*; **manner of articulation**, which refers to airflow – for example, whether the airflow stops, as in *t* in *tip*, or is released through the nose, as in *n* in *note*; and *voicing*, which refers to whether the vocal folds are open as in *s* in *Sue* or moving back and forth as in *z* in *zoo*.

Phonologically, consonants also differ from vowels. As we saw in the sentence, *I felt a pain in my left eye* in Chapter 3, all of the words have a vowel sound; some words, such as *I*, *a*, and *eye*, *only* have vowel sounds. Vowels (or vowel-like sounds) are required in each syllable in a word (see also Chapter 6). Consonants, in contrast, are not required in English syllables, although, as we will see in Chapter 6, some varieties of English have a more complex syllable structure than many languages, in terms of the number of consonants that can occur before and after vowels, as well as the ordering of consonants before and after vowels.

5.3   Characteristics of Consonants

How do we describe individual consonant sounds? Figure 5.1 shows the pulmonic consonant chart of the IPA. Pulmonic refers to consonant sounds that are produced through pushing air out of the lungs and out of the mouth/ nose through the vocal tract. Non-pulmonic consonant sounds also exist in some languages, though not in English; these consonants are produced through an *ingressive* airflow – the air flows inward through the vocal tract. Click consonants, which occur in many languages in Africa, are an example of non-pulmonic consonants. Our discussion in this chapter will focus on pulmonic consonants, as only pulmonic consonants occur in English.

How are consonants classified in the IPA chart? In Chapter 3, we discussed the IPA vowel chart, which positions the possible vowels across all

THE INTERNATIONAL PHONETIC ALPHABET (revised to 2015)

CONSONANTS (PULMONIC)   © 2015 IPA

	Bilabial	Labiodental	Dental	Alveolar	Postalveolar	Retroflex	Palatal	Velar	Uvular	Pharyngeal	Glottal
Plosive	p b			t d		ʈ ɖ	c ɟ	k ɡ	q ɢ		ʔ
Nasal	m	ɱ		n		ɳ	ɲ	ŋ	N		
Trill	B			r					R		
Tap or Flap		ⱱ		ɾ		ɽ					
Fricative	ɸ β	f v	θ ð	s z	ʃ ʒ	ʂ ʐ	ç ʝ	x ɣ	χ ʁ	ħ ʕ	h ɦ
Lateral fricative				ɬ ɮ							
Approximant		ʋ		ɹ		ɻ	j	ɰ			
Lateral approximant				l		ɭ	ʎ	L			

Symbols to the right in a cell are voiced, to the left are voiceless. Shaded areas denote articulations judged impossible.

Figure 5.1 International Phonetic Alphabet pulmonic consonant chart

the world's languages by HAR. The pulmonic consonant chart in Figure 5.1 positions all the possible pulmonic consonants of the world's languages by place of articulation, manner of articulation, and voicing. Place of articulation is shown in the columns while manner of articulation is shown in the rows. When two consonants exist with the same place and manner of articulation (as with [p] and [b], **both bilabial** stops; note: square brackets are used for sounds in the IPA chart unless describing the phonemes of a particular language), the left consonant is voiceless while the right consonant is voiced. Like the IPA vowel chart, the consonant chart places the sounds by place of articulation, from the front of the mouth in the first column to farthest back in the vocal tract in the last column.

Place of articulation refers to the location of the constriction, or narrowing, of the airflow to create different consonant sounds. The places used for consonants are illustrated in Figure 5.2, which shows a labelled vocal tract; 'labial' in Figure 5.1 corresponds to lips, while **dental** means involvement of the teeth. A bilabial consonant is therefore one that uses both lips (bi = two, labial = lips) in articulation, while a **labiodental** consonant employs the upper teeth (dental) and lower lip (labial). Dental sounds refer to consonants articulated with the tip or front of the tongue pushed between the upper and lower teeth or touching the back of the upper teeth. Alveolar sounds are those where the tip of the tongue touches or is close to the alveolar ridge, the hard (bony) area just behind your upper front teeth.

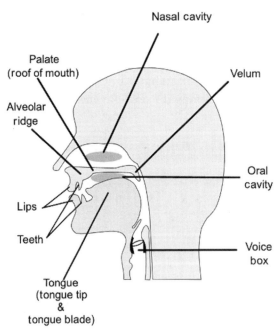

Figure 5.2 Vocal tract

Postalveolar (post = after) consonants are produced slightly farther back in the mouth than the alveolar ridge, but before the palate. Retroflex sounds, as we saw in Chapter 4 in the discussion of rhoticity, are sounds where the tongue is curved back in the mouth, usually in the palatal region but also sometimes in the postalveolar region. Palatal sounds are those where the tongue touches or is close to the palatal region of the mouth, which is the softer area of the roof of the mouth. Velar refers to the region at the back of the mouth, at the velum, while uvular is the region after the velum. Pharyngeal consonants are articulated in the pharynx, a region between the uvula and the glottis, referred to in Figure 5.2 as the voice box. **Glottal** sounds are produced in the glottis ('voice box' in Figure 5.2).

'Manner of articulation' refers to the manner of airflow – the degree and type of constriction or narrowing of the airflow; one important distinction is airflow through the *oral cavity*, or the mouth, and airflow through the *nasal cavity*, or nose. In manner of articulation, consonants categorized as nasals have nasal airflow, whereas the other consonants all have airflow through the oral cavity. Plosive consonants are also called stops; these sounds have a very short stoppage of airflow, hence the term 'stop'; when the airflow is released, a short burst of air can be heard or felt for some sounds, hence the name 'plosive'. Trill consonants occur when there is vibration in airflow between two articulators; this is usually caused by quick movement by one of the articulators (generally the tongue). A tap or flap is when there a very brief contact between the two articulators; it is often considered a brief **stop consonant**. Unlike a stop, however, the flap/tap is very short in duration, with little air build-up and therefore no plosive release. Fricative sounds occur when the two articulators (teeth/lips, tongue/alveolar ridge, for example) are very close together, and the airflow channel narrows as a result, resulting in frication with a palpable hissing or white noise sound for some of these consonants. In **lateral** approximants, air flows along one or both sides of the tongue; for lateral fricatives, the area along both sides or one side of the tongue is narrowed, creating turbulence, or frication. Approximants (including the lateral approximant) are consonants that are similar to vowels, in that the articulators move towards each other but do not create a stop or friction in airflow.

As Figure 5.1 illustrates, for some classes of consonants there is a voicing distinction between consonants. As discussed in Chapter 3, voiceless sounds are those in which the vocal folds remain open as the air passes through the glottis, whereas in voiced sounds, the vocal folds move as the air passes through them, resulting in vibration. Like vowels, nasals, trills, tap/flaps, and approximants are all voiced, while a voicing distinction exists for **plosives** (stops), fricatives, and **affricates** in some varieties of English. The description of consonants follows a specific order: (1) voicing;

(2) place of articulation; (3) manner of articulation. As shown in Figure 5.1, [p] is a voiceless bilabial stop while [b] is a voiced bilabial stop. For consonant classes that only have voiced consonants, such as nasals and approximants, the voicing is implied, and only the place and manner of articulation are needed. The consonant [n] is therefore described only as an alveolar nasal, rather than as a voiced alveolar nasal.

TASK 5.3 International Phonetic Alphabet

📖 Refer to the IPA chart in Figure 5.1 above, to answer the following questions.

(1) What are the IPA symbols for the following consonant sounds?
 (a) voiceless velar stop
 (b) bilabial nasal
 (c) voiced dental fricative
 (d) voiceless glottal fricative
 (e) palatal approximant
(2) How would you describe each of the following consonants using voicing, place of articulation, and manner of articulation?
 (a) t
 (b) z
 (c) l
 (d) θ
 (e) ʒ

How many consonants do languages have? Differences exist in the consonant inventories of languages around the world, with the smallest consonant inventory found in Rotokas, a language in Papua New Guinea, which only has 6 consonants (/p t k b d g/) (Maddieson, 1984). The largest language inventory of 122 consonants can be found in !Xóõ, a Southern Khoisan language spoken in Botswana, Africa; many of these consonants are non-pulmonic clicks. Of the 563 languages surveyed for consonant inventories in WALS, 89 (16%) have a small consonant inventory consisting of 6–14 consonants; 122 (22%) have a moderately small consonant inventory, of 15–18; 201 (36%) have an average consonant inventory, of 19–25; 94 (17%) have a moderately large inventory of 26–33; while 57 (10%) have a large consonant inventory of 34 or more (Maddieson, 2013a). As with vowels, there are some geographical differences in the distribution of consonants; as Maddieson (2013a) notes, average consonant inventories are found dispersed geographically all around the world, including in Europe (English, German, Spanish, and French), Africa (Somali, Mba), Asia (Cantonese, Mandarin Chinese, Sinhala), the Americas (Native American languages Lakhota, Hopi), and Oceania (Australian Aboriginal languages Gooniyandi, Garrwa). In contrast, smaller consonantal inventories are found in the Pacific area, including in languages of South America (Warao, Pirahã), New Guinea (Yareba, Daga), Asia (Tagalog, Japanese), and eastern North America (Cherokee, Chicasaw), as well as in Hawaiian and Te Reo Māori. Larger consonant inventories are found in languages of Africa, including Bantu and Khoisan languages (Hausa, Zulu); in Native American languages of Northwest North America (Squamish, Navajo); and in the middle of the Eurasian landmass (Arabic, Russian, Polish) (Maddieson, 2013a). Irish and Hindi also have larger consonant inventories. As we saw with vowels (Chapter 3), the consonant inventories of substrate languages impact which consonant sounds – and how many – exist in a given variety of English. This will be discussed in more detail below.

Which sounds are most common across languages? The most common consonants cross-linguistically include voiceless stops, nasals, some kind of fricative (usually /s/) and the approximant /j/.

As Table 5.1 shows, more than 90% of languages have a dental/alveolar voiceless stop and bilabial and alveolar nasals; more than 80% of languages have voiceless bilabial and velar stops, the palatal approximant, and a voiceless dental/alveolar fricative. More than 70% have the bilabial approximant /w/, while more than 60% have bilabial and dental/alveolar voiced stops; more than 50% have a voiced velar stop and a velar nasal (Maddieson, 1984). The most common types of consonants by manner of articulation are, in order: stops > fricatives > nasals > approximants > affricates (a combination of stop closure and fricative release); while the most common places of articulation are, in order: alveolar > bilabial > velar > palatal (Maddieson, 1984). The least common places of articulation are dentals, labiodentals, retroflexes, and uvular consonants. The dental fricatives (/θ ð/) are rare, occurring only in 7.1% of the languages (40 out of the 567) in WALS – they occur in many Germanic languages, including English, as well as in Icelandic, as we saw in Chapter 2. As we will see in our discussion of varieties of English below, the Englishes that have 24 consonants have all 3 nasals, and both voiceless and voiced stops and fricatives, including the dental fricatives. Varieties of English with a smaller consonant inventory usually have nasals, but are less likely to have voiced stops and fricatives than voiceless stops and fricatives; they usually do not have dental fricatives as they are often not present in the substratum languages influencing varieties of English.

Table 5.1 Most frequent consonants cross-linguistically

Consonant	Frequency (%)
/n/ – dental or alveolar nasal	99.68
/m/ – bilabial nasal	94.30
/t/ – voiceless dental or alveolar stop	91.00
/k/ – voiceless velar stop	89.30
/j/ – palatal approximant	85.50
/s/ – voiceless dental or alveolar fricative	83.00
/p/ – voiceless bilabial stop	82.60
/w/ – voiced bilabial approximant	75.10
/h/ – voiceless glottal fricative	63.00
/b/ – voiced bilabial stop	62.80
/d/ – voiced dental or alveolar stop	61.51
/g/ – voiced velar stop	55.20
/ŋ/ – velar nasal	52.70

5.4   The Consonants of English Around the World

How many consonants does English have? And how – and why – do English consonant inventories vary across varieties of English? English, used here as an umbrella term, is considered to have 24 consonant sounds. One of the differences between varieties of English, rhoticity, has been discussed in Chapter 4. Table 5.2 shows a consonant chart for English with the 24 most common consonants given. These 24 consonant phonemes exist in many varieties of English and particularly OVEs, including varieties of AmE, AusE, NZE, CanE, and BrE, as well as PCEs such as SgE and JamE, and ethnic varieties of OVEs including AAVE.

TASK 5.4 Phonemes

📖 The word list from Task 5.1 is given below. Each word illustrates one of the consonant phonemes given in Table 5.2. Can you match each word to the phoneme for the underlined sound in each word? Note: sound/spelling correspondence is closer for consonants than it is for vowels. Answers may vary depending on the variety of English.

_p_at	_b_at	_t_ip	_d_ip	_c_ot	_g_ot	_f_ine	_v_ine	_S_ue	_z_oo	_th_ree	_th_ese
_sh_e	A_si_a	_h_ot	_ch_urch	_j_udge	_m_an	_n_ote	si_ng_	_r_ed	_l_ight	_y_ellow	_wh_ite

Table 5.2 English consonants

Manner	Place of articulation															
	Bilabial		Labiodental		Dental		Alveolar		Postalveolar		Palatal		Velar		Glottal	
	Vl	*Vd*	*Vl*	*Vd*	*Vl*	*Vd*	*Vl*	*Vd*	*Vl*	*Vd*	*Vl*	*Vd*	*Vl*	*Vd*	*Vl*	*Vd*
Stop	p	b					t	d					k	g		
Fricative			f	v	θ	ð	s	z	ʃ	ʒ					h	
Affricate									tʃ	dʒ						
Nasal		m						n						ŋ		
Lateral								l								
Approximant		w								r		j				

Fewer differences exist among varieties of English in consonant than in vowel inventories; therefore, the discussion of consonants of English will differ from that of vowels. Each class of consonants will be discussed in turn by manner of articulation, with differences across varieties of English highlighted.

☞ The following discussion is intended to provide a comprehensive overview of consonants across a wide range of Englishes in order to be inclusive in the presentation of English consonants.

The listening tasks to illustrate consonants by varieties of English have been categorized by manner of articulation:

Task 5.5   Stops
Task 5.6   Fricatives, Affricates
Task 5.7   Nasals
Task 5.8   Approximants

Within each task, you can find examples from the following varieties of English:

 (1) Modern RP (Mod RP)
 (2) Northern British English (NBrE)
 (3) Irish English (IrE)
 (4) Midwestern American English (Midwestern AmE)
 (5) Puerto Rican English (PRE)
 (6) AusE speaker from Queensland (Qld AusE)
 (7) New Zealand English (NZE)
 (8) Kenyan English (KenE)
 (9) Zimbabwean English (ZimE)
(10) White South African English (WSAE)
(11) Singapore English (SgE)
(12) Malaysian English (MalE)
(13) Hong Kong English (HKE)
(14) Indian English (IndE)
(15) Pakistani English (PakE)
(16) Sri Lankan English (SLE)
(17) Nepalese English (NepE)
(18) Philippine English (PhlE)

Although you are encouraged to listen to examples of several different varieties of English to expand your understanding of consonants as well as of World Englishes, you may wish to focus your attention on the varieties of English that are of interest to you.

5.4.1   Stops/Plosives

What is a stop consonant? Stop consonants, also called plosives, have complete closure of the airflow, a stoppage of air with a release burst after opening the airflow that may create a slight explosion of air. Figures 5.3 and 5.4 show spectrograms of a Midwestern AmE speaker's production of *say* (Figure 5.3) and *stay* (Figure 5.4). As Figure 5.4 shows, there are no sound waves during the stop closure of *t* in *stay*.

Many varieties of English have a series of six stops, with three places of articulation: bilabial /p b/, produced by closing the mouth / touching both lips together; alveolar /t d/, by placing the tip of the tongue on the alveolar ridge, just behind the upper front teeth; and velar /k g/, by raising the back part of the tongue and touching it to the velum, the soft part of the roof of the mouth towards the back. Consonants like /t d/ (and /s z n l/, see below) are classified as **coronal** consonants as the front – and flexible – part of the tongue is used in their articulation; these consonants have a curving of the front part of the tongue.

As noted above, stops, fricatives, and affricates are classified as voiceless or voiced, though the degree of voicing varies in different Englishes. If you say *Sue* and *zoo* carefully, you may be able to feel the difference in voicing

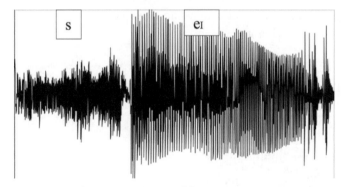

Figure 5.3 Midwestern American English *say*

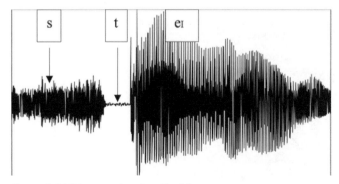

Figure 5.4 Midwestern American English *stay*

if you place one hand in front of your mouth and the other hand on your neck, placed over your glottis.

While voicing may be a useful means of distinguishing consonants phonemically, the actual articulation of stop consonants with regard to voicing is more complicated. For example, if you say the word *pan*, you may feel a puff of air when you release the /p/ at the beginning of the word; the same may occur for the other two voiceless stops, /t/ as in *tea* and /k/ as in *key*. This puff of air, which occurs for voiceless stops at the beginning of a word (and, in some cases, at the beginning of a syllable, as in *pa.per*), occurs in some, though not all, varieties of English. It is called **aspiration** and is noted in IPA transcription with a superscript [ʰ]. Aspiration of voiceless stops occurs because of the build-up of air pressure during the stop closure; once the stop closure is released, the air flows out through the mouth in what can be felt and heard as a puff of air.

An important distinction for stops in initial position in some varieties of English to differentiate the realization of the stop consonants /t/ vs /d/, /p/ vs /b/, and /k/ vs /g/, is **Voice Onset Time**, or **VOT**, which refers to the period of time between the release of the stop closure and the onset of voicing – how long it takes after the stop closure is opened for the vocal folds to begin vibrating. We can measure the VOT through acoustic analysis; in Figures 5.5 and 5.6, you can see an AusE speaker from South Australia pronounce *pan* and *ban*.

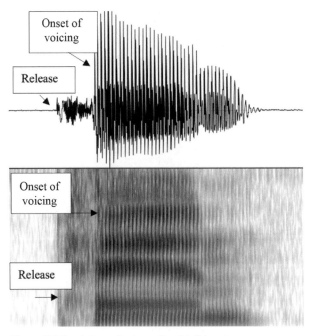

Figure 5.5 South Australia Australian English *pan*

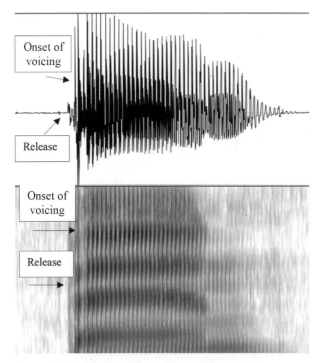

Figure 5.6 South Australia Australian English *ban*

For *pan*, you can see a longer VOT or period of voicelessness between the release of the stop and the onset of voicing. In *ban*, in contrast, this period is quite short, with voicing commencing almost immediately after the release of the stop.

Figure 5.7 shows the actual measurement of VOT in *pan*, which is 0.085 seconds, or 85 milliseconds. We can also measure the VOT for *ban*, which is 0.012 seconds, or 12 milliseconds. Different languages and varieties of English have different VOTs; VOT is best viewed as a continuum of values, as shown in Figure 5.8.

Values between 0 and 30 msec are called **short-lag VOT** and correspond to voiceless (vl) unaspirated stops; a VOT over 30 msec is considered aspirated. In many varieties of English with aspiration, VOT is around 60–120 msec, a **long-lag VOT**, and corresponds to aspirated voiceless stops. Voiced (vd) stops may also have a positive VOT, as we saw with the VOT of *ban* for the SA AusE speaker in Figure 5.6 – this a short-lag VOT of 12 msec. VOT may also be a negative number, when there is pre-voicing before the stop closure release. In Figures 5.9 and 5.10, we can see waveforms and spectrograms of the NepE speaker saying *pat* and *bat*. You can see the relatively short-lag VOT for *pat* and the pre-voicing for *bat*, indicating that NepE distinguishes initial stops by voicing, not aspiration. You may also note the final stop closure and release of [t] for *pat* and *bat* in the figures.

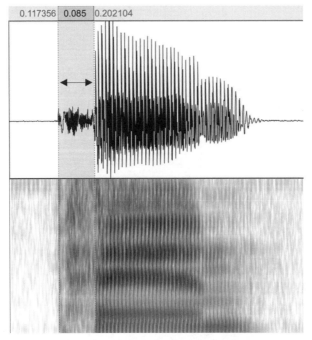

Figure 5.7 South Australia Australian English Voice Onset Time in *pan*

-Negative	0–30 msec	30+ msec	60–120 msec
Pre-voicing	Unaspirated	Aspirated	Aspirated
	Short-lag VOT		Long-lag VOT
	Vl unaspirated stops		Vl aspirated / stops
	Vd stops		

Figure 5.8 Voice Onset Time continuum

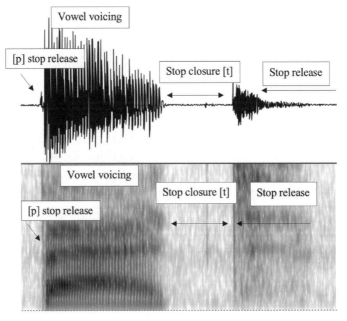

Figure 5.9 Nepalese English *pat*

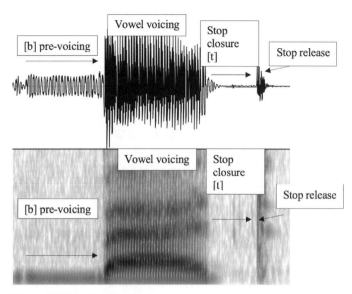

Figure 5.10 Nepalese English *bat*

Table 5.3 Voice Onset Times in different languages

Language	/p/	/b/	/t/	/d/	/k/	/g/
Puerto Rico Spanish	4	-138	9	-110	29	-108
Tamil	12	-74	8	-78	24	-62
Cantonese	[pʰ] 77	[p] 9	[tʰ] 75	[t] 14	[kʰ] 87	[k] 34
English (AmE)	58	1/-101	70	5/-102	80	21/-88
Hindi	[p 13	[b] -85	[t] 15	[d] -87	[k] 18	[g] -63
	[pʰ] 70	[bʰ] -61	[tʰ] 67	[dʰ] -87	[kʰ] 92	[gʰ]-75
			[ʈ] 9	[ɖ] -76		
			[ʈʰ] 60	[ɖʰ] -77		

Based on Lisker and Abramson (1964)

Average VOT values for different languages are shown in Table 5.3; these values are based on Lisker and Abramson (1964), the first study to measure VOT as a means of distinguishing between initial voiced and voiceless stops. As shown in Table 5.3, AmE VOT is either short-lag or negative VOT for /b d g/ and long-lag for /p t k/, indicating that AmE contrasts initial stops by aspiration as well as voicing, in some cases. AusE, as illustrated above, also distinguishes initial stops by aspiration – short- vs long-lag VOT. Both Puerto Rican Spanish (influencing PRE) and Tamil (influencing IndE and SLE) have a 2-way distinction between stops based on voicing – /b d g/ have negative VOT, indicating that pre-voicing exists before the stop release; the VOT values for /p t k/ indicate they do not have aspiration. Cantonese (influencing HKE as well as SgE), in contrast, has a series of unaspirated (short-lag VOT) and aspirated (long-lag VOT) voiceless stops, indicating that initial stops in Cantonese are phonemically voiceless and distinguished by aspiration. Hindi (influencing IndE) has pre-voiced stops as well as short-/long-lag VOT stops. Schachter and Otanes (1972) note that Filipino (influencing PhlE) has a similar voicing pattern to Spanish, with short-lag VOT for voiceless stops and long negative (pre-voicing) for voiced stops.

In varieties of English that distinguish between short- and long-lag VOT for initial stop consonants, the difference between *pan* and *ban*, for example, is not a difference in whether the first sound in *ban* is voiced and the first sound in *pan* is voiceless; instead, the difference is aspiration, or short- vs long-lag VOT. In other words, we listen for the little puff of air to hear a word as *pan* or *ban*. In varieties of English that distinguish initial stops by voicing, voiced stops usually have pre-voicing whereas voiceless stops do not; the hearer is listening for the voicing distinction to differentiate words. If you speak a variety with a short-/long-lag differentiation, it may be difficult to hear the voicing distinction in varieties that do not have long-lag VOT, and vice versa. There is one more important point to note about word-initial voicing in stops: when a consonant precedes the /p t k/, as in *ski* or *spit*, the VOT is shortened and there is no aspiration. For this reason, *sty* and *sdy* are homophones (while *sdy* is not a possible word in English phonologically – see Chapter 6 – there is no articulatory reason why it could not exist; see more below on allophonic variation of voiceless stops).

Which stops are most common in varieties of English? As noted above and as shown in Table 5.4, a series of six stops exists in many varieties of English, including GAmE as well as regional (e.g., Southern, Midwestern, etc.) and ethnic varieties of AmE (including AAVE and ChiE and some NAE); CanE; varieties of BrE (RP, SSBE, among others), as well as IrE, WelE, and ScotE; Englishes in Oceania and the Caribbean, including AusE, NZE, JamE, FijE; and a number of African (BSAE, WSAE, KenE, ZimE, NigE) and Asian Englishes (PhlE, SgE, HKE, MalE). VOT may differ in these Englishes, however: varieties of AmE, BrE, AusE, NZE, and IrE distinguish initial stops by short-/long-lag VOT (aspiration) rather than by voicing. This is also the case for HKE, which has a series of stops that are distinguished by aspiration and not voicing, similar to Cantonese (see Table 5.3). WelE has strongly aspirated stops due to the influence of Welsh (Penhallurick, 2004). In contrast, SSE may have less aspiration for voiceless stops due to influence from Scots, which has unaspirated stops syllable-initially, though research (Stuart-Smith, Sonderegger, Rathcke, & Macdonald, 2015) indicates that

Table 5.4 Stop consonants in varieties of English

Manner	Bilabial		Labiodental		Dental		Alveolar		Postalveolar		Retroflex		Palatal		Velar		Glottal	
	Vl	*Vd*	*Vl*	*Vd*	*Vl*	*Vd*	*Vl*	*Vd*	*Vl*	*Vd*	*Vl*	*Vd*	*Vl*	*Vd*	*Vl*	*Vd*	*Vl*	*Vd*
Stops	p	b					t	d							k	g		
	pat	bat					tip	dip							cot	got		
	pan	ban					tan	Dan							can	go		
							talk											

Place of articulation

a change to a longer VOT is under way and VOT has been lengthening over the twentieth century in SSE. There is more variation in VOT among speakers of NVEs due to both superstrate and substrate influences. A lack of aspiration for initial voiced stops may exist for some speakers of AusAborE, FijE, MāoriE, PasE, IndE, NepE, PakE, PhlE, and Broad WSAE (Bowerman, 2004; Butcher, 2008; Gargesh, 2004; Rajadurai, 2006; Starks, Gibson, & Bell, 2015; Tayao, 2004; Tent & Mugler, 2004; Warren & Bauer, 2004) due to substrate influences leading to voicing, and not aspiration, as a difference word-initially. Place of articulation may differ too: in both SSE and WelE, some speakers may have a more dental articulation for /t d/ due to influence from Scots or Welsh, respectively. This occurs in WAfE as well (Bobda, 2001). ChiE, an ethnic variety of AmE, also often has an apico-dental pronunciation for alveolar stops due to influence from Spanish (Santa Ana & Bayley, 2004). IndE, PakE, and SLE all have retroflex stops, with retroflexion a distinguishing feature of these Englishes (Gunesekera, 2005; Mahboob & Ahmar, 2004; Pandey, 2015). Another feature of IndE, SLE, and PakE is two dental stops /t̪ d̪/ in words with 'th', as in *three* and *these*, as these varieties do not have the dental fricatives /θ ð/ (see below) (the diacritic [̪], which resembles a tooth, symbolizes a dental articulation), giving these varieties two more stop consonants.

Table 5.5 show some of the possible spellings for each of the stop phonemes; this is based on Cruttenden (2014) and is reflective of OVE phonemic inventories. I have added a column entitled 'Other phonemes' to represent the phonemic inventories in other varieties of English. The spellings 't' and 'tt', as examples, have traditionally been seen to represent the /t/ phoneme; they may also represent a voiceless dental stop, an aspirated alveolar stop (phonemically), and a retroflex voiceless stop in some varieties of English.

TASK 5.5 Listening for Stop Consonants

🎧 Listen to the speakers say keywords for each stop consonant. For each speaker/variety, are the initial stop consonants at the same place of articulation distinguished by voicing or by aspiration?

Speaker 1   Mod RP

Speaker 2   NBrE

Speaker 3   IrE

Speaker 4   Midwestern AmE

Speaker 5   PRE

Speaker 6   Qld AusE

Speaker 7   NZE
Speaker 8   KenE
Speaker 9   ZimE
Speaker 10 WSAE
Speaker 11 SgE
Speaker 12 MalE
Speaker 13 HKE
Speaker 14 IndE
Speaker 15 PakE
Speaker 16 SLE
Speaker 17 NepE
Speaker 18 PhlE

Table 5.5 Stop consonant spelling

Consonant	Spellings	Other phonemes	Examples
/p/	p pp	/pʰ/	cup, pen, pill, paper, pepper, apple
/b/	b bb	/p/	banana, ball, rob robber
/t/	t tt th -ed (see Chapter 6)	/tʰ ɾt/	tap, tip, tree, sit little, bitter, matt Thomas, Thames looked, talked
/d/	d dd -ed	/t ɾd/	dip, dell, sad sadder, muddle bombed, banged
/k/	k c cc q ch ck qu /kw/ x /ks/	/kʰ/	kiss, kept, leak cord, can, card occupy, occur cheque, unique choir, chemist chicken, neck quiet, quilt six, X-ray
/g/	g gg gh gu, gue x /gz/	/k/	go, good, geese egg, aggressive ghost, spaghetti guest, guide exempt, exist

You may have noticed that you can hear a puff of air – aspiration – in the production of initial /p t k/ for almost all the speakers; the exceptions are the speakers of IndE, NepE, and PhlE (for /p/ and /t/ only) who do not use aspiration, but instead voicing with pre-voicing of /b d g/ (/p t k/ have a short-lag VOT) to distinguish initial stops. You may also have noticed a retroflex pronunciation of the alveolar stops (as /ʈ ɖ/) for the PakE, IndE, and SLE speakers.

5.4.2   Fricatives and Affricates

What are fricatives? Fricatives have frication – air turbulence – due to a narrow constriction of airflow. Unlike stops, which have complete closure of the airflow, fricatives have continuous airflow, though the constriction can be very narrow. Figure 5.11 shows the Midwestern AmE speaker saying *Sue*. As Figure 5.11 illustrates, the /s/ has strong turbulence; in contrast, we can see clear vocal fold opening/closing cycles for the vowel, as well as four formants. Affricates are consonants that are produced with a stop closure, with a fricative release.

Stops, fricatives, and affricates differ from nasals, approximants, and vowels in a number of ways, including in the greater obstruction of airflow through a full closure or narrow constriction. These three types of consonants are classified as **obstruents** (from 'obstruction'). Nasals, approximants, and vowels, in contrast, are classified as **sonorants**, as the lack of (or lesser) obstruction creates greater amplitude, or acoustic energy or loudness, in production (this is called sonority and will be discussed in

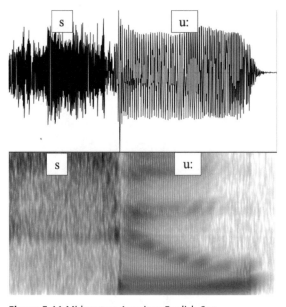

Figure 5.11 Midwestern American English *Sue*

Chapter 6). Another important difference between obstruents and sono-rants is the voicing distinction, as noted above: as the IPA consonant chart (see Figure 5.1) shows, obstruents have a phonemic voicing distinction in all places of articulation, whereas sonorants are all voiced. As we noted above, however, the voiced/voiceless distinction does not accurately repre-sent the articulation of stop consonants in all environments (other voicing differences will be discussed under 'Allophonic Variation', below); the same is true of fricatives and affricates. Another set of terms is often employed to describe the difference in consonant articulation: **lenis** and **fortis**. Fortis consonants are strongly articulated with more force, whereas lenis con-sonants are weakly articulated. Voiceless consonants – /p t k s f θ ʃ tʃ/ in English – are produced with more force, due to the open setting of the vocal folds during articulation; they are fortis consonants. Voiced conso-nants – /b d g v z ð ʒ dʒ/ in English – have a weak articulation, and are lenis consonants.

Due to the variation in fricative inventories cross-linguistically, there is greater variation in fricative inventories across varieties of English, with many Englishes having a smaller set of fricatives, usually /s f h/. Some varieties of English are less likely to have voiced fricatives and the dental fricatives. Table 5.6 shows a possible inventory of fricatives and affricates which exist in many OVEs, including a range of ethnic, social, and regional varieties of AmE (including AAVE), CanE, AusE, NZE, MāoriE, BrE, ScotE, WelE, IrE, as well as some acrolectal and mesolectal varieties of NVEs, such as MalE, JamE, SgE, PhlE, BSAE, and WSAE. As will be discussed below, many of these varieties have allophonic variation for some of these frica-tives, and in particular for the dental fricatives.

The labiodental fricatives /f/ as in *fine* and /v/ as in *vine* are produced by placing the upper teeth on the lower lips; /f/ is voiceless while /v/ is voiced. The airflow passes through the slight opening between the lips and teeth. The dental fricatives /θ/ as in *three* and /ð/ as in *these* are produced by either placing the tip of the tongue between the upper and lower teeth (this is called **interdental** articulation: between the teeth) or the tip of the tongue on the back of the upper front teeth. The alveolar fricatives /s/ as in *Sue* and /z/ as in *zoo* are produced by placing the tip of the tongue very close to (but not touching) the alveolar ridge, with the airflow passing through this narrow gap. The postalveolar fricatives /ʃ/ as in *ship* and /ʒ/ as in *lesion* are produced by placing the front (slightly farther back than the tip) of the tongue close to, but not touching, the region of the roof of the mouth behind the alveolar ridge; the narrow opening between the tongue and the roof of the mouth creates the fric-ation. The affricates /tʃ/ as in *church* and /dʒ/ as in *judge* are articulated by first touching the front (not tip) of the tongue on the postalveolar area

Table 5.6 Fricatives and affricates in varieties of English

	Place of articulation															
	Bilabial		Labiodental		Dental		Alveolar		Postalveolar		Palatal		Velar		Glottal	
Manner	Vl	Vd	Vl	Vd	Vl	Vd	Vl	Vd	Vl	Vd	Vl	Vd	Vl	Vd	Vl	Vd
Fricative			f fine fan	v vine van	θ three thin	ð these then	s Sue see say	z zoo	ʃ she shoe	ʒ Asia lesion					h hot how	
Affricate									tʃ church chew	dʒ judge Joe						

of the roof of the mouth, and then releasing it and holding the tongue close to the roof in the same area. The glottal fricative is produced in the glottis; there may be a slight constriction (vocal folds close together) in the glottis for some speakers/varieties. The fricative /h/ is often considered closer to a vowel, as its articulation is influenced by the vowels that occur before and after /h/.

Many varieties of English have smaller fricative and affricate inventories; as noted above, the dental fricatives are rare cross-linguistically, and, while they exist in English, they do not exist in all varieties of English. These fricatives are often referred to as TH (for /θ/) and DH (for /ð/). The alveolar stops /t d/ or labiodental fricatives /f v/ are often used in place of dental fricatives (*them* to *dem* or *vem*, and *three* to *tree* or *free*); this occurs in many ethnic varieties of AmE, including NAEs such as Navajo, Pima, and Tsimshian Englishes (Coggshall, 2015), as well as in ChiE (Santa Ana & Bayley, 2004). It also occurs in some varieties of AusAborE (Butcher, 2008) and in many Asian Englishes, including basilectal PhlE (Tayao, 2004), IndE, SLE, PakE (Gargesh & Sailaja, 2017), and NepE, as well as African Englishes, including both NigE and BSAE (Bobda, 2001; Van Rooy, 2004). Some varieties of English only have one of the dental fricatives: some speakers of HKE may have /θ/ (Hung, 2012), FijE only has /ð/ (Tent & Mugler, 2004). The realization of /θ ð/ variably as [t d] – a process known as TH/DH-stopping – or as [f v] – known as TH/DH-fronting – is common across many varieties of English; this will be discussed below.

The labiodental fricatives /f v/ also do not exist in all varieties of English: in many varieties, including NAE (Navajo, Pima, and Tsimshian Englishes; Coggshall, 2015), AusAborE (Butcher, 2008), and basilectal PhlE (Tayao, 2004), these fricatives are produced as bilabial stops /p b/, respectively. In IndE, /f/ is often an aspirated /p/ or the bilabial fricative /ɸ/ (Wells, 1982). The phonemes /f/ or /w/ may exist instead of /v/ (HKE: Hung, 2012), as may /ʋ/, a labiodental fricative (IndE, PakE, SLE: Gargesh & Sailaja, 2017), and /f/ or /β/, a bilabial fricative (FijE: Tent & Mugler, 2004). The postalveolar /ʒ/ is also rare cross-linguistically, and occurs only in some varieties of English, as do /z/ and /dʒ/. The fricative /ʒ/ (as well as /z/ and /dʒ/ in some cases) is often produced as /s/ (some NAE: Coggshall, 2015; PhlE: Tayao, 2004; FijE: Tent & Mugler, 2004; IndE, SLE, PakE: Gargesh & Sailaja, 2017; BSAE: Van Rooy, 2004) or /ʃ/ (BrE, AmE, HKE, SLE: Gargesh & Sailaja, 2017; Hung, 2012; Wells, 2008), with /tʃ/ realized as /ʃ/ (PRE). The fricative /h/ does not exist in some varieties of English, including IndE, SLE, and PakE (Gargesh & Sailaja, 2017), as well as AusAborE (Butcher, 2008), nor for Tamil speakers of MalE (Baskaran, 2004). The velar fricative /x/ exists in some varieties of English, due to substrate influences; this includes WelE (from Welsh; Penhallurick, 2004), Quinault English (from Quinault, a

Native American language; Coggshall, 2015) and ScotE (from Scots; Stuart-Smith, 2004). Speakers of WSAE may have the uvular fricative /X/ in words borrowed from Afrikaans (Bowerman, 2004). Table 5.7 shows the spelling of the different fricatives and affricates; this is modified from Cruttenden (2014), with the added 'Other phonemes' based on the inventories discussed above.

TASK 5.6 Listening for Fricatives and Affricates

🎧 Listen to the speakers say keywords for each fricative/affricate consonant. How many of the fricatives/affricates does each speaker have? Do any of the speakers have /t d/ and or /f v/ for the TH and DH? Do you notice any other features discussed above in the speech samples?

Speaker 1   Mod RP
Speaker 2   NBrE
Speaker 3   IrE
Speaker 4   Midwestern AmE
Speaker 5   PRE
Speaker 6   Qld AusE
Speaker 7   NZE
Speaker 8   KenE
Speaker 9   ZimE
Speaker 10 WSAE
Speaker 11 SgE
Speaker 12 MalE
Speaker 13 HKE
Speaker 14 IndE
Speaker 15 PakE
Speaker 16 SLE
Speaker 17 NepE
Speaker 18 PhlE

A number of features discussed above are found in the speech samples: both MalE and HKE speakers have /d/ in DH words, while the SLE, SgE, NepE, PakE, and IndE have /t d/ for both TH and DH (with a dental articulation for the IndE speaker). The PhlE and NBrE speakers have /f/ in TH words. The MalE and SLE speakers have /s/ for /z/. The SLE, IndE, PRE, ZimE, and PhlE speakers have /ʃ/ for /ʒ/, as do the speakers of Midwestern AmE and NBrE in *Asia*. The PRE speaker pronounces the /tʃ/ as /ʃ/ in *chew*, as does the PhlE speaker for the second /tʃ/ in *church*, while the IndE, PakE, and SLE speakers pronounce /v/ as /ʋ/.

Table 5.7 Fricative and affricate spelling

Consonant	Spellings	Other phonemes	Examples
/tʃ/	ch	/ʃ/	chain, much, rich
	tch		fetch, watch
	ti		question, Christian
	tu		nature, statue
/dʒ/	j	/s/	jam, joe, juice
	g		magic, village
	dg		edge, judge
	dj		adjunct, adjective
/f/	f	/p pʰ ɸ/	leaf, friend, selfish
	ff		coffee, effort
	ph		phonetics, physics
	gh		cough, laugh
/v/	v	/f w b ʋ β/	love, view, vine
/θ/ (TH)	th	/t̪ t f s/	three, think, bath
/ð/ (DH)	th	/d̪ d v z/	that, father, breathe
/s/	s/se		skin, snow, see, bus
	ss		kiss, class
	c/ce		advice, decide
	sc/sce		scent, science, acquiesce
	x /ks/		six, reflex
/z/	s/se	/s/	bars, dogs, rose
	ss		dessert, scissors
	z		quiz, zeal, zoo
	x		xerox, xylophone
	x /gz/		exact, anxiety
/ʃ/	sh	/s/	ship, sheep, brush
	ch, chs		chalet, chef, machine, fuchsia
	s, ss + u		sugar, sure
	ce-, ci-, sci-, si-, ti-		ocean, special, conscience, mansion, nation
/ʒ/	g	/s ʃ/	genre
	ge, gi		beige, garage, regime
	si-		vision, division
	s, z + u		closure, leisure, seizure
/h/	h		hello, hot, behave
	wh		who, whose

5.4.3 Nasals

What are nasal consonants? Similar to stop consonants, nasals have stoppage of airflow in the mouth in the same places of articulation as stops: bilabial, alveolar, and velar. The manner of airflow for nasals, however, is through the nasal cavity, rather than through the oral cavity, or mouth.

Try to say /m/ as in *man* (this is a bilabial consonant, so you will need to close your mouth by touching your lips together). You may feel that the air is flowing out of your nasal cavity. Nasals are very common cross-linguistically, as shown above; all the varieties of English surveyed for this volume have minimally two, and often three, nasal consonants. All these varieties have a bilabial nasal, /m/ as in *man*, and an alveolar nasal, /n/, as in *note*. This includes AmE (including regional and ethnic varieties); CanE; BrE (regional, social, and ethnic varieties) and IrE, ScotE, and WelE; African Englishes (BSAE, WSAE, KenE, ZimE); and Asian Englishes (PhlE, HKE, MalE, SgE, IndE, SLE, PakE). Most of these Englishes also have the velar nasal /ŋ/. In some varieties of English, including NBrE (Beal, 2004) and some varieties of IndE (Gargesh, 2004), the velar nasal /ŋ/ only exists as an allophone of /n/ when it occurs before a velar consonant. Table 5.8 shows English nasals by place and manner of articulation, while Table 5.9 shows the spelling of English nasals, including 'Other phonemes' that exist

Table 5.8 Nasals in varieties of English

Manner									

	\multicolumn{17}{c}{*Place of articulation*}
Manner	*Bilabial*	*Labiodental*	*Dental*	*Alveolar*	*Postalveolar*	*Palatal*	*Velar*	*Glottal*
	Vl *Vd*	*Vl* *Vd*	*Vl* *Vd*	*Vl* *Vd*	*Vl* *Vd*	*Vl* *Vd*	*Vl* *Vd*	*Vl* *Vd*
Nasal	m man make			n note no nature			ŋ sing	

Table 5.9 Nasal spelling

Consonant	Spellings	Other phonemes	Examples
/m/	m		woman, number
	mm		summer, committee
	mb		climb, lamb
	mn		column, autumn
/n/	n	/l/	barn, now, no
	nn		connect, funny
	gn		gnaw, champagne
	kn		knee, knife
	pn		pneumonia
/ŋ/	ng	/n/	sing, tongue
	n + k, c (and other consonants)		sink, uncle

in varieties of English, in this case the /l/ for /n/ that exists in HKE, as well as some other varieties of English in China. This is discussed in more detail below.

TASK 5.7 Listening for Nasals

🎧 Listen to the speakers say the keywords for each consonant. Are there major differences in how the speakers pronounce the consonants? What do you notice for Speaker 2's (NBrE) pronunciation of *sing*?

Speaker 1   Mod RP
Speaker 2   NBrE
Speaker 3   IrE
Speaker 4   Midwestern AmE
Speaker 5   PRE
Speaker 6   Qld AusE
Speaker 7   NZE
Speaker 8   KenE
Speaker 9   ZimE
Speaker 10   WSAE
Speaker 11   SgE
Speaker 12   MalE
Speaker 13   HKE
Speaker 14   IndE
Speaker 15   PakE
Speaker 16   SLE
Speaker 17   NepE
Speaker 18   PhlE

You will probably have noticed that there is a great deal of similarity among the speakers/varieties in the production of nasal consonants. You may have noticed a slight stopping at the end of *sing* for the NBrE speaker – her pronunciation of *sing* is [sĩŋg], with a velar stop after the velar nasal. This will be discussed in more detail in Chapter 6 under English syllable structure.

5.4.4   Approximants

What are approximants? There is less constriction for approximants than there is for fricatives, though there is greater constriction than for vowels. As shown in Table 5.10, many varieties of English have four approximants, including social, ethnic, and regional varieties of AmE (including AAVE),

Table 5.10 Approximants in varieties of English

Manner	Place of articulation																
	Bilabial		Labiodental		Dental		Alveolar		Postalveolar		Palatal		Velar		Glottal	
	Vl	Vd	Vl	Vd	Vl	Vd	Vl	Vd	Vl	Vd	Vl	Vd	Vl	Vd	Vl	Vd
Lateral								l light low									
Approximant		w white way witch								r red row rope		j yellow yes					

CanE, AusE (including AusAborE), NZE (including PasE), BrE, IrE, ScotE, WelE, as well as HKE, MalE, SgE, PhlE, and African Englishes including WSAE, BSAE, EAfE, and WAfE. Some differences in place of articulation exist across varieties of English.

We start by looking at /l/ – this is described as an alveolar lateral approximant due to a lateral release of the airflow along the sides of the tongue (the tip of the tongue touches the alveolar ridge, similarly to /t d n/). This is often called an alveolar /l/ or light or clear /l/, in contrast to [ɫ], which occurs as an allophone of /l/ in many varieties of English and is called velar or dark /l/. While most varieties of English have an alveolar /l/, with some allophonic variation to [ɫ] inter- or post-vocalically (see below), some varieties of English, including ScotE, have a velar realization of the lateral approximant /l/ in all positions, in which the back of the tongue is more retracted and the tongue body is lowered during articulation (Stuart-Smith, 2004). In WelE, the articulation of /l/ is regional, with clear /l/ in all positions in the south and midland regions of Wales and dark /l/ in all positions in north Wales (Penhallurick, 2004). /l/ may also be light in all positions in Niuean English (NiuE), a Polynesian variety of English that is spoken by ethnic Niueans in New Zealand (Starks, Christie, & Thompson, 2007), as well as in FijE (Tent & Mugler, 2004) and IndE, SLE, and PakE (Gunesekera, 2005; Wells, 1982).

As discussed in Chapter 4, /r/ (the symbol /r/ is used as an umbrella term for any /r/ sound in English) has many realizations across varieties of English, usually as an alveolar, postalveolar, or retroflex approximant. It may also be rolled or tapped in WelE and PhlE (Penhallurick, 2004; Tayao, 2004); trilled or tapped in FijE, IndE, PakE, NepE, and SLE (Gunesekera, 2005; Tent & Mugler, 2004; Wells, 1982); and trilled for Afrikaans speakers of WSAE (Wells, 1982).

Most varieties of English have a bilabial approximant /w/, which is produced by rounding and narrowing the lips, but without lip closure. MāoriE only has /r w/ and not /l j/. IndE, SLE, NepE, and PakE may not have /w/ as a phoneme, but do have the labiodental approximant /ʋ/, which is often used for /w/, along with the labiodental fricative (Gunesekera, 2005; Pandey, 2015). Conflation of /l/ and /r/ (and to /n/) (where the two consonants are used seemingly interchangeably) occurs in EAfE, including in KenE (Schmied, 2004). This also occurs in HKE for /l/ and /n/, as well as /l/ and /r/, and /r/ and /w/ (Hung, 2012). Table 5.11 shows the spelling patterns for English approximants, including for the 'Other phonemes' discussed above.

Table 5.11 Approximant spelling

Consonant	Spellings	Other phonemes	Examples
/l/	l, le	/r n/	pull, light, table
	ll		balloon, million
/r/	r	/l w ɾ ʈ r/	row, tree, try
	rr		sorry, mirror
	wr		wrist, wrinkle, wrote
	rh		rhyme, rhino
/w/	w	/r v ʋ/	twice, swim, twin
	wh		which, white
	qu /kw/		queen, quiet
	u (after g, s)		suite, linguist, language
/j/	y		yes, you, year
	i		onion, view
	u		cure, music, use
	ue		argue, value
	ew, eu		stew, feud

TASK 5.8 Listening for Approximants

🎧 Listen to the speakers pronounce the keywords for each consonant. What differences, if any, can you notice in the pronunciation of the four approximants by different speakers/varieties?

Speaker 1   Mod RP
Speaker 2   NBrE
Speaker 3   IrE
Speaker 4   Midwestern AmE
Speaker 5   PRE
Speaker 6   Qld AusE
Speaker 7   NZE
Speaker 8   KenE
Speaker 9   ZimE
Speaker 10   WSAE
Speaker 11   SgE
Speaker 12   MalE
Speaker 13   HKE
Speaker 14   IndE
Speaker 15   PakE
Speaker 16   SLE
Speaker 17   NepE
Speaker 18   PhlE

All the speakers, and varieties, shown here have similar productions of /j/; similarly, all have an alveolar /l/ (the velar pronunciation will be discussed below), except for the KenE speaker, who has /n/ for /l/ in *low*. As discussed above, the IndE, PakE, NepE, and SLE speakers do not have /w/, instead producing /w/ as the labiodental fricative /ʋ/. Greater differences exist in the production of /r/ (see also Chapter 4): the WSAE, IndE, NepE, PakE, and SLE speakers have a trilled /r/ while the HKE speaker has /w/ in place of /r/.

Before we examine the allophonic variation that exists in English, we can draw the following conclusions about consonant phoneme inventories across varieties.

- All varieties have a series of stops, using bilabial, alveolar, and velar articulations.
- Most varieties have aspiration for initial voiceless stops.
- All varieties have a bilabial and an alveolar nasal; most, though not all, also have a velar nasal.
- Significant differences exist in the number and type of fricatives and affricates; all varieties have /s/ and most have /f/ (exception: IndE).
- Dental fricatives are less common among varieties of English, as are the voiced labiodental fricative and the voiced postalveolar fricative.
- Most varieties have /j/ and either an alveolar or a velar /l/ or both (see below).
- As seen in Chapter 4, /r/ can be articulated as a tap, a trill, or with a retroflex articulation.
- Not all varieties have /w/.

5.5   Allophonic Variation in English Consonants

Table 5.12 summarizes some of the allophonic variations for consonants across varieties of English. Each of these will be discussed in detail. As noted in the table, speech samples that illustrate the allophonic variation are available in Task 5.9.

Task 5.9 Listening for Consonant Allophones

☞ The following discussion of allophones of consonants is intended to provide a comprehensive overview of such allophones in varieties of English worldwide.

Although you are encouraged to listen to different types of allophonic variation, you may wish to focus your attention on the variation that occurs in the Englishes that are of interest to you.

In Table 5.12, you can find examples of varieties in which the allophonic variation has been found. It may be useful to refer to this list to help guide your reading and listening.

Table 5.12 Allophones of consonants in varieties of English

Rule	Diacritic symbol / examples	Varieties of English	🎧 Listening Task 5.9: Consonant allophones
Devoicing of obstruents	[̥] *tip* vs *dip* *safe* vs *save*	AmE, BrE, AusE, NZE, MalE, SgE Codas only: FijE, NigE, WSAE	(A) Qld AusE, NZE, WSAE compared with MalE, IndE
Aspiration of voiceless stops (VOT)	[ʰ] *key* vs *ski* *top* vs *stop*	AmE, BrE, CanE, AusE, NZE, IrE, ScotE, WelE, HKE, ZimE, MalE (some speakers), PRE, SgE (some speakers), KenE	(B) Appal AmE, NZE, ZimE, SA AusE, CanE
Devoicing of approximants	[̥] *Lear* vs. *clear*	Varieties of English with long-lag VOT, including AmE, BrE, AusE, NZE, HKE, ZimE	(C) Midwestern, Appal AmE, ZimE, HKE, MalE, NBrE
Flapping of /t d/	[ɾ] *butter* *bitter* *city*	AmE (General and all regional varieties), AAVE, NZE, NiuE, AusE, AusAborE, IrE, CanE, MalE, PRE, WSAE	(D) NE, NYC, Calif, Midwestern AmE, SA, Qld NSW AusE, CanE, PRE compared with Mod RP, KenE, SgE
Intervocalic T-glottaling	[ʔ] *city* *water*	Some varieties of BrE (Cockney, Manchester) spreading into other varieties including SW BrE, Midlands BrE, and LonE; ScotE, IrE	(E) EMidBrE
Glottal stopping before a syllabic nasal	[ʔ] *mountain* *button*	AmE, CanE, PRE	(F) Calif, Midwestern, NE AmE, CanE, PRE compared with SA AusE, Mod RP
Final T-glottaling	[ʔ] *pit* *batman*	Word-finally: AmE, BrE, ScotE, IrE, AAVE, NAE, AusE, NZE, NiuE, SgE, MalE Word-medially (pre-consonantal (PreC) favoured): AmE, BrE	(G) Calif AmE, SA AusE, Mod RP, SgE

Rule	Diacritic symbol / examples	Varieties of English	🎧 Listening Task 5.9: Consonant allophones
Dental assimilation	[̪] *month* vs. *mons*	Varieties with final dental fricatives, including AmE, BrE, AusE, NZE, ScotE, WelE, IrE, WSAE	(H) Calif, Midwestern AmE, SA AusE, Mod RP, IrE
TH/DH-stopping	/ð/ → [d] *these* to *dese* /θ/ → [t] *three* to *tree*	Southern/LonBrE, AAVE, NAE, NYC AmE (DH), SAmE, Broad CanE, CaribE, MLE (DH), IrE, SSE (DH), FijE, NZE, MāoriE, PasE, WAfE, EAfE, HKE (DH), SgE, MalE, PhlE	(I) HKE, MalE, SgE
TH/DH-fronting	/ð/ → [v] *Mother* to *mover* /θ/ → [f] *three* to *free*	Most varieties of BrE, including CockneyE, London/SW English, NBrE, ScotE, AAVE, NAE, SAmE, CaribE, NZE, AusE, FijE, NiuE, PasE, MāoriE, HKE, SgE	(J) NBrE, HKE, SgE, MalE
L-velarization	[ɫ]	AusE, AmE, BrE, CanE, NZE, IrE, WelE, ScotE, NigE, WSAE, HKE	(K) Midwestern, Appal AmE, SA AusE, HKE
L-vocalization	[o ow ol u uw]	Southeast BrE, EMidBrE, AmE (GAmE and Midwestern, Southern, NYC AmE), AusE, NZE, HKE, SgE, AAVE, PasE, NiuE, KenE	(K) SA AusE, HKE, SgE
Conflation of /r l w n/	*play* ~ *pray* *line* ~ *nine* *pray* ~ *pway*	/l/ ~ /r/ African Englishes, MalE /l/ ~ /n/ HKE, KenE /r/ ~ /w/ HKE	(L) HKE, KenE
/w/ → [hw] or [ʍ] in <wh-> words	*which* vs *witch*	Southland NZE, SSE, IrE, Trad RP	(M) IrE compared with CanE

Devoicing of obstruents: In some varieties of English in casual speech, the voicing context of a preceding sound (or pause, meaning silence or no voicing) or a following sound can impact the voicing of an obstruent consonant. A word- or syllable-initial voiced obstruent may lose voicing (it may become partially devoiced) if the preceding sound is a voiceless sound or a period of silence or a pause. This is an example of progressive assimilation. For example, in the phrases below, where [...] denotes a pause in speech, the voicing of /b/ in *bring* is affected by the voicing of the preceding sound. In examples (a) and (b), a partial loss of voicing may occur in some varieties of English, as the preceding sound is voiceless or a pause; in contrast, full voicing may occur in (c) as the preceding sound is voiced. This process is called *devoicing.*

Example	Possible realization
(a) ... <u>b</u>ring the car	[b̥ɹĩŋ]
(b) I must <u>b</u>ring the car	[b̥ɹĩŋ]
(c) She can <u>b</u>ring the car	[bɹĩŋ]

The reverse may occur when obstruents are word- or syllable-final, as in /d/ in *good*, below. In this scenario, it is the voicing of the following sound (regressive assimilation) that matters:

Example	Possible realization
(d) Goo<u>d</u> ...	[gʊd̥]
(e) Goo<u>d</u> morning	[gʊd]
(f) Goo<u>d</u> time	[gʊd̥]

In examples (d)–(f), only (e) may be fully voiced for some speakers, as the following word begins with a voiced sound. This process is common in AmE, AusE, NZE, and BrE, as well as in word-final coda position only in FijE, NigE, WSAE. Many varieties of English (see Chapter 6) also have consonant deletion word-finally, along with devoicing. Some varieties also only have voiceless obstruents, as noted above. We use the diacritic [̥] to show that a consonant is devoiced, as in [gʊd̥ tʰãɪm].

In varieties that devoice initial obstruents, aspiration is the key difference between *pie* and *buy* as the /b/ may not be fully voiced in *buy*. In varieties that devoice final obstruents, vowel length may be a key difference in words such as *lag* and *lack* – as we saw in Chapter 3, in some varieties of English, particularly those with a length or tense/lax distinction, vowels are longer before a voiced consonant than a voiceless consonant. The vowel is therefore longer in *lag* than in *lack* in these varieties. In other varieties, these words may be homophones as no length distinction exists for the vowel (see Chapter 3) or voicing distinction for the obstruents. In Task 5.9A, you may be able to hear a slightly longer vowel in *save* than in *safe* and in *lag* than in *lack* for the speakers of Qld AusE, NZE, and WSAE, and, in contrast, little difference for the speakers of IndE and MalE.

Aspiration of voiceless stops and VOT: In Task 5.9A, you can also hear a difference in VOT, and aspiration, for *tip* vs *dip* for the speakers of AusE, NZE, WSAE, and MalE, but not for the speaker of IndE. In varieties with short-/long-lag VOT for initial stops, voiceless stops are aspirated when they are syllable-initial (word-medially) in a stressed syllable; we can also hear this in Task 5.9B for the SA AusE and CanE speakers' production of *attend*, *encounter*, and *employer*, where stress falls on the underlined syllable; in some varieties of English, the /p t k/ are also aspirated when they are at the beginning of an unstressed syllable; both the AusE and CanE speakers have aspiration on the /t/ in *encounter*. If a /s/ precedes the /p t k/ in the same syllable (see Chapter 6), the voiceless stop is realized with short-lag VOT (no aspiration). You can hear the difference in aspiration for /k/ in *key* vs *ski*, /p/ for *pit* vs *spit*, and /t/ in *top*, *tall* vs *stop*, *stall* for the speakers of NZE, Appal AmE, and ZimE in Task 5.9B.

Devoicing of approximants: In varieties of English with a long-lag VOT (aspiration) for initial voiceless stops, full or partial devoicing may occur for the next sound due to the force of the airflow, which continues as the approximant is articulated due to co-articulation effects. In Figures 5.12 and 5.13, we can see a spectrogram of the Appal AmE speaker's production of *Lear* (Figure 5.12) and *clear* (Figure 5.13).

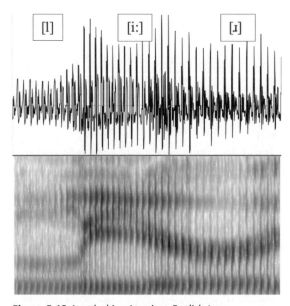

Figure 5.12 Appalachian American English *Lear*

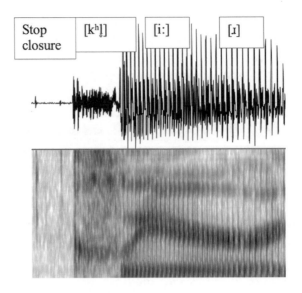

Figure 5.13 Appalachian American English *clear*

In *Lear* (Figure 5.12), there is voicing from the beginning; for *clear*, there is a visible stop closure, followed by aspiration and a partial loss of voicing for [l̥]. You can listen to the speakers of ZimE, NBrE, Midwestern AmE, Appal AmE, HKE, NZE, and MalE say *clear* (some loss of voicing for /l/) and *Lear* (fully voiced /l/) in Task 5.9C.

Intervocalic ~ word-medial /t/: One of the major differences in varieties of English is the realization of /t/ when it is intervocalic (between two vowels, as in *bitter* or *butter*), or word-medially before a syllabic consonant (see Chapter 6) such as 'n' in *mountain*. Possible realizations of /t/ include: (1) it can be aspirated, even if the syllable is unstressed, as discussed above; (2) it can be flapped, which is the production of /t/ as a quick /d/ sound with voicing; or (3) it can be a glottal stop, a process referred to as T-glottaling or T-glottalization.

Flapping of /t d/ when the alveolar stops are intervocalic word-medially, or before /l/ or /r/ word-medially, is a key feature of AmE and CanE, and is one feature that distinguishes these varieties from BrE. It also occurs in other varieties of English, including AusE, AusAborE, NZE, NiuE, some varieties of IrE (which, like AmE and CanE, is also rhotic), PRE, WSAE, and MalE. A flap is symbolized by the symbol [ɾ]; it is a quick tap of the tongue to the roof of the mouth and sounds like a quick 'd'. Flaps are voiced, which means that, for speakers who have a flap intervocalically, *litre* and *leader* may be homophones as the /d/ in *leader* may also be pronounced as a flap. In Task 5.9D, you can hear the NE, NYC, Calif and Midwestern AmE speakers pronounce *leader* and *litre* with flapping, while the speakers of KenE, SgE, and Mod RP have aspiration, not flapping, for /t/ in *litre*. You can also hear the contrast in flapping (SA, Qld NSW AusE, NE, NYC, Calif, Midwestern AmE, CanE, PRE) vs aspiration (Mod RP, SgE, KenE) for words such as *bitter*, *butter*, and *city* in Task 5.9D. As an example, for the word *city*, the CanE, and Qld NSW, SA AusE, speakers say [sɪ.ɾi] whereas the Mod RP speaker says [sɪ.tʰi] and the KenE speaker says [si.tʰi]. Flapping vs aspiration is clearly visible on a spectrogram, as shown in Figures 5.14 and 5.15.

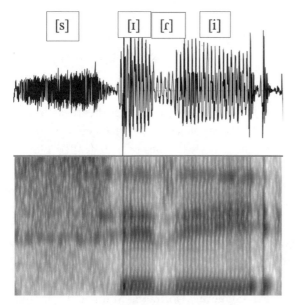

Figure 5.14 Queensland New South Wales Australian English *city*

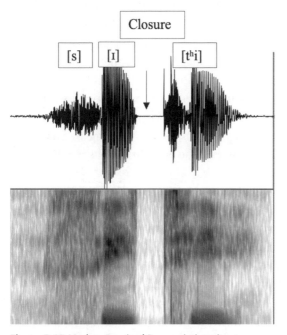

Figure 5.15 Modern Received Pronunciation *city*

In [sɪ.ɾi], as shown in Figure 5.14, there is voicing throughout the stop closure and release whereas in [sɪ.tʰi], as shown in Figure 5.15, there is a period of voicelessness and then aspiration following the release of /t/.

NVEs such as HKE, SgE, and KenE, where the superstrate has historically been BrE, may also have aspiration rather than flapping, while PRE may have flapping as the superstrate has historically been AmE. Task 5.9D also illustrates the different pronunciation of /t/ as either aspirated or flapped. In the word *potato*, you may notice that all the speakers have aspiration for the second syllable, '*ta*', as this is a stressed syllable for some speakers; for the final syllable, '*to*', however, there is a difference by speaker/variety for flapping/aspiration.

T-glottaling, or glottal stopping, refers to the production of a sound through obstruction of airflow in the glottis – it is often heard as a 'uh' on release of the closure, and it is symbolized by [ʔ]. It occurs in many varieties of English in place of the voiceless stops /p t k/ (called glottal replacement) or with the voiceless stops (called glottal reinforcement) at the end of words/syllables, as in *cup, pat,* and *back*. The glottal stop is also an allophone of /t/ intervocalically in some varieties of English – this is called T-glottaling (replacement of /t/ with the glottal stop).

Intervocalic T-glottaling, as in *water* as [wɔː.ʔə] (vs flapped for an AmE or CanE speaker [wɔː.ɾɚ] or aspirated for a Mod RP speaker [wɔː.tʰə]) has historically been present in ScotE and Cockney English, and has spread to regional varieties of English including Northern, Midland (East and West), Southeast, and Southwest BrE, and LonE (Altendorf & Watt, 2004; Baranowski & Turton, 2015; Braber & Robinson, 2018). It is associated with a working-class and young identity, and occurs more often for men than women; it does not occur in Mod or Trad RP. Though its usage is still stigmatized, it is spreading and becoming a marker of a youth norm of LonE, along with L-vocalization and TH-fronting (see below; Alderton, 2020). It also occurs in some varieties of IrE that do not have flapping intervocalically (Hickey, 2004). It does not occur intervocalically in varieties of English, including AmE, AusE, and CanE, that have flapping in this environment. In Task 5.9E, you can listen to the EMidBrE speaker talk about glottal stopping for *latter* and *water*.

Glottal stopping before a syllabic nasal: While AmE and CanE do not have glottal stopping intervocalically, they do have glottal stopping before a syllabic nasal, as in *button* and *mountain*; this variation of /t/, along with flapping, is a key feature distinguishing AmE and CanE from other varieties. Speakers of PRE and other AmE- or CanE-influenced varieties of English may also have glottal stopping in this environment. In Task 5.9F, you can hear the speakers of Mod RP and SA AusE aspirate the 't' in *mountain* and *button* whereas the Calif, Midwestern and NE AmE, CanE, and PRE speakers produce the 't' with glottal stopping.

Final T-glottaling (and/or glottal reinforcement) may occur for many varieties of English, particularly before another consonant (PreC) in the following word (in this environment, glottal stopping is not stigmatized in Trad or Mod RP); though it may also occur before pauses (PreP) and vowels (PreV), though those environments are still stigmatized in some varieties. It may also occur word-medially before another consonant in words like *workload* (for /k/) or *batman* (for /t/). Word-final T-glottaling and glottal reinforcement can occur in varieties of AmE, BrE (word-finally PreC in Trad/Mod RP), LonE (word-finally PreP and PreC), ScotE, IrE, AAVE (Thomas, 2007), NAE (Coggshall, 2015), AusE (Penney, Cox, & Szakay, 2021), and NZE (Warren & Bauer, 2004), as well as SgE (Wee, 2004) and MalE (Baskaran, 2004). It can also occur in Estuary English (LonE) syllable-finally for /t/ – *network* as *ne?work* (Deterding, 2005b) – and in AmE in words such as *batman*, as *ba?man* (Eddington & Taylor, 2009). In Task 5.9G, you can hear speakers of Calif AmE, SA AusE, Mod RP, and SgE say *at this* – there is a sudden stop for /t/ that sounds like 'uh' for the speakers. This indicates there is a closure of the glottis for /t/ and a glottal realization of /t/ as [ʔ]. This is particularly noticeable for the SgE speakers; you may also notice the pronunciation of the *th* as [d] in *this* for the SgE speakers; this is DH-stopping and will be discussed below.

Dental assimilation is a common process in varieties with dental frica-tives; the place of articulation of a postvocalic alveolar (/t d n l/) is assim-ilated to the following dental in words such as *month* and *health*. The diacritic [̪] is used to indicate dental assimilation; *month* may be realized as [mɑ̃n̪θ]. In WSAE, the velar nasal may also become a dental [n̪] before a dental consonant (Bowerman, 2004). Some Englishes, including SLE, PakE, and IndE, also have a retroflexed nasal [ɳ] when an alveolar nasal is before a retroflexed stop as in *aunty* and *band* [aːɳʈiː] (see Gargesh, 2004; Gunesekera, 2005). You can listen to speakers of Calif, Midwestern AmE, SA AusE, Mod RP, and IrE say *month* (with dental assimilation) and *mons* (no dental assimilation) in Task 5.9H.

TH/DH-stopping and TH/DH-fronting: In the discussion of cross-linguistic consonant inventories, we noted that dental fricatives were rare, occurring only in 40 out of the 567 languages in WALS. At the phonemic level, they also do not occur in many varieties of English, while at the phonetic level, many varieties of English that have one or both of the den-tal fricatives have allophonic variation with either TH/DH-stopping (to /t d/), TH/DH-fronting (to /f v/), or both, indicating that there is an ongoing global sound change for the TH/DH sounds, with the likelihood that they will eventually disappear from English.

TH/DH-stopping: Production of the DH in *then* as *den*, and of the TH in *three* as *tree*, occurs in variation with the dental fricatives in many varieties of AmE, including AAVE (particularly in word-initial position as in *dat* for *that*), NYC AmE (with DH-stopping more common than TH-stopping), and SAmE (Thomas, 2007; Wells, 1982). It is considered to be one of the most common features of NAE (Coggshall, 2015). It also occurs in Broad CanE (Wells, 1982), CaribE (Aceto, 2009), varieties of IrE (Popular Dublin, New Dublin, Rural SW/W, Supraregional Southern: Hickey, 2004) and Southern/ LonE (Altendorf & Watt, 2004). DH-stopping also occurs in MLE and may be produced as a flap intervocalically in SSE (Cheshire, Kerswill, Fox, & Torgersen, 2011; Stuart-Smith, 2004). It also occurs in FijE, and in NZE, as well as MāoriE and PasE (Starks, Christie, & Thompson, 2007; Tent & Mugler, 2004), and in some WAfE and EAfE if TH and DH exist in the phonemic inventory of these varieties (Bobda, 2003). This is also the case for mesolectal and acrolectal speakers of PhlE (Tayao, 2004). DH-stopping occurs for speakers of HKE who have the DH phoneme, usually intervocalically (Hung, 2012); both TH and DH may be stopped pre-vocalically in SgE (Wee, 2004). Stopping also occurs in MalE (Baskaran, 2004). You can listen to examples of TH- and DH-stopping for speakers of MalE, SgE, and HKE in Task 4.9I.

TH/DH-fronting: These to *vese* (DH-fronting) and, more commonly, *three* to *free* (TH-fronting), is becoming ubiquitous in English worldwide, both phonemically (see above) and at the level of allophonic variation. TH/DH-fronting is a well-known feature of Cockney English; it is considered to be relatively widespread in BrE (Deterding, 2005b), including in Southern/LonE (Altendorf & Watt, 2004) and northern varieties of BrE (Jansen, 2014). It also occurs in ScotE, along with the variant [h] in words such as *thing* and *think* (Stuart-Smith, 2004). TH-fronting has traditionally been socially stratified and associated with young, working-class men, though it is spreading into the middle class, possibly as a youth norm (Levon & Fox, 2014).

While TH-fronting is less common in varieties of AmE than BrE, it is a well-known feature of AAVE, occurring only word-medially and finally in this variety, with stopping occurring word-initially (Edwards, 2004). TH to [f] can also occur word-medially in some varieties of NAE (Coggshall, 2015) and SAmE (Thomas, 2004). It may also occur in some varieties of CaribE (Aceto, 2009); in varieties of NZE (Wood, 2003), NiuE (Starks, Christie, & Thompson, 2007), and PasE (Starks & Reffell, 2006); as well as in Broad and General AusE (Burridge, 2004) and FijE (Tent & Mugler, 2004). TH (not DH) fronting to [f] is a common feature of HKE (Hansen Edwards, 2018) and also occurs in SgE at the ends of words (Wee, 2004). You can listen to TH-fronting for speakers of NBrE, HKE, SgE, and MalE in Task 5.9J.

L-velarization/vocalization: Most varieties of English have an alveolar (light) /l/ in syllable-initial position. In many of these Englishes, the /l/

becomes velarized (the back part of the tongue is retracted and the tongue body is lowered before the tip of the tongue is raised; see Lee-Kim, Davidson, and Hwang, 2013) after vowels post- or inter-vocalically. This is called L-velarization and is represented by the symbol [ɫ]. L-velarization occurs in varieties of AmE, CanE, BrE, AusE, NZE, IrE, ScotE, WelE, NigE, WSAE, and HKE. Acoustically, an alveolar [l] has a relatively higher F2 and lower F1 than a dark [ɫ] (Carter & Local, 2007). You can hear examples of L-velarization in speakers of Midwestern, Appal AmE, SA AusE, and HKE in Task 5.9K.

L-velarization appears to be a change in progress towards *L-vocalization*, wherein the postvocalic L is produced like a [ow] or [uw] (or [o u]); this appears to be an ongoing natural sound change (Johnson & Britain, 2007). L-vocalization, where *feel* is produced as [fiːu], is a feature of LonE and appears to be spreading in Southeast England and the East Midlands; it also occurs in many varieties of AmE, AusE, and NZE, including PasE, NiuE, and AAVE (Braber & Robinson, 2018; Johnson & Britain, 2007). It is also common in many NVEs in Africa (KenE) and Asia (HKE, SgE) (Bobda, 2001; Hung, 2012; Wee, 2004). In Task 5.9K, you can hear the vocalization in the SgE and HKE speakers' production of *peel* as [pʰiu]; you can also hear examples of L-vocalization for a speaker of SA AusE.

Conflation of /r l w n/: The interchangeable use of some approximants and the alveolar nasal is common in some varieties; Bobda (2001) says /r/ and /l/ conflation (where *play* and *pray* may both mean either word) is common in African Englishes, with a tendency to replace /l/ with /r/ in EAfE. Conflation of /l/ and /n/ may also occur in KenE, and for Chinese speakers of MalE, so *friend* is *fliend* and *ran* is *lan* (Baskaran, 2004). Such conflation is a very common feature of HKE; it stems from conflation of these two sounds in Cantonese, a feature often referred to as 'lazy Cantonese'; /l/ often becomes /n/ in an onset if there is another nasal in the same word (*line* becomes *nine*), a process of assimilation called nasal harmony. In Task 5.9L, you can listen to the HKE speaker say *commu_n_icate* with [l], and *right* and *red* with [w]. You can also hear the KenE speaker pronounce *low* with [n].

/w/ → [hw] or [ʍ]: The hybrid fricative/approximant /ʍ/ has historically existed in English, primarily in varieties of BrE, IrE, and ScotE; it is still retained in SSE and some varieties of IrE (Rural Northern, NDubE, and Supraregional Southern) as well as in Trad RP for some speakers, though its usage is in decline (Hickey, 2004; Wells, 1982). For speakers with this variant, words beginning with <wh->, such as *which*, are produced as [hw], creating a phonemic difference between the first sounds in *Wales* and *whales* as well as *witch* and *which*, which are homophones in other varieties of English. This distinction is also maintained in the Southland region of New Zealand (Gordon & Maclagan, 2004), which, as noted in Chapter 4,

still retains another historical feature of BrE, rhoticity. In Task 5.9M, you can listen to the IrE speaker say *witch* and *which* – he has a noticeable /h/ at the beginning of *which*, in contrast to the speaker of CanE, who pronounces the two words as homophones.

5.6   CHECK YOUR UNDERSTANDING

EXERCISES

(a) Now that we have introduced the vowel and consonant phonemes of English, we can try our hand at phonemic and phonetic transcription. In phonemic transcription, we are concerned with the vowel and consonant phonemes that occur in words – we can transcribe *eat* as /iːt/, for example. We use slant brackets to show this is an idealized pronunciation, with only the vowel and consonant phonemes shown. Importantly, it does not show us the actual realization of the vowel and the consonant – the actual phone of each phoneme. We know that, in some varieties of English, a vowel is shortened before a voiceless consonant; we also know that /t/ may have different realizations in different environments. If we want to show how a speaker actually pronounces the word *eat*, we have to use phonetic transcription, using diacritics and square brackets. As a speaker of GAmE, I would produce *eat* as [iˑt], with a slightly shorter vowel length.

Your turn: Try to transcribe each of the following words into, first, a phonemic transcription, and then a phonetic transcription based on how you would say the word. This may be different from how your classmates pronounce the words.

speak
man
fine
that
pill

(b) How many ways can you transcribe the following words, based on different phonemic and phonetic inventories in varieties of English? For example, the word *three* can be transcribed as (among other ways):

Word	Transcription 1	Transcription 2	Transcription 3
three	θɹi	tʰɹi	fɹi
Varieties:	AmE, Mod RP	MalE	HKE, NBrE
Features:	Dental fricative	TH-stopping	TH-fronting

Give one example of a **variety** of English for each transcription of each word. Try to find at least three realizations, written in phonetic transcription, of each word.

Word	Transcription 1	Transcription 2	Transcription 3
pill			
Varieties			
Features			
zoo			
Varieties			
Features			
fit			
Varieties			
Features			

DISCUSSION QUESTIONS

(a) Which consonants are more common cross-linguistically and also across varieties of English?

(b) Which consonants are less common cross-linguistically and across varieties of English?

(c) Why are some consonants more common and others less common? Can you think of articulatory (how difficult/easy they are to articulate) and acoustic (how easy/hard they are to hear) reasons why some consonants are more or less common than others?

EXPAND YOUR UNDERSTANDING

Throughout this chapter, as well as in Chapter 3, we have discussed the phonemic inventories of varieties of English, as well as cross-linguistic inventories. As we noted in both this chapter and Chapter 3, some vowels and consonants are more common cross-linguistically, probably because they are easier articulatorily and more salient acoustically. If you were to invent your own language, which vowels/consonants would you select?

(a) Which vowels would your language have (you should reference the IPA vowel chart in Chapter 3). Select at least five vowels. Explain why you selected these vowels.

(b) Which consonants would your language have (you should reference the IPA consonant chart in this chapter)? Select at least ten consonants. Explain why you selected these consonants.

(c) Construct at least ten words using your vowel and consonant inventories. What does each word mean?

(d) Give at least one allophone for your vowels and one for any of the consonants. What is the phonological rule for each allophone?

(e) Finally, give your language a name!

For example, in my language, which I call Hansenish, I have the word *bunta* – /bʌnta/ – (in my language, I have the vowels /ʌ a/, and others, and the consonants /b t n/ and others). This is phonetically transcribed to [bʌndã] – in my language, /t/ is voiced to [d] after a nasal, and vowels are nasalized if there is a preceding nasal in the word. The meaning of the word is *button*. This is a real Hansenish word in my family language (my familect). When my daughter was very young, she called a belly button a *belly bunta*. We still refer to belly buttons as *belly buntas* in our house.

ANALYSE YOUR OWN PRONUNCIATION

In Appendix A, you will find the instructions on how to record a word list for consonants.

(a) What other languages do you speak? What is the consonant inventory of the languages? You may need to do some online research to access this information.

(b) What variety of English do you think you speak? What are the consonants of your variety?

(c) What predictions can you make about your own consonant inventory?

(d) How many consonant phonemes can you identify in your own English? Why do you think you have this number of consonants? What do you think are the main influences on your English consonants?

(e) Do you have any of the features discussed in this chapter, including short- or long-lag VOT (aspiration), /l r w n/ conflation, TH/DH-fronting, TH/DH-stopping? In your opinion, why do you have these features?

(f) Which vowel and consonant phonemes and allophones can you find in your English, based on your transcription of your pronunciation of the words in Appendix A?

6 | English Syllable Structure

TASK 6.1 PRE-READING

How many of the following consonants can you add to the beginning and the end of words to create real English words? You can use any vowel.

Consonant phonemes: /s p t l r/

Example words: *tree*, *let*

- Which sound combinations are allowed together at the beginning/ends of words?
- Which combinations are not allowed? (For example, can you find an English word that begins with 'str'? What about 'stl'?)
- What is the maximum number of consonants you can group together at the beginning of a word? At the end of a word?

6.1   Introduction to the Chapter

In this chapter, we move from discussing English **segmentals** – individual consonant and vowel sounds – to **suprasegmentals**, the units of sound above the level of the segment. This includes stress, pitch, and tone, and extends above individual vowels and consonants to syllables, words, phrases, and sentences. At the core of our discussion of suprasegmentals is the **syllable**, which can be defined as a unit of organization for sound sequences. Every word is made up of minimally one syllable; in some languages, including English, words often contain multiple syllables.

We begin the chapter by examining what we mean by 'syllable', and the components of a syllable including the **onset, nucleus**, and **coda**. We then examine syllable inventories cross-linguistically, with a special focus on the languages that influence varieties of English. An overview of English syllable structure is then provided, with a focus on how syllable structure varies across varieties of English. In the final section of the chapter, you will be guided through exercises designed to check your understanding of the content of the chapter and to analyse your own English syllable inventory.

6.2   Defining the Syllable

TASK 6.2 Listening for Syllables

🎧 Listen to the speakers of SA AusE, CanE, KenE, and SgE say the following words:

teacher	*act*	*telephone*	*happy*
unhappy	*visionary*	*king*	*congratulate*

- How many syllables are there in each word?
- How do you know? (What are you listening for to help you determine the number of syllables?)

What is a syllable? You may have noted that both *act* and *king* are one-syllable words, while *teacher* and *happy* have two syllables, *telephone* and *unhappy* have three, and *congratulate* and *visionary* have four syllables each. How did you know? A simple trick is to clap for each beat that you hear in the word. In *act* and *king*, there is only one beat or clap, while in *happy* and *teacher* there are two. For both *happy* and *teacher*, there is a short break within each word; this break is a syllable boundary. If we transcribe each of these words phonemically, we can use a period (or full stop) to denote the syllable boundary (note: we do not need to use phonetic transcription to analyse syllables; the transcriptions are based on a GAmE pronunciation of the words). Look closely at each word and the syllables within each word: which kind of sound does every syllable contain?

act	king	happy	teacher	telephone	unhappy	congratulate	visionary
/ækt/	/kɪŋ/	/hæp.i/	/tiː.tʃɚ/	/tel.ə.foʊn/	/ʌn.hæp.i/	/kən.grætʃ.ə.leɪt/	/vɪʒ.ə.ner.i/

In all the words, each syllable has a vowel; in fact, a syllable is required to have a vowel or vowel-like sound; we can say that vowels (or a vowel-like sound) are *obligatory* in syllables. We can further say that each syllable can contain only one vowel (where diphthongs and triphthongs are also considered to be one vowel). This vowel is called the *nucleus* of the syllable – the centre, or core. If each syllable must contain one nucleus, and each syllable can contain *only* one nucleus, we can further state that we can count the number of syllables in a word by the number of nuclei in a word. In *act* and *king*, there is only one nucleus; both words are one-syllable words. In *congratulate*, in contrast, there are four nuclei (including /ə/, a weak vowel, which we will explore more in Chapter 7). This is, therefore, a four-syllable word.

Each syllable above may contain zero (no) consonants before or after the nucleus, or one or more consonants. Unlike vowels, however, consonants are not obligatory in syllables – the words *I* and *eye*, as examples, can be transcribed as /aɪ/, with no consonants before or after the vowel. A number of syllables in the words above also do not contain consonants before or after the vowel nucleus. Consonants, therefore, are *optional* in English syllables. Any consonants that occur before the nucleus in a syllable are called the *onset*, the beginning, while the consonants that occur after the nucleus are called the *coda*, or finish. If the syllable does not have any consonants before the nucleus, we call it a *zero onset*; this is the case with *act* /ækt/, which has a zero onset before the nucleus, and two consonants, /kt/, in the coda: the consonants after the nucleus. Similarly, if there are no consonants after the nucleus, we call this a *zero coda*, as in the last syllable in *happy* /hæp.i/. Syllables with a zero coda are called open syllables while syllables with a consonant in the coda are called closed syllables. As we saw in Chapter 3 on English vowels, there are differences in some varieties of English about which types of vowels can occur in open or closed syllables; in varieties that have a short/long vowel distinction (e.g., /ɪ/ ~ /iː/, as in *bit* /bɪt/ vs *beat* /biːt/), only vowels that are considered long or tense, as well as diphthongs and triphthongs, can occur in open syllables, such as *tree* /triː/ or *try* /traɪ/. These vowels can also occur in closed syllables as in *beat*. In contrast, short/lax vowels can only occur in closed syllables. These varieties often have weak vowels (see Chapter 7), which are reduced vowels that are not considered vowel phonemes. Weak vowels may occur in open syllables, as in the second syllable of *telephone*, which has the weak vowel /ə/, as shown above. This will be discussed in Chapter 7.

We can use the following notation to represent a syllable: V for vowel, or the nucleus of the syllable, and C for consonant. While VCC represents the syllable structure of *act*, CVC represents the syllable structure of *king* in many varieties of English. Both *happy* and *teacher* have two syllables, and we therefore have to represent the structure of each syllable separately: *happy* has CVC for /hæp/ and a V for /i/. The structure is therefore CVC.V, with the full stop denoting the boundary between syllables. *Teacher* would be CV for the first syllable /tiː/, and CVC for the second syllable for a rhotic speaker /tʃɚ/ and CV for a non-rhotic speaker /tʃə/.

TASK 6.3 Syllable Structure

📖 Using C to represent a consonant and V for a vowel, describe the syllable structure in each syllable of the following words:

telephone	unhappy	congratulate	visionary
/tel.ə.foʊn/	/ʌn.hæp.i/	/kən.grætʃ.ə.leɪt/	/vɪʒ.ə.ner.i/

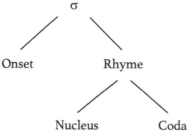

Figure 6.1 Syllable tree

We can draw a simple syllable tree (Figure 6.1) to illustrate syllable structure, with the Greek letter σ, called *sigma*, denoting a syllable.

As the syllable tree shows, the nucleus and coda together comprise a **rhyme** (also called **rime**). You may be familiar with the term 'rhyme' from poetry; when we say two words rhyme, we mean they have a repetition of sound. The repetition of sound is of the vowel and the consonants after the vowel – the nucleus and the coda, which form the rhyme or rime. Only the sounds before the vowel, in the onset, are different. The words *prey*, *may*, *tray*, *stray*, *lay*, *play* all rhyme; while each has a different onset, the rhyme is the same for all the words, as the following possible phonemic transcriptions show:

prey /preɪ/   *may* /meɪ/   *tray* /treɪ/   *stray* /streɪ/   *lay* /leɪ/   *play* /pleɪ/

TASK 6.4 Rhyme

📖 The first stanza of Shakespeare's poem *Venus and Adonis* is given below. Rhyme is often used at the end of sentences. Which words rhyme in this stanza?

> COME away, come away, death,
> And in sad cypres let me be laid;
> Fly away, fly away, breath;
> I am slain by a fair cruel maid.
> My shroud of white, stuck all with yew,
> O prepare it!
> My part of death, no one so true
> Did share it.

We can diagram words using the syllable tree. The word *king*, which may be pronounced as /kɪŋ/, /kiŋ/, or /kɪŋg/, among other ways, depending on the variety of English, has a CVC syllable structure for /kɪŋ/ and /kiŋ/, one

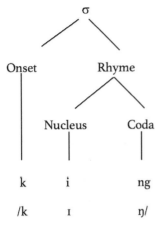

Figure 6.2 Syllable tree of *king*

of the most common syllable structures in the world (for /kɪŋg/, the syllable structure would be CVCC).

6.3 Syllable Structures across Languages

What are the most common syllable structures across languages? While all spoken languages organize sounds by syllables, there is a great deal of variation in syllable structures cross-linguistically. As Maddieson (1984) notes, all languages have a CV syllable structure (as in *he* /hi/ in English), with CV the only allowable syllable structure in some languages, including in Hawaiian, Yareban (Papua New Guinea), and Mba (Democratic Republic of Congo). As Maddieson also notes, some languages have an optional consonant in the onset, symbolized as (C), with an allowable syllable structure of (C)V. This occurs in Fijian (influencing FijE and Ibgo (a substrate language of NigE)). Both CV and (C)V syllable structures are considered simple syllable structures.

CVC and CCV are moderately complex syllable structures. Languages have rules about which consonants, and in which sequence, can occur in an onset and coda. This is called the **phonotactics** of a language. In sequences with two consonants in the onset, the second of the two consonants is often an approximant; we can see this in the English words *tree* /triː/ and *play* /pleɪ/ (Maddieson, 1984). More complex syllable structures involve up to three consonants before the nucleus, as in CCCV, and up to four consonants after the vowel, as in VCCCC, with CCCVCCCC (e.g., in *strengths* /streŋkθs/) a possible structure in some languages, including English.

Of the 486 languages surveyed for syllable structure in WALS, 61, or 13%, have a simple syllable structure; 274, or 56%, have a moderately complex syllable structure; and 151, or 31%, have a complex syllable structure (Maddieson, 2013c). Simpler syllable structures are found in languages closer to the equator, including in Africa, New Guinea, and South America. This includes Kiswahili (influencing KenE), Igbo (influencing NigE), Māori (influencing MāoriE), and Fijian (influencing FijE). A moderately complex syllable structure is common among languages in Africa, the eastern part of Asia, and in Australia; this includes many of the Aboriginal languages in Australia, such as Pitjantjatjara (influencing AusAborE), Filipino (influencing PhlE), Cantonese (influencing HKE and SgE), Mandarin Chinese (influencing SgE and MalE), Spanish (influencing PRE), Zulu (influencing SAE), Hausa (influencing NigE), and Native American languages including Cherokee and Navajo (influencing NAE). Complex syllable structure is found in languages of North America and northern Eurasia, including in Bengali and Hindi (influencing IndE), Native American languages such as Hopi and Lakhota (influencing NAE), and Irish (influencing IrE). While there exists variation in syllable structures and phonotactics across varieties of English, as we will see below, English is considered to have a complex syllable structure.

6.4   English Syllable Structure

Which syllable structures exist in English? As we saw in Task 6.4, English has minimally the following syllable structures: CVC, V, VC, CCVC, with CVC the most common in the words in this table:

telephone	unhappy	congratulate	visionary
/tel.ə.foʊn/	/ʌn.hæp.i/	/kən.grætʃ.ə.leɪt/	/vɪʒ.ə.ner.i/
CVC.V.CVC	VC.CVC.V	CVC.CCVC.V.CVC	CVC.V.CVC.V

In the pre-reading task (Task 6.1), you were asked to create beginnings (onsets) and endings (codas) of real English words using any vowel and the consonants /s p t l r/ in any combination. How many consonants did you arrange in the onset before the vowel nucleus? In the coda after the nucleus? Which combinations of consonants were possible? Which were not possible? You may have created words similar to the ones listed here:

> zero onset: *at, all*
> C onsets*: see, tea, row, pea, leap*
> CC onsets: *tree, plea, sleep, trip*
> CCC onsets: *spree, street, split*
> zero coda: *tea, see, pea*
> C coda: *at, all, sip, pear, loss*
> CC coda: *apt, ask, tilt, tears, leaps, leapt, pulls, trips*
> CCC coda: *asks, tilts*

Based on the five consonant phonemes, /s p t l r/, we can create a zero onset, a single-consonant onset (C), a two-consonant onset (CC), and a three-consonant onset (CCC). For codas, we can create a zero coda, a single-consonant coda (C), a two-consonant coda (CC), and a three-consonant coda (CCC). As we noted above, English syllable structure is complex, with the following onsets and codas possible (note: a four-consonant coda is possible in some words, as in *texts* or /teksts/):

Onsets	Codas
Zero	Zero
C	C
CC	CC
CCC	CCC
	CCCC

Syllables can have both complex onsets and complex codas, with the possible English syllables shown in Table 6.1.

Table 6.1 Possible English syllable structures

Syllable structure	Example word	Possible transcription
V	I	/aɪ/
CV	tea	/tiː/
CCV	tree	/triː/
CCCV	stray	/streɪ/
VC	at	/æt/
VCC	ask	/æsk/
VCCC	asks	/æsks/
VCCCC	*ersts	*/eɪsts/
CVC	leap	/liːp/
CCVC	sleep	/sliːp/
CCCVC	street	/striːt/
CVCC	task	/tæsk/
CVCCC	tasks	/tæsks/
CVCCCC	bursts	/bɜːɹsts/
CCVC	trip	/trɪp/
CCVCC	trips	/trɪps/
CCVCCC	prints	/prɪnts/
CCVCCCC	*blursts	*/blɜːɹsts/
CCCVC	street	/striːt/
CCCVCC	sprint	/sprɪnt/
CCCVCCC	sprints	/sprɪnts/
CCCVCCCC	strengths	/streŋkθs/

*These are possible syllable structures but lack exemplars in English. We can construct possible words such as *ersts* and *blursts* for a rhotic speaker of English.

Can all consonants occur in the onset of a syllable and in the coda of a syllable? As with all languages, English has a series of rules that govern which consonants, how many, and in which order, can occur in the onset and the coda of a syllable. These are called the *phonotactic rules* governing the syllable structure of a language. It is important to note that, while many Englishes follow the same phonotactic rules, some Englishes, as we will see below, have less complex syllable structures and more restrictive rules regarding which consonants can occur together in an onset and coda. We will explore this below.

TASK 6.5 English Onsets and Codas

📖 Based on the onsets in the words given below, can you create rules governing in which order consonants can occur in CC and CCC onsets in English?

CC: *steep, spin, skin, black, cream, twin, prey*
CCC: *street, splint, sprint, scream*

As you can see in *street, splint, sprint, scream*, CCC onsets have the voiceless alveolar stop /s/ as the first sound. This is followed by one of the voiceless stops, /p t k/, and then one of the four approximants, /r l w j/. This is a phonotactic rule in many varieties of English: this means we can create the possible CCC onsets in English shown in Table 6.2 (based on Roach, 2009). Note: there is variation across varieties in the realization of /sCj/ clusters such as /stj/ in *stew*, as will be discussed in more detail below, with either yod dropping (deletion of /j/ in a Cj or CCj onset) or yod coalescence (assimilation of /dj tj sj zj/ to [dʒ tʃ ʃ ʒ]), as well as /stj/ to [ʃt] in some varieties of English.

As you can note, the combinations /stl/, /spw/, and /stw/ are not possible in English; while /skl/ does occur in *sclerosis*, it is rare.

Table 6.2 CCC onsets in English				
/s/ plus:	/l/	/r/	/w/	/j/**
/p/	spl splint	spr spring	*	spew
/t/	*	str street	*	stew
/k/	skl sclerosis	skr script	skw square	skewer

*not possible; **variation across varieties of English

TASK 6.6 Listening for CCC Onsets

🎧 Listen to the speakers of Calif AmE, Mod RP, KenE, and SA AusE pronounce the CCC onsets in the words in Table 6.2.

You may notice that the speakers have vowel differences in some of the words.

- Can you notice the FLEECE/KIT merger for the speaker of KenE, as well as the TRAP/BATH merger for the speaker of Calif AmE?
- Can you hear the Calif AmE speaker pronounce the /stj/ cluster as [st] (she has yod dropping in this cluster)? You can compare this to her pronunciation of /skj/ in *skewer* and /spj/ in *spew*, where she pronounces the /j/.
- You might also hear yod coalescence for the Mod RP and SA AusE speakers for /stj/ to [ʃt].
- The KenE speaker, in contrast, pronounces /j/ as [i].

What about CC and C onsets? If we examine the words in Task 6.5 – *steep, spin, skin, black, cream, twin, prey* – we can see that the CC onsets form the building blocks of CCC onsets, either /s/ plus /p t k/, as in *steep, spin, skin*, or a consonant plus /r l w j/, as in *black, twin, prey*. This gives us two possible combinations for CC onsets: (a) /s/ plus a consonant; or (b) a consonant plus an approximant. There are more combinations for CC onsets than CCC onsets, with the combinations in Tables 6.3 and 6.4 possible (based on Roach, 2009).

The second combination is any of the consonants in Table 6.4 plus /l r w j/ (note: some combinations are not possible or are very rare, as marked by *) (based on Roach, 2009).

TASK 6.7 Listening for CC Onsets

🎧 Listen to the speakers of Calif AmE, Mod RP, KenE, and SA AusE pronounce CC onsets for some of the words in Tables 6.3 and 6.4.

- Do any of the speakers have yod dropping or yod coalescence for any of the /Cj/ clusters? Which clusters and which speakers?

Table 6.3 /s/ plus consonant onsets in English

	/p/	/t/	/k/	/f/	/n/	/m/
/s/	spy	start	sky	sphere	snow	Smurf

Table 6.4 Consonant plus /l r w j/ onsets in English

	/l/	/r/	/w/	/j/**
/p/	play	pry	*	pew
/t/	*	try	twin	tune
/k/	clean	cream	queen	queue
/b/	blue	breath	*	beauty
/d/	*	dream	dwell	dew
/g/	gloves	green	*Gwen	*gules
/f/	fly	fry	*	few
/θ/	*	throat	thwack	*
/s/	sleep	*Sri Lanka	swam	shoo
/ʃ/	*	shriek	*schwa	*
/h/	*	*	*	huge
/v/	*	*	*	view
/m/	*	*	*	music
/n/	*	*	*	news
/l/	*	*	*	lewd

*rare or not possible in English; **variation across varieties of English
(*Source:* based on Roach, 2009)

You may notice that the Calif AmE speaker has yod dropping for /tj/ and /dj/, while the Mod RP speaker has yod coalescence for both; the SA AusE speaker has yod dropping in /dj/ and coalescence in /tj/. The KenE speaker pronounces /j/ as [i]. None of the speakers has a /lj/ or a /nj/ cluster, pronouncing the onset as [l] or [n], respectively (the KenE speaker pronounces /lj/ and /nj/ as [li] and [ni], respectively).

For C onsets, all English consonants can occur in an onset with the exception of /ŋ/ (and /ʒ/ is rare and occurs only in borrowed words such as *genre* from French, which may also be pronounced with /dʒ/ for some speakers).

TASK 6.8 Listening for C Onsets

🎧 Listen to the speakers of Calif AmE, Mod RP, KenE, and SA AusE pronounce all the C onsets in keywords.

- Can you hear the [n] in *low*, for the KenE speaker?
- Only the Calif AmE and KenE speakers have /ʒ/ in *genre*.

English consonant codas also follow phonotactic rules; all English consonants can occur syllable-finally, in the coda, with the exception of

/h j w/. This gives us the following possible C codas (note: not all Englishes have these consonants, as we saw in Chapter 5, and therefore not all these C codas):

Stops:	/p/	/b/	/t/	/d/	/k/	/g/		
	stop	*rob*	*late*	*sad*	*back*	*bag*		
Fricatives:	/s/	/z/	/f/	/v/	/θ/	/ð/	/ʃ/	/ʒ/
	kiss	*buzz*	*leaf*	*leave*	*bath*	*bathe*	*wish*	*beige*
Affricates:	/tʃ/	/dʒ/						
	which	*edge*						
Nasals:	/m/	/n/	/ŋ/					
	some	*can*	*sing*					
Approximants:	/l/	/r/						
	tall	*bear*						

TASK 6.9 Listening for C Codas

🎧 Listen to the speakers of Calif AmE, Mod RP, KenE, and SA AusE pronounce C codas for the examples given.

- Which speakers have a C coda in *bear*?
- Which speakers have a zero coda instead?
- Why is there a difference among speakers for this coda?

CC codas in English come in two forms: (a) /m n ŋ l s/ plus a consonant; or (b) a consonant plus /s z t d θ/. This creates the following codas (based on Roach, 2009):

(a) /m n ŋ l s/, with /r/ included for rhotic Englishes, plus a consonant:

  Examples: /ŋk/ *think* /lt/ *salt* /nt/ *point* /nd/ *hand* /mp/ *grump* /st/ *last* /rt/ *start*

(b) a consonant plus /s z t d θ/:

  Examples: /ft/ *lift* /ld/ *peeled* /ks/ *bikes* /vd/ *loved* /nθ/ *month* /gz/ *dogs*

TASK 6.10 Listening for CC Codas

🎧 Listen to the speakers of Calif AmE, Mod RP, KenE, and SA AusE pronounce CC codas for the examples given.

- Which speakers have a CC cluster in *start*?
- Which speakers have a C coda instead?
- Why is there a difference among speakers for this cluster?

The CC coda rules form the building blocks of CCC codas. CCC codas come in two forms: /m n ŋ l s r/ plus a consonant plus /s z t d θ/ (a combination of both CC rules); and (b) consonant plus /s z t d θ/ plus /s z t d θ/.

(a) /m n ŋ l r s/ plus a consonant plus /s z t d θ/

Examples: /ntʃt/ *lunched* /lkt/ *milked* /lks/ *milks* /mps/ *bumps* /rnz/ *turns*

(b) consonant plus /s z t d θ/ plus /s z t d θ/

Examples: /nθs/ *months* /sks/ *flasks* /sts/ *lasts* /ksθ/ *sixth* /kst/ *taxed*

In most varieties of English, **Consonant Cluster Reduction (CCR)** or simplification is a natural process that occurs, typically in faster speech. In this process, some consonants are deleted in order for the speech to be more fluent. This occurs more often when the next word begins with the same consonant (as in *first time*, where the /t/ in *first* may be deleted); both /t/ and /d/ are often deleted in fast speech when they are word-final in the cluster (this is called /t d/ deletion and is discussed in more detail below) or when they occur in the middle of a cluster (medially – as in /CtC/, /CdC/), in words such as *lasts* /sts/ or *wands* /ndz/. CCR occurs across most, if not all, varieties of English in fast speech.

TASK 6.11 Listening for CCC Codas

🎧 Listen to the speakers of Calif AmE, Mod RP, KenE, and SA AusE pronounce CCC codas for the examples given.

- Which speakers have a CCC cluster in *turns*?
- Which speakers have a CC cluster instead?
- Why is there a difference among speakers for this cluster?
- Can you hear CCR in the /sts/ coda for the Calif AmE speaker in *lasts*?

The CCCC rules combine both CCC rules to form two types of clusters: (a) /m n ŋ l r s/ plus a consonant plus /s z t d θ/ plus /s z t d θ/, or (b) a consonant plus /s z t d θ/ plus /s z t d θ/ plus /s z t d θ/.

Examples: /lfθs/ *twelfths* /ksts/ *texts* /mpts/ *prompts* /ksθs/ *sixths* /rldz/ *worlds*

TASK 6.12 Listening for CCCC Codas

🎧 Listen to the speakers of Calif AmE, Mod RP, KenE, and SA AusE pronounce CCCC codas for the examples given.

- Which speakers have a CCCC cluster in *worlds*?
- Which speakers have a CCC cluster instead?
- Why is there a difference among speakers for this cluster?
- Can you hear CCR in the /ksts/ coda for the Calif AmE and KenE speaker in *texts*?
- Can you hear CCR in the /ksθs/ coda for the speakers of Calif AmE, SA AusE, and Mod RP?

As you saw in Tasks 6.9–6.12, varieties (and/or speakers) of English that are non-rhotic will not have final C codas with /r/, or CC, CCC, CCCC clusters where the first consonant in the coda is /r/.

TASK 6.13 Cluster Rules

📖 Why do you think /s z t d θ/ are common final consonants in CC, CCC, and CCCC clusters? Let's look at some words that end with /s z t d θ/. Which function do these sounds perform in these words?

/s/: *asks, walks, tips, cats, books*
/z/: *runs, drives, dogs, beds, words*
/t/: *talked, helped*
/d/: *planned, jumped*
/θ/: *fifth, twelfth, hundredth*

You may have noticed that /s z t d θ/ have a grammatical function in the words given in Task 6.13; /s z/ are used to inflect words for third person singular as well as plural (and the possessive/genitive case as in *John's*); /t d/ inflect for regular past tense; and /θ/ is used for ordinal numbers in contrast to cardinal numbers, such as *five* vs *fifth*, *twelve* vs *twelfth*, and *hundred* vs *hundredth*. These endings are morphophonemic – morphological endings that carry grammatical meaning but are realized phonologically.

6.5   Polysyllabic English Words

How many syllables can English words have? English words have a minimum of one syllable, which can be as short as a V syllable, as in *eye* /aɪ/, or as long as a CCCVCCCC syllable, as in *strengths*, /strɛŋkθts/ in some varieties of English. While *eye* has a zero onset and a zero coda, and *strengths* has the maximum allowable number of consonants in the onset (three) and coda (four) in any variety of English, both syllables have one nucleus and therefore both are one-syllable words. As this shows, the number of syllables in words does not depend on the number of consonants; rather, as explained above, it is based on the number of nuclei in the word. There are many polysyllabic words in English, with two, three, and four syllables common.

act	king	happy	teacher	telephone	unhappy	congratulate	visionary
/ækt/	/kɪŋ/	/hæp.i/	/tiː.tʃə/	/tel.ə.foʊn/	/ʌn.hæp.i/	/kən.grætʃ.ə.leɪt//	/vɪʒ.ə.ner.i/

How do we know where the syllable boundary is in a word? In the polysyllabic words given above, a syllable boundary is marked with a full stop [.]. In *happy*, for example, the syllable boundary is between the /p/ and the /i/, creating /hæp.i/. But how do we know this is the correct boundary? Sometimes we can hear where the boundary is – where the break is between syllables in words. If you say *congratulate*, for example, you may be able to hear that you stop after /kən/ and then after /grætʃ/ and /ə/ and /leɪt/. Where do you hear the syllable boundary for *basket*? You may hear a break between the /s/ and the /k/, leaving a syllabification of *basket* as /bæs.kət/. Another rule of thumb is to avoid creating onsets and codas that are not possible in English – to follow English phonotactic rules. If we have the word *abstract* as an example, and transcribe it as /æbstrækt/, we can note it has two vowels and therefore two nuclei, making it a two-syllable word (which we can hear as well, if we pronounce it out loud). Where would we place the syllable boundary? You may be able to hear a syllable break between /b/ and /s/, placing the boundary as follows: /æb.strækt/. Does this follow English phonotactic rules? This syllabification creates a coda in the first syllable of /b/ and an onset in the second syllable of /str/, which is allowable in English. If we moved the syllable boundary between the vowel and the /b/, would this be possible in English – /æ.bstrækt/? You may note this breaks English phonotactic rules in two ways – one, it creates a four-member onset of /bstr/, which is not possible in English. It also creates an onset with a string of consonants in an order which is not possible in English.

To understand the phonotactic constraints of English and other languages, it is helpful to know about the principle of sonority. Sonority can be defined as the relative loudness of a speech sound in comparison to other sounds with the same pitch, stress, and length (Ladefoged & Johnson, 2014). In other words, some speech sounds are louder than other speech sounds, all else being equal.

The Sonority Sequencing Principle (SSP) (Clements, 1990), which is often employed to explain phonotactic constraints in English and other languages, states that: every syllable contains exactly one peak of sonority,

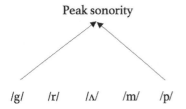

/g/ /r/ /ʌ/ /m/ /p/

Figure 6.3 Sonority hierarchy of *grump*

contained in the nucleus (Parker, 2011, p. 2). Peak sonority is in the nucleus of a syllable, in the vowel or vowel-like sounds; sonority rises in the onset, reaching a peak in the nucleus, and then falling in the coda. In the word *grump* for example (see Figure 6.3), we can see a rise in sonority from the first sound in the onset, /g/, which is less sonorous than /r/, to the peak in the vowel nucleus, falling in the coda from /m/, which is more sonorous than /p/.

For this reason, a /gr/ onset and /mp/ coda are considered to be well formed, as they conform to the SSP. Though there are tendencies cross-linguistically to conform to SSP in phonotactics and syllabification, some languages violate the SSP for some onsets and codas. English, as an example, has numerous onsets and codas that violate the SSP, including CC and CCC onsets that begin with /s/ (as the following stop consonant is less sonorous than /s/), and codas ending with /s z/, as in /sks/ in *flasks* and /sts/ in *tests*.

Cross-linguistically, onsets are preferred over codas, and zero onsets and closed codas are disfavoured; for example, in a sequence of VCV, most languages of the world would break down the syllables in the sequence as V.CV rather than VC.V, to create an onset rather than a coda (Steriade, 2002).

The preference for onsets over codas is often expressed as the Maximum Onset Principle (MOP), a principle for assigning consonants between nuclei as onsets or codas. The MOP states that the onset should be assigned as many consonants as possible without violating phonotactic constraints. In some varieties of English, this includes not allowing short/lax vowels to be in open syllables, and conforming to the English onset and coda rules, including in number and order. Looking again at our polysyllabic words from Task 6.3, how can the MOP plus English phonotactic constraints help explain the example syllable-boundary parsing in each word?

happy	teacher	telephone	unhappy	congratulate	visionary
/hæp.i/	/tiː.tʃə/	/tel.ə.foʊn/	/ʌn.hæp.i/	/kən.grætʃ.ə.leɪt/	/vɪʒ.ə.ner.i/

In the examples, a GAmE transcription is given. In *happy* /hæp.i/, the vowel is a short vowel and therefore it requires a closed syllable (and therefore a coda). In *teacher* /tiː.tʃɚ/, we can maximize the onset and place /tʃ/ as the onset of the second syllable. In *unhappy* /ʌn.hæp.i/ both /ʌ/ and /æ/ are short vowels and require a coda; in *congratulate* /kən.grætʃ.ə.leɪt/ /æ/ requires a coda. While /ə/ is considered a weak vowel (see Chapter 7) and does not require a coda, we cannot create an onset with the cluster /ngr/ and therefore /n/ becomes a coda of the first syllable while /gr/ is the onset of the second. The fourth syllable is given the onset /l/. In *visionary* /vɪʒ.ə.ner.i/, both /ɪ/ and /e/ require codas.

Discussions of the MOP for English have focused on OVEs. It is not clear whether it is applicable to all varieties of English, given the differences in varieties in syllable inventories, long/short or tense/lax vowels, and weak/strong vowels and syllables (see Chapter 7). As with the SSP, the MOP is best seen as a tendency for syllabification in varieties of English, dependent on variety-specific phonotactic rules.

6.6   Syllable Structures across Varieties of English

Do all Englishes have the same syllable structures? Many of the languages that influence varieties of English have simpler syllable structures, as we saw above; as a result, there are differences in the types of syllable onsets and codas allowed in varieties of English. While many OVEs – including non-ethnic varieties of AmE, CanE, BrE, AusE, NZE, JamE, among others – have the syllable structures detailed above, many NVEs as well as ethnic varieties of OVEs may have simpler or moderately complex syllable structures due to substrate influences. In addition, variation in the realization of syllable structures, and particularly syllable codas, exists across all Englishes.

TASK 6.14 Listening for Syllable Structures in Varieties of English

🎧 Listen to the speakers of HKE, NBrE, NepE, SLE, ZimE, and MalE pronounce the following onset and coda clusters:

Onsets: /st/ *stay* /str/ *stray*
Codas: /mp/ *bump* /lfθ/ *twelfth* /ksθs/ *sixths*

- Do the speakers pronounce all the consonants in each cluster?
- Are other sounds pronounced before or within each cluster?

In Task 6.14, you may have heard differences in how the different speakers realized the CC and CCC onsets and codas; for both *stay* and *stray*, for example, the SLE speaker added a vowel sound before the /s/, so that the words sounded like *istay* and *istray*; this also makes the words *stay* and *stray* two-syllable words for the SLE speaker, as the words have two vowels, or nuclei. A vowel was also inserted between the /t/ and the /w/ in *twelfth* by the NepE speaker, so it sounded like *tuwelfth* (this also creates a two-syllable word for the NepE speaker). Vowel insertion is known as **vowel epenthesis** when it occurs between two consonants, as in *tuwelfth* for the NepE speaker, and **vowel prothesis** when it occurs before the first consonant in the onset, as in *istay* and *istray* for the SLE speaker. It can also occur at the end of a word, at the coda; you can hear this in *twelfth* for the MalE speaker (also creating a two-syllable word). It is called **vowel paragoge** when it occurs syllable- or word-finally. You may also have heard CCR; this can be heard on *sixths* and *twelfth* for the NepE speaker. Both processes occur in many varieties of English to resolve differences in onset and coda length and phonotactic constraints between the substrate language(s) and the English superstrate variety or varieties. As discussed above, CCR is also frequent as a simplification process in many varieties of English that have complex clusters, usually during faster and/or more casual speech. Other speech processes, including substitution due to assimilation effects, are also common across varieties of English. We will look at each of these processes, as well as other phonological processes in syllable realization, below. A summary of the different processes is given in Table 6.5, with reference to listening tasks for each type of variation.

☞ The following discussion of syllable structure variation is intended to provide a comprehensive overview of the syllables in Englishes worldwide.

Although you are encouraged to listen to different types of syllable structure variation, you may wish to focus your attention on the variation that occurs in the Englishes that are of interest to you.

In Table 6.5, you can find a list of varieties in which variation has been found. It may be useful to refer to this list to help guide your reading and listening.

TASK 6.15 Listening for Syllable Structure Variation

🎧 In Task 6.15, you can listen to a range of speakers of different varieties of English illustrate syllable structure variation.

These features and speakers are listed in Table 6.5.

Table 6.5 Syllable structure variation

Rule	Examples	Varieties of English	🎧 Listening Task 6.15: Syllable Structure Variation
Vowel epenthesis: insertion of vowel between consonants	*store → sitoa* *cream → kirimu* *film → filam*	AusAborE, FijE, IndE, PakE, EAfE, NigE, NBrE, SgE	(A) NepE, SgE
Vowel prothesis: insertion of vowel before first consonant in an onset	*stay → istay*	SLE, IndE, PakE, NepE, PhlE	(B) SLE, PakE, NepE
Vowel paragoge: insertion of vowel at the end of a word	*sent → senti*	EAfE, SAfE, HKE, MalE	(C) HKE, MalE
Consonant Cluster Reduction	*start → tart* *desk → des* *limp → lim* *self → sef*	AusAborE, FijE, NigE, EAfE, BSAE, AAVE, CaribE, ChiE, IndE, PhlE, SgE, MalE, HKE, NepE, EMidBrE Universal across varieties of English in fast speech	(D) Calif AmE, SA AusE, Mod RP, KenE, NepE, MalE, SgE, HKE
/t d/ deletion in word-final codas	*fast → fas* *hand → han*	AusAborE, FijE, NZE, NiuE, AAVE, AmE, ChiE, BrE, ScotE, IrE, CanE, CaribE, HKE, SgE, NigE, MalE, PhlE, WAfE, BSAE	(E) SgE, Midwestern AmE
Yod coalescence, dropping, and retention	Coalescence: /dj tj sj zj/ → [dʒ tʃ ʃ ʒ] Dropping: /nju tju dju/ → [nu tu du]	Coalescence: RP, LonE, Southern BrE, EMidBrE, CanE, AusE, IrE, WSAE Dropping: LonE/Southern BrE (/nj/), Cockney English, WelE, most varieties of AmE, FijE, NigE, AusE	(F) Mod RP, SA AusE, IrE, Calif AmE
NG-coalescence and retention ING-variation	*sing → [sɪŋ]* *swimming, talking → [ɪŋ], [in]*	Retention: NBrE, WMidBrE, Broad AusE, African Englishes, some varieties of AmE Variation: AmE, BrE, ScotE, AusE, AusAborE (/-an/)	(G) Calif, Midwestern, Appal AmE, NBrE
Metathesis	*ask → aks* *grasp → graps*	FijE, NigE, AAVE, SgE, HKE	(H) HKE, SgE
/str/ clusters	/stj/ and /str/ assimilation to [ʃtC]	NZE, NBrE	(I) NZE, NBrE

Vowel insertion: Vowel epenthesis, the insertion of a vowel between consonants, occurs in AusAborE to break up onsets as many of the Aboriginal languages that influence this variety of English have shorter onsets (Butcher, 2008). It also occurs in FijE, with *sitoa* for *store*, *kirimu* for *cream*, and *filam* for *film* common (Tent & Mugler, 2004). The weak vowel /ə/ may also be inserted between /s/ and /k/ in /sk-/ onsets in IndE and PakE (Gargesh & Sailaja, 2017) and between the voiced bilabial stop and alveolar lateral approximant in /bl-/ onsets in PakE, so that *blue* is [bɪlju] (Mahboob & Ahmar, 2004). It may also occur in SgE. In Task 6.15A, you can hear vowel epenthesis for speakers of NepE and SgE for <u>twelfth</u> (vowel inserted between /t/ and /w/) and <u>texts</u> (vowel inserted between /t/ and /s/).

In Southeast Asian varieties of English, including IndE (particularly in North India), NepE, PakE, and SLE, the initial CC clusters /sp-/, /st-/, /sk-/, as well as CCC beginning with /s/, are not tolerated and are resolved by insertion of [i] before the cluster, or vowel prothesis – so *station* becomes *istation* and *sloth* becomes *isloth* (Bobda, 2001; Gargesh & Sailaja, 2017). Consonant clusters are also rare in PhlE due to influence from Filipino, with the favouring of V, CV, VC, and CVC syllables in PhlE; like other Southeast Asian Englishes, onset clusters with /s/ are often simplified through [i] insertion before the /s/, so that *start* is *istart* (Tayao, 2004). In Task 6.15B, you can hear speakers of SLE, PakE, and NepE insert a vowel before /s/ in <u>spit</u>, <u>split</u>, <u>stay</u>, <u>stray</u>, <u>strop</u>, <u>square</u>.

In EAfE, plosive + plosive codas such as /kt/, /gd/, are resolved through the insertion of a vowel between the consonants; vowel insertion of [ɪ ʊ] also occurs after a C coda so *book* is [bʊkʊ] (Schmied, 2004). In NigE, consonant clusters in the coda (and CCC in the onset) are also disfavoured, and resolved through insertion of [u] or [i] (Gut, 2004). In South India varieties of English, vowels may be inserted in /nst/ codas so that *against* is [ageːnəst] (Gargesh, 2004). Vowel insertion between /l/ and nasals also occurs in codas in NBrE (Beal, 2004). Vowel paragoge, the insertion of a vowel at the end of a coda, also occurs in many varieties of English, including HKE, MalE, and PakE. Vowel paragoge may also occur in EAfE and SAfE at the end of a cluster in a coda, so that *sent* becomes *senti* (Bobda, 2003). In Task 6.15C, you can hear speakers of HKE and MalE insert a vowel at the end of the coda in *sixths, twelfths*.

Consonant Cluster Reduction: CCR is a common process across varieties of English. It occurs in both onsets and codas in AusAborE (Butcher, 2008), FijE (Tent, 2001), NZE, and NiuE (Starks, Christie, & Thompson, 2007); it also occurs widely in EAfE, as many African languages have strict phonotactic rules and only allow CV syllables, and consonant clusters are resolved through CCR and/or vowel insertion (Schmied, 2004). In NigE, some syllable structures never occur, including CCC onsets, and CCC and CCCC codas (Gut, 2004). Word-initial clusters are also disfavoured in some varieties of CaribE, changing *start* to *tart*, and *stop* to *top* (Aceto, 2009). While onset clusters may be allowed in SAE, /r/ may be deleted in onset clusters for speakers of BSAE (Van Rooy, 2004). The onset cluster /kw/ is often reduced to /k/ in NigE (Gut, 2004). In EMidBrE, CCR may occur both word-finally and word-medially, so that *exactly* becomes [ɛzakli] and *asked* becomes [ast] (Braber & Robinson, 2018). As noted above, CCR is also a fast speech phenomenon that is universal across varieties of English (see Tasks 6.11 and 6.12).

In AAVE, final CCR may occur when a coda cluster ends a monomorphemic word and the next word begins with a consonant, so we have deletion of *left* to *lef*, *desk* to *des* (Edwards, 2004). CCR also occurs more frequently in ChiE than other varieties of English; final consonants can also be deleted in ChiE when they are not in a cluster, so that *night* becomes [nai] (Fought, 2006). In EAfE, plosives are deleted in final position in codas if the preceding consonant is a fricative (Schmied, 2004). Final clusters are resolved in IndE through deletion of the final consonant (Gargesh & Sailaja, 2017); this also occurs in NepE. In final clusters with /s/ plus consonants in PhlE, the final consonant is dropped (Tayao, 2004). While SgE allows CCC onsets, it only allows CC or CCC clusters in the coda, with reduction – such as *texts* to [teks] – often occurring to resolve CCCC clusters (Wee, 2004). Final stops are deleted after continuants (nasals or approximants) in clusters such as /mt mp nt/ so that *sent* is *sen* and *limp* is *lim* (Wee, 2004). CCR is also common in MalE, with CCC reduced to CC medially or finally, as in *glimpse* /mps/ to [ms], and *amidst* /dst/ to [ds]; /l/ is often deleted if it is the first consonant of a cluster, so *self* is *sef* (Baskaran, 2004). Final TH is also often lost in clusters in MalE, so that *sixth* is *six* (Baskaran, 2004); the final consonant in CC clusters may also be deleted (Hashim, 2020). CCR also occurs in HKE (Hansen Edwards, 2016c). In Task 6.15D, you can hear CCR for speakers of SgE, HKE, Calif AmE, MalE, SA AusE, Mod RP, and KenE in the following words: *bumps* (/p/ deleted in /mps/ coda); *fifth, grump* (final consonant deleted: /θ/ in /fθ/ coda and /p/ in /mp/ coda); *flasks* (SgE: final consonant deleted: /s/ in /sks/; HKE: last two consonants deleted: /ks/ in /sks/); *grump* (/p/ deleted in /mp/ coda); *hiked* (/k/ deleted in /kt/ coda); *lasts* (/t/ deleted in /sts/ coda); *salt* (/l/ deleted in /lt/ coda); *sixth* (/θ/ deleted in /ksθ/ coda); *texts* (/ts/ deleted in /ksts/ coda); *sixth* (/θs/ deleted in /ksθs/ coda).

/t d/ deletion is a type of CCR that occurs frequently in syllable codas word-finally across varieties of English, particularly in more casual, conversational speech; it is likely a universal process across varieties of English. It has been found to occur in AusAborE when there is more than one obstruent in a cluster, as in *fast* to *fas*, or after a nasal, as in *hand* to *han* (Butcher, 2008; Malcolm, 2004). This also occurs in FijE (Tent & Mugler, 2004), NZE, NiuE (Starks, Christie, & Thompson, 2007); AAVE (Edwards,

2004); as well as most varieties of AmE (Kretzschmar, 2004), including ChiE (Santa Ana & Bayley, 2004); varieties of BrE (Tagliamonte & Temple, 2005), IrE (Hickey, 2004), ScotE (Smith, Durham, & Fortune, 2009), CanE (Hoffman & Walker, 2010); CaribE (Aceto, 2009); and for NVEs of English including HKE (Hansen Edwards, 2016c), SgE (Gut, 2004), MalE (Baskaran, 2004), PhlE (Tayao, 2004), WAfE (Bobda, 2003), BSAE (Van Rooy, 2004), and NigE (Gut, 2004).

Many varieties of English, including most AmE varieties, favour /t d/ deletion in monomorphemic endings – for example, in *fast* and *hand* – in contrast to past tense endings such as *walked, explained, wept* due to the loss of morphological information in the latter. In some varieties, however, including AAVE, /t d/ deletion occurs even in past tense clusters, so that *I walked to his house yesterday* becomes *I walk to his house yesterday* with the grammatical information given by the context of the sentence (Edwards, 2004). In CaribE, the final /t/ is usually retained when the preceding consonant is a nasal as in *tent* (Aceto, 2009). In Task 6.15E, you can hear /t d/ deletion for speakers of Midwestern AmE and SgE in *field, hand, lapsed, last, lift, point, taxed*, and *wished*.

Yod dropping and coalescence: Yod is the name for the palatal approximant /j/. In onset clusters such as /tj dj sj nj/, referred to as a Cj onset, the /j/ is often deleted (this is referred to as *yod dropping*); in the clusters, /dj tj sj zj/ may undergo coalescence to create [dʒ], [tʃ], [ʃ], and [ʒ], respectively; coalescence means that the two sounds merge into one sound through the processes of assimilation and deletion. This is referred to as *yod coalescence* (see also above). Yod coalescence is a feature of RP English (Upton, 2004) and occurs variably in LonE, Southern BrE, and EMidBrE, and may occur in AusE, IrE, WelE, and CanE (Braber & Robinson, 2018; Wells, 1982). Yod dropping may occur in /nj/ clusters, as in *news* /njuːz/ to [nuːz], in London/Southern BrE (Altendorf & Watt, 2004), and is a feature of Cockney English (Wells, 1982). It also occurs in FijE in /Cju/ syllables (Tent, 2001). In some WAfE, including NigE and Liberian English, yod is inserted in clusters between velars and non-high vowels so that *catch* becomes *cjatch* (Bobda, 2003). Yod dropping may also occur in /hj/ and /pj/ onsets for Igbo speakers of NigE (Gut, 2004). Most AmE varieties prefer yod dropping, with [tu du nu] in *tune, duke, new* common (Kretzschmar, 2004; Thomas, 2004); it is also sometimes deleted in AAVE (Edwards, 2004). Yod has been retained in varieties of SAmE due to a longer period of contact with BrE (Thomas, 2004). Yod is also retained in clusters in ScotE (Stuart-Smith, 2004). In Task 6.15F, you can listen for yod dropping, retention, and coalescence as follows: *beauty, few, music:* /Cj/ yod retention for all four speakers (also notice the flap for /t/ for the Calif AmE speaker in *beauty*); *tune:* yod dropping for the Calif AmE and IrE speakers, and coalescence for the SA AusE and

Mod RP speakers; *dew:* yod dropping for the Calif AmE, SA AusE, and IrE speakers, and coalescence for the Mod RP speaker.

NG-coalescence refers to a historical sound change in which the cluster 'ng', in words such as *sing* and *rang*, became /ŋg/ through assimilation of the /n/ to the following velar; this resulted in a loss of the final /g/ in some varieties of English, with the 'ng' realized as [ŋ]. Across varieties of English, NG-coalescence is common. Retention of /g/ occurs in some varieties of English, such as NBrE and EMidBrE (Beal, 2004 – see also discussion of /ŋ/ in NBrE in Chapter 5; Braber & Robinson, 2018), including in Manchester English (Baranowski & Turton, 2015), as well as in the West Midlands (Clark, 2004). It also occurs in some varieties of AmE. In Broad AusE, [ŋk] may also be used in words such as *nothing, something, anything, everything* (Burridge, 2004). NG is also often articulated as [ŋg] in many African Englishes due to spelling of <g> in words such as *singer, hanger* (Bobda, 2001).

ING-variation is also common between articulation of ING as [ɪŋ] or [in] in words such as *walking* and *swimming*, with [in] considered a less formal variant of ING. It occurs in varieties of AmE, BrE, ScotE, and AusE, most commonly in progressives (e.g., *walking, swimming, talking*) (Adamson & Regan, 1991; Schleef, Meyerhoff, & Clark, 2012). In AusAborE, /-an/ is often used in place of /-in/ in words like *singing*, which may be pronounced as *singan* (Malcolm, 2004). In Task 6.15G, you can hear two speakers of AmE pronounce *singer* and *hanger*. One of the speakers (Midwestern AmE) has retained the /g/ and pronounces both words with a [ŋg] for <-ng>, whereas the other speaker (Calif AmE) has NG-coalescence and pronounces the <-ng> as [ŋ]. You can also hear NG retention for the speaker of NBrE for *sing*, which she pronounces as [sĩŋg]. You can also hear the Appal AmE speaker talk about ING-variation.

Metathesis refers to the transposition of two sounds in a word: when two consonants in a syllable are put into a different order. Metathesis occurs for /ks/ in FijE (Tent & Mugler, 2004) and NigE (Gut, 2004), so that *ask* is realized as *aks*. It also occurs in AAVE in /s/ + stop clusters like /sk/ and /sp/, so *ask* is *aks* and *grasp* is *graps* (Edwards, 2004). It also occurs in /sp/ codas, which change to [ps], so *lisp* to *lips*, in SgE (Wee, 2004). It may also occur in HKE. In Task 6.15H, you can listen to metathesis of the /sp/ coda to [ps] for speakers of SgE and HKE.

In NZE, as well as NBrE, /str/ and /stj/ clusters may be realized as [ʃtr], [ʃtʃ], respectively, due to a process of assimilation (Bauer & Warren, 2004). You can hear /str/ assimilation for speakers of NZE and NBrE in *straight, street, stray, strop, strip* in Task 6.15I.

6.7   CHECK YOUR UNDERSTANDING

EXERCISES

(a) The following words are given in phonemic transcription. What is the syllable structure for each word? What is a possible English word for each of the transcriptions?

/sprɪŋ/

/hjuːdʒ/

/splæʃt/

/blaɪnd/

/iːt/

/spɪld/

/sneɪk/

/tækst/

/lʌntʃ/

/tiː/

(b) What process does each of the following transcriptions evidence? The processes include: metathesis, CCR, /t d/ deletion, vowel epenthesis, vowel prothesis, vowel paragoge, /str/ assimilation, yod dropping, yod coalescence, NG-retention, ING-variation.

Word	Phonetic realization
risk	[rɪks]
string	[istrɪŋ]
text	[tekəstə]
newt	[nuːt]
walking	[wɔːkin]
tube	[tʃuːb]
string	[sitrɪŋ]
text	[tekstə]
singing	[sɪŋgɪŋ]
text	[teks]

DISCUSSION QUESTIONS

In this chapter, the SSP and the MOP were discussed in relation to syllabification of polysyllabic words. Differences in syllabification exist across varieties of English, however, due to differences in vowel, consonant, and syllable inventories. How would you syllabify the following words? First, transcribe each word phonemically, and then add a period or full stop [.]

to mark where you would place the syllable boundary for each word. What was the basis of your decision for each word?

language
phonetics
phonology
linguistics
symbol
understanding

EXPAND YOUR UNDERSTANDING

In Chapter 5, you determined the consonant and vowel inventories for your invented language. In this chapter, we have examined possible syllable structures in varieties of English. Which syllable structures are possible in your invented language? Specifically:

(a) Which onset clusters would your language have – how many consonants can occur in the onset: zero, C, CC, CCC? Which types of consonants can occur in a C onset, and in which combination can consonants occur in the CC and CCC onsets, if your language has them? Be sure to use only the consonants you selected for your language in Chapter 5.

(b) Which coda clusters would your language have – how many consonants can occur in the coda: zero, C, CC, CCC, CCCC? Which types of consonants can occur in a C coda, and in which combination can consonants occur in the CC, CCC, CCCC coda, if your language has them? Be sure to use only the consonants you selected for your language in Chapter 5.

(c) What is the minimum syllable structure in your language (e.g., V or CV)? What is the maximum syllable structure (e.g., CCCVCCCC)?

(d) What are all the possible syllable structures in your language? Give an example word for each.

(e) How many syllables can a word have in your language? What is the minimum number of syllables and the maximum number of syllables for words in your language?

ANALYSE YOUR OWN PRONUNCIATION

(a) What syllable structures are possible in the languages you speak, other than English? You may need to do some online research to access this information.

(b) What variety of English do you speak? What are the syllable structures in this variety of English?

(c) What predictions can you make about your own syllable structure inventory?

(d) In Appendix A, you will find sample words to illustrate different syllable structures. Following the instructions in Appendix A, record yourself
reading these words and then phonemically and phonetically transcribe
your recordings.

(e) How many syllable structures can you identify in your own English?
Why do you think you have these syllable structures? What do you
think are the main influences on your English syllable structure?

(f) Do you have any of the features discussed in this chapter, including
CCR, /t d/ deletion, vowel epenthesis/prothesis/paragoge, metathesis,
yod dropping/coalescence/retention? Why do you think you have these
features?

7 | English Stress and Rhythm

TASK 7.1 PRE-READING

Listen to the speakers of SA AusE, Mod RP, Calif AmE, IrE, SgE, MalE, SLE, and HKE pronounce the word *record* as a noun (as in the sentence: 'She set a new Olympic *record* in the high jump') versus as a verb, as in the sentence 'She wants to *record* a new music album'). You may notice that some speakers have a slightly different pronunciation of *record* when it is a noun (noted as N), versus as a verb (noted as V).

- Which speakers have a notable difference in their pronunciation of *record* as an N vs a V?
- What is the difference in the pronunciation (what can you hear that is different)?
- Why do you think some speakers/varieties have this difference and others do not?

7.1 Introduction to the Chapter

This chapter will introduce you to the concepts of *stress* and *rhythm* in relation to languages and varieties of English. The chapter begins by defining stress both acoustically and articulatorily, and then examining stress across varieties of English. This is examined first at the level of the syllable through a focus on **strong** vs **weak syllables** in English, and the relationship between strong/weak syllables and stress. The discussion then focuses on the concept of word stress in varieties of English, after which rhythm and **pitch accent** are introduced, through an examination of stress- and syllable-timing in different languages as well as varieties of English. This discussion will also present information about the function of stress and pitch accent in various substrate languages for different varieties of English, such as Cantonese, Malay, Filipino, Spanish, among others, to help you understand the different stress and rhythm patterns that exist across varieties of English. In the final section of the chapter, you will be guided through exercises designed to check your understanding of the content of the chapter.

7.2   Defining Stress

What do we mean by stress? And how do we articulate and perceive stress? In Task 7.1, you listened to speakers of different varieties of English pronounce the word *record* as an N and as a V. You may have noted that the speakers of SA AusE, Calif AmE, IrE, and Mod RP pronounced the word differently as an N and as a V, with more emphasis on the first syllable as an N, as *REcord* (upper case will be used in this book to denote a stressed syllable), versus more emphasis on the second syllable as a V, as *reCORD*. In contrast, the SgE, SLE, MalE, and HKE speakers had a less noticeable difference in their pronunciation of *record* as an N or V. What is the difference that some speakers had in the pronunciation of *record* as an N or V? You may answer that some speakers stressed the first syllable of *REcord* when they pronounced it as an N and the second syllable *reCORD* as a V, whereas other speakers had less noticeable stress differences in the pronunciation of the word. We can see these differences if we analyse the pronunciation of these words acoustically. In Figures 7.1–7.4, you can see the pronunciation of *record* by an IrE speaker as an N (7.1) and a V (7.2), and by an SLE speaker as an N (7.3) and a V (7.4).

You can see a physical difference in the two syllables for *record* for the IrE speaker: as an N, the first syllable is longer than in *record* as a V; it also has greater **intensity**, which corresponds to the amplitude of the utterance, a rough correlate with loudness (though not an exact equal) – the power of a sound relative to other sounds. This is expressed

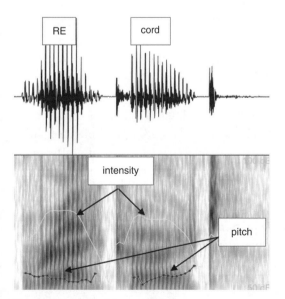

Figure 7.1 Irish English *record* (N)

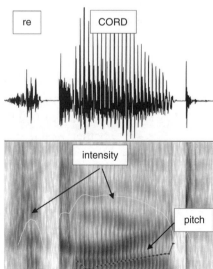

Figure 7.2 Irish English *record* (V)

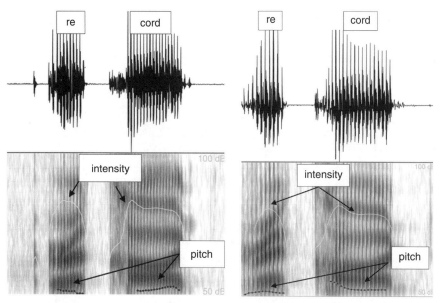

Figure 7.3 Sri Lankan English *record* (N)   **Figure 7.4** Sri Lankan English *record* (V)

in decibels – dB on the spectrogram. The spectrogram also shows *pitch*, which is the fundamental frequency (or F0) of a sound – the number of times the vocal folds vibrate per second, expressed in hertz (see also Chapter 3). Although the pitch differences in the first and second syllables of *record* as an N are not large, there is a notable pitch difference in *record* as a V, as shown in Figure 7.2; you may also note that there is no pitch track on the first syllable in *record* in Figure 7.2, indicating that the pitch was lower than the pitch range set in Praat. In addition, as a V, the second syllable has longer duration and greater intensity. You may also notice stop closure for [k] in both words.

For the SLE speaker, in contrast, there is little acoustic difference between the realization of *record* as an N or as a V, as Figures 7.3 and 7.4 illustrate. The first syllable is roughly equal in duration, intensity, and pitch regardless of whether *record* is articulated as an N or as a V. This difference between the N and V articulations for the IrE speaker is called *stress*: the IrE speaker places stress on the first syllable of *record* as an N and on the second syllable as a V. In addition, the IrE speaker reduces or weakens the vowel in the second syllable of *record* as an N and in the first syllable when it is a V, creating a notable difference in duration, vowel quality, and intensity between the two syllables in each word and between the two words. Stressed syllables have higher intensity than unstressed syllables, are longer in duration, and have higher (or lower) pitch than unstressed syllables. They also have full vowel phonemes (see Chapter 3) in the nucleus in the syllable. We can therefore say that, acoustically, a stressed syllable has greater *prominence* relative to other syllables, and that prominence, while differing cross-linguistically, may include loudness, length, vowel quality, and pitch. In other words, to make a syllable more prominent perceptually to listeners, a speaker may make the syllable louder, longer, use a full vowel sound, and either raise or lower the pitch. We can also make the vowel sound stronger by weakening or reducing the vowel quality of surrounding vowels. This prominence takes more muscular energy to realize physically, creating articulatory differences in stressed and unstressed syllables as well. This brings us to our next topic – the difference between strong and weak syllables, and the relationship among stressed and unstressed syllables and weak and strong syllables.

7.3   Strong vs Weak Syllables

What is a weak syllable? And how do speakers reduce syllables? Strong syllables are longer in duration than weak syllables, have full vowel phonemes as the nucleus of the syllable (see Chapter 6), and have greater intensity (and/or loudness). They can also receive additional prominence through stress. Weak syllables, in contrast, are shorter in duration, have less intensity/loudness, and have a weak vowel or syllabic consonant (see below) as the nucleus. The most common weak vowel is the schwa, symbolized as [ə]; [ɚ] is used to symbolize a rhotic pronunciation of the schwa. The schwa is a mid central vowel, a short 'ugh' sound, and is often quite similar to the full vowel phoneme /ʌ/, a low central vowel that exists in some varieties of English. There is also a weak version of the high front vowel, usually [ɪ] but also [i], and a weak vowel for a high back vowel sound, [u]. Many NVEs, as well as ethnic varieties of English, may not have weak vowels, or if the variety has weak vowels, may not reduce syllables as frequently or in the same manner as OVEs. Even within OVEs, there are differences in strong/weak syllable rules, as we will see below. We return to Wells' Lexical Sets (Wells, 1982; see Chapter 3). There are three Lexical Sets for weak vowels – the second syllables of happY, lettER, and commA. Table 7.1 presents common realizations of these vowels across varieties of English; as noted in Chapter 4, the symbol /r/ is used to denote a rhotic pronunciation for some of the varieties in Table 7.1. The actual realisation of rhoticity varies both across and within varieties of English.

Table 7.1 Weak syllables in varieties of English

Variety	happY/daddY	lettER	commA/AsiA
Mod/Trad RP (Upton, 2015)	i (Mod) ɪ (Trad)	ə	ə
LonE (Altendorf & Watt, 2004)	ɪi	ə	ə
WMidBrE (Clark, 2004)	ɪi, i, ɪ i:	ə	ə
EMidBrE (Braber & Robinson, 2018)	ɪ ~ ɛ ~ i	ə ~ ɒ ~ ɐ	ə ~ ɒ ~ ɐ
NBrE (Beal, 2004)	ɪ ~ ɛ ~ i	ə ~ ɒ ~ ɐ	ə ~ ɒ ~ ɐ
IrE (Hickey, 2004) (NDubE)	i	əɹ	ə
ScotE (Stuart-Smith, 2004; Wells, 1982)	e	ɪr, ər	ʌ, ə
WelE (Penhallurick, 2004)	i:	ə ~ ʌ	ə ~ ʌ
G/StAmE (Kretzschmar, 2004)	i	ɚ	ə
Rural SAmE (Thomas, 2004)	ɪ ~ i	ɚ ~ ə	ə
AAVE (Thomas, 2007)	ɪ ~ i	ə	ə
CanE (Boberg, 2004; Wells, 1982)	i	ɚ	ə
JamE (Devonish & Harry, 2004)	i	o ~ ə:	o ~ ə:
PRE (my data)	i	ɚ	ɑ
AusE (Horvath, 2004; Wells, 1982)	i:	ə	ə
AusAborE (Malcolm; 2004)	i	a ~ ʌ > ə	a
NZE (Hay, Maclagan, & Gordon, 2008; Wells, 1982)	i:	ə	ə
FijE (Tent & Mugler, 2004)	i	ɐ	ɐ
EAfE (Schmied, 2004)	ɪ	a	a
ZimE (my data)	i	ɜr	a
NigE (Gut, 2004)	i	a	a
WSAE (Bowerman, 2004)	ɪ ~ i	ə	ɐ, ə
BSAE (Van Rooy, 2004)	ɪ	ä	ä
SgE (Wee, 2004)	i	ə	ə
MalE (Baskaran, 2004)	i	ə(r)	ə > ʌ
HKE (Deterding, Wong, & Kirkpatrick, 2008)	i	ə(r)	ə
IndE (Gargesh, 2004; Wells, 1982)	ɪ ~ i	ə(r)	a, ə
PakE (Mahboob & Ahmar, 2004)	ɪ	ʌr, er, ər	ʌ
SLE (my data)	i	ə(r)	a, ə
NepE (my data)	i	ər	a, ə
PhlE (Tayao, 2004)	ɪ	ɛr	ɑ

TASK 7.2 Weak Syllables

📖 In Table 7.1, you will find the common pronunciations for the second syllables in happY, lettER, and commA for different varieties of English.

- Which varieties have a schwa in lettER and commA?
- What other vowels exist in these syllables for other varieties of English?
- Which vowels are common for the second syllable in happY?

We start by looking at the second syllable in happY. The two most common articulations of the second syllable are both high front vowels – either the high front (tense/long) vowel [i] or [iː], or the high front (lax/short) vowel [ɪ]. As we noted in Chapters 3 and 6, in many varieties of English that have a tense/lax vowel distinction, only tense vowels are allowed in open syllables, without a coda. The exception is weak syllables, as in the second syllable of happY, which is a weak syllable in many varieties of English, and particularly OVEs, including varieties of AmE, BrE, AusE, CanE, WelE, ScotE, WSAE, NZE, and IrE. More common, however, is the realization of the vowel in the second syllable of happY as either [i] or [iː], for two reasons: as discussed in detail in Chapter 3, many varieties of English have a FLEECE/KIT merger, with only the FLEECE (/i/ or /iː/) vowel in its inventory. This includes many NVEs including KenE, NigE, BSAE, HKE, SgE, MalE, PhlE, some varieties of IndE, and FijE, as well as ethnic varieties of English including ChiE, AusAborE, and MāoriE, due to substrate influences.

The second reason for the prevalence of the pronunciation of the second syllable of happY as [i] or [iː] is that varieties that have a tense/lax distinction, including varieties of AmE, BrE, NZE, AusE, IrE, and WelE, have undergone or are undergoing a process called *happY tensing*, in which the final weak vowel in words in the happY Lexical Set is realized as the tense vowel [i] or [iː], rather than the lax vowel [ɪ]. This appears to be a global sound change in progress.

The second syllable in lettER commonly has a schwa realization [ə] in many non-rhotic varieties of English, and particularly OVEs, as well as some NVEs. This includes varieties of BrE, AusE, NZE, WelE, WSAE, AAVE, HKE, MalE, IndE, NepE, and SLE. Rhotic varieties of English may have a rhoticized schwa realization of the second syllable of lettER as [ɚ]. This exists in most varieties of AmE, CanE, PRE, Edinburgh ScotE, some varieties of IndE, SLE, HKE, NepE, and IrE. Other varieties may have another weak vowel (e.g., ScotE has [ɪ]) or a full vowel in the second syllable. This includes AusAborE [a ~ ʌ > ə], FijE [ɐ], JamE [o ~ əː], NigE and KenE [a], BSAE [ä], ZimE [ɜr], PakE [ʌr ~ er ~ ər], NBrE [ə ~ ɒ ~ ɐ], ScotE [ɪr ~ ər] and WelE [ə ~ ʌ]. The realization of the second syllable of commA largely follows that of the second syllable of lettER, minus the rhoticity for the rhotic varieties of English. In some varieties, such as PRE, WSAE, ZimE, IndE, NepE, SLE, and MalE, a full vowel may exist in commA whereas a schwa exists in lettER.

TASK 7.3 Listening for Strong and Weak Syllables

🎧 You can listen to speakers of the following varieties of English pronounce the second syllable in the happY, commA, and lettER Lexical Sets:

Mod RP, EMidBrE, NBrE, IrE, GAmE, CanE, PRE, SA AusE, NZE, KenE, ZimE, SNigE, WSAE, SgE, MalE, HKE, IndE, PakE, SLE, NepE, PhlE

- Based on the information given in Table 7.1, which varieties/speakers do you expect to have a strong/weak syllable structure in happY, lettER, and commA?
- For which varieties/speakers can you hear a notable difference in the two syllables in happY, lettER, or commA for any of the following: (a) syllable length (duration); (b) intensity (loudness); and/or (c) a full vowel sound?

Based on your listening, you may have noted that some speakers, in particular the speakers of GAmE, CanE, BrE (all three speakers), IrE, SA AusE, NZE, and WSAE, have a stronger first syllable in each word, whereas speakers of other varieties, including the KenE, ZimE, SNigE, SgE, MalE, HKE, IndE, PakE, NepE, and PhlE speakers, may have more equal syllables in terms of duration and loudness, regardless of whether they use a weak or strong vowel in the second syllable. As we can hear, some varieties have a clear contrast between the two syllables, with reduced vowels in the second.

7.4   Stress, Tone, and Pitch

Do all languages have stress? Before we look at stress and weak/strong syllables in varieties of English, it is helpful to examine stress, tone, and pitch across languages. Languages are generally classified as having one of the following prosodic features: (1) lexical word stress – this includes English and German; or (2) tone – where each syllable has a separate pitch, which distinguishes meaning; the latter includes many Asian languages, including Cantonese and Mandarin Chinese. A third, and often controversial, category is: (3) **pitch–accent languages**, which use pitch accent (change in pitch) to create prominence for one syllable in a word, in contrast to duration and loudness in stress languages. This includes languages such as Norwegian and Japanese (see Hyman, 2009, for a discussion of pitch vs tone and stress languages). These languages are sometimes categorized as simpler tone languages (see Maddieson, 1984).

Stress patterns also vary across languages; according to Goedemans and van der Hults (2013), of the 502 languages analysed for stress in WALS, 220 (or 44%) do not have fixed stress. This includes tone languages such as Mandarin Chinese which rely on tone, and not stress, for meaning, as well as European languages such as Spanish, French, German, and English; Native American languages such as Navajo and Hopi; Asian languages such as Malay, Hindi, and Sindhi; and Pacific Island languages such as Fijian, Māori, and Tongan. Another 92 languages (18%) prefer stress on the first syllable; this includes Irish, Bengali, and many Australian Aboriginal languages. Only a few languages prefer stress on the second syllable (16, or 3%); this pattern exists primarily in Australian Aboriginal languages or Native American languages. Only Winnebago, a Native American language, has stress on the third syllable. Few languages prefer stress on the antepenultimate (third syllable before the end, or two syllables before the final syllable): only 12, or 2%, of the languages have this pattern, including Greek and Macedonian. More common is stress on the penultimate (second to last) syllable; this pattern exists for 110, or 22%, of the languages, including a few Celtic languages, such as Welsh, Breton, and Cornish; African languages including Kiswahili; Asian languages including Tagalog and Indonesian; and languages of South America and Austronesia. A number (51, or 10%) have fixed stress on the ultimate syllable. This includes languages in South America and in Austronesia. These different stress patterns result in unique stress patterns in the varieties of English that are influenced by these languages.

7.5   Word Stress in Varieties of English

What is the difference between strong/weak syllables and word stress?
As we saw above, some varieties of English distinguish between strong and weak syllables, with weak syllables realized with a weak vowel,

shorter length, and less intensity. Other varieties of English may not reduce syllables but realize multiple syllables in a word with relatively similar intensity and length, and with full vowel phonemes. English also utilizes stress to differentiate syllables in words (and sentences); like strong syllables, stressed syllables have more **prominence**, what is often called an *accent*. Importantly, in varieties with strong and weak syllables, only strong syllables can be stressed, and receive more prominence, while weak syllables are always unstressed. In words with more than one strong syllable, as in *communicate*, one of these syllables may have more prominence, receiving primary stress, whereas another strong syllable may receive secondary stress. If we transcribe *communicate* into phonemic transcription based on GAmE, for example, the pattern for strong/weak syllables is WSWS, where W denotes a weak syllable and S a strong syllable. In *communicate* the first syllable is weak, with a schwa, the second is strong, the third is weak, and the fourth is strong. Only one of the strong syllables can receive the most prominence – the primary stress – and this is the second syllable in *communicate*, as indicated by ['] in the possible transcription of *communicate*. The last syllable, the second strong syllable, also receives some prominence but this is secondary to the syllable receiving primary stress. This is considered secondary stress and is indicated by [ˌ] in the transcription.

Word	Possible transcription
communicate	/kəˈmjuː.nəˌkeɪt/
	W S W S
	Primary Secondary
	Stress Stress

In varieties that have strong/weak distinction, in two-syllable words such as happY, lettER, and commA, the first syllable is both a strong and a stressed syllable, giving a strong–weak (SW) syllable pattern, and a stressed (S) unstressed (U) word stress pattern. This latter pattern is called **trochaic stress**; when the stress falls on the second syllable in a two-syllable word, the stress pattern is called **iambic stress**, with WS syllables and a US stress pattern In Task 7.1, *record* was used as an example of a word that may have a different stress pattern depending on the variety of English. In some varieties of English, including AmE, CanE, BrE, AusE, NZE, and IrE, *record* has a trochaic pattern (SW/SU) as an N, as ˈREcord. In contrast, it has an iambic (WS/US) stress when it is used as a V, as in reˈCORD. As we saw above, not all varieties of English utilize stress in this manner, however.

Noun	Verb
'REcord	re'CORD
S W	W S
S U	U S
Trochaic	Iambic

Largely based on descriptions of OVEs such as AmE and BrE, English is considered to be a lexical stress language, with word stress. English has both fixed and free word stress: most varieties of English have fixed stress on the same word regardless of the context it occurs in; for example, the word *communicate* has a fixed primary stress on the second syllable regardless of the context in which it is used. English also has free stress, in that stress differs across words based on origin, affixes, and grammatical category. Most one-syllable words that are content words (this includes nouns, verbs, adjectives, and adverbs) are strong syllables; in varieties of English that have both strong and weak syllables, words that are grammatically categorized as function words, which includes pronouns, auxiliary verbs, articles, conjunctions, and prepositions, may be weak syllables. Varieties of English that make greater use of stress, including many OVEs such as AmE, CanE, BrE, and AusE, dislike sequences of similar syllables – for example, WW or SS – preferring to alternate strong and weak syllables, with stress therefore ultimately falling only on a strong syllable, with secondary stress possible in some words. Alternation between stress and unstressed and strong/weak syllables is called a stress-timed rhythm, and will be discussed in more detail below, along with syllable-timing.

Table 7.2 provides a summary of some of the word stress patterns in varieties of English based on the available research. For varieties of English that make greater use of word stress, stress rules can be complex, and are based on word origin (*ballet*, for example, as a two-syllable N, would typically have a trochaic stress pattern; however, *ballet* may be pronounced with iambic stress in some varieties of English, including GAmE), affixation, and grammatical category. A full description of English stress patterns that are followed by many OVEs, including most varieties of AmE, AusE, CanE, and BrE, can be found in Roach (2009) and Cruttenden (2014).

☞ The following discussion is intended to provide a comprehensive overview of word stress in varieties of English worldwide.

Word stress patterns are organized by variety of English in Table 7.2. Although you are encouraged to read about different types of word stress, you may wish to focus your attention on the stress patterns that occur in the Englishes that are of interest to you.

Table 7.2 Word stress in varieties of English

Variety	Unstressed syllables	Word stress
RP / Southern BrE (Roach, 2009; Upton, 2004)	Reduced vowels	Tendency to stress 1st syllable in verbs with -*ize* suffix (AmE stresses syllable preceding -*ize*): '*ADvertize*; 1st syllable on noun and 2nd on verb for words such as *record*; -*ate*-suffixed words tend to have stress on 2nd syllable. Complex word stress based on affixation, grammatical category, and origin (see Roach, 2009)
NBrE (Beal, 2004)	May have full vowels in unstressed syllables	Northeast: tendency for equal or main stress on 2nd element in compounds: '*STAKE'FORD*; tends not to reduce vowels in unstressed prefixes from Latin such as *con-, ex-*
EMidBrE (Braber & Robinson, 2018)	Definite article reduction: *the* reduced to a consonant, commonly [t ʔ]	Word-initial weak syllable deletion: *about* to *bout, avoid* to *void*. Word-medial weak syllable deletion: *company* to *compny, normally* to *normly*
IrE (Hickey, 2007)	Reduced vowels	Tendency to shift stress to long final vowels in trisyllabic verbs such as *testi'FY* 1st syllable on noun and 2nd on verb for words such as *record*
ScotE (Cao & Jin, 2017; Wells, 1982)	Disyllabic words have one long and one short syllable (Scottish Snap or Scotch Snap) – *table* may have short 1st syllable and long 2nd syllable; SVLR (see Chapter 3)	Stress on final -*ize* suffix in verbs: *adver'TIZE*; 1st syllable on noun and 2nd on verb for words such as *record*
WelE (Penhallurick, 2004)	Final unstressed syllables not reduced for some speakers; final unstressed vowel in happY tends to be long; vowel may be lengthened in a stressed syllable or shortened, with the coda lengthened	Penultimate stress is preferred if it is trisyllabic: *main'TENance*. Antepenultimate stress is preferred if it is tetrasyllabic: *co'ROnary*

Variety	Unstressed syllables	Word stress
G/StAmE (Kretzschmar, 2004; Roach, 2009)	Stress on strong syllables; weak syllables reduced	Tendency for stress on 1st syllable for 2-syllable nouns/adjectives – 'PERfect, 'RObot and on the 2nd syllable on verbs – a'TTACH, re'SIST; 3-syllable words: verbs receive stress on last syllable if strong; nouns may receive stress on 1st syllable if strong; preserves more secondary stress, and more fully realized vowels, than BrE: SECreTARY in AmE versus SECretry in BrE; -ate-suffixed words tend to have stress on 1st syllable
SAmE (Kretchmar, 2004; Thomas, 2004)	Southern Drawl = extreme lengthening of stressed vowels	Strong initial stress: 'Insurance, 'POlice, in contrast to other AmE varieties
AAVE (Edwards, 2004)	Reduced vowels	Strong initial stress: 'INsurance, 'POlice, in contrast to other AmE varieties
ChiE (Fought, 2006; Santa Ana & Bayley, 2004)	/i/ and /u/ are not reduced; less reduction of unstressed syllables than GAmE	Word stress may appear idiosyncratic – often in compound words and polysyllabic words where stress patterns differ from GAmE: Thanks'GIVing day, type'WRITer, 'SHOW up
CanE (Boberg, 2004)	Reduced vowels	Follows word stress patterns from BrE and AmE. Stress on 1st syllable on noun and 2nd on verb for words such as record
AusE (Horvath, 2004)	Reduced vowels	Follows BrE for word stress. Stress on 1st syllable on noun–verb pairs such as 'REcord
AusAborE (Butcher, 2008; Malcolm, 2004)	Unreduced vowels	Preference for trochaic stress / stress on the 1st syllable: 'REferee, 'KANgaroo. Words like along, suppose, police pronounced without the 1st unstressed syllable: long, spoz, plis
NZE (Hay, Maclagan, & Gordon, 2008)	Some use of full vowel in unstressed grammatical words and polysyllabic words	Generally follows BrE for word stress; some stress on 1st syllable in noun-verb pairs such as 'REcord
MāoriE (Warren & Bauer, 2004)	Unreduced vowels	Generally follows NZE
NiuE (Starks, Christie, & Thompson, 2007)	Less/no reduction of vowels	Generally follows NZE; stress on last syllable if the last vowel is long; in words with more than one stress, no clear difference between primary and secondary stress

Table 7.2 (Cont.)

Variety	Unstressed syllables	Word stress
FijE (Tent & Mugler, 2004)	Unreduced vowels	Unpredictable word stress patterns; often stress on penultimate syllable if vowel in last syllable is short; sometimes words of 3 syllables or more have equal stress on all syllables
EAfE, WAfE, SAfE (Bobda, 2001; Schmied, 2004)	Tendency for unreduced vowels	Word stress in -ism words: stress almost always on preceding syllable, and on the suffix in SAfE and EAfE. Some speakers may have stress on 1st syllable on noun and 2nd on verb for words such as *record*. Stress on the same syllable on stem: *adMIRE, adMIRation, adMIRable* in EAfE
WSAE (Bowerman, 2004)	Reduced vowels	Stress on 1st syllable on noun and 2nd on verb for words such as *record*
BSAE (Van Rooy, 2004)	Tendency for unreduced vowels	Stress on penultimate syllable as in *se'VENty* except when the final syllable is superheavy (it has a diphthong) and a coda, or a V + coda cluster, in which case stress shifts to last syllable (*cam'PAIGN* and *con'TRAST*)
NigE (Gut, 2004)	Tendency for unreduced vowels	Differs from AmE and BrE: tendency for stress to shift to the right (*sa'LAD*); verbs tend to have stress on the last syllable if they have final obstruents (*inter'PRET*) or contain the affixes -*ate*, -*ise*, -*ize*, -*fy*, -*ish*; stress on the following affixes: -*ative*, -*ature*, -*itive/-utive*, -*man*, -*day*, -*atory/-utory*, -*cide*, -*land*, -*phone*. Strong consonant clusters may also shift stress to the preceding syllable as in *an'CEstor*; 2nd element stressed in compounds as in *fire'WOOD, proof'READ*
SgE (Low, 2012; Wee, 2004)	Unreduced vowels	Lacks secondary and primary stress and instead assigns equal stress to each syllable: BrE *cele'BRAtion* vs SgE *'ce'le'bra'tion*. If a word has more than one stressed syllable, it is the last syllable that carries primary stress. No distinction in stress on noun–verb pairs such as *record*. Compound nouns stress on final syllable unlike AmE and BrE: *desk'LAMP* and *math teach'ER*

Variety	Unstressed syllables	Word stress
MalE (Baskaran, 2004; Hashim, 2020)	Unreduced vowels	No distinction in stress on noun–verb pairs such as *record* May have more or fewer stresses than BrE; words with secondary stress in BrE may have primary stress on 2 syllables in MalE. May have lengthening or stressing of particular syllables for emphasis or contrast. Shift in stress from antepenultimate syllable (as in BrE) to penultimate syllable: ˈCAmera in BrE to caˈMEra in MalE; ˈINdustry in BrE to inˈDUSstry in MalE
HKE (Deterding, Wong, & Kirkpatrick, 2008; Hung, 2012)	Tendency for unreduced vowels; vowel reduction is often absent in function words so a full vowel occurs in *for, to, as*	Variable lexical primary stress patterns; full vowel in 1st syllable in words such as *accept* and *consider*. No distinction in stress on noun–verb pairs such as *record*
IndE (Gargesh, 2004)	Unreduced vowels	Heavily influenced by substrate languages: all monosyllabic words are stressed. In bisyllabic words, the primary stress tends to fall on the 1st syllable unless followed by an extra-heavy syllable (with long vowel and/or onset/coda cluster), in which case the stress falls on the last syllable. In words of 3 syllables, the primary stress falls on the penultimate syllable if it is heavy (onset and long vowel; short vowel and coda); otherwise, it falls on the 1st syllable
PakE (Mahboob & Ahmar, 2004)	Vowel reduction limited to some function words (*the, a, was*) in fast speech	Tendency not to produce differential stress in noun–verb pairs such as *record*
SLE (Mendis & Rambukwella, 2010)	Tendency not to reduce unstressed vowels	Tendency for primary stress on 1st syllable of a word. Tendency not to produce differential stress in noun–verb pairs such as *record*
PhlE (Dayag, 2012; Tayao, 2004)	Tendency for unreduced vowels	Lexical stress patterns vary in terms of acrolect, mesolect, and basilect; acrolect group is most similar to GAmE

As Table 7.2 shows, there is a great deal of variation across Englishes with regard to syllable and word stress patterns, largely due to substrate influences. Like Spanish (and English), ChiE does not have fixed stress patterns; this is also the case for FijE, due to the influence of Fijian, and MalE, due to the influence of Malay. AusAborE varieties prefer a trochaic stress pattern on two-syllable words, and stress on the first syllable on multisyllabic words, probably due to influence from Aboriginal languages where stress falls on the first syllable. A preference for stress on the penultimate syllable is found in WelE for some words, likely due to the influence of Welsh. Despite these differences across varieties, it is possible to draw a few conclusions:

- Many OVEs, including many varieties of AmE, CanE, BrE, and IrE, reduce vowels in unstressed syllables, with a clear contrast between stressed and unstressed syllables.
- Most NVEs, including most African Englishes (EAfE, SAfE, BSAE) and Asian Englishes (HKE, SgE, PhlE, MalE, IndE, PakE, and SLE) and many ethnic varieties of English (MāoriE, ChiE, AusAborE, NiuE), tend to use full vowels in unstressed syllables, with few reductions to weak vowels.
- Some varieties, such as WelE, ChiE, and NZE, may have unique patterns or have less syllable reduction than other OVEs but more than many NVEs.
- Stress patterns for N vs V for words such as *record* and *import* differ across varieties of English. Many OVEs, including varieties of AusE, AmE, CanE, IrE, and BrE, follow a trochaic (SU) pattern for nouns, and iambic (US) for verbs. Compound nouns/adjectives also tend to have stress on the first element, as in *DESK lamp*.
- Other varieties of English tend to stress the first syllable of both nouns and verbs such as *record* and *import*; this includes HKE, SgE, SLE, PakE, and MalE.
- Many regional, ethnic, and NVE varieties tend to stress words on the first syllable, regardless of grammatical category; this includes: AusAborE, SAmE, AAVE, and SLE.

TASK 7.4 Listening for Word Stress

🎧 You can hear speakers of the following varieties of English pronounce words of two syllables of more:

Speakers: Midwestern AmE, Qld AusE, EMidBrE, HKE, NZE, MalE, SLE, WSAE, ZimE

- Which speakers have a difference of pronunciation for *rebel* as a noun (N) vs a verb (V)?
- Which speakers have a more equal pronunciation of all the syllables in each word vs a contrast between unstressed/stressed syllables?

  Words

  absent-minded

  affect

  department

  fact-finding

  rebel (N) vs *rebel* (V)

You may notice that the speakers of Midwestern AmE, EMidBrE, Qld AusE, WSAE, and ZimE stress the first syllable on *rebel* when it is an N and on the second syllable when it is a V. The HKE, MalE, NZE, and SLE speakers have a less noticeable difference in *rebel* as an N vs a V, with the HKE and NZE speakers placing more emphasis on the second syllable for *rebel* as both an N and a V. You may also have noticed a more uneven or up and down rhythm in the pronunciation of the words *department* (with most prominence on PART), *absent-minded* (with the most prominence on MIND), *affect* (with prominence on FECT) and *fact-finding* (with prominence on FACT), and weaker/reduced syllables for the other syllables, most noticeably for the speakers of Midwestern AmE and Qld AusE, with some differentiation for speakers of EMidBrE, NZE, WSAE (she stresses the first syllable of *affect*), and ZimE, and least differentiation for speakers of HKE, MalE, and SLE. The MalE speaker, in particular, has a very even realization for every syllable in each word; this can be contrasted with the speaker of Midwestern AmE, who has a clear differentiation among syllables in each word.

It is important to note that what constitutes stress in a variety of English may vary; we noted above that there appear to be four main ways in which languages, including English, create prominence, which we label as stress: (1) pitch change (raising or lowering the pitch of a syllable); (2) full vowel quality; (3) longer syllable duration; and (4) greater intensity/amplitude. How varieties (and languages in general that utilize word stress) use these features, however, may differ. This may result in some varieties being perceived as not having word stress as their acoustic signals for stress may not be heard as such by listeners whose variety of English marks stress differently. For example, AmE has larger durational differences and amplitude differences in stressed and unstressed syllables than some varieties of IndE; while IndE does use duration and amplitude to signal stress, the differences between unstressed and stressed syllables for duration and amplitude may not be as great as those for AmE (Wiltshire & Moon, 2003). As Pickering and Wiltshire (2000) found, many varieties of Southeast Asian Englishes, including some varieties of IndE and PakE, may not rely as much on amplitude to mark stress; instead, these varieties primarily mark stress with pitch, and – unlike AmE, as an example – use a low frequency (pitch) to mark stress, in contrast to a high frequency as found in many OVEs. NigE may also primarily use tone to indicate stress, with a high pitch/tone used for stressed syllables and a low tone/pitch for unstressed syllables (Gut, 2004).

Varieties of English that have a clear contrast between stressed and unstressed syllables through vowel reduction may also have **syllabic consonants**. As we noted in Chapter 6, all syllables must contain a nucleus, which is a vowel or a vowel-like sound. As we also noted in Chapter 6, sounds such as nasals and approximants are more sonorous than other consonants, but less sonorous than vowels. These consonants – and particularly /n/ and /l/ – may serve as the nucleus of a syllable when the syllable is weakened/reduced and the weakened vowel is deleted. This often occurs in words with 'le' in the spelling that is preceded by an alveolar consonant, as in *little* or *bottle*; it occurs less commonly with a non-alveolar consonant preceding the 'le' as in *trouble* (see also Roach, 2009). The nasal /n/ is most frequently syllabic in syllables with an alveolar plosive or fricative plus 'en', 'on', or 'ain', where the vowel is a schwa, as in *button* and *mountain*. In rhotic varieties of English, /r/ can also become syllabic in weak syllables.

How do we mark syllabic consonants? If a syllable is pronounced with a syllabic consonant, we use the diacritic [ˌ] underneath the syllabic consonant: [n̩ l̩ r̩] represent syllabic /n/, /l/, and /r/ respectively. The phonemic and phonetic transcription of *button* is shown below for a speaker who has both flapping and syllabic /n/.

Word	Possible phonemic transcription	Possible pronunciation
button	/bʌt.ən/	[bʌɾ.n̩]

Which varieties of English have syllabic consonants? As syllabic consonants are part of the process of syllable weakening and reduction, they occur in varieties of English that have a clear differentiation between strong and weak syllables; this includes varieties of AmE, BrE, CanE, ScotE, IrE, and AusE. They are rarer or not possible in varieties that do not reduce unstressed syllables, including SgE and MalE.

What does a syllabic consonant sound like? In words with syllabic consonants, the preceding syllable, as in *lit* in *little* or *but* in *button*, is a strong and stressed syllable; for the second syllable, you may hear only a [n] or a [l], signifying a syllabic realization for this consonant (the vowel is deleted/reduced).

TASK 7.5 Listening for Syllabic Consonants

🎧 Listen to the speakers of Midwestern AmE, CanE, IrE, HKE, Mod RP, and SgE pronounce *bottle* and *button*, both of which may be pronounced with syllabic consonants for some speakers.

- Which speakers have a syllabic /l/ in *bottle*?
- Are there any other realizations for /l/ in these words by some speakers?
- Which speakers have syllabic /n/ in *button*?
- Do the same speakers have syllabic consonants in both words?
- What other features do you notice in the words (think about the pronunciation of /t/)?

You may be able to hear that the CanE, Midwestern AmE, and IrE speakers have a noticeable syllabic pronunciation of 'le' as [l̩] whereas the Mod RP speaker has a weak syllable [əɫ]. The SgE and the HKE speakers have L-vocalization in place of /l/. The Midwestern AmE, CanE, and IrE speakers have syllabic /n/ in *button*, while the Mod RP speaker has a weak syllable with a schwa. The SgE and HKE have two syllables of equal strength in *button*. You may also have noticed flapping in *bottle* and glottal stopping in *button* for the Midwestern AmE and CanE speakers (see Chapter 5).

7.6 Rhythm in Varieties of English

What is rhythm? As we saw in the previous discussion, varieties of English (and languages) have different stress patterns in syllables and words. Languages and varieties of English also differ in respect to **rhythm** – one aspect of the prosody of the language/variety. One of the earliest discussions of this difference was by Pike (1946), who differentiated between languages that had *stress-timed rhythm* and languages that had *syllable-timed rhythm*. Languages that were labelled as stress-timed by Pike and other scholars were categorized as having relatively equal intervals between stressed syllables; these languages make use of both strong and weak syllables to create a more uneven rhythm, with prominence and reduction of syllables occurring across words and phrases. In other words, syllables vary in prominence and the syllables are uneven in terms of being strong/weak and having stress. Languages that were viewed as having **stress-timing** include German, Dutch, and English, all of which are Germanic languages.

Other languages have relatively equal syllables, with all syllables equal in duration; these languages, which include many Asian languages, and particularly tone languages (see above and Chapter 8), were categorized as having **syllable-timing**. A third category of languages have **mora-timing**, for example Japanese, where every mora is equal; the mora is a phonological unit based on syllable weight.

While these categories are still widely used to describe languages, and, more recently, varieties of English, the distinction of stress- vs syllable-timing does not accurately represent rhythm. Subsequent research found, as Thomas and Carter (2006, p. 335) state, that 'inter-stress durations do not differ significantly between syllable-timed and stress-timed languages and that syllable durations differ greatly in syllable-timed languages'. Instead, stress/syllable-timing should be viewed as a continuum, and encompasses not only timing in languages/varieties, but other features as well. Dauer (1983) argued that timing is based on the phonology of a language, with stress-timed languages (and, for our purposes, varieties of English) tending to have: (1) a greater range of syllable types, including complex onsets and codas; (2) a larger range of vowels in unstressed syllables, including reduced/weak vowels; and (3) lexical stress, in contrast to pitch accent in tone languages such as many Asian languages. In contrast, languages (and varieties) that are more syllable-timed may have: (1) a simpler syllable structure, and more CV syllables; (2) full vowels in all syllables; and (3) less lexical stress or tendency to realize accent through variation in pitch contour.

Based on this categorization, English (used here as an umbrella term, but largely referring to OVEs such as AmE, BrE, CanE, and AusE) has been categorized as being stress-timed, as English has a range of syllables and complex syllable structures, both strong and weak vowels in syllables, and uses lexical stress (as in *record* as a noun or a verb) (Dauer, 1983). Spanish and French, in contrast, have been labelled as more syllable-timed, as they have relatively simpler syllable structures, favouring a CV syllable structure, and less reduction of vowels in unstressed syllables (Dauer, 1983). Some languages, such as Polish and Catalan, are considered mixed, falling between syllable- and stress-timing, as they have features of both types: Catalan has simpler syllable structure but also reduction of unstressed syllables, whereas Polish has complex syllable structures but no reduction of unstressed syllables (Thomas & Carter, 2006).

In current research on rhythm, many researchers use the Pairwise-Variability Index (PVI), devised by Low and Grabe (1995) and Low, Grabe, and Nolan (2000), to analyse the rhythm of languages and varieties. In this approach, the duration of the nucleus in adjacent syllables is measured, and the absolute value of the difference in duration between syllables is divided by the mean of their duration. This is then averaged for a complete utterance (a phrase or sentence) and multiplied by 100, allowing for a comparison across varieties of English with speaking rate controlled (Thomas and Carter, 2006). The PVI is increasingly used in World Englishes research to compare rhythm across varieties of English. Table 7.3 shows some of the values, based on current research. The PVI is often presented as an nPVI, a normalized PVI in which (as opposed to a raw PVI, or rPVI) a higher number for the PVI indicates more variability in duration across vowels (or syllables, in some instances), and thus a more stress-timed rhythm, whereas a lower number indicates less variability and a more syllable-timed rhythm. Note: I have listed the languages/varieties for each study in descending order by nPVI. I have also noted which type of speech data was used in each, as this may impact the results (see below).

Table 7.3 PVI values across languages and varieties of English

Language/variety	nPVI/PVI
Thomas & Carter (2006) *Interviews*	
AAVE	53.0
AmE (European)	52.0
JamE	40.0
ChiE	40.0
Spanish	20.0
Shousterman (2014) *Interviews*	
PRE	45.0 (younger); 41.0 (older)
Coggshall (2008) *Interviews*	
Lumbee NAE	51.0 (older); 40.0 (younger)
Cherokee NAE	38.0
Cherokee	19.0
Carter (2005) *Interviews*	
African American English	55.15
AmE (European)	53.04
ChiE	42.64
Spanish	27.98
Jian (2004) *Reading task*	
AmE	43.4 (reduced vowels); 51.3 (full vowels)
Taiwan English	38.4 (reduced vowels); 39.8 (full vowels)
Deterding (2011) *Reading task*	
BrE	58.82
Standard Malay	44.37
Tan & Low (2014) *Reading and spontaneous speech tasks*	
SgE	47.30 read speech; 48.14 spontaneous speech

Table 7.3 (Cont.)

Language/variety	nPVI/PVI
MalE	41.21 read speech; 43.67 spontaneous speech
Grabe & Low (2002) *Reading task*	
Thai	65.8
Dutch	65.5
German	59.7
BrE	57.2
Tamil	55.8
Malay	53.6
SgE	52.3
Greek	48.7
Welsh	48.2
Rumanian	46.9
Polish	46.6
Estonian	45.4
Catalan	44.6
French	43.5
Japanese	40.9
Spanish	29.7
Mandarin Chinese	27.0
Szakay (2006) *Reading task and spontaneous speech*	
NZE	58.7
MāoriE	47.3
Torgersen & Szakay (2011) *Interviews*	
BrE (Anglo)	53.70
MLE	51.41
Fuchs (2016) *Reading task and spontaneous speech*	
BrE	61.3 read speech; 58.3 spontaneous
IndE	55.6 read speech; 52.4 spontaneous
Mok & Dellwo (2008) *Reading task*	
BrE	69.67
Mandarin Chinese English	60.67
HKE	57.65
German	56.42
Italian	54.78
French	49.47
Mandarin	45.95 telling story; 45.02 reading
Cantonese	36.77 telling story; 34.32 reading

Table 7.4 presents a summary of rhythm for varieties of English based on the available research. As Tables 7.3 and 7.4 show, and as is illustrated in Figure 7.5, AmE is relatively stress-timed in comparison to JamE as well as ChiE and PRE, both of which are influenced by Spanish, which has a more syllable-timed rhythm. African Englishes also tend to be more syllable-timed. Some varieties of NAE, and particularly Cherokee NAE, also have a more syllable-timed rhythm, the latter due to the influence of Cherokee. Younger speakers of Lumbee NAE also appear to be moving towards a more syllable-timed rhythm whereas older speakers have a more stress-timed rhythm, similar to European speakers of AmE and AAVE speakers. Varieties of English influenced by Chinese languages, including

Table 7.4 Rhythm in varieties of English

Variety	Stress/syllable-timing continuum
RP / Southern BrE (Altendorf and Watt, 2004)	Stress-timed
MLE (Torgersen & Szakay, 2011)	More syllable-timed than BrE
G/StAmE (Kretzschmar, 2004)	Strong stress-timing
AAVE (Thomas & Carter, 2006)	Very stress-timed, like GAmE
NAE (Coggshall, 2008)	More syllable-timed than GAmE (variety- and age-dependent)
ChiE (Thomas & Carter, 2006)	Syllable-timed
CanE (Boberg, 2004)	Strong stress-timed language
JamE (Thomas & Carter, 2006)	Syllable-timed
AusE (Horvath, 2004)	Tendency towards stress-timing, but less so than AmE
AusAborE (Butcher, 2008; Malcolm, 2004)	Tendency towards syllable-timing
NZE (Hay, Maclagan, & Gordon, 2004)	Less stress-timed than AmE and BrE; becoming more syllable-timed
MāoriE (Szakay, 2006)	Syllable/mora-timed
NiuE (Starks, Christie, & Thompson, 2007)	Syllable-timed
FijE (Tent & Mugler, 2004)	Syllable-timed
EAfE (Schmied, 2004)	Tendency towards syllable-timed rhythm
SAfE (Bobda, 2010)	Syllable-timed
BSAE (Van Rooy, 2004)	Syllable-timed
NigE (Gut, 2005)	Syllable-timed
IndE (Fuchs, 2016)	Syllable-timed
PakE (Mahboob & Ahmad, 2004)	Syllable-timed
SgE (Tan & Low, 2014)	Syllable-timed
MalE (Tan & Low, 2014)	May be more syllable-timed than SgE
HKE (Mok & Dellwo, 2008)	Syllable-timed
PhlE (Tayao, 2004)	Syllable-timed

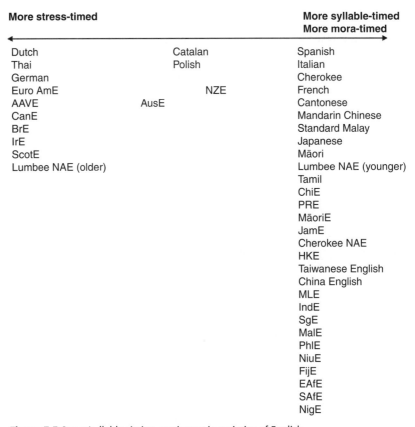

More stress-timed

More syllable-timed
More mora-timed

More stress-timed			More syllable-timed / More mora-timed
Dutch	Catalan		Spanish
Thai	Polish		Italian
German			Cherokee
Euro AmE		NZE	French
AAVE	AusE		Cantonese
CanE			Mandarin Chinese
BrE			Standard Malay
IrE			Japanese
ScotE			Māori
Lumbee NAE (older)			Lumbee NAE (younger)
			Tamil
			ChiE
			PRE
			MāoriE
			JamE
			Cherokee NAE
			HKE
			Taiwanese English
			China English
			MLE
			IndE
			SgE
			MalE
			PhlE
			NiuE
			FijE
			EAfE
			SAfE
			NigE

Figure 7.5 Stress/syllable-timing continuum in varieties of English

Mandarin Chinese (Taiwanese English, China English) and Cantonese (HKE) are also more syllable-timed, as are Chinese languages. Standard Malay is also more syllable-timed than BrE; Malay influences both MalE and SgE, both of which are syllable-timed, although MalE may be more syllable-timed than SgE. Other varieties of Asian English also appear to be more syllable-timed than BrE or AmE; this includes PhlE and IndE.

Even among varieties of English that are considered more stress-timed, there are differences; while AusE is stress-timed, it is less stress-timed than AmE (Horvath, 2004).

NZE has often been described as less stress-timed than BrE and AmE; research (Szakay, 2006) suggests it is more stress-timed than MāoriE, though it appears to be in the process of becoming more syllable-timed, as younger speakers of NZE are more syllable-timed than older speakers of NZE. MLE, which is influenced by Jamaican Creole, among other languages, also appears to be syllable-timed in comparison to other varieties of BrE.

In summary, many NVEs as well as ethnic varieties of OVEs tend towards a syllable-timed rhythm, due to the influence of substrate languages such as Tamil, Malay, Spanish, and Chinese languages that are syllable- or mora-timed, such as Japanese. In contrast, OVEs, and particularly CanE, AmE, and BrE, are more stress-timed. The languages/varieties that are more syllable-timed also tend to have simpler syllable structures and lack weak vowels in unstressed syllables, whereas the languages and varieties that are more stress-timed have more complex syllable structures and often have weak vowels in unstressed syllables, as we saw in previous chapters.

TASK 7.6 Listening for Timing in Varieties of English

🎧 You can listen to speakers of Appal AmE, EMidBrE, Qld AusE, NZE, SLE, IndE, NepE, HKE, MalE, WSAE, and ZimE read the following sentences:

He caught a cod.
Let us meet at the square on the north end.
He is going to dip her food into the sauce.
The father is sitting on his cot thinking the world is a fine place.

- Which speakers/varieties tend to be more stress-timed? Syllable-timed?
- You may wish to pay attention to the syllables/words that are underlined (they are potential weak/unstressed syllables/words) – are they reduced or pronounced with the same duration as the other syllables?

As Task 7.6 illustrates, timing is not absolute, but rather a continuum with more stress- or more syllable-timing. Even varieties that are more syllable-timed may reduce weak syllables, and varieties that are more stress-timed may use full vowels in unstressed syllables. Speech tasks such as reading tasks may also impact timing – a reading task is more likely to elicit careful speech, which may be more syllable-timed for some speakers. In general, however, you can hear a difference in rhythm between the speakers of Appal AmE, EMidBrE, Qld AusE, and NZE on the one end, and speakers of HKE, IndE, MalE, NepE, and SLE, on the other, with the speakers of ZimE and WSAE falling between these two groups. The speakers of Appal AmE, EMidBrE, Qld AusE, and NZE tend to reduce the underlined words in Task 7.6; these are all grammatical function words (articles, prepositions, pronouns, auxiliary verbs). The second syllables of *sitting, going, father,* and *thinking,* also underlined, are also unstressed and weak in these varieties of English. In contrast, the speakers of HKE, IndE, MalE, NepE, and SLE have less reduction and more equal emphasis on each syllable.

7.7   CHECK YOUR UNDERSTANDING

EXERCISES

(a) What is the difference between a weak and a strong syllable? Which vowels are usually found in weak syllables? Which varieties of English have weak syllables?

(b) For varieties of English that have weak and strong syllables, what is the relationship between word stress and weak/strong syllables?

(c) What is a syllabic consonant? Which consonants can be syllabic? Why can these consonants (as opposed to other consonants) be syllabic?

(d) What is trochaic stress? Iambic stress?

DISCUSSION QUESTIONS

What is the relationship between Shakespeare and hip hop? In Chapter 6, we explored syllable structure and rhyme in poetry. In this chapter, we noted that some words in English have an iambic stress pattern, which consists of one weak/unstressed syllable followed by a strong/stressed syllable, as in *deCIDE*. The most common metre (or basic rhythmic structure) in poetry used by Shakespeare and other famous English poets, including Geoffrey Chaucer, William Wordsworth, and John Milton, is called **iambic pentameter** – a series of five (*penta*) words with iambic stress in a row, to form:

> *kaBOOM kaBOOM kaBOOM kaBOOM kaBOOM*

An example of this can be found in Shakespeare's Sonnet 18:

> Shall <u>I</u> / com<u>pare</u> / thee <u>to</u> / a <u>sum</u> /mer's <u>day</u>
> Thou <u>art</u> / more <u>love</u> /ly <u>and</u> / more <u>tem</u> / pe<u>rate</u>
> Rough <u>winds</u> / do <u>shake</u> / the <u>dar</u> / ling <u>buds</u> / of <u>May</u>
> And <u>sum</u> / mer's <u>lease</u> / hath <u>all</u> / too <u>short</u> / a <u>date</u>

Each line has a series of ten syllables, which can be divided into five groups of two syllables, with each set of two syllables having iambic stress, as shown above, with / denoting the break between iambic groups, and the stressed syllable underlined. This rhythm does create stress on function words, such as *to*. Try to read aloud each line, using iambic pentameter. Why do you think iambic pentameter was popular in poetry? One reason may be that it approximates human speech, leading to the speech sounding more natural when the play is performed on the stage or when a poem is recited aloud.

You may also have noticed that the poem has a series of end-rhymes, with the last syllables of each line rhyming in alternate lines: *day* rhymes with *May* and the last syllable of *temp<u>erate</u>* rhymes with *date*. This is a common poetic device. Poets and song writers may also use internal rhymes in their songs. An internal rhyme occurs inside a line, across several lines of the poem or song. A famous example of this is the song *Hey Jude*, by The Beatles (rhymes have been marked through underlining, bolding, and italics). As you can see, The Beatles rhymed the last word in a line with an internal word in the subsequent line, so that *bad* and *sad*, *better* and *let her*, and *heart* and *start* form rhymes:

Hey Jude, don't make it <u>bad</u>
Take a <u>sad</u> song and make it **better**
Remember to **let her** into your *heart*
Then you can *start* to make it **better**

Here is the next verse of *Hey Jude*. Following the pattern above, can you mark the rhymes in the verse?

Hey Jude, don't be afraid
You were made to go out and get her
The minute you let her under your skin
Then you begin to make it better

This brings us to hip hop and rap. Hip hop is a type of music that emerged within the African American, Jamaican, and Latino American community in New York City in the 1970s. A key feature of hip hop is the rhythmic music and the chanted or spoken rhyming speech, called rapping. The raps of hip hop are highly complex and creative, with hip hop artists increasingly being viewed as poets (Bradley, 2021). Consider the following line from Eric B. and Rakim's 1986 song, *Eric B. Is President*, as analysed by Vox (Caswell, 2016).

But can you <u>detect</u> what's coming <u>next</u>, from the <u>flex</u> of the **wrist**
Say *indeed* and I'll *proceed* 'cause my **man made a mix**
If he *bleed* he won't *need* no **band-Aid to fit**

As you can see, the artists blend internal and end rhymes, both across and within sentences. Even more complex is Eminem's *Lose Yourself*, the first rap song to win an Academy Award (rhymes within each line are marked with italics, bold, and underlining):

His **palms** are <u>sweaty</u>, *knees weak*, **arms** are hea<u>vy</u>
There's **vomit** on his <u>sweat</u>er <u>already</u>, **mom's** spa<u>ghetti</u>

He's *nervous,* but on the *surface* he looks **calm** and ready
To drop **bombs,** but he keeps on forgetting

In just four lines, almost every word rhymes with another word, from *palms,*
arms, vomit, mom's, calm, bombs, sweaty, heavy, already, ready, spaghetti,
knees, weak, among others (see Caswell, 2016).

Which rhymes can you find in the following passage from Rakim's song
My Melody (see King, 2015):

My unusual style will confuse you a while
If I were water, I'd flow in the Nile
So many rhymes you won't have time to go for yours
Just because of applause I have to pause
Right after tonight is when I prepare
To catch another sucker-duck MC out there
My strategy has to be tragedy, catastrophe
And after this you'll call me your majesty

The rhythmic nature of the lyrics and music is one reason for the suc-
cess of hip hop music, as is the story-telling (for an in-depth analysis of
rap lyrics, see Alim, 2003). In fact, the popularity of hip hop has inspired
teachers to use hip hop to bring Shakespeare to life, by setting sections of
Shakespeare's plays, as well as his sonnets, to music (Korbey, 2016).

EXPAND YOUR UNDERSTANDING

In Chapters 5 and 6, you were asked to construct your own language,
selecting vowels, consonants, and syllable structure for it. You were also
asked to select the minimum and maximum number of syllables for words
in your language.

(a) Is your language more syllable-timed or stress-timed?
(b) Are some syllables in your language reduced, with weak vowels? For
    example, you may decide that all one-syllable words have weak vowels,
    or that all final syllables in words of three syllables have weak vowels.
(c) Which vowels, if any, represent weak vowels in your language?

ANALYSE YOUR OWN PRONUNCIATION

(a) What variety of English do you speak? What are the stress patterns in
    this variety of English? Is your variety more or less syllable-timed?
(b) What predictions can you make about your own stress patterns?

(c) In Appendix A, you will find sample words to illustrate different stress patterns. Following the instructions there, record yourself reading these words and then do a phonemic and phonetic transcription, and an acoustic analysis using Praat.

(d) Do you have a weak vowel in happY, commA, or lettER? Why or why not?

(e) Do you have the same stress patterns on N/V pairs such as *record* and *rebel*? Or do you have a trochaic pattern for nouns and iambic for verbs?

(f) Do you have syllabic consonants in words such as *bottle* and *button*?

(g) Do you alternate strong and weak syllables in multiple-syllable words and sentences? Do you weaken unstressed words/syllables?

(h) Why do you think you have these patterns?

8 Intonation in Varieties of English

TASK 8.1 PRE-READING

🎧 Listen to the speakers of Midwestern AmE, Qld AusE, EMidBrE, HKE, MalE, NepE, and WSAE read two sentences: a declarative statement and a yes/no question.

He hid the letter under the hat. Declarative statement
Will you pay for the opera King Lear? Yes/no question

- What did you notice at the end of the question vs the end of the declarative statement?
- For which of the two sentences did the pitch of the speakers' voices fall?
- For which of the two sentences did the pitch of the speakers' voices rise?

8.1 Introduction to the Chapter

Building on the discussion of suprasegmentals in Chapter 6 ('English Syllable Structure') and 7 ('English Stress and Rhythm'), this chapter introduces the concept of **intonation**. The chapter begins by defining intonation both articulatorily and acoustically, with a focus on the relationship among pitch, tone, and intonation. The chapter then provides an overview of methods of analysing intonation, including acoustic analysis and the widely used Tone and Break Indices (ToBI) System. It then examines intonational systems in different varieties of English by first describing GAmE and SSBE sentence intonation and **pitch accent** patterns, to provide a framework through which to examine other varieties of English. The intonation and pitch accent patterns from different varieties of English are then discussed, as is the pitch range of different varieties of English. The chapter then examines two global phenomena in detail as they are spreading across varieties of English – **High Rising Terminal** on declarative statements, or **uptalk**; and **creaky voice**, also commonly called **vocal fry**. The chapter ends with exercises to check your understanding of the content of the chapter, as well as to expand your knowledge through an analysis of the intonation and pitch accent patterns in your own variety of English.

8.2 Defining Intonation

What is intonation? In Task 8.1, you listened to speakers of different varieties of English say two sentences, a declarative statement (*He hid the letter under the hat*) and a yes/no question (*Will you pay for the opera King Lear?*). You may have noticed that, for the declarative statement, the speakers' pitch fell or was lowered at the end, while for the yes/no question, their pitch rose at the end. We can visualize this through an acoustic analysis using Praat. Figures 8.1 and 8.2 show the speaker of MalE saying the declarative sentence (Figure 8.1) and the yes/no question (Figure 8.2).

For the speakers in Task 8.1, and as illustrated by the pitch contours on the spectrograms in Figures 8.1 and 8.2, these sentences have different intonation contours, with a falling pitch at the end of the statement and a

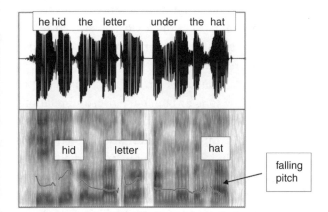

Figure 8.1 Malaysian English *He hid the letter under the hat*

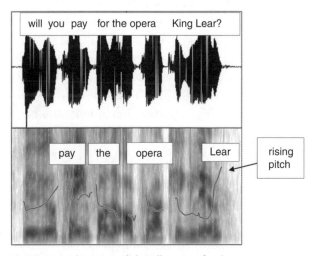

Figure 8.2 Malaysian English *Will you pay for the opera King Lear?*

rising pitch at the end of the yes/no question. In other words, the speakers are lowering or raising their pitch at the end of each sentence, which can indicate to the listener whether their utterance is a statement or a question. Different languages and varieties of English use pitch to signal meaning, including whether the speaker is asking a question, or is uncertain, expressing surprise, or making a statement. Before we examine the way different languages and varieties of English use intonation to signal meaning, we first have to define pitch and intonation.

In this book, I will follow Ladd's (2008, p. 4) definition of intonation; as he states, intonation 'refers to the use of *suprasegmental* phonetic features to convey "postlexical" or *sentence-level* pragmatic meanings in a *linguistically structured* way' (p. 4). As Ladd further notes, *suprasegmental* refers to fundamental frequency or F0 – the cycles of opening and closing of the vocal folds per second, expressed in hertz – and intensity and duration. *Postlexical* and/or *sentence-level* refer to a phrase- or sentence-level unit which excludes stress, tone, and accent used at the lexical level to differentiate the meaning of words (as in word stress in some varieties of English for N/V pairs such as *REcord* (N) vs *reCORD* (V) – see Chapter 7). Finally, as Ladd (2008, p. 4) notes: linguistically, structures 'are organised in terms of categorically distinct entities (e.g., low tone or boundary rise) and relations (e.g., stronger than/weaker than)'.

What is the relationship between pitch and intonation? Pitch refers to the F0 of a segment of speech while intonation refers to the patterns of pitch (rise and fall) across an utterance or stretch of speech, often called an **intonation phrase** (IP). Pitch can be classified as High (H) or Low (L) in English. As we can see in Figures 8.1 and 8.2, the MalE speaker has a series of high and low pitches across both sentences, with a higher pitch on *hid* and a lower pitch on *hat* in Figure 8.1, and a higher pitch on *pay*, *the*, *opera*, and *Lear* in Figure 8.2. The speaker also has a slightly higher rise on the second syllable of *letter* in Figure 8.1. Each noticeable rise or fall is a change in pitch; the pattern of rises and falls across an utterance is the intonation of that utterance, and called an intonation phrase, or IP.

Do all languages have intonation? Intonation is universal across languages, in part because intonation has an important function in language. One function for many languages is the use of falling intonation to signal the end of an utterance or statement (Hirst & Di Cristo, 1998). Despite intonation being universal, differences exist not only cross-linguistically but also across varieties of English in terms of the intonation range (or pitch range) used by speakers of a given variety, as well as how intonation is used to establish meaning.

It is useful here to make a distinction between languages that are classified as tone languages and those that are intonation languages. As we noted in Chapter 7, at the word level, we can distinguish among three different types of languages – languages that use: (1) lexical word stress (e.g., English and German); (2) tone – where each syllable has a separate pitch, which distinguishes meaning (e.g., Mandarin Chinese, Thai, and Yoruba); and, in some analyses, (3) pitch-accent languages, which use pitch accent (change in pitch) to create prominence for one syllable in a word (e.g., Japanese and Norwegian). While tone and stress are lexical or word-level features of language, and not included in our definition of intonation as in Ladd (2008), intonation is non-lexical, and occurs at the level of the syllable/word as well as across longer stretches of speech in intonation phrases. Languages that make use of intonation to signal meaning, including whether the utterance is a statement or a question, are often called **intonation languages**, in contrast to **tone languages**, which use tone at the word or syllable level to change meaning. One useful distinction between tone and intonation languages is whether the phonological pitch distinctions are spread across a word (a tone or pitch-accent language) or across the entire IP (intonation languages) (see van der Hulst, 1988).

Most accounts of English, based on OVEs including AmE, BrE, CanE, AusE, and NZE, among others, label English as an intonation language, similar to many other Germanic languages such as Dutch and German. However, it is important to note that many of the languages that influence varieties of English use tone to distinguish meaning in words and syllables. We can distinguish among languages as having a system of no tones, a simple tone system (usually with a high vs a low contrast in tone), or a complex tone system of three or more tone contrasts. Of the 527 languages surveyed for tone in WALS, 307, or 58%, do not have tones, while 132, or 25%, have a simple tone system, and 88, or 17%, have a complex tone system (Maddieson, 2013c). Languages with no tone include many European languages, such as Irish, English, Spanish, German, and French, as well as indigenous languages of Australia and North and South America. Languages with simpler tone systems include some North American indigenous languages such as Oneida and Cherokee; many languages in Africa, including Zulu, Hausa, Igbo; and languages of Asia, including Japanese (also categorized as a pitch-accent language). Languages with complex tone systems predominate in Africa and Asia, and include languages influencing varieties of English such as Cantonese, Mandarin Chinese, and Yoruba (Maddieson, 1984). Some varieties of English that have substrate tone languages, including HKE, SgE, NigE, and Ghanaian English, may be best interpreted as tone languages (see Gussenhoven, 2014; Lim, 2009).

While English has traditionally been classified as an intonation language, it is more accurate to state that some varieties of English are tone languages while others are intonation languages. In terms of the relationship between rhythm and tone, tone languages are usually more syllable-timed, as there is tone on every syllable. Many of the varieties of English that can be classified as more syllable-timed (see Chapter 7, and below) are influenced by substrate tone languages.

8.3   Analysing and Interpreting Intonation

How do we analyse intonation? As you saw above, we can analyse a speech segment for intonation by acoustically examining pitch rises and falls across an utterance. While this is a common method for intonation analysis, not all pitch changes are clearly visible on a spectrogram and therefore auditory (hearing) analysis is also often employed to find any patterns that may not be as clearly visible acoustically but are noticeable to the listener.

Regardless of which method is used – auditory or acoustic, or both – we need a notation system for interpreting intonation and pitch. While different approaches have been developed for the labelling of intonation contours, the ToBI System is often employed in research on English intonation. The ToBI System, developed by Pierrehumbert, Beckman, and colleagues (see Beckman & Pierrehumbert, 1986; Pierrehumbert, 1990), is based on an Autosegmental Metrical (AM) approach to intonation, and uses a binary system of High (H) or Low (L) levels of pitch. A ToBI analysis can consist of four tiers: (1) the Tone tier, with pitch accents and boundary and phrase tones; (2) an Orthographic tier, for the transcription of speech; (3) a Break-Index tier, to show boundaries between words and phrases; and (4) a Miscellaneous tier, for any supplementary information. A brief description of ToBI is given below.

We first look at what has been called sentence stress, nuclear stress, and tonic stress, among other things, in other accounts of intonation. ToBI uses the terminology of *pitch accent* for any prominent (stressed) syllable; this syllable is marked with an *, with either H* or L* pitch accents possible, or rising or falling accents, as shown below, based on Beckman and Elam (1997) and Pierrehumbert and Hirschberg (1990). It is important to note that H and L are relative to other pitches in the IP, and that there is no absolute H or L.

H*	peak accent; peak F0 slightly after or within the accented syllable; rise from middle F0 to F0 in upper range of speaker's pitch range
L*	low accent; low valley of F0; lower range of speaker's pitch range
L*+H	scooped accent; low tone in lower range of speaker's pitch range on accented syllable followed by sharp rise to a high

	tone in upper range of speaker's pitch range; may mean uncertainty or incredulity
L+H*	rising peak accent; a high peak on the accented syllable, preceded by sharp rise from valley in lowest part of speaker's pitch range
H+!H*	clear step down to accented syllable from high pitch (! signals a downstep); downsteps may mark information that exists or can be inferred from the discourse context

In ToBI, all accented (stressed) syllables are labelled with a pitch accent; if the syllable is not accented, it does not receive a pitch accent. All IPs in traditional accounts of English (primarily GAmE in ToBI) are considered to have at least one pitch accent, with more possible depending on the speaker/meaning of the utterance. The pitch accent (rise or fall) often extends over subsequent syllables if these syllables are unstressed. As noted in Chapter 7, pitch changes are not the only dimension of prominence; prominence can also include lengthening of the syllable, greater intensity, and full vowel sounds; ToBI, however, focuses only on pitch. All pitch accents are equal in the AM approach; in reality, however, it may be that one syllable is the most prominent in an IP.

The edges of the intonation phrase receive a % so that beginning boundary tones are marked as %L (Low) or %H (High) while final (end of IP) tones are marked as L% or H%. A non-final (intermediate) phrase can also be marked as High or Low with L- or H- (from Port, 1999).

Phrasal tones

L- or H-	phrase accent; occurs at an intermediate phrase between the pitch accent and a boundary tone; fills the space between the pitch accent and the boundary tone; an H- upsteps the boundary tone, creating a higher boundary tone than an L-
L% or H%	(final) boundary tone; occurs at every IP boundary
%H	high initial boundary tone
%L	low initial boundary tone

As full IPs have two final tones, the following boundary tones may occur in some varieties of English, including GAmE, upon which ToBI was developed:

L-L%	standard declarative sentence; there will be a sharp decrease in the intonation contour from the pitch accent to the boundary tone

He hid the letter under the hat.
L-L%

L-H%   a continuation rising boundary tone (common in a list of items to indicate incompleteness of list, as in *chips* and *pies* vs *fries*):
He bought chips, pies, and fries.
L-H% L-H%   L-L%

H-H%   a high rise on yes/no questions:
Will you pay for the opera King Lear?
H-H%

!H-L%   final plateau – a falling intonation where a preceding H* upsteps the final L% to a higher level:
I just ASKED you why.
L+H*   !H-L%

The Break-Index tier is used to mark word and phrase boundaries and comprises five levels:

0	no word boundary
1	normal word–word boundary
2	strong juncture with no tonal marking
3	intermediate phrase boundary
4	intonational phrase boundary

The following ToBI annotation is taken from Gussenhoven (2014, p. 4). As the example shows, the speaker has an H*L pitch accent on the syllables in capital letters, a low tone (%L) on the first word of the utterance, and a low tone (L%) at the utterance-final boundary:

He's a member of both associations.
He's a MEMber of BOTH associATions
%L   H*L   H*L   H*LL%

This indicates the speaker has a low pitch when starting the utterance, and a falling pitch on the end of the utterance. Three words in the IP have a pitch accent – the stressed syllable of *member*, the word *both*, and the stressed syllable of *associations*. This speaker is using a high pitch accent to give prominence to keywords in the IP (see also Chapter 7). Here, the utterance is spoken as a declaration – a statement of fact, as indicated by the speaker's falling intonation at the end of the utterance.

ToBI has been used to transcribe and annotate speech for intonation patterns and other prosodic elements; while it was developed based on intonation patterns of GAmE, it has been modified for use in other languages, including Japanese, Greek, Portuguese, and Hong Kong Cantonese, and varieties of English, including RP and some Australian varieties. As Lim (2009) notes, ToBI was developed based on OVE standards and therefore may not be appropriate for all varieties of English.

How do we analyse pitch and intonation acoustically? Acoustically, intonation is measured through fundamental frequency, or F0, which corresponds to the number of vocal fold vibrations per second, or hertz (Hz). We often call this *pitch*; as Gussenhoven (2004, p. 1) states, 'Pitch is the auditory sensation of tonal height.' As noted above, we can hear pitch auditorily by ear and we can analyse pitch acoustically through software programs such as Praat. Men and women have different pitch ranges, as do children, so it is important that pitch settings are modified to adjust for the possible pitch ranges of the speaker: for men, a standard setting may be between 75 and 300/400 Hz, while for women, a standard setting is usually 100–500 Hz. Children's pitch may be as high as 600 Hz (as a comparison, sopranos can sing at as high as 2,000 Hz); both women and men may have pitch as low as 40 Hz if they use creaky voice (see below) (Gussenhoven, 2004). The F0 rise is usually greater on a salient syllable; it can also be relatively lower on a salient syllable. What is important to note is that there is no absolute value for the F0 to be considered H or L – a high pitch accent or boundary tone is higher than the preceding/following syllables; conversely, a low or lowered pitch or boundary tone is lower than preceding/following syllables. For this reason, an acoustic analysis may not always display what a listener hears as low or high if the rise/fall is slight (though it may still be interpreted by the hearer as a rise/fall). Another important point to consider in acoustic analyses of intonation is that it is normal for a pitch to start higher at the beginning of the IP and gradually fall across the IP (Levis & Wichman, 2015).

In Praat, a Textgrid can be created to show the four ToBI tiers, as shown in Figure 8.3 for the NepE woman reading the declarative sentence *He hid the letter under the hat* from Task 8.1. In Figure 8.4, the sentence has been analysed using ToBI. Notice also that the pitch settings are 100–500 Hz as this is a woman speaking. You can note that she has several pitch accents – *hid, letter, hat* – with a falling tone at the boundary. You can also note the use of the Orthographic tier (text) to give the transcription of the words said; the Break-Index shows that there is a normal word boundary after each word and final intonational phrase boundary after *hat*. The miscellaneous (Misc) tier can be used for supplementary notes.

8.4   Intonation in Varieties of English

Do all varieties of English have the same intonation and pitch accent patterns? We start by looking at the general patterns found in GAmE and SSBE, not because these patterns should be viewed as being the

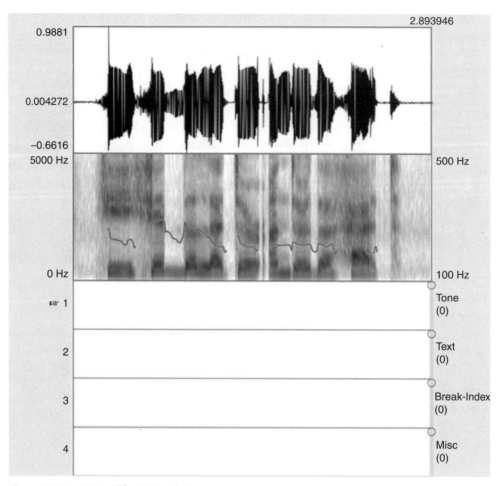

Figure 8.3 Praat Textgrid for ToBI analysis

norm or the standard, but because they provide a useful springboard for introducing possible intonation patterns in varieties of English. Some of these have already been introduced above for GAmE in the discussion of ToBI; these are based on Cruttenden (2014). As Table 8.1 shows, declarative statements, wh-questions, and exclamations typically take a falling intonation in SSBE and GAmE, while yes/no questions and echos on declarative statements have a rise in pitch. When items are presented in a list, as in *He brought apples, pears, and grapes*, each item is usually given a rising pitch to indicate incompleteness of the list (more items will be listed), with a falling pitch on the last item to indicate finality. Other sentence types, notably imperatives and tag questions, may have either a rising or falling intonation depending on the meaning of the utterance.

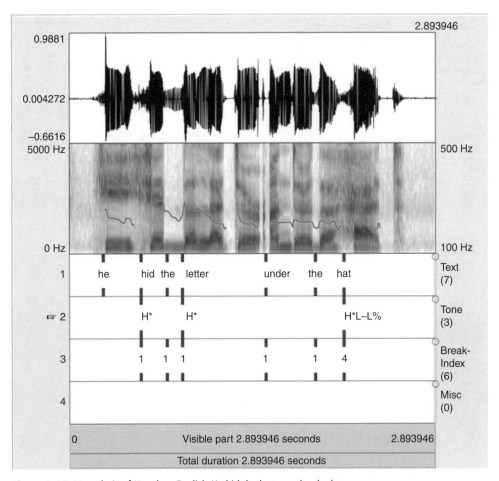

Figure 8.4 ToBI analysis of Nepalese English *He hid the letter under the hat*

TASK 8.2 Listening for Sentence Types

🎧 Listen to the speakers of GAmE and Mod RP read aloud the following sentences. Can you hear the falling or rising intonation patterns for each sentence type?

(1) Declarative statement: *All of this takes willpower.* (falling intonation)

(2) Yes/no question: *Should he spend all of his time just studying?* (rising intonation)

(3) Wh-question: *Where should he live?* (falling intonation)

(4) Tag question: *This long-awaited feeling doesn't develop suddenly, does it?* (rising intonation)

(5) List of items: *At first, it is not easy for him to be casual in dress, informal in manner, and confident in speech.* (rise rise fall)

Table 8.1 Intonation patterns in General American English and Standard Southern British English

Sentence type	Pattern	Example sentences
1 Declarative statements	high fall or low fall high fall: more liveliness/ involvement fall-rise: reservation, contrast, warning	*The train leaves at midnight.*
2 Echos/declarative questions	high rises	*So you didn't go?*
3 Yes/no questions	low rise (BrE) or high rise (AmE) rise-fall marks yes/no as exclamation	*Is this your bag?*
4 Wh-questions	low fall or high fall low rise (BrE) or high rise (AmE) more tentative	*Who is going to the lunch?*
5 Tag questions	high fall / low fall (statement) low rise (question)	*This is your car, isn't it?*
6 Imperatives	falling tone: abrupt imperatives rising tone (mostly low rise): polite imperatives	*(What should I do now?) Go and wash the car.*
7 Exclamations	fall tone (can include rise-fall)	*What a beautiful day!*
8 List of items	rise rise fall: rise on each subsequent item and fall on last item	*He brought apples, pears, and grapes.*

In GAmE and SSBE, pitch accents create more prominent syllables, usually to highlight key information or new information; this is commonly on the last content word in the IP; content words include nouns, verbs, adjectives, adverbs, in contrast to function words, which include pronouns, prepositions, conjunctions, articles, auxiliary verbs, and articles. For contrastive purposes, however, any word may become the bearer of the tonic syllable. A pitch accent is usually on the word that is most important – prominent – in the IP: the *focus* of the information. In English grammar, which follows a topic–comment structure, new information is often on the last content word. For example, in the declarative statement *She drove the blue car*, the neutral (also called non-contrastive) pitch accent pattern would be on *car*, as shown in example 1 below. As examples 2–5 show, stress can be moved to highlight different information, such as the car being *blue* (the colour is important), that the subject of the sentence *drove* (not rode in) the car, that the subject was the *driver* (and not someone else), or that she drove a *particular* blue car.

(1) Non-contrastive: She drove the blue *car*.
(2) Contrastive: She drove the *blue* car. (It was not the red or green car.)
(3) Contrastive: She *drove* the blue car. (She was the driver, not the passenger.)
(4) Contrastive: *She* drove the blue car. (She drove the car, not someone else.)
(5) Contrastive: She drove *the* blue car. (She drove a particular blue car.)

The last word may not always be a content word; if the speaker and hearer have been discussing cars, for example, *car* may be replaced by a pronoun, as shown in example 6:

(6) She drove the *blue* one.

Here, the speaker places the pitch accent on *blue*, rather than *one*, to highlight the colour, and also because *blue* is the last content word (as *one* is a function word). Once a word has been replaced by a pronoun, it is considered *old information*, and therefore is generally not emphasized in GAmE and SSBE. This is called *deaccenting* (see Ladd, 2008) and can also occur when stress is expected on a word and it does not occur. This may occur in different varieties of English (see below).

TASK 8.3 Listening for Pitch Accent

🎧 In this task, you can listen to a speaker of GAmE read the example sentences discussed above.

(1) Non-contrastive: She drove the blue *car*.
(2) Contrastive: She drove the *blue* car (not the red or green car).
(3) Contrastive: She *drove* the blue car. (She was the driver.)
(4) Contrastive: *She* drove the blue car (not someone else).
(5) Contrastive: She drove *the* blue car (the special blue car).
(6) Final pronoun: She drove the *blue* one.
(7) Yes/no question: She drove the blue *car*?
  • Can you hear the prominence of the italicized words in each sentence? (These words receive the high pitch accent in each sentence.)
  • Can you hear the falling intonation in sentence 1 versus the rising intonation in sentence 7?

In Figures 8.5 to 8.7, waveforms and spectrograms of some of the sentences from Task 8.3 are given. To simplify the analysis, only the pitch accents and final boundary tones are marked though you may note the higher intonation on all three sentences at the initial phrase boundary (%H). Figure 8.5 shows the spectrogram and waveform for sentence (1), the non-contrastive statement; the pitch accent is on the last content word in this extract, on *car*, and the boundary tone is an L-L% for a declarative statement.

Figure 8.6 shows an acoustic analysis of the same sentence when the pitch accent is placed on *blue*, with an L pitch rising to an H pitch (L+H*) and a falling pitch on *car* (L-L%).

Figure 8.7 shows the same speaker placing the pitch accent on *the*, which has a notably higher pitch than the preceding and following words, and a falling boundary tone on *car*.

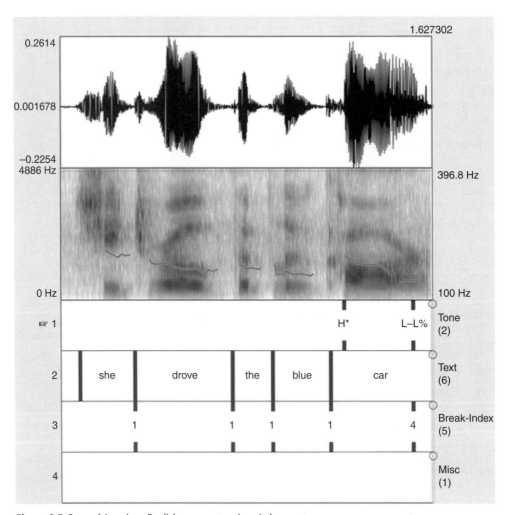

Figure 8.5 General American English non-contrastive pitch accent on *car*

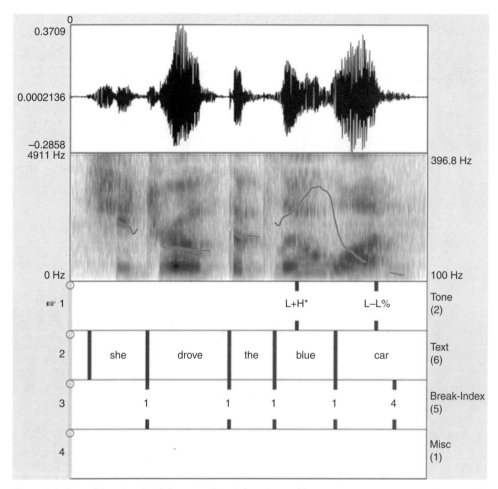

Figure 8.6 General American English contrastive pitch accent on *blue*

As noted previously, not all varieties of English are intonation languages; as Lim (2009) and Gussenhoven (2014) argue, varieties of English that are influenced by tone languages, including SgE, NigE, and HKE, may themselves best be interpreted as tone languages. NigE, for example, has a system of H or L tones, with more level pitch on syllables and less complex pitch accents than BrE (Gut, 2005). HKE and SgE, among other varieties, have a Medium tone (M) due to substrate influences; HKE, MalE, and SgE also use discourse particles like *lah* and *meh*, usually at the end of the IP, with tone due to influence from Chinese languages, and particularly Cantonese (see Lim, 2009, and Low, 2012). Even within distinctive varieties of English such as AmE and BrE, intonation patterns can vary widely, with some varieties of both AmE (particularly Calif AmE / Western AmE) and BrE (Southern BrE) having a final rise on declarative statements (see below), while some varieties of English in Northern England, Northern Ireland, and

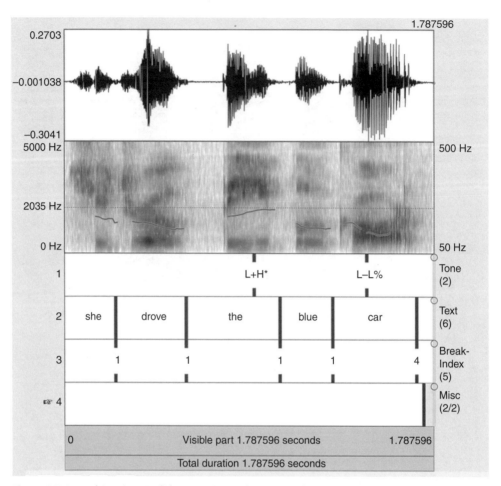

Figure 8.7 General American English contrastive pitch accent on *the*

parts of Scotland, part of the Urban North British English (UNBE) dialect area, also have a distinctive rise pattern on declarative statements.

Varieties of English may also have different pitch ranges; pitch range can be understood as the distance between the highest and the lowest pitch level for a speaker and/or a speaker's average pitch level (Malarski & Jekiel, 2018). Some varieties of English, including MāoriE (see Warren & Bauer, 2004) and FijE (Tent & Mugler, 2004), have a relatively higher pitch overall. Some NAE as well as NigE may have a smaller pitch range (Gut, 2005; Newmark, Walker, & Stanford, 2016); IndE appears to have a smaller pitch range in read speech but a wider pitch range in conversational speech and a higher pitch level than BrE (Fuchs, 2018). In contrast, IrE (Hickey, 2004) and AAVE have a wider pitch range; AAVE also has falsetto (see below) and a frequent shift in pitch levels (Thomas, 2007). Within AmE, SAmE has a wider pitch range than Midwestern AmE while varieties of English in Northern Scotland, England and Ireland have a narrower pitch range than Southern BrE varieties (Malarski & Jekiel, 2018).

Table 8.2 presents a summary of intonation patterns across varieties of English. Available speech samples are referenced in the table. Generally, as outlined in the above discussion of GAmE and SSBE / RP English, most varieties of English have a rising intonation on yes/no questions and a rise/rise/fall intonation for a list of items. While many varieties also have a falling intonation on declarative statements, some varieties have a rising intonation on declaratives (this is called High Rising Terminal (HRT) or uptalk, and will be discussed in detail below); similarly, while some varieties have a falling intonatlon on wh- questions, in some varieties all questions have a rise at the end. Only notable differences in intonation are highlighted in the table as well as in the discussion below.

☞ The following discussion of intonation is intended to provide a comprehensive overview of the intonation in Englishes worldwide.

Although you are encouraged to listen to different types of intonation patterns, you may wish to focus your attention on the intonation patterns that exist in the Englishes that are of interest to you.

In Table 8.2, listening tasks illustrating intonation patterns are listed for each variety as relevant. Listening Task 8.4 in Table 8.2 presents a range of intonation patterns for speakers of different varieties of English, as shown in the table. You may also wish to re-listen to Tasks 8.2 and 8.3, which have been previously introduced in this chapter. Listening tasks 8.5–8.7 will be discussed in detail in later sections of the chapter.

It may be useful to refer to this list to help guide your listening.

TASK 8.4 Listening for Intonation in Varieties of English

🎧 In Task 8.4, you can listen to a range of speakers illustrate intonation patterns in different varieties of English. The varieties and intonation patterns are listed in Table 8.4. Table 8.4 also makes reference to other listening tasks when relevant.

Table 8.2 Intonation in varieties of English

Variety	Intonation systems	🎧 Listening tasks
RP English / SSBE (Cruttenden, 2014)	Falling contour for declarative statements and wh-questions. Rising contours for yes/no questions. Given information is deaccented. Uptalk emerging in some varieties of Southern BrE.	8.2, 8.4A
NBrE (Cruttenden, 2014)	UNBE: Greater use of intonation rises in Northern BrE, in contrast to falling intonation in Southern BrE on declarative statements.	8.4A

Table 8.2 (Cont.)

Variety	Intonation systems	🎧 Listening tasks
EMidBrE (my data)	Lengthening of final stressed syllable in IP. Uptalk for some speakers.	8.4A
IrE (Hickey, 2004)	Large intonational range characterized by a noticeable drop in pitch on stressed syllables. UNBE: Greater use of intonation rises in Belfast (Northern Ireland). High pitch a primary cue to prominence in Belfast.	8.4B
WelE (Penhallurick, 2004)	May have a high degree of pitch movement on an unaccented syllable after a pitch accent. A sequence of rising contours (L H, H H) that has an ultimately rising nuclear contour.	
G/StAmE (Kretzschmar, 2004)	High tone at beginning of a sentence, either as a boundary tone %H or as a high initial pitch accent H*. Declarative sentences and wh-questions typically end in a low tone L–L%. Rising tone in yes/no questions. Given information is deaccented. Uptalk and creaky voice in some varieties/speakers.	8.2, 8.3, 8.4C, 8.5, 8.6, 8.7
Appal AmE (Lai & van Hell, 2020)	Regional pattern of pitch accent is default high tone (H*). More rising pitch accent (L+H*) (uptalk) in declarative sentences than other varieties. Creaky voice.	8.4C, 8.6, 8.7
Rural SAmE (Thomas, 2004)	Exaggerated pitch rises are main intonational contour of white SAmE; this occurs in heavily stressed syllables.	
AAVE (Edwards, 2004; Thomas, 2007)	Yes/no questions sometimes omit final rise, with level or falling contour. Wider pitch range, with falsetto, and frequent shift in pitch. More level and rising final contours than European AmE. Yes/no questions may have falling final contours in formal situations but level or rising in informal situations. High frequency of primary stresses.	
NAE (Coggshall, 2008; Newmark, Walker, & Stanford, 2016)	Pitch contour in some words: stressed syllable is low and the following syllable is high (L*+H). End of intonation units may have high-rising (uptalk), mid, or high-falling contour, rather than falling as in GAmE. Smaller pitch range.	
ChiE (Santa Ana & Bayley, 2004)	A rising glide which can occur anytime in a contour. Lengthening of syllables with pitch accent. Final rise for declarative statements (uptalk).	

Variety	Intonation systems	🎧 Listening tasks
CanE (Boberg, 2004)	Similar to GAmE. Final rise for declarative statements (uptalk). Creaky voice for some speakers.	8.4D, 8.5, 8.6, 8.7
PRE (my data)	Generally follows AmE (acrolectal). Uptalk for some speakers.	8.4E, 8.6
AusE (Horvath, 2004; my data)	Final rise for declarative statements (HRT)/Australian Questioning Intonation (AQI) (uptalk). Creaky voice for some speakers.	8.4F, 8.5, 8.6, 8.7
AusAborE (Butcher, 2008; Jespersen, 2015)	Little systematic research on intonation of AusAborE. Uptalk for some speakers.	
NZE (Bauer & Warren, 2004)	Final rise for declarative statements (uptalk).	8.4G, 8.5, 8.6
MāoriE (Warren & Bauer, 2004)	Relatively high pitch in MāoriE overall. More uptalk among Māori women than Pakeha (European) women. More uptalk in MāoriE than NZE.	
NiuE (Starks, Christie, & Thompson, 2007; Warren, 2015)	Last syllable or stress group has falling pitch. Uptalk from NZE.	
FijE (Tent & Mugler, 2004)	Overall higher pitch patterns than in GAmE or BrE. Yes/no questions start at high pitch and end with very rapid rise and then fall in pitch. Last syllable or stress group is indicated by a fall in pitch.	
KenE (Schmied, 2004)	Influenced by tone languages. A general lowering of pitch through the course of a sentence, combined with a weakening of the intensity. May have relatively even pitch/tone throughout the IP.	8.4H
BSAE (Van Rooy, 2004)	Tone/information units may be shorter so more syllables and words receive pitch accent. A general lowering of pitch throughout the course of a sentence.	
WSAE (Grice, German, & Warren, 2020; my data)	May follow BrE intonation patterns for wh-questions, tag-questions, list of items, and yes/no questions. Uptalk and creaky voice for some speakers.	8.4I, 8.6, 8.7
ZimE (my data)	May follow BrE for wh-questions, declarative statements, yes/no questions, list of items. Some speakers may have uptalk. Tendency for pitch accent to fall on first content word of IP and for %H boundary tone.	8.4J, 8.6

Table 8.2 (Cont.)

Variety	Intonation systems	🎧 Listening tasks
NigE (Gut 2005; Zerbian, 2013)	Tone is grammatically determined – content (lexical) words receive a high tone on the stressed syllable, and function (non-lexical) words receive a low tone. Smaller pitch range than BrE. Rising tones are rare and occur mostly in yes/no and tag questions. Stress is rarely used for emphasis or contrast. Given information is not deaccented. Preference for pitch accent on final word in IP.	
SgE (Lim, 2009; Low, 2012; Wee, 2004; my data)	Smaller number of pitch contrasts than RP. Speakers do not generally use pitch variations to express contrastive meaning. Final syllable may be lengthened; may also be louder and have higher pitch (word-final high boundary tone). Both new and given information may receive stress; more difficult to distinguish stressed, unstressed, and pitch accented syllables as more syllables receive stress. Rise-fall tone may indicate greater emphasis. May have H, M, L tone. Use of discourse particles (*hor, leh, lor, ma, meh*) with original tone from Cantonese. Some speakers may have creaky voice and/or final rise in intonation.	8.4K, 8.6, 8.7
MalE (Baskaran, 2004; Nayan and Setter, 2016)	Does not have as many patterns of intonation. Particles such as *lah, man, ah(uh)* signal questions, attitudes, emotions, instead of intonation. Loudness may be used for emphasis. Pitch direction does not change within accented word (as fall or as a rise) and may stay level across a word. Cooperative Rise (CR).	8.4L, 8.6
HKE (Wee, 2016; my data)	The pitch accent tends to occur at the end of an utterance. Emphatic words may not receive pitch accent. Smaller number of pitch contrasts. Repeated information – pronouns and determiners, for example – may not be deaccented. May have H, M, L tone; tone may stay level across a word. May have rising tone on yes/no and wh-questions. Use of discourse particles (*lah, hor, leh, lor, ma, meh*) with original tone from Cantonese. Rising final tone on declarative statements for some speakers.	8.4M, 8.6

Variety	Intonation systems	🎧 Listening tasks
IndE (Gargesh, 2004; Wiltshire & Harnsberger, 2006; Fuchs, 2016, 2018)	Falling intonation in statements, commands, and exclamations. Rising intonation occurs in yes/no questions, tag questions, some wh-questions, and in dependent clauses. Use of pitch to indicate an accented syllable. May have several pitch accents on words; these multiple pitch accents are a salient feature of IndE. Given information is not deaccented. Smaller pitch range in read speech, wider in conversational speech, and higher pitch range than BrE.	8.4N
PakE (Mahboob & Ahmar, 2004)	Falling intonation in statements, commands, and exclamations. Rising intonation occurs in yes/no questions, tag questions, some wh-questions, and dependent clauses. Accented syllables marked with lower pitch. Amplitude does not mark stress; use of pitch to mark accented syllables.	8.4O
SLE (Fery, 2010)	From Tamil: an H rise tone at the phrase boundary.	8.4P, 8.6
NepE (my data)	An H pitch rise at the phrase boundary for some speakers.	8.4Q
PhlE (Tayao, 2004)	Final rising-falling intonation in statements and final rising in questions for some speakers (no distinction in intonation between yes/no and wh-questions).	8.4R

We start by looking at different varieties of BrE. The intonation patterns for RP/SSBE have also been described above and can be heard in Tasks 8.2 and 8.4A. Northern England, along with parts of Northern Ireland and northern parts of Scotland, are part of the Urban North British English (UNBE) dialect area. One key feature of this dialect is a rising intonation which is similar to but not the same as uptalk/HRT on declarative statements. Less research has been done on the intonation of EMidBrE; my own analysis of data suggests that uptalk may exist for some speakers and that there is lengthening on the final stress syllable in the IP. This can be heard in Task 8.4A. Southern varieties of IrE generally follow SSBE/RP sentence patterns; a key feature of this variety, however, is the large intonation range and drop in pitch on stressed syllables. This can be heard in Task 8.4B (listen for the drop in pitch on the stressed word *more* in Conversation Intonation Range 2). As noted in Chapter 7, WelE has more pitch movement on unaccented syllables that occur after a pitch accent in an IP. Some varieties of ScotE may follow UNBE with a rise on declarative statements.

We now turn to varieties of AmE. In addition to the patterns discussed for GAmE previously, some varieties may have a *High Rising Intonation* (HRT) on declarative statements (this is also called *uptalk*) as well as a lower phonation register called *creaky voice* or *vocal fry*. Both of these will be discussed in detail separately below. Differences in intonation patterns can be found in Appal AmE, which has more rising intonation than other varieties of AmE, as well as Rural SAmE, which has more exaggerated pitch rises, particularly on stressed syllables. AAVE has more uptalk than many varieties of AmE, and greater frequency of primary stresses (pitch accents) across an IP. NAE also has uptalk as well as a pattern of L pitch accent on stressed syllables followed by an H pitch (L*+H). ChiE also has uptalk as well as the possibility of a rising glide anywhere in an IP. CanE follows GAmE patterns; some speakers have uptalk and creaky voice. PRE follows GAmE intonation patterns, particularly in the acrolectal variety. Some speakers also have uptalk. In Tasks 8.4C, 8.4D, and 8.4E, you can listen to speakers of GAmE, Calif AmE, Midwestern AmE, and Appal AmE, as well as CanE and PRE, illustrating the main intonation patterns of these varieties, including uptalk and creaky voice, which will be examined in more detail separately, below.

A key feature distinguishing Australian and New Zealand varieties of English, including AusAborE and MāoriE, is the uptalk on declarative statements, which will be discussed more below. NiuE may also have uptalk, probably influenced by NZE. Both NiuE and FijE have a falling pitch on the last syllable or stress group; FijE also has a rapid rise and then fall in pitch on yes/no questions, which tend to start on a higher pitch. In Tasks 8.4F and 8.4G, you can listen to speakers of AusE and NZE illustrate the intonation patterns of these varieties of English, and particularly the uptalk on declarative statements.

We now move to the discussion of African Englishes. KenE is influenced by tone languages and has a more syllable-timed rhythm (see Chapter 7), with a relatively even pitch or tone throughout the IP. This can be heard in Task 8.4H. BSAE tends to have shorter IP, which may increase the number of words/syllables receiving a pitch accent. WSAE generally follows BrE intonation patterns, also described above, and some speakers may have creaky voice and/or uptalk; this can be heard in Task 8.4I. ZimE may also follow BrE intonation patterns; in my own analysis of ZimE data, I noted a tendency for a %H boundary tone in the IP, with an H pitch accent on the first content word in the IP, and then a low level pitch across the IP; this can be heard in Task 8.4J and seen in Figure 8.8.

In NigE, tone is grammatically determined – content (lexical) words receive a high tone on the stressed syllable, and function (non-lexical) words receive a low tone, with stress rarely used for emphasis or contrast. Pitch accent is also often used on the final word in the IP. Most IPs end in falling tones, with rising tones only used in yes/no and tag questions.

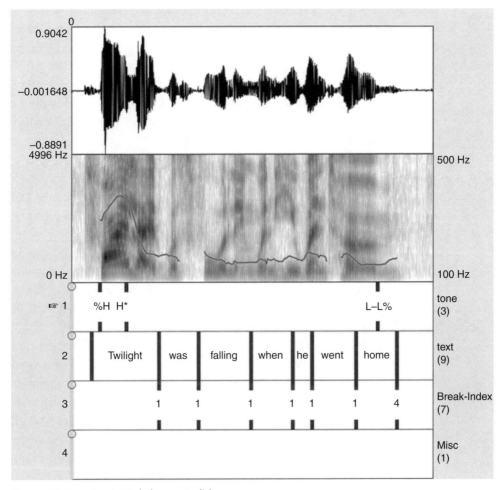

Figure 8.8 Intonation in Zimbabwean English

Some Asian Englishes, including HKE, SgE, and MalE, may also best be categorized as tone and not intonation varieties of English, as discussed above. These varieties are also more syllable-timed and have less pitch movement across syllables, similar to KenE. SgE has a more level tone across the IP, with a smaller number of pitch contrasts than BrE. SgE may also have an M tone, and place more stress on syllables without deaccenting unstressed syllables or given information. I also found a final rise in intonation in SgE, as well as in MalE and HKE, possibly due to influence from substrate languages; it may also be uptalk, which is spreading globally across Englishes. You can listen to two speakers of SgE in Task 8.4K. MalE has similar features to HKE and SgE; it also has a feature called a Cooperative Rise (CR), which is a rise in tone at the end of the IP. You can listen to two speakers of MalE in Task 8.4L, including an example of the CR. One of them also talks about the 'flatter' nature of tone in MalE. HKE may also have an H, M, or L, rather than an H–L tone contrast; the tone may stay level within a word, leading to a more monotone sound, as described by speakers of HKE (Hansen Edwards, 2018). Tone may also be used on discourse particles found at the end of the IP, such as *lah, leh, lor*, which are borrowed from Cantonese. HKE may also not use pitch accent to stress keywords but rather place the pitch accent at the end of the IP. HKE may have a rising intonation in both yes/no and wh-questions; this can be heard in Task 8.4M. Some speakers of HKE may have a rising intonation on declarative statements; it is not clear whether this is uptalk or a use of an H tone, influenced by Cantonese. This can also be heard in Task 8.4M.

A key feature of IndE is the use of several pitch accents in an IP, as well as a lack of deaccenting of given information, giving more syllables and words prominence than in many other varieties of English; this can be heard in Task 8.4N. Similarly, PakE uses pitch to mark accented syllables and may have lower pitch on these. You can listen to the PakE speaker in Task 8.4O. Little has been written about the intonation of SLE; it is possible that SLE has an H% tone at the phrase boundary, which is a feature of Tamil, one of the substrate languages influencing SLE, giving SLE a high rise at the end of each phrase or intonation unit. This resembles uptalk, though the High Rising Terminal is likely influenced by Tamil. This can be heard in the speech of the SLE speaker in Task 8.4P. Similarly, little has been written about the intonation of NepE; my data from the speaker of NepE indicates a pattern of a rising pitch at the end of phrases may exist in this variety as well; this can be heard in the speech samples in Task 8.4Q. Acrolectal PhlE generally follows AmE; in mesolectal and basilectal varieties, statements have a falling intonation and both wh- and yes/no questions have a rising intonation. You can listen to a speaker of PhlE in Task 8.4R.

8.5 Uptalk and High Rising Intonation

TASK 8.5 Listening for Uptalk

🎧 Listen to the speakers of AmE, CanE, AusE, and NZE in conversation. For each sentence given below, what do you notice about the intonation and pitch? What happens on the words given in bold in each sentence?

(1) I'm from United States of **America**. (Calif AmE)
(2) I don't really know if I have an accent so that's why I say standard American **English**. (Calif AmE)
(3) Australian ... **English** I'm not too sure I just know how it sounds **like**. (Calif AmE)

(4) It's a very smally **populated** there's not a lot of **people.** (Midwestern AmE)
(5) Hong Kong is very **polluted.** (CanE)
(6) I think the people here ... like they're very **nice.** (CanE)
(7) I'm from uh Wellington New **Zealand.** (NZE)
(8) Ummm it's a harbour city much like **Hong Kong.** (NZE)
(9) Mmm I do double major in accounting and international **business.** (NZE)
(10) My uni has an agreement with umm **CUHK.** (SA AusE)
(11) Like we were saying before I was enjoying it when it was warmer. (SA AusE)
(12) **Australia.** (Qld AusE)

In our discussion of intonation patterns above, we noted that declarative statements have a falling intonation in many varieties of English. In Task 8.5, all the speakers are making statements but, in each case, they use a rising pitch on the words in bold. This is a global phenomenon called *High Rising Terminal* (HRT) or, more commonly, *uptalk.*

What is High Rising Terminal / uptalk? Before we discuss the phenomenon of a high rise on declarative statements, it is important to clarify what we mean by HRT and uptalk. HRT is the name given to the phenomenon of a rising intonation at the end of statements, where otherwise it would be a falling intonation. As Warren and Britain (2000) state, HRT can be defined as 'salient rises in pitch at the end of non-interrogative intonational phrases' (p. 153). The use of the term 'high' in the label is somewhat misleading, as the rise may begin L rather than H for some speakers and varieties. The term 'uptalk' is used synonymously with HRT, and is likely a better term as it refers to the realization of the end of the IP with a rising intonation, either from an L or an H start. For this reason, the term 'uptalk' will be used in this book. Both HRT and uptalk have been used in some research also to refer to the use of a rising intonation on questions and confirmation checks; in this volume, the terms will only be used to refer to a rising intonation on declarative statements.

As mentioned above, both UNBE end rises and uptalk are two types of intonation variation that occur in varieties of English. While the UNBE intonation is restricted to areas of Northern Ireland, Scotland, and England, uptalk occurs globally. Both the UNBE rises and uptalk involve rising intonation on declarative sentences, which would take a falling intonation in other varieties of English. However, as researchers (Cruttenden, 2014; Ladd, 2008) note, they should not be considered the same phenomenon; it is possible that the UNBE rise, along with other features common in Northern England, parts of Scotland, and Northern English comprising the UNBE dialect group, is influenced by Irish (Ladd, 2008). The UNBE rise consists of a rise on declaratives, with the rise either continuous or a rise with a plateau, with possible downdrift at the end (Cruttenden, 2014). It has been found in northern cities in England including Liverpool, Birmingham, Manchester, and Newcastle, as well as in Glasgow, Scotland, and Belfast, Northern Ireland.

What is the difference between uptalk and UNBE rises? Research (Cruttenden, 2014) shows both phonetic and pragmatic differences in uptalk and UNBE rises. In many varieties of English, uptalk coexists with a falling intonation; this means the speaker has a *choice* in the use of a rise or fall for declarative statements; in UNBE, in contrast, the rising intonation is the *only* realization for a declarative statement. Phonetic differences exist as well; while the uptalk intonation contour consists of a rise from the pitch accent to the end of the utterance, the UNBE consists of a rise and often a fall, which Cruttenden (2007) calls a *rise–plateau–slump*, which can be expressed in ToBI as L+H* H L%, L*+H H L%, or L* HL% – a low or low-rising pitch accent, a high phrase accent, and a low boundary tone (Ladd, 2008).

In which varieties of English does uptalk occur? Uptalk is a well-established linguistic phenomenon across varieties of English, as shown in Table 8.2. It has been documented as a feature of AusE since the 1960s (Warren, 2015) and is referred to as Australian Questioning Intonation (AQI) in AusE. It was also documented in NZE as early as the 1960s, particularly among MāoriE speakers as well as in NiuE and other varieties of NZE (Warren, 2015). In the US, it is considered a notable feature of Southern California (SoCal) AmE, as part of Valley Girl speech that has emerged in the San Fernando Valley area of California. Uptalk exists in other varieties of AmE, including Western, Midwestern, Southern, Northern, and Appal AmE, as well as ChiE, AAVE, and NAE. It has also been found in CanE, and in Southern varieties of British English, including LonE and Mod RP; it also occurs in WelE (Warren, 2015). It may also occur in some NVEs, including WSAE, ZimE, HKE, SgE, SLE, and PRE, though many of the languages that influence these varieties of English are tone or pitch-accent languages, and the final rise may be a feature from the substrate language. Uptalk may also be spreading into NVEs through the media.

What is the function of uptalk? While a rising intonation is most commonly used to signal a question or as a confirmation check, uptalk is defined in this volume as occurring in contexts where the speaker is not asking a question. Following Levon (2020), this discussion focuses on contexts where a rising intonation would not have occurred historically or in prescriptive accounts of the variety. Uptalk is often viewed as signalling uncertainty or hesitation (Levon, 2016). Research (e.g., Levon, 2016, 2020; Warren, 2015), however, indicates that uptalk has both discourse and affective functions, and does not often signal hesitancy. Uptalk most commonly occurs at the end of an IP, though it can also occur medially. One function of uptalk is to hold the floor, to signal that more information is forthcoming. Research (see Levon, 2020) on the types of speech acts involving uptalk also suggests that, for LonE women, uptalk is used most frequently in the telling of narratives and less so for opinions, descriptions, and explanations, and least on facts. As Levon (2020) argues, uptalk may be used as a device to organize complex interactions, with narratives requiring more development and sentence structure coordination than statements of facts, with greater use of uptalk in narratives aiding the organization of the content. Men and women may also use uptalk for different communicative purposes in some varieties of English: in LonE, uptalk may have an instrumental function for women, as described above, while for men, it may have a referential or affective function to build solidarity with interactants (Levon, 2020). Research in AusE and NZE also suggests that uptalk is used more often in complex narratives, as a mechanism of floor holding and seeking confirmation from listeners (Levon, 2016). Affectively, it may also function as a politeness marker in NZE, to emphasize in-group solidarity (Levon, 2016); in the UK, it may also be a solidarity marker for women speakers of RP, as well as a discourse marker to emphasize both new and important information (Bradford, 1997).

Who uses uptalk? Uptalk is often stereotyped as being a feature of young women's speech; however, gender differences in uptalk are not consistent across varieties or by speech task or type. Research suggests that, while women may use more uptalk than men to hold the floor in SoCal AmE, there may not be as much difference in the use of uptalk between men and women in statements (Ritchart & Arvaniti, 2014). It is associated with young women speakers of RP in the UK (Bradford, 1997). In research on uptalk in LonE, Levon (2020) also found that uptalk is associated with ethnicity; while Asian and Black speakers in his study used some uptalk, they did not do so as regularly as white speakers of LonE. Interestingly, Levon also found a higher rate of uptalk among white London men than white London women. In New Zealand, higher rates of uptalk have been found for Māori men than Māori women, though Pakeha (European) women have higher rates of uptalk than Pakeha men (Britain, 1992). In NZE and AusE, as well as in Calif AmE, the use of uptalk is not associated with social class, indicating that it has spread to the general population (Warren, 2015). In the UK, as well as in Western AmE, in contrast, it is associated with a middle class, with less usage among the working class (Warren, 2015). Though it is often associated (negatively) with younger women, particularly in the US, age does not appear to be a significant factor in use of uptalk in many varieties of English (Shokeir, 2008).

How is uptalk realized phonologically? As Levon (2020) notes, it is not always possible to find evidence of uptalk through an acoustic analysis of data alone as what the hearer perceives as a final rise may not appear as such acoustically. Therefore, a combination of both acoustic and auditory analysis is better with this type of data. Table 8.3 presents a summary of uptalk patterns across varieties of English, as well as for use in questions (a question intonation) and with declarative statements when the data is available.

The acoustic realization of the rise can be anywhere from less than 50 Hz to over 100 Hz, and it can also occur only on the final syllable of the IP, over several syllables of the last word, or across more than one word (Warren, 2015). Figure 8.9 shows a ToBI analysis of the utterance *I'm from United States of America* as spoken by a Calif AmE woman (you can listen to her say the sentence in Task 8.5). As you can see in Figure 8.9, the speaker has a rise across her realization of *America*, making it sound as if she is asking the question *I'm from United States of America?* rather than making a statement about her place of origin.

Uptalk appears to be spreading globally, with some suggestions that it may be occurring in some NVEs, including SgE, ZimE, WSAE, HKE, and SLE (see Task 8.6). In MalE, a unique type of rise occurs, which Nayan and Setter (2016) label a Cooperative Rise or CR, in declarative sentences, which starts with a relative low pitch and increases across a longer duration than a regular rise. As they note, this CR is used to show solidarity

Table 8.3 Uptalk in varieties of English

Variety	Uptalk – declarative statements	Questions
AusE (Fletcher, Grabe, & Warren, 2005)	L* H-H% (most common) H* H-H%	H* H-H% (most common) L* H-H%
NZE (Fletcher, Grabe, & Warren, 2005)	L+H* H-H% L* H-H%	L* H-H% L* L-H%
SoCal AmE (Ritchart & Arvaniti, 2014)	L* H-H% L* L-H% H* H-H% (occasionally)	H* H-H% L* H-H%
Midwestern AmE (Prechtel & Clopper, 2016)	L* L-H% L* H-H% H* L-H%	
Northern AmE ((Prechtel & Clopper, 2016)	L* L-H% L* H-H% H* L-H%	
CanE (Prechtel & Clopper, 2016)	L* H-H% H* L- H%	
BrE (Arvaniti & Atkins, 2016)	L-H% (floor holds, statements) H-H% (statements)	H-H%

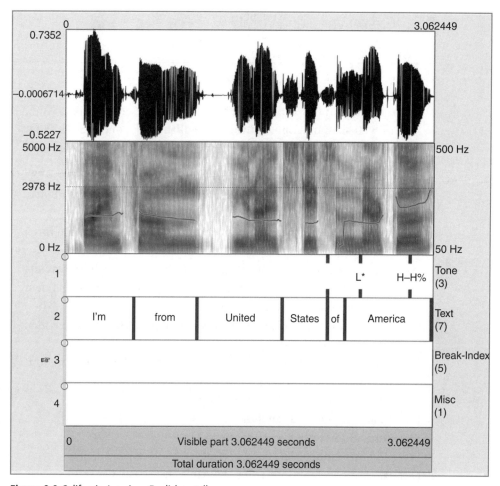

Figure 8.9 California American English uptalk

and cooperation, and may be used either as a confirmation check or to ask simple questions (as part of question intonation) or in statements, the latter of which is similar to uptalk.

TASK 8.6 Listening for Uptalk in Varieties of English

🎧 You can listen to speakers of Appal AmE, SA AusE, CanE, HKE, MalE, EMidBrE, Midwestern AmE, NZE, PRE, SgE, SLE, WSAE, and ZimE in conversation. All the speakers have a rising pitch at the end of their utterances, all of which are declarative statements.

You can also listen to the Calif AmE speaker talk about the Valley Girl SoCal AmE accent, and its features of uptalk, breathy voice, and creaky voice (see below).

8.6   Creaky Voice and Vocal Fry

TASK 8.7 Listening for Creaky Voice

Listen to the extracts from speakers of Appal AmE, Midwestern AmE, Qld NSW AusE, CanE, SgE, Taiwanese English (TaiE), and WSAE. What do you notice about their pronunciation of the words in bold in each of the extracts?

(1)   I am from Asheville, North Carolina, which is in the United States of **America**. (Appal AmE)

(2)   And after Wilmington, I was in Charlottesville, Virginia for a **year**. (Appal AmE)

(3)   I'm from the western part of North Carolina which is in the mountains and that that region has a has really has its kind of its own particular **dialect**. (Appal AmE)

(4)   And then a really nice contrast was going out to **Tai O** ... which was lovely. (Qld NSW AusE)

(5)   Yeah a lot of people say that we're going to a job when we get **out** but. (CanE)

(6)   **Ah yes**, cause I really love **biology**. (CanE)

(7)   I did **last year** though. (CanE)

(8)   **And** a little little bit of **Japanese**. (TaiE)

(9)   Right **pronunciation** maybe. (TaiE)

(10) All my educators are from the same **area**, usually. (Midwestern AmE)

(11) We don't get that much chances in **Singapore** yeah. (SgE)

(12) So perhaps cer certain of the things I say might not **be** exactly 100 **per cent** South African **English**. (WSAE)

(13) I've spent errrm a large part of my life **outside** of South Africa. (WSAE)

You may notice that the speakers' pronunciation of the words in bold included a popping or cracking sound; it may also sound rough. This is a type of production of speech sounds, or phonation, called *creaky voice*. Creaky voice is a type of phonation in which the vocal folds are compressed, resulting in aperiodic vocal pulses and a low F0. Henton and Bladon (1988, p. 10) suggest it sounds like 'popping corn'.

What do we mean by phonation? Before we examine creaky voice in detail, it is useful to look at the different phonation types in language.

Phonation refers to the different glottal configurations during speech production. We have already discussed the difference between voiceless and voiced sounds in relation to consonants (see Chapter 5). Modal phonation is the average F0 for a speaker – the normal speaking and singing pitch – while creaky voice is produced with more glottal closure and a lower F0; on the other side of the spectrum is a voiceless phonation, with a breathy/whispery voice produced with voicing but more open vocal folds, resulting in a murmured or sighing sound during production. Pitch range varies not only by speaker and variety/language, but also between women's and men's voices as well as between children and adults; as Borrie and Delfino (2017) note, the mean F0 for modal phonation is approximately 85–180 Hz for men and 165–265 Hz for women; creaky voice, in contrast, can have an F0 as low as 7–78 Hz, with little difference in vocal range for men and women.

Are creaky voice and vocal fry the same? The terms 'creaky voice' and 'vocal fry' are often used synonymously to describe the same phenomenon, though some linguists (see Keating, Garellek, & Kreiman, 2015) differentiate between the two phonation types; Keating et al. (2015) note that, while both creaky voice and vocal fry have a lower F0, vocal fry may not have irregular or aperiodic glottal pulses, unlike creaky voice. In this book, the terms will be used to refer to the same phenomenon. In the past, this type of phonation was considered to be a speech disorder; in a seminal article, Hollien, Moore, Wendahl, and Michel (1966) argued that it was a normal phonation mode for many speakers. Creaky voice occurs in many varieties of English; it also occurs in many languages as a phonemic contrast for vowels and consonants and on glottal stops; it is also often connected with tone – as an example, often Cantonese tone 4 and Mandarin tone 3 have creaky voice (Davidson, 2020).

In which varieties of English does creaky voice occur? Creaky voice occurs in many varieties of English; it was originally associated with a type of Valley Girl SoCal AmE. Creaky voice has been found in a range of AmE, including Calif AmE, ChiE, AAVE, SAmE, Western AmE, Midwestern AmE, and Appal AmE; it has also been found in varieties of CanE, BrE, and ScotE, including in RP, NBrE, MLE; and in AusE, NZE, and MāoriE (Davidson, 2020; Hornibrook, Ormond, & Maclagan, 2018; Szakay, 2012; Szakay & Torgersen, 2016). In my data, I also found creaky voice in SgE and WSAE.

Who uses creaky voice and why? Gender and ethnic differences have been found in the use of creaky voice; in New Zealand, for example, women have been found to use more creaky voice than men; it is also widely perceived to occur most often among young American women than American men (Yuasa, 2010); research on BrE, in contrast, found that creaky voice was more common among men than women in both RP and NBrE (Henton & Bladon, 1988). It has also been widely perceived to occur more often with younger than older women, though research on AmE speakers has not found an age effect, with both younger and middle-aged women exhibiting similar rates of creaky voice (Davidson, 2020). Creakiness has also been associated with more standard speech in Edinburgh English while a more breathy phonation has been associated with more working-class speech (Esling, 1978). In the US, in particular, creaky voice may be a symbol of being educated, upwardly mobile, and urban among young women (Lai & van Hell, 2020), whereas in NBrE, it may be used by men to sound hyper masculine (Henton & Bladon, 1988). It is important to note that creaky voice (and particularly with reference to the term 'vocal fry') has been widely criticized in the media, most often in relation to its use by young American women. Perceptions may be changing, however, as creaky voice spreads not only into different varieties of AmE but also globally, probably through the movie, television, and music industries (Yuasa, 2010). For both men and women, it is becoming associated with a more urban, educated, and higher social-class identity (Henton & Bladon, 1988; Yuasa, 2010). As Yuasa (2010) argues, young American women may increasingly adopt creaky voice to project a more contemporary, upwardly mobile identity and more authoritativeness. There is some evidence that, as creaky voice lowers the F0, it may help a speaker assert authority, possibly because speakers who have a lowered pitch may be viewed as more dominant in the workplace (Yuasa, 2010). For example, Greer and Winters (2015) have found that the use of creaky phonation can increase authoritativeness ratings for women speakers, and ratings of authoritativeness, coolness, and attractiveness for men speakers.

Its use appears to be increasing, particularly among young women in both America and New Zealand; in New Zealand, creaky voice may also be a marker of ethnicity as speakers with creaky voice are perceived to be Māori, whereas those with breathy voice are perceived to be Pakeha (European) (Szakay, 2012). In the US, creaky vs breathy voice has also been associated with ethnicity, with European American men having more creaky voice than African American men who, in turn, have more breathy voice than European American men (Thomas & Reaser, 2004).

When do speakers use creaky voice? Creaky voice is more commonly found at the end of sentences or IPs, as it is often used as a linguistic marker of sentence or paragraph boundaries – to signal to the listener that the utterance has ended (Wolk, Abdelli-Beruh, & Slavin, 2012), though it can also occur sentence-medially. It also occurs more commonly in falling intonation contexts. In BrE, and particularly RP English, speakers may use a combination of creaky voice and falling intonation to signal turn-taking (Laver, 1980). It may also occur more often on unstressed over stressed syllables, as the latter have a higher F0 as one means to mark prominence

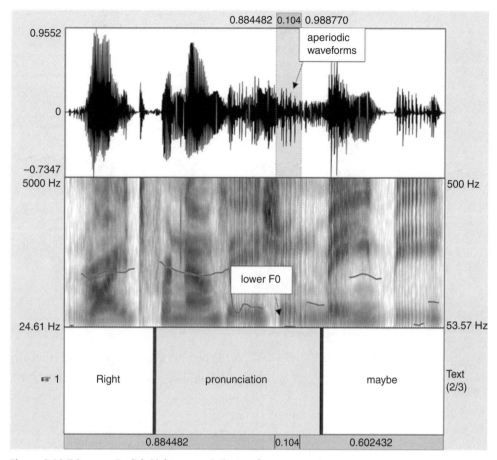

Figure 8.10 Taiwanese English *Right pronunciation maybe*

(Gibson, 2017). It may also be used in AmE to introduce phrases that are parenthetical or explanatory, as in the phrase *like solar power* in the sentence *Renewable energy, like solar power, is becoming more popular.*

How can we measure creaky voice? To find instances of creaky voice, we can listen for the popping sound in a speaker's voice and/or a lowering of pitch; acoustically, we can also look for evidence of creaky voice on a spectrogram, by looking for a lowered F0 as well as aperiodic pulse (vocal fold vibration) on the waveform, and a longer period between glottal openings. A more complex acoustic measure of phonation is to compare the amplitude of the first harmonic (H1) and second harmonic (H2) in a vowel; this is also called spectral tilt. Creaky voice has lower spectral tilt values, while breathy voice has higher spectral tilt values (see Keating et al., 2015, for further details). Figure 8.10 shows a speaker of Taiwanese English (TaiE) saying the sentence *Right pronunciation maybe* that you can hear in Task 8.7.

We can note the aperiodic (irregular cycle) waveform on *pronunciation*; on the spectrogram, we can note that the F0 lowers to 53.57 Hz during the speaker's production of *pronunciation*.

8.7   CHECK YOUR UNDERSTANDING

EXERCISES

(a) What is intonation?

(b) What is the difference between an intonation and a tone language?

(c) What does ToBI stand for? What are the four indices in ToBI?

(d) What do we mean by pitch accent?

(e) What does phonation mean? What are three different types of phonation in English?

(f) What does F0 stand for? What does it mean?

DISCUSSION QUESTIONS

(a) What is creaky voice / vocal fry? When does it usually occur? Is creaky voice common in your variety of English? Do you or your peers have creaky voice / vocal fry? If you do, what do you think has influenced you or your peers' use of creaky fry?

(b) What is uptalk? When does it occur? Is uptalk common in your variety of English? Do you or your peers have uptalk? If you do, what do you think has influenced you or your peers' use of uptalk?

(c) While English is generally considered an intonation language, Lim (2009) and Gussenhoven (2014) argue that some varieties of English, including HKE, NigE, and SgE should be considered tone languages, or varieties of English that use tone, in contrast to varieties of English, including AmE and BrE, that use intonation. Do you agree with this differentiation among varieties of English?

EXPAND YOUR UNDERSTANDING

In Chapter 7, you were asked whether your invented language is more syllable- or more stress-timed. You should refer to your answer to that question when you respond to the following questions:

(a) What are the intonation contours in your language for the following sentence types?

    (1) Yes/no questions

    (2) Wh-questions

(3) Declarative statements

(4) List of items

(5) Tag questions

(b) Does your language use H or L pitch to ask questions or make a statement? Is the intonation of wh- and yes/no questions the same?

(c) Does your language use pitch accent for contrastive stress?

(d) Does your language have non-contrastive stress on a particular word in a sentence?

(e) Is your language a tone or an intonation language (you should refer to your answers about your language in Chapter 7).

ANALYSE YOUR OWN PRONUNCIATION

(a) Which variety of English do you speak? What intonation, tone, and pitch patterns exist in your variety of English?

(b) What predictions can you make about your own use of tone, pitch, and intonation?

(c) In Appendix A, you will find a list of sentences to illustrate different intonation and pitch accent patterns. Record yourself reading these sentences. To supplement this data, you are also prompted to record yourself answering a few open-ended questions.

(d) You can listen to yourself and use Praat to analyse your intonation and pitch in the sentences.

(e) What pitch and intonation patterns do you observe in your own speech? Are these the same as or different from what you predicted you might find? If they are different, why do you think this is the case?

(f) If you said you have uptalk, can you find examples of uptalk in your recording?

(g) If you said you have creaky voice, can you find examples of creaky voice in your recording?

9 Investigating English Phonetics and Phonology

TASK 9.1 PRE-READING

Discuss the following questions with your classmates and teacher:

- What surprised you the most in your reading of this book?
- Based on your reading of the chapters in this book, how would you define *accent*?
- Is your answer to this question different from your answer before you read the book?
- Which linguistic features comprise an accent?
- What did you learn about your own accent and your variety of English?
- How would you describe your own accent?

9.1 Introduction to the Chapter

In the final chapter of this book, we return to the concept of *accent*, by looking at how we develop and use our accent across time and space. The chapter then provides you with resources for more advanced study of English and phonology, by presenting a range of online websites and databases with speech samples, as well as movies and TV series to provide exposure to different varieties of English. The discussion then focuses on pragmatic considerations in data collection, including the use of free software programs such as Audacity and Praat to record and analyse speech. The chapter then reviews different types of data that can be collected for phonetic and phonological analysis, including word lists, reading passages, and conversational data, with a discussion of the benefits and drawbacks of using each type of data. In the final section of the chapter, you are guided through exercises to check your understanding of its content.

9.2   Acquiring and Using an Accent

This book began with the question *How would you define the word accent?*

In Chapter 1 of the book, we stated that we can define accent as the way different phonetic and phonological features are realized in a given language or variety and/or for a particular speaker. As has been shown in this book, these features include vowel and consonant phonemes and allophones, syllable structure, speech rhythm, and stress, pitch, and intonation patterns, among others. While every person's accent is by nature idiosyncratic – we all speak a different idiolect – specific features, in frequency and/or combination, can signal a particular regional, ethnic, and social identity. As an example, GAmE may be more saliently signalled by intervocalic flapping, rhoticity, a TRAP/BATH merger, and LOT as unrounded [ɑ:], whereas RP (Mod and Trad) has the TRAP/BATH split, aspiration for medial /t/, LOT as a low back rounded vowel, and is non-rhotic.

How did we get these features and our unique accent? Lippi-Green (2012) uses the metaphor of the Sound House to describe both first and second phonological acquisition. Below is an excerpt from her description of the building of a Sound House for a child learning their first language, which provides a useful starting point for our discussion:

> First, think of all the sounds which can be produced by the human vocal apparatus as a set of building materials. The basic materials, vowels and consonants, are bricks. Other building materials (wood, mortar, plaster, stone) stand in for things like tone, vowel harmony, and length.... Children are born with two things: a set of language blueprints wired into the brain, which gives them some intuitive understanding of very basic rules of language. They also have a set of tools which goes along with these blueprints. Now think of the language acquisition process as a newborn who begins to build a Sound House. The Sound House is the 'home' of the language, or what we have been calling accent – the phonology – of the child's native tongue. At birth the child is in the Sound House warehouse, where a full inventory of all possible materials is available to her. She looks at the Sound Houses built by her parents, her brothers and sisters, by other people around her, and she starts to pick out those materials, those bricks she sees they have used to build their Sound Houses.... Maybe this child has parents who speak English and Gaelic, or are natives of Cincinnati and speak what they think of as Standard American English, as well as African American English Vernacular. The parents each have two Sound Houses, or perhaps one Sound House with two wings. She has two Sound Houses to build at once. Sometimes she mixes materials up, but then sorts them out.... The child starts to socialize with other children. Her best friend has a slightly different layout, although he has built his Sound

House with the exact same inventory of building materials.... She wants to be like her friends, and so she makes renovations to her Sound House.

(Lippi-Green, 2012, p. 48)

Lippi-Green's Sound House metaphor offers a useful example of how we build up our individual sound system and how this system can change across time. We can modify this metaphor to illustrate how you use your accent in different social contexts by imagining that the accent you build across time and space comprises a box of phonetic and phonological tools. You acquire different consonants and vowels, stress, tone, and other prosodic features throughout your life, through your environment, including the accents of your parents, peers, and educators, as well as through exposure to other languages and varieties in media, education, and travel. We all have this toolbox of features; we may pull out different sounds or prosodic patterns to use in different situations and with different people. We all have more than one way to say the same thing, and we vary the use of these different ways of sounding based on the context. While our toolbox may resemble the toolbox of our friends, siblings, and peers as well as other members of our community, our toolbox is uniquely ours, representing our unique lived linguistic experiences, needs, and aspirations. It is our idiolect. We may share some unique features within our family; this is our familect. The toolbox is not locked – the contents can be added to or changed through exposure to new sounds and features.

These different accent features have social meaning, and different groupings of these accent features provide listeners with information about our identity, including our ethnicity, age, gender, social class, where we grew up and/or have lived. We can modify these features to sound more like our peer groups and/or for different social purposes; in other words, we actively make linguistic choices to speak with different accent features across different social situations based on the available tools in our toolbox. Some speakers have a repertoire of features – they can both flap and aspirate the /t/ in *water* and may choose either aspiration or flapping depending on the situation; others may use more or less rhoticity, TH-fronting, GOOSE-fronting, uptalk, or creaky voice depending on where they are and with whom they are speaking.

Accent features have social meaning. It is important to understand that there is no linguistic superiority in the pronunciation of *water* with flapping, glottal stopping, or aspiration, just as there is no linguistic superiority in saying *car* with or without rhoticity and *three* with TH-fronting, TH-stopping or with the dental fricative. Social meaning, however, is assigned to the use of these different features, though these meanings differ across speech communities. Importantly, social meaning can change – TH-fronting to [f], as an example, has historically been viewed in the UK as symbolic of a working-class (less educated) accent and associated with men; it has now become more synonymous with an urban or street accent in the UK (Levon & Fox, 2014). Part of this spread is through the media, including both TV and music. For example, TH-stopping, associated with MLE, is a feature of the British rap style called Grime, and may spread in usage to British Anglos through music to enact an identity associated with Grime, or being street or tough (Drummond, 2018). Similarly, in the US, DH-stopping, in particular, is associated with AAVE and has become a feature of Hip Hop Nation Language (Alim, 2004), which may further spread the use of this feature beyond African Americans also to enact a hip hop / rap identity, as research (Cutler, 1999) suggests.

As new or innovative features spread across different communities of speakers, the social stigma is often lessened and may eventually disappear. Both uptalk and creaky voice, as we saw in Chapter 8, have been criticized in the US media as examples of the deterioration of English language standards; these two features are spreading across the US, as well as globally, partly through mass media generated in California, and, as they become more commonplace, they may gradually become more accepted as the social meaning attached to the features changes.

Any meaning that a particular feature or group of features is given has been assigned based on the use of a feature by a particular group. Speech patterns that are not the standard are often viewed negatively against the standard, and speakers with these features may be discriminated against. In fact, the standard features are not linguistically better and the standard variety is not more linguistically complex – saying *fink* or *tink* rather than *think* is not of a lesser linguistic quality or complexity, and does not mean that the speaker has less ability or intelligence than if the speaker said *think* with the dental fricative. As we saw in Chapter 2, these norms and standards have arisen when one particular dialect is given power, and the speech patterns of the group in power are codified in dictionaries and reference books, thereby becoming educational (and prescriptive) tools. As we also saw in Chapter 2, this standard is usually the variety spoken by the people in power in a particular region. It is no accident that the prestige French standard is based on the Paris dialect; in England, the prestige dialect changed to Southeast England, notably London upper-class speech, when the seat of power shifted. As such, which variety is deemed the standard – and which ones are labelled as non-standard or regional – has nothing to do with quality of the variety or language itself. Instead, this is an accident of geography, with the seat of power often in the most geographically suitable location in a country or region for finance and commerce, like London in England; Paris in France; and, from the 1960s, California in the US, which holds significant power both in the US and globally through Hollywood movies and TV.

Variation across Englishes – both across a country as in the United States and England as well as across the world – illustrates the creativity and culture of its speakers. Just like other languages, English is dynamic, and always in a state of change. It will continue to evolve and change as new ideas, concepts, and things enter the world, and through contact with other languages and cultures. That so many different varieties of English exist is a testimony to the resilience of English; as we saw in Chapter 2, the seeds of English were sown first in England by the Anglo-Saxons, and later across the world through migration and colonial expansion of the British, and then American, Empire. We can also think of seeds as a metaphor for language: as these seeds were planted, new varieties sprouted, nourished by the different languages that make up the soil in which the seed was planted. As new trees grew from the seeds, they in turn sprouted different branches, which eventually developed into new varieties. These new varieties sprouted new and unique fruits and seeds – different sounds, words, and grammatical structures, among other things. These varieties all have a common ancestor – Old English, which itself is derived from West Germanic – but each variety has absorbed unique linguistic and cultural features in the region in which it grew. These varieties inject English with new vocabulary, morphological and grammatical features, sound patterns, and pragmatic and sociolinguistic rules.

In many cases, particularly in regions of the United Kingdom, Ireland, and North America, varieties that are considered non-standard (e.g., regional, ethnic, and working-class varieties) have features that were historically present in English but may have disappeared in other varieties. Rhoticity in some varieties of BrE is one example of a historical remnant that still exists, though its use is in decline. The standard varieties are also in a state of change – even the Queen of England did not always speak the Queen's English, a common nickname for Trad RP. For example, a study by Harrington, Palethorpe, and Watson (2000) examined the pronunciation of English monophthong vowels by Queen Elizabeth II from 1952 to 1988 through the analysis of the Queen's annual Christmas speech. They found that the Queen's vowels had shifted over the 36-year period of the study towards a more modern or mainstream RP (Mod RP in our book), in line with the general changes in SSBE.

To conclude, rather than assessing the English of speakers who do not speak what is considered to be the prestige or standard variety and/or NVEs against a standard American or British English (e.g., GAmE and Trad RP), as has been the norm, we should value and celebrate linguistic diversity, and explore why these differences exist and how they bring the culture of various regions and speakers alive.

TASK 9.2 Accents and Social Meaning

📖 In Chapter 1, these key tenets of this book were given:

- Everyone speaks with an accent.
- No accent – or variety of English – is inherently better than another accent or variety.
- The social meaning of different accent features varies across contexts.
- Accents can change across time.
- No linguistic feature is inherently better than another.

In your own words, explain what these tenets mean, using examples from your reading of this book as well as your own experiences.

9.3 Resources for Varieties of English

In this section, various resources to deepen your understanding of English accents worldwide, as well as to support research in English phonetics and phonology, are presented and discussed. Table 9.1 presents a list of online resources to supplement the listening tasks in this book; these online resources can also be used for research purposes. Many of these websites have been referenced in various discussions in this book; they are listed together here for easy reference.

Tables 9.2 and 9.3 list movies and TV shows that authentically present a range of English accents (Table 9.2) as well as indigenous and invented languages (Table 9.3). The movies and TV shows given in Table 9.2 can be useful in expanding your understanding of the different varieties of English, through listening practice and analysis of which linguistic features that exist in a given variety of English are present in the speech of different characters. Music is also a wonderful means of exploring variation across varieties of English. For examples of Hip Hop Nation Language, which evolved from the language of African Americans but is considered to be the language of a borderless hip hop community, you can listen to the music of Mystikal, Ludacris, and Missy Elliott, among others (Alim, 2004). For examples of Grime, the British rap style that incorporates features of MLE, you can listen to the music of Bugzy Malone, Kano, Lady Leshurr, and Stormzy.

Table 9.1 Online resources for varieties of English

Title and website link	Content
International Phonetic Association www.internationalphoneticassociation.org	Website of the IPA.
University of Victoria Linguistics IPA Lab http://web.uvic.ca/ling/resources/ipa/charts/IPAlab/IPAlab.htm	IPA charts with sound files for each consonant and vowel.
WALS: *The World Atlas of Language Structures* https://wals.info	Database of linguistic features including phonological features of over 500 languages.
UPSID: UCLA Phonological Segment Inventory Database Simpler interface: http://web.phonetik.uni-frankfurt.de/upsid_info.html	Database with phonological information on 451 languages.
The History and Spread of English Worldwide www.eng.cuhk.edu.hk/ENGE-MAP	Background on development and spread of English worldwide. Speech samples and background information on AmE, CanE, NZE, AusE, MalE, PhlE, HKE, SgE, NigE, IndE, JamE, KenE, PRE, and IrE.
Sound Comparisons https://soundcomparisons.com/#home	Database of pronunciations of words in historical and current varieties of English, as well as in Germanic, Romance, Slavic and Baltic, Celtic languages, and languages of the Andes and Brazil.
VADA: The Visual Accent and Dialect Archive https://visualaccentdialectarchive.com	Collection of video clips of speakers of English from around the world, including Africa, the Americas, Asia, the Caribbean, Europe, and Oceania. Aims to provide visual information on English accents to aid theatre professionals.
English Accents Worldwide www.eng.cuhk.edu.hk/ENGE-EAWW	Recordings of word lists, reading passages, and conversation from speakers of AmE, BrE, AusE, NZE, CanE, PRE, SgE, and KenE. Primarily focuses on vowels of different varieties of English.
The Speech Accent Archive https://accent.gmu.edu	Extensive database featuring recordings of speakers from all over the world reading the same passage, *Please Call Stella*. Includes recordings from Africa, Asia, Australia–Oceania, the Caribbean, Central America, Europe, the Middle East, North America, South America. Phonetic transcription of speech.

Title and website link	Content
The Audio Archive www.alt-usage-english.org/audio_archive.html	Recordings of spoken texts from speakers of AusE, AmE, CanE, BrE, IndE, IrE, WelE, NZE. Texts include: *Arthur the Rat, Bother Father ..., The Rainbow Passage, The North Wind and the Sun, I Teach Ferdinand ..., Comma Gets a Cure.*
IDEA: International Dialects of English Archive www.dialectsarchive.com	Recordings of English dialects and accents from around the world; includes recordings from Africa, Asia, Australia–Oceania, the Caribbean, Central America, Europe, the Middle East, North America, South America.
University College London (UCL) Speaker Database www.phon.ucl.ac.uk/shop/uclspeaker.php	Recordings of 45 speakers of BrE with a Southeastern accent. Recordings include word lists, sentence and passage reading, and semi-spontaneous speech.
British Library – British Accents and Dialects https://sounds.bl.uk/Accents-and-dialects	Recordings of speakers of different dialects of British, Scottish, Welsh, and Northern Irish English.
British National Corpus www.natcorp.ox.ac.uk	Collection of spoken and written samples of dialects of BrE with over 100 million words.
The IViE Corpus: English Intonation in the British Isles www.phon.ox.ac.uk/files/apps/IViE	Recordings of 9 urban dialects spoken in the British Isles, including Northern Ireland (Belfast), Ireland (Dublin), Wales (Cardiff), and England (London, Cambridge, Liverpool, Bradford, Leeds, and Newcastle).
Santa Barbara Corpus of Spoken American English www.linguistics.ucsb.edu/research/santa-barbara-corpus	Recordings and transcriptions of speakers of AmE from all over the United States.
Wellington Corpus of Spoken New Zealand English http://korpus.uib.no/icame/manuals/WSC/INDEX.HTM	A corpus of both written and spoken NZE.
The NIE Corpus of Spoken Singapore English https://videoweb.nie.edu.sg/phonetic/niecsse/index.htm	Recordings of interviews and reading passages from speakers of SgE. Extracts and transcripts are available.
Telling Stories: Linguistic Diversity in Hong Kong www.eng.cuhk.edu.hk/ENGE-TellingStories	Database of sound files from 40 languages, including African languages such as Afrikaans and Kiswahili; Asian languages including Cantonese, Hindi, Mandarin Chinese, Tagalog; Celtic languages including Irish, Scots, and Scottish Gaelic; and 29 varieties of English, including AmE, AusE, BrE, HKE, IrE, PhlE, ScotE, WSAE, among others.

Table 9.2 English accents in movies and TV

Variety	Movie/TV show
African American English / African American Vernacular English	*Boyz n the Hood*
	Precious
	Straight Outta Compton
	Bamboozled!
	Why Did I Get Married?
	Hustle and Flow
	Welcome Home Roscoe Jenkins
	Something New
	The Wire
Southern American English	*Sling Blade*
	The Apostle (also AAVE)
	Mud
	No Country for Old Men
	Selma
Midwestern & Northern American English	*Mare of Eastown* (Pittsburgh AmE)
	My Cousin Vinny (NYC AmE)
	Spotlight (Boston AmE)
	Fargo (Minnesota AmE)
Appalachian American English	*Mountain Talk*
Native American English	*Smoke Signals*
	Reservation Dogs
Chicano English	*Gentefied*
	East Los High
	East Side Sushi
	My Family / Mi Familia
Valley Girl Southern California English	*Valley Girl* (1983)
California American English	*Clueless*
Australian English	*Muriel's Wedding*
	Goldstone
	Mystery Road
	The Castle
	The Adventures of Priscilla, Queen of the Desert
	Upright
	Gallipoli
	Strictly Ballroom
	Black and White (also AusAborE)
Australian Aboriginal English	*Rabbit Proof Fence*
	Mabo
	Goldstone
	Charlie's Country
	Sweet Country
	Samson and Delilah
	The Sapphires
	Black and White

Variety	Movie/TV show
New Zealand English	*Hunt for the Wilderpeople*
	Outrageous Fortune
	Eagle vs Shark
	Flight of the Conchords
	Shearing Gang
Pasifika English	Samoan: *Samoan Wedding / Sione's Wedding*
Māori English	*Whale Rider*
	Once Were Warriors
	Boy
	White Lies
Jamaican English	*Cool Runnings*
	The Harder They Come
	Rockers
Scottish English	*Trainspotting*
	Shallow Grave
	Sweet Sixteen
	Limmy's Show
	Braveheart
Irish English	*In Bruges*
	In the Name of the Father (NIrE)
	Waking Ned Devine
	Derry Girls (NIrE)
Welsh English	*Gavin and Stacey*
	Twin Town
	Pride
British English	*Love, Actually* (various, including Southern BrE, IrE)
	Four Weddings and a Funeral (Southern BrE, ScotE)
	The Crown (RP)
	This is England (Midlands, Liverpool)
	The Full Monty (Sheffield, Midlands)
	Downton Abbey (RP)
	Lock, Stock and Two Smoking Barrels (Liverpool, Cockney)
	Billy Elliott (Geordie, NBrE)
	Eastenders (Cockney)
	Brassed Off (Yorkshire, NBrE)
	My Fair Lady (phonetician Henry Higgins is based on phonetician Henry Sweet)
	Riff Raff (working-class accents)
Nigerian English	*Omo Ghetto: The Saga*
	The Wedding Party
	Chief Daddy
Kenyan English	*Nairobi Half Life*
	Rafiki
	Supa Modo
	Just in Time

Table 9.2 (Cont.)

Variety	Movie/TV show
South African English	*Tsotsi*
	Gangster's Paradise: Jerusalema
	Max and Mona
	Blood & Water
Indian English	*Monsoon Wedding*
	The Namesake
	Bride and Prejudice
	Slumdog Millionaire
Pakistani English	*021*
	Khuda Kay Liye
Singapore English	*Tiong Bahru Social Club*
	Ah Boys to Men
	Crazy Rich Asians
	If Movies Were in Singlish (parody)
Malaysian English	*Ola Bola*
	Pisau Cukur
	Sell Out!
Philippine English	*Toto*
	Everything about Her
	Four Sisters and a Wedding

Table 9.3 Indigenous/endangered and invented languages in movies and TV

Indigenous/endangered languages	The Americas
	Sooyii (Blackfoot)
	Windtalkers (Navajo)
	Atanarjuat: The Fast Runner (Inuktitut)
	Four Sheets to the Wind (Creek)
	The Missing (Apache)
	Daughters of the Dust (Gullah)
	The Last of the Mohicans (Iroquoian)
	Dances with Wolves (Lakhota)
	The New World (Algonquin)
	Sgaawaay K'uuna / Edge of the Knife (Haida)
	Embrace of the Serpent (Cubeo, Huitoto, Ticuna, Wanano)
	Moana (dubbed into Hawaiian)
	Star Wars (dubbed into Navajo)
	A Fistful of Dollars (dubbed into Navajo)
	Finding Nemo (dubbed into Navajo)
	Oceania
	Ten Canoes (Yolngu Matha)
	Warrarman Ngarranggarni / Warmun Dreaming (Gija)
	The Orator / O Le Tulafale (Samoan)
	Maori (Waru)

| | **Europe**
Kings (Irish Gaelic)
Arracht/Monster (Irish Gaelic)
Seachd: The Inaccessible Pinnacle (Scottish Gaelic)
Calon Gaeth (Small Country) (Welsh)
The First King: Birth of an Empire (Old Latin)
Gypsy (Romani)
The Passion of the Christ (Old/Middle Aramaic, Latin, and Hebrew)
Nummioq (Greenlandic)
Inuk (Greenlandic)
My Brilliant Friend (Neapolitan dialect of Italian)
Documentaries on language endangerment
The Miracle of Little Prince (documentary on how translations of *The Little Prince* into endangered languages can help language preservation)
Last Whispers: Oratorio for Vanishing Voices, Collapsing Universes and a Falling Tree (featuring a range of endangered languages in speech, song, and whispers)
The Linguists (documentary about language endangerment and preservation)
Language Matters (documentary on endangered languages) |
| **Invented languages**
(Obias, 2017) | *Star Trek* (Klingon)
Lord of the Rings (Elvish, from Finnish, Welsh, Greek, and Latin)
Star Wars: Return of the Jedi (Huttese, from Quechua)
Despicable Me (Minionese, from Spanish, Italian, Japanese, Bahasa Indonesian, as well as Indian and Chinese languages)
Harry Potter (Parseltongue, invented by a phonetician, Francis Nolan)
Game of Thrones (Dothraki, from Spanish, Kiswahili, Arabic, and Estonian)
Avatar (Na'Vi, from Māori and Ethiopian languages)
The Interpreter (made-up language based on Shona and Kiswahili) |

The movies and TV shows given in Table 9.3 may be of interest if you wish to deepen your understanding of language endangerment as well as to listen to how these less common languages are spoken. In many cases, these languages are at severe risk of extinction and these movies provide one means of recording the languages for preservation. The movie *Sgaawaay K'uuna / Edge of the Knife*, as an example, is in two dialects of Haida, an endangered language of the indigenous Haida people in Canada that is spoken by only twenty people in the world today (Alberge, 2019). There are also a number of indigenous artists who sing primarily or exclusively in indigenous, and often endangered, languages, including Alien Weaponry (New Zealand Māori-language metal band); Shellie Morris and the Borroloola

Songwomen (Australian Yanuwa, Garrawa, Mara, and Guanji languages); Geoffrey Gurrumul Yunupingu (an Aboriginal singer songwriter from Australia who performed in his native Yolngu language); Baker Boy (an Aboriginal Australian rapper who raps in English and Yolngu Matha); Portavoz (a Chilean rapper who performs in Mapudungun); The Halluci Nation (a Canadian electronic music group that performs powwow-step, a mix of First Nation pow wow and electronic music); Renata Flores Rivera (a Peruvian singer who performs some of her music in Quechua); Brô MCs (indigenous rap group from Brazil who perform in Portuguese and Guarani); and Nanook (a rock band from Greenland that performs in Greenlandic) (Condon, 2019; Woodman, 2017). Table 9.3 also includes a list of movies with invented languages; these languages follow linguistic principles and are often based on existing languages and their structures.

9.4   Resources for Researching English Phonetics and Phonology

In this section, we will review and expand our discussion on useful data collection methods and tools for researching English phonetics and phonology. We will first look at software for speech data collection and analysis. Throughout this book, we have used Praat as a tool for data analysis; instructions on how to use Praat for various purposes have been given in Appendix A as well as in individual chapters. Praat is one of the most commonly used and comprehensive acoustic analysis software programs for speech analysis; as we have seen throughout this book, Praat is useful for spectrographic and waveform analysis of sounds, words, and sentences. Audacity is another program commonly used in speech research, primarily for recording both longer and shorter stretches of speech directly onto a computer; Audacity is also useful for parsing and editing speech files, for extracting shorter sections of speech (words or sentences) from longer recordings, and for acoustic analysis of waveforms and spectrograms. WaveSurfer also allows for the recording of speech samples, as well as acoustic analysis of waveforms. The Speech Analyzer from SIL also allows for more sophisticated acoustic analysis of speech, like Praat; it is available for Windows only. All these programs are free and easy to download and use. Links are given in Table 9.4.

Table 9.5 highlights the different types of speech data collection tasks, from word lists and sentence reading tasks to more conversational data. While each type has specific benefits, each also has drawbacks. Word lists, sentence readings, and reading passages can be useful to elicit particular phonetic or phonological features; however, they may not elicit the full

Table 9.4 Free online software programs for recording and analysing speech

Tools/website	Purpose
Praat www.fon.hum.uva.nl/praat Guide in English: https://wstyler.ucsd.edu/praat/ UsingPraatforLinguisticResearchLatest.pdf	Recording short speech samples; editing files; acoustic analysis through both waveforms and spectrograms See use of Praat in this book in Chapters 3–5, 7–8; Appendix A
Audacity www.audacityteam.org/download	Recording short and long speech samples; extracting words/sentences from longer passages; editing speech files; waveform and spectrogram analysis
WaveSurfer www.speech.kth.se/wavesurfer	Recording speech samples; annotation and transcription; acoustic analysis; speech editing
The Speech Analyzer from SIL https://software.sil.org/speech-analyzer	Acoustic analysis (F0, spectrogram, waveform). Windows only

Table 9.5 Speech data collection tasks

Type	Strengths	Weaknesses	Examples	Resources
Word lists	Focus on specific phonetic and phonological features; can control for other factors. Ideal for phonetic analysis of specific speech features.	Controlled environment so may not elicit a range of phonetic realizations of a feature.	Wells' Lexical Sets [hVd] keywords	Vowels: Table 3.3; Table 10.1 Rhoticity: Table 10.2 Consonants: Tables 5.4–5.11; 10.3 Syllable structure: Table 10.4 Weak/strong syllables and word stress: Table 10.5
Sentence reading	Focus on specific phonetic and phonological features.	Controlled environment so may not elicit a range of phonetic realizations of a feature.	*Bother, father caught the hot coffee in the car park* (rhoticity, vowels)	Rhoticity: Table 10.2 Stress/rhythm: Table 10.5 Intonation: Table 10.6 Pitch accent: Table 10.7

Table 9.5 (Cont.)

Type	Strengths	Weaknesses	Examples	Resources
Reading passages	Focus on specific phonetic and phonological features.	Controlled environment so may not elicit a range of phonetic realizations of a feature.	*The Boy Who Cried Wolf* *The Rainbow Passage* *The North Wind and the Sun*	Deterding (2005a) Fairbanks (1960) International Phonetic Association (1999)
Interview questions / conversation	Most closely resembles everyday speech. Useful for exploration of linguistic and social factors that constrain linguistic variation.	May not elicit all the speech sounds under study.	*Did you ever have a dream that really scared you?*	Table 10.8; Tagliamonte (2006)

range of phonetic realizations for a given speech feature. More conversational interview data more closely resembles everyday speech and may elicit a wider range of phonetic realizations, but is messier as it is harder to control different variables. In addition, it may be more time-consuming to transcribe and analyse and, unless specifically elicited, participants may not produce many instances – or any – of a particular feature under study. For these reasons, many researchers use several data tasks in their research in order to maximize their data set: more controlled speech tasks such as word lists, sentences, and reading passages to elicit sufficient examples of the feature under study, and more naturalistic conversational/interview data to elicit a broader range of realizations for the feature/s under study.

9.5   CHECK YOUR UNDERSTANDING

The book concludes with a list of questions for general discussion and for consideration for further study in English phonetics and phonology:

(1) What do you think are the key features in sounding like a speaker of your variety of English? Are some phonetic and/or phonological features more salient than others?

(2) Which features of the variety of English that you and your peers speak are in variation? Do speakers of English in your region/community have variable rhoticity? GOOSE-fronting? TH/DH-stopping or fronting? Uptalk or creaky voice? Which linguistic and social factors do you think constrain this variation in your community? If you are not sure, how could you find out?

(3) Can you add any movies, TV shows, and/or musical artists to those given in this chapter to highlight different varieties of English, languages, and linguistic features?

(4) Which languages and/or dialects (including of English) are spoken in your country or region?

(5) Does linguistic discrimination exist in your country/region for speakers of any of these languages/dialects?

(6) Using the UNESCO Endangered Languages List (Moseley, 2010), research the status of each language/dialect spoken in your country/region. Are any of the languages/dialects endangered? Why do you think these languages/dialects are endangered? What can be done to protect these languages/dialects?

APPENDIX A

Recording and Analysing Your Own Pronunciation

To record your own word list, you will need a recording device; this can be an external or internal microphone on a computer, iPad, or smartphone. To optimize the recording quality, you are advised to find a quiet room and to use an external microphone if available. As we will be using Praat to analyse our speech samples, you are advised to record your speech using Praat. You can download Praat for both the Mac and the PC here: www.fon.hum.uva.nl/praat. You can find instructions on how to record a sound on the Praat Intro Menu, www.fon.hum.uva.nl/praat/manual/Intro.html; Figure 10.1 shows the recording interface of Praat.

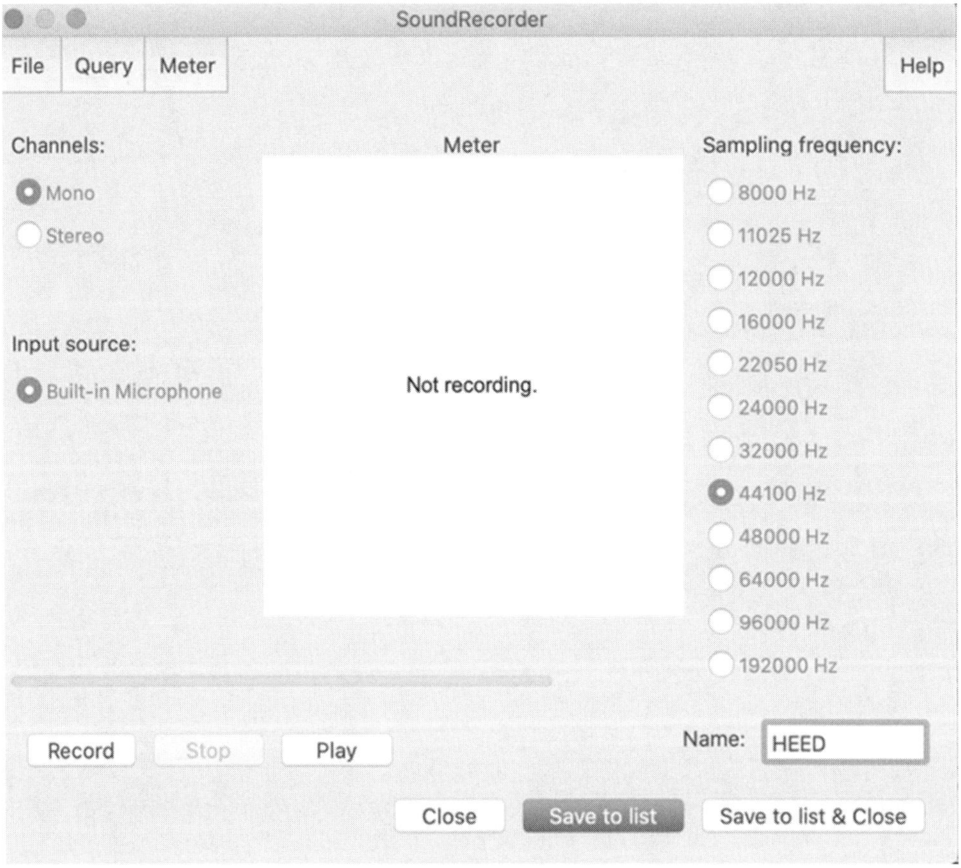

Figure 10.1 Recording words and sentences in Praat

Chapter 3:   The Vowels of English

To investigate your vowel phonemes, you will be recording separate speech files of each word. To neutralize the environment, you are advised to record your speech files using a carrier sentence, as in: *I say [hVd]/[bVt] again* (*I say <u>heed</u> again / I say <u>beat</u> again*).

Table 10.1 gives a series of sample words for each of Wells' (1982) Lexical Sets. As much as is feasible, these words are minimal pairs. You are advised to record one word for each of the Lexical Sets, using either the [hVd] or the [bVt] list. For all your recordings, try to speak naturally, with a normal rate of speech. It is fine to record each word several times before you are satisfied with the recording. Try to pronounce each word as you would normally say it.

Table 10.1 Word list for vowels

Wells' Lexical Sets	[hVd]	[bVt]
FLEECE	heed	beat
KIT	hid	bit
DRESS	head	bet
TRAP	had	bat
GOOSE	who'd	boot
FOOT	hood	book
STRUT	hudd/hud	but
GOAT	hoed/hode	boat
FACE	hayed	bait
START	hard	Bart
LOT	hod	bot/cot/pot
FORCE	hoard	boar/bored/court
BATH	dance/staff/ask/bath	
NURSE	heard	Bert
PALM	father/ma/bra/spa/pa	
THOUGHT	haught(y)/hawk/hawed	caught/bought/taught
CLOTH	soft/lost/cough/boss/off/cloth	
PRICE	hide	bite
CHOICE	hoid/void	boyt/boy
MOUTH	howd	bout
NEAR	heered	beard
SQUARE	hared	bared
NORTH	horde	short/tort
CURE	hured	boor/poor

Once you have recorded your speech sample, you need to view the sound to begin your analysis. To do this, follow the instructions in Praat on 'Viewing and Editing a Sound':

www.fon.hum.uva.nl/praat/manual/Intro_2_2__Viewing_and_editing_ a_sound.html.

Once you click on 'View and Edit', a waveform and spectrogram appear. You can click on any of the bars under the spectrogram to listen to the recording. This can help you identify which words are visualized for each waveform. This is shown in Figure 10.2.

As shown in Figure 10.3, I have identified the shaded area as HEED. To analyse the formants for this word, I first select the relevant section of the waveform by clicking my mouse on the beginning section of HEED and dragging my mouse across the waveform for HEED. Then click on 'sel' on the bottom left. To see the formant values, click on 'Formant' at the top right if they are not visible. If they are already visible, you will see red dots along the spectrogram in the bottom of each picture; these dots, in greyscale, can be seen in Figure 10.4.

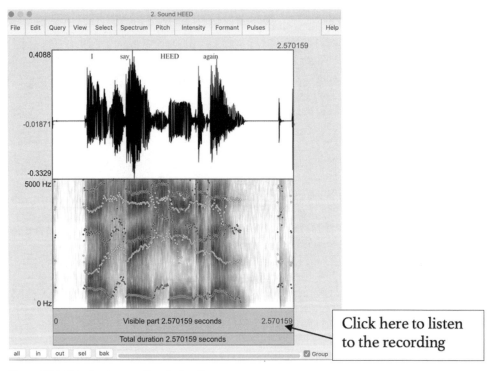

Figure 10.2 Listening to recordings in Praat

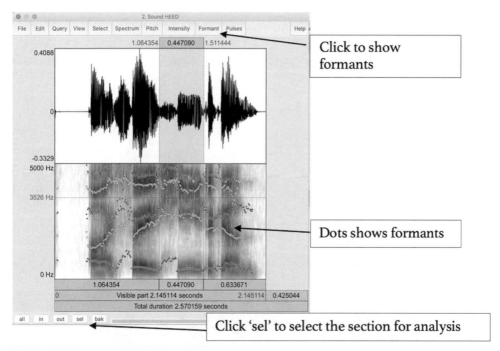

Figure 10.3 Formant analysis in Praat

We will now place the cursor in the middle of the vowel articulation; we are trying to locate the most 'steady' articulation of the vowel that is not influenced by either the initial [h] or the ending [d]. Once you have selected what you believe is the optimal part of the vowel for analysis, click on 'Formant', and then on 'Formant listing'; this is shown in Figure 10.5.

A new window will pop up with Time (section of the recording from which you extracted the formant values), and the values for F1–F4, as shown in Figure 10.6. For HEED, the F1 is 472.84 and F2 is 2825.60. We will plug these numbers into an Excel file, which you can download in the online link in the speech files folder for Chapter 3. This Excel file, shown in Figure 10.7, has the values I have extracted from my own vowels as well as a blank spreadsheet for you to input your vowel formants. This spreadsheet automatically converts the F1 and F2 values to a Bark Scale, and places them onto a vowel chart. Continue to do this for all the vowels except for the vowels in the 'r' Lexical Sets and diphthongs. Your vowel template should look something like Figure 10.7.

The spreadsheet automatically generates a vowel chart, as shown in Figure 10.8. You need to adjust both the vertical and horizontal axis numbers to display all the vowels. As an example, my F2 Bark values range

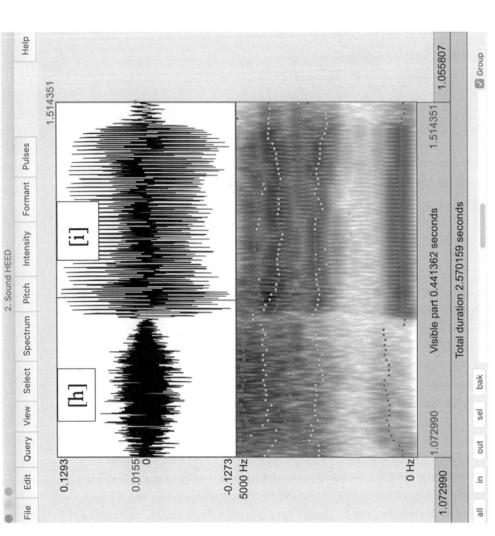

Figure 10.4 Formants in HEED

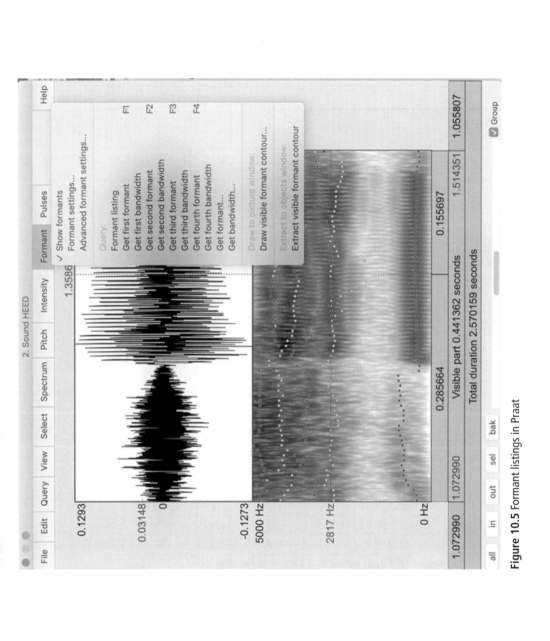

Figure 10.5 Formant listings in Praat

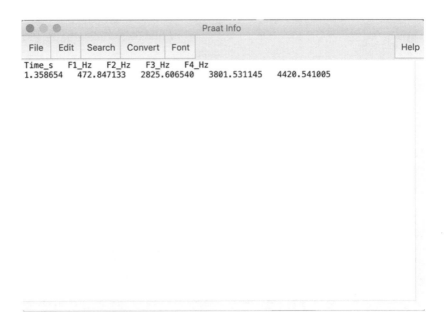

Figure 10.6 Formant values

	F1 (Hz)	F2 (Hz)	F1 (Bark)	F2 (Bark)
HEED (FLEECE)	430	2805	4.120	15.204
HID (KIT)	445	2317	4.251	14.038
HEAD (DRESS)	591	1949	5.513	12.938
HAD (TRAP)	773	1933	6.945	12.881
WHO'D (GOOSE)	411	1624	3.944	11.732
HOOD (FOOT)	542	1535	5.101	11.352
HUD (STRUT)	768	1464	6.905	11.036
HOD (LOT)	693	1149	6.334	9.412
FATHER (PALM)	729	1370	6.612	10.589
HOED (GOAT)	516	1360	4.875	10.540
CLOTH	675	1016	6.189	8.610
HAWED (THOUGHT)	635	1004	5.873	8.533
BATH	704	1895	6.420	12.752

Figure 10.7 Excel spreadsheet for Bark Scale values for vowel formants

from 8.533 to 15.204 so my horizontal axis should be set for a minimum of 8 and maximum of 16 (I have set it for 7 to 17) in the template. My F1 axis should range from a minimum of 3; I have set it for 2 to 8. This can easily be changed by clicking on the vertical and horizontal axes on the figure. You should also label each vowel by keyword for easy reference (to locate

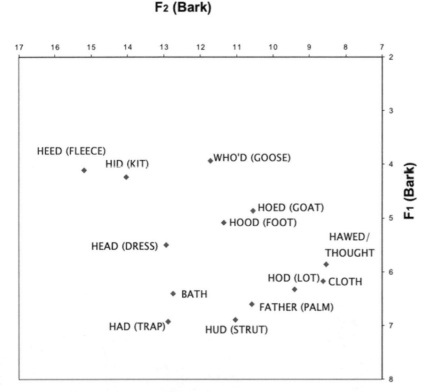

F₂ (Bark)

Figure 10.8 Vowel chart generated in Excel

which vowel each dot represents, hover your mouse over the dot until the F1 and F2 numbers are displayed).

To measure the formant values of diphthongs, we need to create two measurements per diphthong, one for the 1st target and one for the 2nd target. In other words, we need two F1 and two F2 measurements per diphthong to show the transition from the 1st to the 2nd target. For some vowels, like FACE, the transition may be very slight; it is easier to see the transition for CHOICE (HOID); Figure 10.9 shows a waveform and spectrogram for my pronunciation of HOID (CHOICE). There is a clear change in the F2 of CHOICE as it increases in frontness (higher F2) for the 2nd target.

As shown in Figure 10.10, an increase in F2 can also be seen in the F2 of HIDE (PRICE), also showing the movement towards a fronter articulation in the 2nd target.

For HOWD (MOUTH) in Figure 10.11, there is a lowering of the F2 in the 2nd target.

There is a smaller shift in the 1st and 2nd targets for HAYED (FACE), as shown in Figure 10.12, given the smaller change from the 1st to the 2nd target.

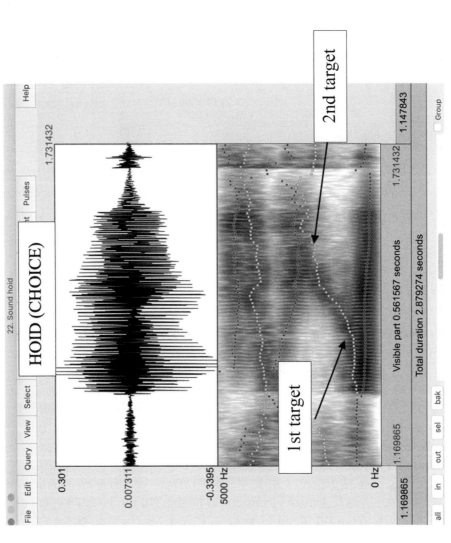

Figure 10.9 Formants in HOID

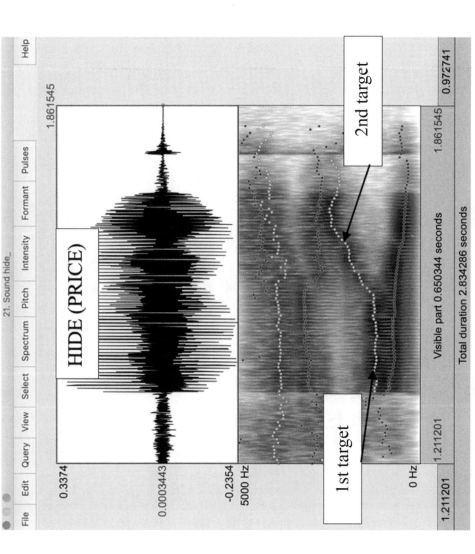

Figure 10.10 Formants in HIDE

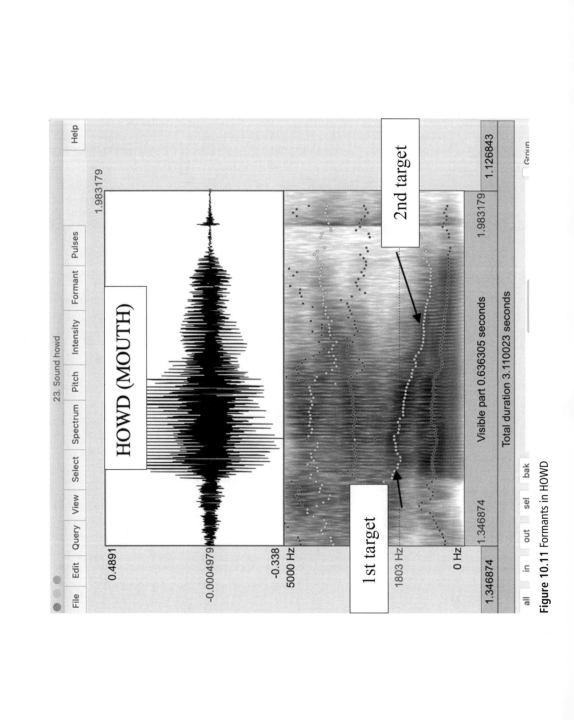

Figure 10.11 Formants in HOWD

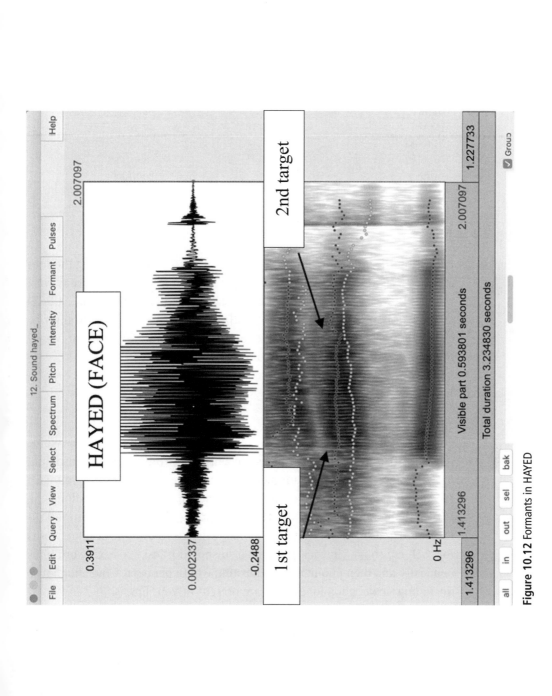

Figure 10.12 Formants in HAYED

Chapter 4:   Rhoticity in Varieties of English

Table 10.2 Word list / sentence for rhoticity

Wells' Lexical Sets	[hVd]	[bVd]/[bVt]
FORCE	hoard	boar/bored/court
NURSE	heard	Bert
START	hard	Bart
NEAR	heered	beard
SQUARE	hared	bared
NORTH	horde	short/tort
CURE	hured	boor/poor
lettER	header	better
Sentence:	*Bother, father caught hot coffee in the car park.*	

Following the guidelines above for vowels, record yourself reading the sentence as well as the words in the 'r' Lexical Sets in Table 10.2. You may wish to record the actual keywords in each Lexical Set (like FORCE and NURSE) or the words in the [hVd] and/or [bVd]/[bVt] lists. You can also transcribe each word phonemically and phonetically to examine both your vowel inventory and rhoticity after different vowels.

Chapter 5:   The Consonants of English

Following the guidelines above for vowels, record yourself reading the words in Table 10.3. You may wish to record only one word for each consonant, to determine which consonant phonemes exist in your English. If you wish to examine allophonic variation in your English, including short-/long-lag VOT, flapping, glottal stopping, TH/DH-stopping and fronting, light/dark /l/ variation, and /r l w j/ variation, you may wish to record one or more words for each consonant in each position. You should transcribe each word phonemically and then phonetically, to examine both phonemes and allophones (including vowel allophones) that are present in your English.

Chapter 6:   English Syllable Structure

Following the guidelines above for vowels, record yourself reading the words in Table 10.4. You should transcribe your pronunciation both phonemically and phonetically, to analyse your syllable structure and any syllable structure variation that exists in your English.

Table 10.3 Word list for consonants

Phoneme and keyword	Allophonic variation	Words
/p/ – pat	Initial	*pot*
	After /s/	*spot*
	Medial	*repeat*
	Final	*slip*
/b/ – bat	Initial	*boy, bit*
	Medial	*a rebel* (N), *to rebel* (V)
	Final	*rob*
/t/ – tip	Initial	*top*
	After /s/	*stop*
	Medial	*bitter, better, button,*
	Final	*mountain*
		at this
/d/ – dip	Initial	*Dan*
	Medial	*middle, muddle*
	Final	*bad*
/k/ – cot	Initial	*can*
	Medial	*a record* (N), *to record* (V)
	Final	*back*
/g/ – got	Initial	*gave*
	Medial	*bagged*
	Final	*bag*
/f/ – fine	Initial	*fan*
	Medial	*a perfect* (adj.), *to perfect* (V)
	Final	*leaf*
/v/ – vine	Initial	*van*
	Medial	*having*
	Final	*gave*
/θ/ – three	Initial	*think, thought*
	Medial	*something, anything*
	Final	*bath, breath*
/ð/ – these	Initial	*that, the*
	Medial	*mother, father*
	Final	*bathe, breathe*
/s/ – Sue	Initial	*see*
	Medial	*buses*
	Final	*kiss*
/z/ – zoo	Initial	*xerox*
	Medial	*lazy*
	Final	*buzz*
/ʃ/ – she	Initial	*shoes*
	Medial	*wishes, gracious*
	Final	*brush*

Table 10.3 (Cont.)

Phoneme and keyword	Allophonic variation	Words
/ʒ/ – Asia	Initial	*genre*
	Medial	*pleasure*
	Final	*rouge*
/h/ – hot	Initial	*how, hello*
	Medial	*ahead*
/tʃ/ – church	Initial	*chew*
	Medial	*teacher*
	Final	*which*
/dʒ/ – judge	Initial	*Joe*
	Medial	*enjoy*
	Final	*edge*
/m/ – man	Initial	*make*
	Medial	*summer*
	Final	*some*
/n/ – note	Initial	*nine*
	Medial	*minor*
	Final	*bean*
/ŋ/ – sing	Medial	*singer*
	Final	*thing*
/r/ – red	Initial	*red, right*
	After aspirated /p t k/	*pray, tree*
	Medial	*roaring*
	Final (see above also)	*lear*
/w/ – white	Initial	*witch, way*
	<wh->	*which, where*
/l/ – light	Initial	*lear, line*
	After aspirated /p t k/	*play, clear*
	Medial	*taller, smaller*
	Final	*pull, pool, pill*
/j/ – yellow	Initial	*you*
	After aspirated /p t k/	*tune, pew*

Table 10.4 Word list for syllable structure

Syllable structure	Example word	Possible transcription
V	I	/ai/
CV	tea	/tiː/
CCV	tree	/triː/
CCCV	stray	/streɪ/
VC	at	/æt/
VCC	ask	/æsk/
VCCC	asks	/æsks/

Syllable structure	Example word	Possible transcription
VCCCC	*ersts	*/eɪsts/
CVC	leap	/liːp/
CCVC	sleep	/sliːp/
CCCVC	street	/striːt/
CVCC	task	/tæsk/
CVCCC	tasks	/tæsks/
CVCCCC	bursts	/bɜːɹsts/
CCVC	trip	/trɪp/
CCVCC	trips	/trɪps/
CCVCCC	prints	/prɪnts/
CCVCCCC	*blursts	/blɜːɹsts/
CCCVCC	sprint	/sprɪnt/
CCCVCCC	sprints	/sprɪnts/
CCCVCCCC	strengths	/streŋkθs/

*These are possible syllable structures but lack exemplars in English. We can construct possible words such as *ersts* and *blursts* for a rhotic speaker of English.

Chapter 7: English Stress and Rhythm

Following the guidelines above for vowels, record yourself reading the words and sentences in Table 10.5. You may want to transcribe the words phonemically and phonetically. You can also do an acoustic analysis of your pronunciation of the words and sentences using Praat: you can examine the pitch, intensity, and duration of each syllable of the words in the weak vowel Lexical Sets and the N/V pairs, to determine whether your pronunciation of each syllable in the Lexical Sets words, as well as the words as an N or as a V, is the same. You can also examine whether one or more syllables have more prominence through pitch, intensity, and duration in the multiple-syllable words and the sentences.

Chapter 8: Intonation in Varieties of English

Following the guidelines above for vowels, record yourself reading the sentences in Table 10.6 (sentences in italics were used in the speech samples). Please record each sentence as a separate speech file.

Sentences for contrastive/non-contrastive stress: Read the sentences in Table 10.7 as you would normally say them.

It is also useful to record more naturalistic data, as some features, including uptalk and creaky voice, may not be as common in more formal speech tasks such as word lists and sentence reading. Therefore, you can record yourself answering the questions in Table 10.8, from Chapter 1.

Table 10.5 Word/sentence list for stress and rhythm

Feature	Words/sentences
Weak vowels	Wells' Lexical Sets: happY, commA, lettER
Noun/verb pairs	A *record* (N) as in 'She set a new Olympic *record* in the high jump' To *record* (V) as in 'She wants to *record* a new music album' A *rebel* (N) as in 'He is a *rebel*' To *rebel* (V) as in 'He is going to *rebel*'
Polysyllabic words	*absent-minded* *affect* *department* *fact-finding*
Syllabic consonants	*button* *bottle*
Stress-timed/ syllable-timed rhythm	<u>He</u> caught <u>a</u> cod. Let <u>us</u> meet <u>at the</u> square <u>on the</u> north end. <u>He</u> <u>is</u> <u>going</u> <u>to</u> dip <u>her</u> food <u>into the</u> sauce. <u>The</u> fath<u>er</u> <u>is</u> sitt<u>ing</u> <u>on his</u> cot think<u>ing</u> <u>the</u> world <u>is a</u> fine place.

Table 10.6 Sentence list for intonation

Sentence type	Example sentences
1. Declarative statements	The train leaves at midnight. *All of this takes willpower.* *He hid the letter under the hat.*
2. Echos/declarative questions	So you didn't go?
3. Yes/no questions	Is this your bag? *Should he spend all of his time just studying?* *Will you pay for the opera King Lear?*
4. Wh-questions	Who is going to the lunch? *Where should he live?*
5. Tag questions	This is your car, isn't it? *This long-awaited feeling doesn't develop suddenly, does it?*
6. Imperatives	(What should I do now?) Go and wash the car.
7. Exclamations	What a beautiful day!
8. List of items	He brought apples, pears, and grapes. *At first, it is not easy for him to be casual in dress, informal in manner, and confident in speech.*

Table 10.7 Sentence list for pitch accent

Sentence type	Example
Non-contrastive	She drove the blue car.
Contrastive	She drove the blue car. (Not the red or green car)
Contrastive	She drove the blue car. (She was the driver, not the passenger)
Contrastive	She drove the blue car. (Not someone else)
Contrastive	She drove the blue car. (The special blue car)
Final pronoun	She drove the blue one.

Table 10.8 Open-ended questions for interview/conversation data

(1) Where are you from? What is your home town and country?
(2) Where else have you lived? How long have you lived in each place?
(3) What other languages (other than English) do you speak?
(4) Which variety/ies of English do you speak?

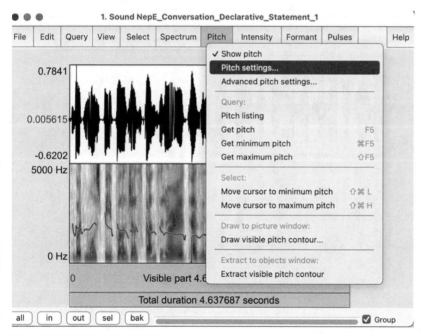

Figure 10.13 Pitch settings in Praat

To examine pitch and intonation, open each sentence file in Praat (open a speech file and click on 'View and Edit'). Then click on 'Show pitch' in the top bar under 'Pitch', as shown in Figure 10.13.

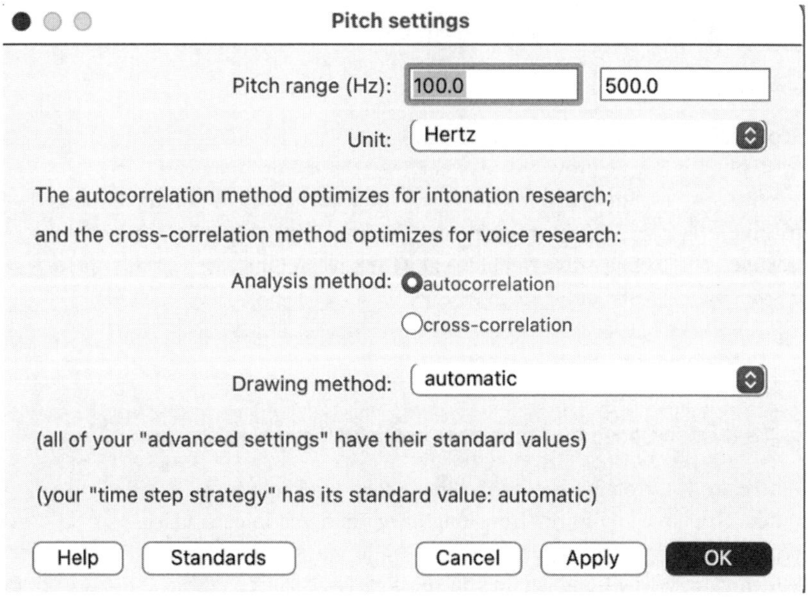

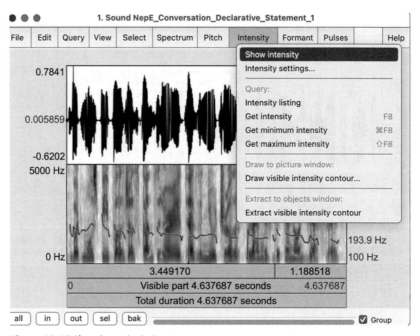

Figure 10.14 Pitch range in Praat

Figure 10.15 Show intensity in Praat

You may need to adjust the pitch setting: 75–300 for male voices and 100–500 for female voices. To do this, click on 'Pitch' on the top bar, and then on 'Pitch settings', as shown in Figure 10.14.

You can then change the pitch range as necessary.

It may also be helpful to show intensity (see Chapter 7); this can be done by clicking on 'Show intensity'. This is shown in Figure 10.15, and will give you a spectrogram with both pitch and intensity.

APPENDIX B

Answers to the Task Questions

Chapter 1:   Introduction

Tasks 1.1–2
Answers may vary.

Task 1.3
Speaker 1

(1) Hanoi, Vietnam
(2) New Hampshire and Virginia in the US for 3 years
(3) Vietnamese
(4) Americanized English with a New Hampshire accent
(5) Because of living in the US
(6) Living in the US
(7) First studied a British English accent and then changed to American English to try to sound more American
(8) Deciding to study in the US

Speaker 2

(1) Taipei, Taiwan
(2) She spent 2 years in kindergarten (preschool) in Canada and completed her secondary school in New Zealand
(3) Chinese (Mandarin), Russian, German, a little bit of Polish
(4) She speaks a mix of American and British English
(5) She learned American English in Taiwan and British English in New Zealand
(6) Teachers, education, movies/TV
(7) Yes, from American English to a mix of American and British English
(8) Moving to New Zealand

Speaker 3

(1) Moscow, Russia
(2) Russia until age 15; she then moved to Thailand, where she lived for 4 years; she has been living in Hong Kong for 3 years

(3) Russian, a bit of German, and she is learning Mandarin Chinese. She speaks just a few words in Thai
(4) No particular accent but speaks a mixture of American and British English
(5) Learning English in Russia and then attending international school in Thailand
(6) Friends, teachers, movies/TV
(7) Her accent changed when she moved to Thailand; she also changes her accent depending on with whom she is speaking
(0) Environment

Speaker 4

(1) Canberra and Melbourne, Australia
(2) She was born in Edinburgh, Scotland; her family then moved to England, where she lived until she was 3. When she was 3, her family moved to Melbourne, Australia, where she lived for 6 years. She then lived in Canberra for 8 years. She has lived in Sydney for the past 2 years.
(3) No answer
(4) Australian English; British English for spelling; she also has some British English pronunciations
(5) Because she grew up in Australia. British English comes from her parents
(6) Moving from the UK to Australia
(7) Yes, she had a very English accent when she lived in the UK
(8) Moving to Australia at age 3

Speaker 5

(1) New York, USA
(2) She was born in Hong Kong but her family immigrated to the US during her early adolescence
(3) Cantonese and Mandarin Chinese
(4) New York American English / mixed English
(5) Learned American English when she moved to the US
(6) Education, peers, movies/TV
(7) Yes, from more Cantonese-influenced Hong Kong English to more Americanized English
(8) The environment

Speaker 6

(1) Asheville, North Carolina, USA
(2) He lived in Asheville until he was 18; he then spent 1 year in Washington DC, and then 3 years in Winston-Salem, North Carolina. He also lived

in China for 2 years and then in Chicago, Illinois, USA, for 3 years; Wilmington, North Carolina for 1 year; Charlottesville, Virginia for 1 year; and Hong Kong for 3 years

(3) German, some Mandarin Chinese, and a little Cantonese

(4) Appalachian American English

(5) He grew up in the Appalachia region of the US

(6) His parents and where he grew up

(7) No answer

(8) No answer

Speaker 7

(1) Surabaya, East Java, Indonesia

(2) East Java, Java, and Borneo, Indonesia; Switzerland when she was 26 years old, for 2 years; 6 months in South Korea, then Hong Kong

(3) Three Indonesian languages: East Java, Central Java, and South Borneo. She studied German when living in Switzerland

(4) American English

(5) Due to influence of watching American media. She feels she has less of an Indonesian accent than her friends

(6) Media and books and needing to use English when living in Switzerland

(7) No answer

(8) No answer

Speaker 8

(1) Almaty, Kazakhstan

(2) Outside Kazakhstan: 8 months in the US, 4 months in Austria, and 2 years in Hong Kong

(3) Kazakh and Russian; intermediate German; some French, Spanish, and Putonghua

(4) A mix of American and British English

(5) She was taught British English in high school in Kazakhstan but learned American English when she lived in the US

(6) Living in the US for 8 months. Also influence from Russian, Kazakh, and German.

(7) Yes, from more British English to more American English

(8) Environment and peers

Speaker 9

(1) Jinan, Shandong Province, China

(2) Moved to North Carolina at age 14, for 4½ years, and then to Minnesota for 2½ years for university

(3) Mandarin Chinese; Japanese and Spanish; learning Cantonese

(4) North Carolina American English

(5) He learned English at age 14 in North Carolina

(6) Learning English in the US, interacting with American peers

(7) No answer

(8) No answer

Speaker 10

(1) Bangkok, Thailand, but born in India

(2) Born in India and lived there until age 2; has lived in Thailand since age 2

(3) Thai, Hindi

(4) Indian English (a southern variety of Indian English)

(5) She speaks English with her mother, who is from the southern part of India

(6) Her mother, and also high school as she went to school with many children who were from India. She also studied Hindi, and that influences her English as well

(7) No answer

(8) No answer

Speaker 11

(1) Kaohsiung, Taiwan

(2) 18 years in Kaohsiung

(3) Putonghua, a little Taiwanese, and a little bit of Japanese

(4) She feels she speaks Taiwanese English, but others tell her she has American English features

(5) Other people tell her she sounds more American

(6) Her English teacher, as she had one-on-one English lessons with a teacher who studied in the US. She studied with this teacher for 4 years. Also listening to American pop music.

(7) Yes, she feels she may be picking up some British English features in Hong Kong

(8) Listening to her teachers in Hong Kong, many of whom speak British English

Check Your Understanding
Exercises

(a) *Accent* refers to pronunciation features, while *dialect* includes not only pronunciation features but also other linguistic features, including vocabulary, grammar, and morphology.

(b) There are many regional, social, and ethnic varieties of different Englishes, including in American and British English.

(c) (1) Answers will vary – examples include Northern or Southern British English; Ulster English; Southern American English.
(2) Answers will vary – examples include Māori English, Native American English, Chicano English.

Discussion Questions and Expand Your Understanding

Answers may vary.

Chapter 2   The History and Spread of English Worldwide

Task 2.1

Answers may vary.

Task 2.2

The three English words are *mother, father, three*. It is likely that kinship terms such as *mother* and *father* as well as numbers such as *three* evolved from Proto-Indo-European (PIE) due to their similarities, as well as the probability that these words existed in PIE. You may have noted that one difference between *father* in Germanic vs Romance languages is the *f* vs *p* at the beginning of the word. Linguists, including Jacob Grimm (who, along with his brother Wilhelm Grimm, wrote *Grimms' Fairy Tales*), postulate that this was part of the First Germanic Sound Shift, also known as Grimm's Law, in which a number of consonant changes took place as Germanic languages evolved from PIE. Linguists posit that *p* as in *pader* existed in PIE; the *p* shifted to *f* in Germanic languages.

Task 2.3

Shakespeare wrote in Early Modern English. See text, page 25.

Task 2.4

(1) bite
(2) name
(3) house
(4) bone

Task 2.5

Answers in the text on page 34.

Check Your Understanding
Exercises

(a) (1) hundred
   (2) moon
   (3) bath
   (4) thunder
   (5) wool
   (6) right
(b) (1) Early Modern English

   1450/1500 CE – 1650 CE
   High level of readability – close in spelling to Late Modern English,
      with a few exceptions (heauen, kingdome)

   (2) Old English

   Circa 450 CE – 1100/1150 CE
   Use of 'þ', 'ð', 'æ'
   Difficult to understand unless trained in Old English
   No f/v distinction (heofonum)
   {-an} inflection

   (3) Late Modern English

   1650 CE – present day
   Represents modern-day spelling

   (4) Middle English

   Circa 1100/1150 CE – 1450/1500 CE
   Change of 'þ', 'ð' to 'th'
   Emergence of 'ou' spelling, f/v distinction (as 'u' in heuenes)
   Loss of {-an} inflection
(c) The *i*-mutation was a phonological change that took place in 7 CE,
   leading to the plural forms of *foot* as *feet* and *goose* as *geese*. The plural
   form {-iz} was added to some nouns, with the vowel *i* leading to a shift
   in the first vowel of *o* to ē, due to vowel harmony.
(d) The Great Vowel Shift took place from the fifteenth to seventeenth centuries, from Middle to Modern English. The long vowels went through a
   process of raising; some vowels became diphthongs. As a result, Modern
   English spelling and pronunciation are not as closely related as they
   were in the Old and Middle English periods.

Discussion Questions

Answers may vary.

Expand Your Understanding

Speaker 1	NZE, Inner Circle English, OVE, native speaker of English
Speaker 2	WSAE, Outer Circle English, NVE, Postcolonial English, native speaker of English
Speaker 3	German English, Expanding Circle English, NVE, native speaker of German; not a native speaker of English
Speaker 4	MalE, Outer Circle English, NVE, Postcolonial English, native speaker of English and Malay
Speaker 5	ZimE, Outer Circle English, NVE, Postcolonial English, native speaker of English and Shona
Speaker 6	AmE, Inner Circle English, OVE, native speaker of English
Speaker 7	IndE, Outer Circle English, NVE, Postcolonial English, native speaker of English and Hindi
Speaker 8	AusE, Inner Circle English, OVE, native speaker of English
Speaker 9	China English, Expanding Circle English, NVE, native speaker of Mandarin Chinese (Putonghua); not a native speaker of English
Speaker 10	BrE, Inner Circle English, OVE, native speaker of English
Speaker 11	ChilE, Expanding Circle English, NVE, a native speaker of Spanish; not a native speaker of English
Speaker 12	Korean English, Expanding Circle English, NVE, a native speaker of Korean; not a native speaker of English
Speaker 13	HKE, Outer Circle English, NVE, Postcolonial English, a native speaker of Cantonese; not a native speaker of English
Speaker 14	Kyrgyzstan English, Expanding Circle English, NVE, a native speaker of Russian and the Kyrgyz language; not a native speaker of English
Speaker 15	PakE, Outer Circle English, NVE, Postcolonial English, a native speaker of Urdu and Sindhi; not a native speaker of English

Chapter 3:   The Vowels of English

Task 3.1

Answers may vary.

Task 3.2

Listening task

Task 3.3

(1) (a) ɑ (b) ʉ (c) e (d) ɔ (e) o
(2) (a) open-mid back unrounded vowel
(b) open front rounded vowel
(c) close front unrounded vowel
(d) close back unrounded vowel
(e) open front unrounded vowel

Task 3.4
Listening task

Task 3.5
Answers given in the text on pages 62–3.

Task 3.6
The speakers of Mod RP, IrE, WSAE, and AusE have a length distinction for *bead* and *bid* whereas the speakers of SgE and KenE do not have a length difference.

Task 3.7
Answers may vary.

Tasks 3.8–3.25
Listening tasks, answers may vary.

Task 3.26

MOUTH: 1st target fronted in AusE, NZE; 2nd target centralized in NZE, lowered in AusE
PRICE: 1st target backed and 2nd target lowered in AusE and NZE
GOAT: 1st target lowered in NZE and WSAE; 2nd target is centralized or fronted in NZE, AusE, WSAE
FACE: 1st target lowered in AusE, NZE and retracted (backed) in WSAE; 2nd target lowered in NZE
GOOSE: fronted in WSAE, NZE, Mod RP, and AusE
FLEECE: pronounced as a high front long vowel by all the speakers

Task 3.27

Answers in text on page 104

Task 3.28

Listening task

Check Your Understanding
Exercises

(a) Refer to vowel chart in Chapter 3

(b)

    High: refers to vowels that are articulated with the tongue raised high in the mouth

    Mid: refers to vowels that are articulated with the tongue raised to a mid point in the mouth

    Low: refers to vowels that are articulated with the tongue lowered in the mouth

    Open: refers to an open jaw

    Mid: refers to a mid (slightly) open jaw

    Close: refers to a closed or nearly closed jaw

    Front: means that the front part of the tongue is lowered or raised

    Central: refers to neutral tongue placement

    Back: means that the back part of the tongue is lowered or raised

(c) Back vowels tend to be rounded while front vowels tend to be spread or neutral.

(d) /æ/   Open/low front unrounded vowel

    /ɛ/   Open-mid front unrounded vowel

    /ɪ/   Close/high front unrounded vowel

    /ʉ/   Close/high central rounded vowel

    /ɜ/   Open-mid central unrounded vowel

    /ʊ/   Close/high back rounded vowel

    /ɔ/   Open-mid back rounded vowel

(e) FI is the first formant and correlates with Height.

    F2 is the second formant and correlates with Advancement (front/backness).

(f) The following sets of words form minimal pairs:

sleep/slip	*ship/sheep*	*lit/let*
pal/pill	*sheep/steep*	*man/moon*
feel/fill	*steep/stop*	*man/map*
fill/pill		

    Latte, tea, and *many* do not form minimal pairs with any of the words. Minimal pairs are words with one phonemic difference; the words must have the same number of phonemes.

(g)

    Sam [sæ̃m] vs *sad* [sæd] – vowel nasalization preceding a nasal in the same syllable

sat [sæ̆t] vs *sad* [sæd] – vowel shortening preceding a voiceless consonant in the same syllable

hike [hʌɪk] vs *hide* [haɪd] – 'Canadian Raising' of vowels in PRICE/
MOUTH Lexical Sets before voiceless consonants in the same syllable

too [tʉ:] vs *coo* [ku:] – GOOSE-fronting after /t/ (coronal consonant)

Discussion Questions

(a) If a language only has 3 vowels, it is more likely to have /i a u/, and for
5 vowels, /i e a o u/. The vowels are the most maximally distinctive in
terms of HAR.

(b) Cultivated accents (as in AusE, for example) are closer to RP, while
Broad has the most local features and General is the most common (and
Standard) accent, free of most regional and sociocultural features.

Acrolectal (as in PhlE, for example) means closest to the superstrate,
while basilectal has the most substratum influences. The mesolectal has
unique linguistic features but is closer to the superstrate than the basilectal variety.

(c) The superstrate is the variety or varieties of English that influence an
NVE; for PhlE, this is AmE, while in HKE, this has historically been
BrE. The substrates are the local languages that influence the NVE;
for PhlE, this is Filipino as well as other languages and dialects of the
Philippines; for HKE, this has historically been Cantonese but may also
increasingly be Mandarin Chinese.

Expand Your Understanding

(a) Like NBrE, EMidBrE has a FOOT/STRUT merger and the TRAP/BATH
merger as /a/. The speaker also has a fronted GOOSE.

(b) Some answers may vary. FLEECE/KIT are merged for this speaker;
GOOSE and FOOT are merged; and GOOSE and FOOT also appear to be
fronted in some contexts, with less fronting before /l/ as in PULL/POOL.
DRESS/TRAP are not merged for this speaker.

Chapter 4:   Rhoticity in Varieties of English

Task 4.1–4.2

Answers may vary.

Task 4.3

Answers in the text, page 126

Task 4.4

Answers in the text, page 127

Task 4.5

Answers in the text, page 130

Task 4.6

Answers in the text, page 131

Task 4.7

Answers in the text, pages 132–3

Task 4.8

Answers in the text, pages 133–4

Task 4.9

Answers in the text, page 135

Task 4.10

Answers in the text, page 136

Task 4.11

Answers in the text, pages 136–7

Task 4.12

Answers in the text, page 137

Task 4.13

Answers in the text, page 138

Check Your Understanding
Exercises

(a)

[ɹ] – retroflex approximant – varieties of AmE, ScotE

[ʁ] – voiced uvular fricative – varieties of ScotE

[ɾ] – alveolar tap or flap – varieties of ScotE, WelE

[ɻ] – voiced retroflex approximant – varieties of English in the West of England; IrE, NIrE

(b) Speaker 1 is from SA, Australia (see Figure 10.16). He is non-rhotic; there is no lowering of the F3.

Speaker 2 is from Chicago, Illinois, USA. She is rhotic (note the lowering of the F3 in Figure 10.17).

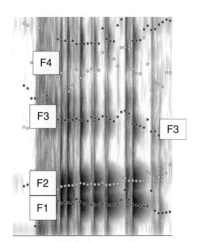

Figure 10.16 Speaker 1: rhoticity

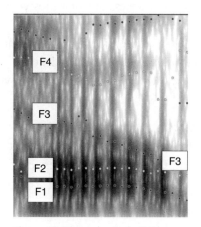

Figure 10.17 Speaker 2: rhoticity

Discussion Questions

Answers may vary.

Expand Your Understanding

The speaker is rhotic.

Chapter 5:   The Consonants of English

Tasks 5.1–2

Answers may vary.

Task 5.3

(1)

  (a) Voiceless velar stop /k/
  (b) Bilabial nasal /m/
  (c) Voiced dental fricative /ð/
  (d) Voiceless glottal fricative /h/
  (e) Palatal approximant /j/

(2)

  (a) t – voiceless alveolar plosive (stop)
  (b) z – voiced alveolar fricative
  (c) l – (voiced) lateral approximant
  (d) θ – voiceless dental fricative
  (e) ʒ – voiced postalveolar fricative

Task 5.4

The following correspondences exist in many, though not all, varieties of English. Other answers are possible depending on the variety of English.

  p̱at /p/
  ḇat /b/
  ṯip /t/
  ḏip /d/
  c̱ot /k/
  g̱ot /g/
  f̱ine /f/
  v̱ine /v/
  S̱ue /s/
  ẕoo /z/
  ṯhree /θ/
  ṯhese /ð/
  s̱he /ʃ/
  As̱ia /ʒ/
  ḫot /h/

c̲hurch /tʃ/
j̲udge /dʒ/
m̲an /m/
n̲ote /n/
sin̲g̲ /ŋ/
r̲ed /r/
l̲ight /l/
y̲ellow /j/
w̲hite /w/

Task 5.5
Answers in the text, page 162

Task 5.6
Answers in the text, page 166

Task 5.7
Answers in the text, page 169

Task 5.8
Answers in the text, page 173

Task 5.9
Listening task

Check Your Understanding
Answers may vary.

Chapter 6: English Syllable Structure

Task 6.1
Answers may vary; see also page 192.

Task 6.2
Answers in the text, page 188

Task 6.3

telephone	*unhappy*	*congratulate*	*visionary*
/tel.ə.foʊn/	/ʌn.hæp.i/	/kən.grætʃ.ə.leɪt/	/vɪʒ.ə.ner.i/
CVC.V.CVC	VC.CVC.V	CVC.CCVC.V.CVC	CVC.V.CVC.V

Task 6.4
death/breath
laid/maid
yew/true
it/it (not a pure rhyme)

Task 6.5
Answers in the text, pages 194–6

Task 6.6
Listening task

Task 6.7
Answers in the text, page 196

Task 6.8
Listening task

Task 6.9
Only the Calif AmE speaker has /r/ after the vowel in *bear* as she is a rhotic speaker of English. The KenE, Mod RP, and SA AusE speakers have zero coda in *bear*, as they are non-rhotic speakers of English (see also Chapter 4).

Task 6.10
Only the Calif AmE speaker has the CC cluster in *start* as she is rhotic. The SA AusE, KenE, and Mod RP speakers have a C coda in this word as they are non-rhotic.

Task 6.11
Only the Calif AmE speaker has the CCC cluster in *turns* as she is rhotic. The SA AusE, KenE, and Mod RP speakers have a CC coda in this word as they are non-rhotic.

Task 6.12
Only the Calif AmE speaker has the CCCC cluster in *worlds* as she is rhotic. The SA AusE, KenE, and Mod RP speakers have a CCC coda in this word as they are non-rhotic.

Task 6.13
Answers in the text, page 199

Task 6.14
Answers in the text, page 203

Task 6.15
Listening task

Check Your Understanding
Exercises
(a) /sprɪŋ/   CCCVC *spring*

   /hjuˑdʒ/   CCVC *huge*

   /splæʃt/   CCCVCC *splashed*

   /blaɪnd/   CCVCC *blind*

   /iːt/   VC *eat*

   /spɪld/   CCVCC *spilled*

   /sneɪk/   CCVC *snake*

   /tækst/   CVCCC *taxed*

   /lʌntʃ/   CVCC *lunch*

   /tiː/   CV *tea*

(b)

Word	Phonetic realization	Process
risk	[rɪks]	Metathesis
string	[istrɪŋ]	Vowel prothesis
text	[tekəstə]	Vowel epenthesis and paragoge
newt	[nuːt]	Yod dropping
walking	[wɔːkin]	ING-variation to [n]
tube	[tʃuːb]	Yod coalescence
string	[sitrɪŋ]	Vowel epenthesis
text	[tekstə]	Vowel paragoge
singing	[sɪŋgɪŋ]	NG retention
text	[teks]	CCR

Discussion Questions and Expand Your Understanding

Answers may vary.

Chapter 7:   English Stress and Rhythm

Task 7.1

Answers in the text, page 213

Task 7.2

Answers in the text, pages 217–18

Task 7.3

Answers in the text, page 218

Task 7.4

Answers in the text, page 227

Task 7.5

Answers in the text, page 229

Task 7.6

Answers in the text, page 235

Check Your Understanding
Exercises

(a) Some varieties of English have strong and weak syllables. Strong syllables have a full vowel phoneme as the nucleus of the syllable, and usually have greater intensity and/or loudness, and longer duration. Weak
syllables are shorter in duration, and usually have less intensity and/or
loudness, and may have a weak vowel such as a schwa /ə/, a high front
vowel /i ɪ/, or a high back vowel /u/. Many OVEs, including varieties of
AmE, CanE, BrE, IrE, WelE, ScotE, WSAE, AusE, and NZE, among others,
have weak syllables.

(b) Weak syllables are always unstressed; strong syllables may be stressed
or unstressed, but only strong syllables can receive stress.

(c) Nasals and approximants, and most commonly /l/ and /n/, can become
the nucleus of a syllable when in a weak syllable and the weak vowel is
deleted. These consonants can be the nuclei of a syllable because they
are sonorous, like vowels, in contrast to obstruents.

(d) A trochaic stress is a pattern of stress where a stressed syllable is followed
by an unstressed syllable. This occurs for many two-syllable nouns and
adjectives in some varieties of English, including *water, happy, shep-
herd*, and *English*. An iambic stress pattern has an unstressed syllable
followed by a stressed syllable. This pattern occurs for many two-
syllable words, and particularly verbs and adverbs, in some varieties of
English, including *attend, relax, suggest*, and *collect*.

Discussion Questions
The Beatles *Hey Jude*

> Hey Jude, don't be <u>afraid</u>
> You were <u>made</u> to go out and **get her**
> The minute you **let her** under your *skin*
> Then you be*gin* to make it **better**

Rakim *My Melody*

> My **unusual style** will **confuse you a <u>while</u>**
> If I were water, I'd flow in the **<u>Nile</u>**
> So many *rhymes* you won't have *time* to go for yours
> Just <u>because</u> of <u>applause</u> I have to <u>pause</u>
> *Right* after *tonight* is when I <u>prepare</u>
> To catch another sucker-duck MC <u>out there</u>
> My **strategy has to be tragedy**, **catastrophe**
> After this you'll call me your **majesty**

Chapter 8: Intonation in Varieties of English

Task 8.1

Answers in the text, page 241

Tasks 8.2–8.6

Listening tasks

Task 8.7

Answer in the text, page 268

Check Your Understanding
Exercises

(a) Intonation is the pattern of pitch across a stretch of speech.

(b) Tone languages use tone at the level of the syllable or word to change word meaning; tone is a word or lexical feature of language. Intonation languages use intonation across stretches of speech to signal meaning.

(c) ToBI stands for the Tone and Break Indices System, a widely used system to label intonation and pitch in languages and varieties of English.

It has four tiers: (1) the Tone tier; (2) the Break-Index tier; (3) the Orthographic tier; and (4) the Miscellaneous tier.

(d) Pitch accent refers to a prominent rise or fall in pitch on a syllable, or across a word, to signal stress or accent.

(e) Phonation refers to the different glottal configurations during speech production. This may include breathy (a whispery voice with voicing but more open vocal folds), modal (normal mode), creaky (more glottal closure during production).

(f) F0 stands for fundamental frequency. It is the number of cycles of the vocal fold opening and closing per second, expressed in hertz.

Discussion Questions and Expand Your Understanding

Answers may vary.

Chapter 9:   Investigating English Phonetics and Phonology

Check Your Understanding

Answers may vary

Tasks 9.1–9.2

Answers may vary.

Glossary

Accent: The pronunciation of speech sounds, words, and phrases; in this book, accent is used to refer to the way speakers of a given variety of English produce speech sounds, words, and phrases.

Acrolectal variety: A variety of a language that is closer to the superstrate and/or standard language; it is often spoken by more highly educated speakers.

Advancement: In reference to vowel articulation, advancement refers to the placement of the tongue, whether it is pushed forward (front), pulled back (back), or in the central area of the mouth (central). This is also called front/backness of the tongue.

Affricate: A consonant produced with a stop closure and fricative airflow release.

Allophones: The physical realizations, or phones, of a phoneme.

Alveolar: Consonants articulated with the tip of the tongue touching or nearly touching the alveolar ridge.

Approximant: A consonant that is produced with movement of the articulators towards each other without turbulence. Approximants have less constriction than other consonants, but have greater constriction than vowels.

Articulator: Also called articulatory organ; an organ used to produce speech sounds, including lips, teeth, and tongue.

Articulatory organ: See **articulator**.

Aspiration: A burst of air after the release of some consonants.

Assimilation: A process in which a preceding (progressive or forward assimilation) or following (regressive or backward assimilation) speech sound(s) influences the realization of a sound. For example, in many varieties of English, a vowel may take on a more nasal realization if followed by a nasal consonant in the same syllable.

Back vowel: A vowel articulated with a back tongue placement, or retraction.

Basilectal variety: A variety of a language with the most features from the local language influencing it; it is closer to the substrate language and the most distinctive variety from the acrolect and/or standard.

Bilabial: A consonant articulated with both lips.

Central vowel: A vowel articulated with a more centralized tongue; the tongue is neither advanced to the front of the mouth nor pulled to the back of the mouth.

Checked vowel: A vowel that can only occur in a closed syllable.

Close vowel: A vowel with a high tongue height; close refers to the position of the jaw, which is nearly closed. This is also called a high vowel.

Closed syllable: A syllable in which a consonant(s) follows the vowel in a syllable.

Coda: Any consonants that occur after the nucleus in a syllable.

Complementary distribution: When a speech sound has different physical realizations, or phones, in non-overlapping linguistic environments. The different phones are in complementary distribution as they do not overlap.

Consonant Cluster Reduction (CCR): Deletion of one or more consonants in an onset or coda; this occurs widely across varieties of English, due to substrate influences and/or speech simplification processes.

Contrastive distribution or meaning: Sounds are phonemes if they create words with different or contrastive meaning if the sounds are placed in the same linguistic environment. This means the sounds are in contrastive distribution and are different phonemes in a language.

Coronal: An articulation using the tip or front of the tongue.

Creaky voice: Also referred to as vocal fry. A type of phonation in which the vocal folds are compressed, resulting in aperiodic vocal pulses and a low F0.

De facto official language: A language that has become a widely accepted official language due to common usage but that does not have legal status.

De jure **official language:** An official language with legal status.

Deaccenting: When a word or syllable that would typically receive prominence or stress is not emphasized, usually because it is repeating known information.

Dental: A consonant realized with the tip of the tongue touching the back of the upper front teeth, or with the tip of the tongue between the upper and lower teeth, which is also referred to as interdental.

DH: Refers to the English voiced dental fricative.

Dialect: A regional, ethnic, or social variety of language; it comprises specific accent, grammar, spelling, and vocabulary features, among others, shared by a particular group of speakers.

Diphthong: A vowel that has movement from one vowel sound to a second vowel sound, as in /ai/ in *eye*.

English: An umbrella term for hundreds of Englishes that are spoken around the world due to social, geographic, sociopolitical, and linguistic factors.

Ethnolect: An ethnic variety or dialect of a language, including English.

Expanding Circle Englishes: Englishes that have been developed in countries due to globalization. English is typically not widely used or an official language in these countries. These Englishes include China English, Chilean English, German English, and Japanese English.

F0: Fundamental frequency, see below.

F1: First formant; the lowest band of energy. It corresponds to tongue height: high vowels have a lower F1 and low vowels have a higher F1.

F2: Second formant; the second band of energy. It corresponds to advancement (front/backness) of vowels: the higher the F2, the more fronted the tongue advancement of the vowel.

F3: Third formant; the third band of energy. It corresponds to both lip rounding and rhoticity, with a lowered F3 indicating a rhotic realization for some speakers/ varieties of English.

F4: Fourth formant; the fourth band of energy.

Formant: A band of energy that can be measured acoustically; formants are often used to analyse vowels. The first formant, F1, corresponds to tongue height, while the second formant, F2, corresponds to advancement.

Fortis: Refers to consonants that are produced with more force. It may also refer to voiceless obstruents in English.

Free vowel: A vowel that can occur in an open or closed syllable.

Fricative: A consonant with frication – or air turbulence – during articulation due to a narrowing or constriction of the airflow.

Front vowel: A vowel articulated with a front tongue advancement.

Fundamental frequency: Is often written as F0; it is the rate of vocal fold opening and closing per second. We hear F0 as pitch. It is expressed in hertz.

Glottal: A consonant articulated using the glottis, usually with a movement or constriction of the vocal folds.

HAR: Height, Advancement, and Rounding – features that distinguish vowel sounds from each other.

Height: In reference to the articulation of vowels, height refers to the placement of the tongue in the mouth, from high (near the roof), to mid, and low in the mouth.

High Rising Terminal: See also **uptalk**. The use of a rising intonation at the end of a non-interrogative intonation phrase.

High vowel: A vowel articulated with the high tongue height. High vowels are also called close vowels in reference to the nearly closed position of the jaw.

Homophones: Words that sound the same but have a different spelling and meaning; *here* and *hear* are examples of homophones.

Iambic pentameter: Metre often used in poetry; it consists of a series of five (*penta*) words with iambic stress.

Iambic stress: A stress pattern in which the stress falls on the second of two syllables, as in *inVITE*, where the second syllable is given more prominence.

Inner Circle Englishes: The English of countries in which English is a *de jure* or de facto official language and in wide usage among the population. These Englishes are also considered Old Varieties of English and are typically the standard-bearers or norm-providing Englishes in education. These Englishes include American, Australian, British English, and Irish English.

Intensity: An acoustic measurement of the power of a sound relative to other sounds. It is measured in decibels and is a rough correlate of loudness.

Interdental: Consonants articulated with the tip of the tongue between the upper and lower teeth.

Intonation: Patterns of pitch rises and falls.

Intonation languages: Languages that make use of intonation to signal meaning.

Intonation phrase (IP): The patterns of pitch rises and falls across an utterance or stretch of speech.

Intrusive-/r/: Usually occurs in non-rhotic varieties of English. It occurs when there is no actual 'r' spelling or /r/ sound in a word. It is an overgeneralization of linking-/r/; a /r/ sound is inserted after a vowel (usually a non-high vowel or diphthong with a non-high off glide) and before another vowel in the next syllable or word.

Koineization: A process in which different dialects of a language mix to form a unique new variety of that language.

Labiodental: Consonants articulated with the upper teeth and lower lips.

Language isolate: A language that does not appear to be related to any other language and is therefore not classified as part of a language family, but instead as a language family in its own right.

Lateral: Articulation with airflow along the sides of the tongue. In English, this refers to the lateral approximant /l/.

Lax vowel: A vowel that is articulated with relaxed tongue muscles; they may be labelled as short vowels in some varieties of English.

Lenis: Refers to consonant articulation. Lenis consonants are more weakly articulated than fortis consonants. *Lenis* may also be used to refer to voiced obstruents in English.

Linking-/r/: Usually occurs in non-rhotic varieties of English. The postvocalic and syllable- or word-final /r/ is realized at the beginning of the next syllable or word if the next syllable or word begin with a vowel.

Long-lag VOT: A Voice Onset Time of 60–120 milliseconds; this corresponds to aspirated voiceless stops in English.

Long vowel: Some varieties of English have pairs of vowels that have similar height and advancement but are different in duration when placed in the same linguistic context. The longer vowel in the pair is called a long vowel in these varieties.

Low vowel: A vowel articulated with low tongue height. These vowels are also called open vowels, in reference to the openness of the jaw during articulation.

Manner of articulation: Used to classify consonants; it refers to the way in which the airflow is affected as it flows from the lungs through the mouth and/or nose.

Mesolectal variety: A variety that has unique features from the substrate language; it is often spoken by educated speakers. It is considered to be in-between the acrolectal and the basilectal varieties.

Mid vowel: A vowel articulated with the tongue height in the middle of the mouth.

Minimal pair test: A test to determine whether a pair of sounds are phonemes or phones in a language.

Monophthong: A vowel that consists of a single vowel sound, as in /i/ in the word *tea*.

Mora-timing: This refers to the rhythm of languages, such as Japanese, where every mora is equal. A mora is a phonological unit based on syllable weight.

Nasals: Consonants produced with airflow through the nasal cavity.

New Varieties of English (NVEs): Varieties of English that emerged through colonialism and globalization; these include Singapore English, Hong Kong English, Indian English, Nigerian English, Japanese English, and China English.

Non-rhotic: When a variety or speaker of English does not retain the /r/ pronunciation after vowels in the same syllable, as in *hear*.

Nucleus: The nucleus is the vowel or vowel-like sound that is obligatory in a syllable.

Obstruent: A classification for consonants that have greater obstruction in airflow through full closure or a narrow constriction. In English, stop, fricative, and affricate consonants are classified as obstruents. Some varieties of English have pairs of obstruents with the same place and manner of articulation but a difference in voicing.

Old Varieties of English (OVEs): Varieties of English that emerged in the first spread of English globally; this includes English in England, Ireland, Scotland, Wales, Northern Ireland, Canada, the United States, Australia, and New Zealand.

Onset: Any consonants that occur before the nucleus in a syllable.

Open syllable: A syllable that does not have a consonant after the vowel; the vowel is the last sound in the syllable.

Open vowel: Vowels that are realized with an open jaw. Also called low vowels.

Outer Circle Englishes: Englishes that have developed in former American or British colonies, including Singapore, Hong Kong, India, and Kenya. They may have official language status. They are New Varieties of English and also often referred to as Postcolonial Englishes.

Palatal: Relating to the roof of the mouth, between the alveolar ridge and velum.

Phonation: Different ways in which air can pass through the vocal folds.

Phone: The actual physical realization of a sound; this depends upon its linguistic environment (the sounds that surround the phoneme).

Phoneme: A distinct unit of sound; vowels and consonants that can distinguish one word from another in a language.

Phonetics: Individual vowel and consonant sounds of a language.

Phonology: The way in which individual speech sounds pattern in a language, including where each speech sound occurs, in which combination the sounds can occur together, and how the nature of speech sounds may change based on where they occur in a syllable or word.

Phonotactics: Rules in languages regarding how speech sounds can pattern in syllables. Also referred to as phonotactic rules.

Pitch: The fundamental frequency (or F0) of a sound – the number of times the vocal folds vibrate per second. This is expressed in hertz.

Pitch accent: A prominent or stressed syllable.

Pitch-accent languages: Languages that use a change in pitch (pitch accent) to create prominence for one syllable in a word.

Place of articulation: Used to classify consonants; it refers to the location of the constriction or narrowing of the airflow by different articulatory organs during production of the consonant.

Plosives: Also called stop consonants; consonants with a complete closure of the airflow.

Postalveolar: Consonants produced with the front of the tongue touching or close to the area of the roof of the mouth behind the alveolar ridge.

Postcolonial Englishes: Englishes that have emerged in former American or British colonies due to contact between English and local languages. These varieties are also called Outer Circle Englishes.

Postvocalic: A speech sound occurring immediately following a vowel.

Prevocalic: A speech sound occurring before a vowel.

Progressive assimilation: Also called forward assimilation; when a preceding sound influences the realization of a speech sound.

Prominence: In English, some syllables may have greater strength or salience than other syllables; this may also be called an accent on a syllable. This is usually achieved through longer duration, greater intensity, and pitch changes. The use of prominence varies across varieties of English.

Pronunciation: How we say words; the production of speech sounds.

r-colouring: When realization of the postvocalic /r/ begins on the preceding vowel, resulting in F3 lowering during the production of the vowel.

r-dropping: Also called r-loss. A non-rhotic pronunciation of /r/ after vowels in the same syllable.

/r/-sandhi: Refers to two types of linking phenomena, linking-/r/ and intrusive-/r/.

Regressive assimilation: Also called backward assimilation; when a following sound influences the realization of a speech sound.

Retroflex: Articulation with the tongue curled back or concave.

Rhotic: When a variety or speaker of English retains the /r/ pronunciation after vowels in the same syllable, as in *hear.*

Rhoticity: Realization of the /r/ after vowels in the same syllable as in words such as *hear* and *car.*

Rhyme (or rime): A sequence of sound repetition in syllables and words; rhymes are created when syllables or words have different onsets but the same nucleus (vowel) and coda, as in *late* and *mate.*

Rhythm: One aspect of prosody; it refers to the cadence or pattern of strong and weak syllables in a language. Languages can be more stress-timed, syllable-timed, or mora-timed.

Rounded vowel: A vowel that has a more rounded lip shape; this contrasts with an unrounded, or neutral, lip shape.

Segmentals: Used in phonetics and phonology to describe individual consonant and vowel sounds.

Short-lag VOT: A Voice Onset Time of 0–30 milliseconds; this corresponds to voiceless unaspirated stops in English.

Short vowel: Some varieties of English have pairs of vowels that have similar height and advancement but are different in duration when placed in the same linguistic context. The shorter vowel in the pair is called a short vowel in these varieties.

Singlish: Colloquial Singapore English.

Sonorants: Speech sounds that either lack, or have a lesser degree of, obstruction of airflow. In English, nasals, approximants, and vowels are categorized as sonorants.

Sonority: Refers to the degree of amplitude, or loudness, of speech sounds relative to other sounds.

Stop consonants: Also called plosives; consonants with a complete closure of the airflow.

Stress: Refers to the prominence of a syllable or word relative to other syllables/words. In English, prominence may be achieved through a higher intensity, longer duration, pitch change, and use of full vowel phonemes.

Stress-timing: This refers to the rhythm of languages or varieties that use both strong and weak syllables to achieve an uneven rhythm; stress-timed languages and varieties also tend to have a greater range of syllable types and larger range of vowels in unstressed syllables, and make use of lexical stress.

Strong syllable: In English, strong syllables have full vowel phonemes and greater intensity and may be longer in duration than weak syllables. They may also receive stress.

Substrate: A language that influenced another language through contact; in this book, substrate refers to the local languages that have influenced English, as in the influence of Kiswahili on Kenyan English and Cantonese on Hong Kong English.

Superstrate: A language that undergoes changes due to contact with another language; in this book, superstrate typically refers to American or British English, and their colonial spread globally.

Suprasegmentals: Units of sound beyond the level of the segment.

Syllabic consonant: A consonant that can take the place of a vowel as the nucleus in a weak syllable. In English, sonorant consonants, and particularly nasals and approximants, can become syllabic.

Syllable: Unit of organization for sound sequences. Minimally consists of one vowel or vowel-like sound.

Syllable-timing: This refers to the rhythm of languages or varieties in which syllables are more equal in duration; these languages/varieties also tend to have simpler syllable structures and more CV syllables, full vowels in all syllables, and less lexical stress.

Tense vowel: A vowel that is articulated with tensing or tightening of the tongue muscles; tense vowels may be labelled as long vowels in some varieties of English.

TH: Refers to the English voiceless dental fricative.

Tone languages: Languages that use tone at the word or syllable level to change meaning.

Triphthong: A vowel with movement from a first to a second, and finally a third, vowel sound. This occurs in some varieties of English.

Trochaic stress: A stress pattern in which the stress falls on the first of two syllables in a word or phrase, as in *STUdent*, with more prominence on the first syllable.

Unrounded vowel: A vowel with a more spread or neutral lip shape.

Uptalk: Often used synonymously with the term High Rising Terminal. Uptalk refers to the use of a rising intonation/pitch at the end of a non-interrogative intonation phrase – when the speaker is making a statement and not asking a question.

Variably semi-rhotic: When the /r/ after the vowel in the same syllable is retained in some but not all environments.

Varieties of English: An umbrella term for the ways English is spoken around the world.

Variety: Often used synonymously with *dialect* to refer to the different dialects or accents of a language, including different Englishes around the world. In this book, the term 'variety' is used to refer to the English spoken in a country or region, such as Singapore English in Singapore, Nigerian English in Nigeria, and Australian English in Australia.

Velar: Consonants produced with the back of the tongue raised up and touching or nearly touching the velum.

Vocal fry: See creaky voice.

Voice Onset Time (VOT): The period of time between the release of the stop closure and the onset of voicing.

Voiceless: A mode of phonation in which the vocal folds are open as the air passes through them.

Voicing: A mode of phonation in which the vocal folds move or vibrate as the air passes through them.

Vowel epenthesis: Insertion of a vowel sound between two consonant sounds.

Vowel paragoge: Insertion of a vowel sound syllable- or word-finally.

Vowel prothesis: Insertion of a vowel sound before the first consonant in an onset.

Weak syllables: In English, weak syllables are syllables with a weak or reduced vowel or syllable consonant; they are usually shorter in duration and have less intensity than strong syllables.

World Englishes: The different varieties of English spoken around the world.

References

Aceto, M. (2009). Caribbean Englishes. In B. Kachru, Y. Kachru, and C. Nelson (eds.), *The Handbook of World Englishes* (pp. 203–22). Oxford: Wiley Blackwell.

Adamson, H. D. and Regan, V. M. (1991). The acquisition of community speech norms by Asian immigrants learning English as a second language. *Studies in Second Language Acquisition*, 13(1), 1–22.

Alberge, D. (2019, 28 March). Canadian film made in language spoken by just 20 people in the world. *The Guardian*: www.theguardian.com/world/2019/mar/28/canadian-film-made-in-haida-language-spoken-by-just-20-people-in-the-world.

Alderton, R. (2020). Speaker gender and salience in sociolinguistic speech perception: GOOSE-fronting in Standard Southern British English. *Journal of English Linguistics*, 48(1), 72–96.

Alim, H. S. (2003). On some serious next millennium rap ishhh: Pharoahe Monch, Hip Hop poetics, and the internal rhymes of Internal Affairs. *Journal of English Linguistics*, 31(1), 60–84.

Alim, H. S. (2004). Hip Hop Nation language. In E. Finegan and J. R. Rickford (eds.), *Language in the USA* (pp. 387–409). Cambridge: Cambridge University Press.

Altendorf, U. and Watt, D. (2004). The dialects in the South of England: phonology. In B. Kortmann, E. W. Schneider, K. Burridge, R. Meshtrie, and C. Upton (eds.), *A Handbook of Varieties of English 1: Phonology* (pp. 178–203). Berlin: Mouton de Gruyter.

Arvaniti, A. and Atkins, M. (2016). Uptalk in Southern British English. Paper presented at the Speech Prosody 2016, Boston.

Asprey, E. (2007). Investigating residual rhoticity in a non-rhotic accent. *Leeds Working Papers in Linguistics and Phonetics*, 12, 78–101.

Baranowski, M. (2017). Class matters: the sociolinguistics of GOOSE and GOAT in Manchester English. *Language Variation and Change*, 29, 301–39.

Baranowski, M. and Turton, D. (2015). Manchester English. In R. Hickney (ed.), *Researching Northern Englishes* (pp. 293–316). Amsterdam and Philadelphia: John Benjamins.

Baskaran, L. (2004). Malaysian English: phonology. In B. Kortmann, E. W. Schneider, K. Burridge, R. Meshtrie, and C. Upton (eds.), *A Handbook of Varieties of English 1: Phonology* (pp. 1034–46). Berlin: Mouton de Gruyter.

Bauer, L. and Warren, P. (2004). New Zealand English: phonology. In

B. Kortmann, E. W. Schneider, K. Burridge, R. Meshtrie, and C. Upton (eds.), *A Handbook of Varieties of English 1: Phonology* (pp. 580–602). Berlin: Mouton de Gruyter.

Beal, J. (2004). English dialects in the north of England. In B. Kortmann, E. W. Schneider, K. Burridge, R. Meshtrie, and C. Upton (eds.), *A Handbook of Varieties of English 1: Phonology* (pp. 113–33). Berlin: Mouton de Gruyter.

Becker, K. (2009). /r/ and the construction of place identity on New York City's Lower East Side. *Journal of Sociolinguistics*, 13(5), 634–58.

Becker, K. (2014). (r) we there yet? The change to rhoticity in New York English. *Language Variation and Change*, 26(2), 141–68.

Beckman, M. E. and Elam, G. A. (1997, March). Guidelines for ToBI labelling: www.ling.ohio-state.edu/research/phonetics/E_ToBI.

Beckman, M. E. and Pierrehumbert, J. (1986). Intonational structure of English and Japanese. *Phonology Yearbook*, 3, 255–309.

Benson, L. D. (2008). The Geoffrey Chaucer Page: https://chaucer.fas.harvard.edu/pages/general-prologue-0.

Bobda, A. S. (2001). East and Southern African English accents. *World Englishes*, 20(3), 269–84.

Bobda, A. S. (2003). The formation of regional and national features in African English pronunciation: an exploration of some non-interference factors. *English World-Wide*, 24(1), 17–42.

Bobda, A. S. (2010). Word stress in Cameroon and Nigerian Englishes. *World Englishes*, 29(1), 59–74.

Boberg, C. (2004). English in Canada: phonology. In B. Kortmann, E. W. Schneider, K. Burridge, R. Meshtrie, and C. Upton (eds.), *A Handbook of Varieties of English 1: Phonology* (pp. 351–65). Berlin: Mouton de Gruyter.

Boersma, P. and Weenink, D. (2021). Praat: doing phonetics by computer (Version 6.1.39). University of Amsterdam: Phonetic Sciences: www.fon.hum.uva.nl/praat.

Bolton, K. and Kwok, H. (1990). The dynamics of the Hong Kong accent: social identity and sociolinguistic description. *Journal of Asian Pacific Communication*, 1(1), 147–72.

Borrie, S. A. and Delfino, C. R. (2017). Conversational entrainment of vocal fry in young adult female American English speakers. *Journal of Voice*, 31(4), 513.e525–513.e532.

Bowerman, S. (2004). White South African English: phonology. In B. Kortmann, E. W. Schneider, K. Burridge, R. Meshtrie, and C. Upton (eds.), *A Handbook of Varieties of English 1: Phonology* (pp. 931–42). Berlin: Mouton de Gruyter.

Braber, N. and Robinson, J. (2018). *East Midlands English*. Berlin: Mouton de Gruyter.

Bradford, B. (1997). Upspeak in British English. *English Today*, 13(1), 29–36.

Bradley, A. (2021, 4 March). The artists dismantling the barriers between rap and poetry. *New York Times*

Style Magazine: www.nytimes.com/2021/03/04/t-magazine/rap-hip-hop-poetry.html.

Britain, D. (1992). Linguistic change in intonation: the use of high rise terminals in New Zealand English. *Language Variation and Change*, 4, 77–104.

Burridge, K. (2004). Synopsis: phonetics and phonology of English spoken in the Pacific and Australasian region. In B. Kortmann, E. W. Schneider, K. Burridge, R. Meshtrie, and C. Upton (eds.), *A Handbook of Varieties of English 1: Phonology* (pp. 1089–97). Berlin: Mouton de Gruyter.

Burridge, K. (2010). 'A peculiar language': linguistic evidence for early Australian English. In R. Hickey (ed.), *Varieties in Writing: The Written Word as Linguistic Evidence* (pp. 295–348). Amsterdam: John Benjamins.

Butcher, A. (2008). Linguistic aspects of Australian Aboriginal English. *Clinical Linguistics & Phonetics*, 22(8), 625–42.

Cao, R. and Jin, S. (2017). Phonological differences between Received Pronunciation and Standard Scottish English. *Advances in Social Science, Education and Humanities Research*, 113, 121–30.

Carter, P. (2005). Quantifying rhythmic differences between Spanish, English, and Hispanic English. In R. Gess and E. J. Rubin (eds.), *Theoretical and Experimental Approaches to Romance Linguistics* (pp. 63–75). Amsterdam: John Benjamins.

Carter, P. and Local, J. (2007). F2 variation in Newcastle and Leeds English liquid system. *Journal of the International Phonetic Association*, 37(2), 183–99.

Caswell, E. (2016, 19 May). Rapping, deconstructed: the best rhymers of all time. *Vox*: www.vox.com/2016/5/19/11701976/rapping-deconstructed-best-rhymers-of-all-time.

Chambers, J. K. (2010). English in Canada. In E. Gold and J. McAlpine (eds.), *Canadian English: A Reader* (pp. 1–37). Kingston, Ont.: Queen's University.

Chand, V. (2010). Postvocalic (r) in urban Indian English. *English World-Wide*, 31(1), 1–39.

Cheshire, J., Kerswill, P., Fox, S., and Torgersen, E. (2011). Contact, the feature pool and the speech community: the emergence of Multicultural London English. *Journal of Sociolinguistics*, 15(2), 151–96.

Clark, U. (2004). The English West Midlands: phonology. In B. Kortmann, E. W. Schneider, K. Burridge, R. Meshtrie, and C. Upton (eds.), *A Handbook of Varieties of English 1: Phonology* (pp. 134–62). Berlin: Mouton de Gruyter.

Clements, G. N. (1990). The role of the sonority cycle in core syllabification. In J. Kingston and M. Beckman (eds.), *Between the Grammar and Physics of Speech* (pp. 282–333). Papers in Laboratory Phonology 1. Cambridge: Cambridge University Press.

Coggshall, E. L. (2008). The prosodic rhythm of two varieties of Native American English. *University of Pennsylvania Working Papers in Linguistics*, 14(2), 1–9.

Coggshall, E. L. (2015). American Indian English. In J. P. Williams, E. W. Schneider, P. Trudgill, and D. Schreier (eds.), *Further Studies in the Lesser-Known Varieties of English* (pp. 99–127). Cambridge: Cambridge University Press.

Condon, D. (2019, 8 August). 5 artists preserving Indigenous language through their amazing music. ABC: www.abc.net.au/doublej/music-reads/features/artists-making-music-in-indigenous-language/11391512.

Cox, F. (2006). Australian English pronunciation into the 21st century. *Prospect*, 21(1), 3–21.

Cox, F. and Palethorpe, S. (2007). Australian English. *Journal of the International Phonetic Association*, 37(3), 341–50.

Cox, F. and Palethorpe, S. (2019). Vowel variation in a standard context across four major Australian cities. In S. Calhoun, P. Escudero, M. Tabain, and P. Warren (eds.), *Proceedings of the 19th International Congress of Phonetic Sciences, Melbourne, Australia 2019* (pp. 577–81). Canberra: Australasian Speech Science and Technology Association Inc.

Crowley, J. P. (1986). The study of old English dialects. *English Studies*, 67(2), 97–112.

Cruttenden, A. (2007). Intonational diglossia: a case study of Glasgow.

Journal of the International Phonetic Association, 37(3), 257–74.

Cruttenden, A. (2014). *Gimson's Pronunciation of English, 8th Edition*. Abingdon: Routledge.

Crystal, D. (2005). *The Stories of English*. Woodstock, NY: Overlook Press.

Crystal, D. (2019). *The Cambridge Encyclopedia of the English Language* (3rd ed.). Cambridge: Cambridge University Press.

Cutler, C. (1999). Yorkville Crossing: White teens, hip hop and African American English. *Journal of Sociolinguistics*, 3(4), 428–42.

Dauer, R. M. (1983). Stress-timing and syllable-timing reanalyzed. *Journal of Phonetics*, 11, 51–62.

Davidson, L. (2020). The versatility of creaky phonation: segmental, prosodic, and sociolinguistic uses in the world's languages. *WIREs Cognitive Science*, 12(3), 1–18.

Dayag, D. T. (2012). Philippine English. In E. Low and A. Hashi (eds.), *English in Southeast Asia: Features, Policy, and Language Use* (pp. 91–9). Amsterdam: John Benjamins.

Denison, D. and Hogg, R. (2006). Overview. In D. Denison and R. Hogg (eds.), *A History of the English Language* (pp. 1–42). Cambridge: Cambridge University Press.

Deterding, D. (2005a). The North wind versus a wolf: short texts for the description and measurement of English pronunciation *Journal of the International Phonetic Association*, 36(2), 187–96.

Deterding, D. (2005b). Listening to Estuary English in Singapore. *TESOL Quarterly*, 39(3), 425–40.

Deterding, D. (2011). Measurements of the rhythm of Malay. Paper presented at the International Congress of Phonetic Sciences 17, Hong Kong.

Deterding, D., Wong, J., and Kirkpatrick, A. (2008). The pronunciation of Hong Kong English. *English World-Wide*, 29(2), 148–75.

Devonish, H. and Harry, O. G. (2004). Jamaican Creole and Jamaican English: phonology. In B. Kortmann, E. W. Schneider, K. Burridge, R. Meshtrie, and C. Upton (eds.), *A Handbook of Varieties of English 1: Phonology* (pp. 450–80). Berlin: Mouton de Gruyter.

Drummond, R. (2018). Maybe it's a grime [t]ing: TH-stopping among urban British youth. *Language in Society*, 47(2), 171–96.

Dryer, M. S. and Haspelmath, M. (eds.) (2013). *The World Atlas of Language Structures Online*. Leipzig: Max Planck Institute for Evolutionary Anthropology.

du Plessis, D. and Bekker, I. (2014). To err is human: the case for neorhoticity in White South African English. *Language Matters*, 45(1), 23–39.

Eberhard, D. M., Simons, G. F., and Fennig, C. D. (2020). Ethnologue: languages of the world (23rd ed.): www.ethnologue.com.

Eckert, P. (2008). Where do ethnolects stop? *International Journal of Bilingualism*, 12(1–2), 25–42.

Eddington, D. and Taylor, M. (2009). T-glottalization in American English. *American Speech*, 84(3), 298–314.

Edwards, W. F. (2004). African American Vernacular English: phonology. In B. Kortmann, E. W. Schneider, K. Burridge, R. Meshtrie, and C. Upton (eds.), *A Handbook of Varieties of English 1: Phonology* (pp. 383–92). Berlin: Mouton de Gruyter.

Encyclopedia Britannica (2021). British Empire timeline. In *Encyclopedia Britannica*.

Esling, J. H. (1978). Voice quality in Edinburgh: a sociolinguistic and phonetic study (Ph.D. thesis). University of Edinburgh, Edinburgh.

Esposito, C. M. and Khan, S. u. D. (2020). The cross-linguistic patterns of phonation types. *Language and Linguistics Compass*, 14(12), 1–26.

Espy-Wilson, C., Boyce, S., Jackson, M., Narayanan, S., and Alwan, A. (2000). Acoustic modeling of American English /r/. *Journal of the Acoustical Society of America*, 108, 343–56.

Fairbanks, G. (1960). *Voice and Articulation Drillbook* (2nd ed.). New York: Harper & Row.

Feagin, C. (1990). Dynamics of sound change in Southern States English: from r-less to r-ful in three generations. In J. Edmonson, C. Feagin, and P. Mühlhäuser (eds.), *Development and Diversity: Language Variation across Time and Space: A Festschrift for Charles-James N. Bailey* (pp. 129–46). Arlington: SIL / University of Texas.

Fery, C. (2010). The intonation of Indian languages: an areal phenomenon. In I. Hasnain and S. Chaudhury (eds.), *Problematizing Language Studies: Festschrift for Rama Agnihotri* (pp. 288–312). Delhi: Aakar Books.

Fletcher, J., Grabe, E., and Warren, P. (2005). Intonational variation in four dialects of English: the High Rising Tune. In S. Jun (ed.), *Prosody Typology: The Phonology of Intonation and Phrasing* (pp. 391–409). Oxford: Oxford University Press.

Fought, C. (2006). *Language and Ethnicity.* Cambridge: Cambridge University Press.

Fuchs, R. (2016). *Speech Rhythm in Varieties of English: Evidence from Educated Indian English and British English.* Singapore: Springer.

Fuchs, R. (2018). Pitch range, dynamism and level in postcolonial varieties of English: a comparison of educated Indian English and British English. Paper presented at Speech Prosody 9, Poznań.

Gargesh, R. (2004). Indian English: phonology. In B. Kortmann and E. W. Schneider (eds.), *A Handbook of Varieties of English* (pp. 993–1002). Berlin: Mouton de Gruyter.

Gargesh, R. and Sailaja, P. (2017). South Asia. In M. Filppula, J. Klemola, and D. Sharma (eds.), *The Oxford Handbook of World Englishes* (pp. 1–26). Oxford: Oxford University Press.

Gibson, T. A. (2017). The role of lexical stress on the use of vocal fry in young adult female speakers. *Journal of Voice,* 31(1), 62–6.

Goedemans, R. and van der Hulst, H. (2013). Fixed stress locations. In M. S. Dryer and M. Haspelmath (eds.), *The World Atlas of Language Structures Online.* Leipzig: Max Planck Institute for Evolutionary Anthropology. (Available online at http://wals .info/chapter/14.)

Gordon, E. and Maclagan, M. (2004). Regional and social differences in New Zealand: phonology. In B. Kortmann, E. W. Schneider, K. Burridge, R. Meshtrie, and C. Upton (eds.), *A Handbook of Varieties of English 1: Phonology* (pp. 603–13). Berlin: Mouton de Gruyter.

Gordon, M. J. (2004). The West and Midwest: phonology. In B. Kortmann, E. W. Schneider, K. Burridge, R. Meshtrie, and C. Upton (eds.), *A Handbook of Varieties of English 1: Phonology* (pp. 338–50). Berlin: Mouton de Gruyter.

Grabe, E., and Low, E. L. (2002). Durational variability in speech and the rhythm class hypothesis. *Papers in Laboratory Phonology,* 7, 515–46.

Greenblatt, S. and Abrams, M. H. (eds.) (2006). *The Norton Anthology of English Literature* (8th ed., Vol. I). New York: W. W. Norton & Company.

Greer, S. D. F. and Winters, S. J. (2015). The perception of coolness: difference in evaluating voice quality in male and female speakers. Paper presented at the International Congress of Phonetic Sciences 2015, Glasgow.

Grice, M., German, J. S., and Warren, P. (2020). Intonation systems across varieties of English. In C. Gussenhoven (ed.), *The Oxford Handbook of Language Prosody* (pp. 1–16). Oxford: Oxford University Press.

Gunesekera, M. (2005). *The Postcolonial Identity of Sri Lankan English*. Columbo: Katha Publishers.

Gussenhoven, C. (2004). *The Phonology of Tone and Intonation*. Cambridge: Cambridge University Press.

Gussenhoven, C. (2014). On the intonation of tonal varieties of English. In M. Filppula, J. Klemola, and D. Sharma (eds.), *The Oxford Handbook of World Englishes* (pp. 1–39). Oxford: Oxford University Press.

Gut, U. B. (2004). Nigerian English: phonology. In B. Kortmann, E. W. Schneider, K. Burridge, R. Meshtrie, and C. Upton (eds.), *A Handbook of Varieties of English 1: Phonology* (pp. 813–30). Berlin: Mouton de Gruyter.

Gut, U. B. (2005). Nigerian English prosody. *English World-Wide*, 26(2), 153–77.

Hagiwara, R. (1995). Acoustic realizations of American /r/ as produced by women and men. *UCLA Working Papers in Phonetics*, 90.

Hall-Lew, L. (2009). Ethnicity and phonetic variation in a San Francisco neighborhood (Ph.D. thesis). Stanford University, Stanford, California (3382940).

Hansen Edwards, J. G. (2016a). Accent preferences and the use of American English features in Hong Kong: a preliminary study. *Asian Englishes*, 18(3), 197–215.

Hansen Edwards, J. G. (2016b). Defining 'native speaker' in multilingual settings: English as a native language in Asia. *Journal of Multilingual and Multicultural Development*, 38(9), 757–71.

Hansen Edwards, J. G. (2016c). The deletion of /t, d/ in Hong Kong English. *World Englishes*, 35(1), 60–77.

Hansen Edwards, J. G. (2018). TH variation in Hong Kong English. *English Language and Linguistics*, 23(2), 439–68.

Harrington, J., Palethorpe, S., and Watson, C. (2000). Monophthongal vowel changes in Received Pronunciation: an acoustic analysis of the Queen's Christmas broadcasts. *Journal of the International Phonetic Association*, 30(1/2), 63–78.

Hartmann, D. and Zerbian, S. (2009). Rhoticity in Black South African English – a sociolinguistic study. *Southern African Linguistics and Applied Language Studies*, 27(2), 135–48.

Hashim, A. (2020). Malaysian English. In K. Bolton, W. Botha, and A. Kirkpatrick (eds.), *The Handbook of Asian Englishes* (pp. 373–98). Hoboken, NJ: John Wiley & Sons, Inc.

Hay, J., Maclagan, M., and Gordon, E. (2008). *New Zealand English*. Edinburgh: Edinburgh University Press.

Hay, J. and Sudbury, A. (2005). How rhoticity became /r/-sandhi. *Language*, 81(4), 799–823.

Hazen, K. (2018). The contested southernness of Appalachia. *American Speech*, 93(3–4), 374–408.

Heggarty, P., Shimelman, A., Abete, G., et al. (2019). Sound comparisons: exploring diversity in phonetics across language families: https://soundcomparisons.com/#home.

Henton, C. G. and Bladon, R. A. W. (1988). Creak as a sociophonetic marker. In L. M. Hyman and C. Li (eds.), *Language, Speech and Mind: Studies in Honour of Victoria A. Fromkin* (pp. 3–29). New York: Routledge.

Hickey, R. (2004). Irish English: phonology. In B. Kortmann, E. W. Schneider, K. Burridge, R. Meshtrie, and C. Upton (eds.), *A Handbook of Varieties of English 1: Phonology* (pp. 68–97). Berlin: Mouton de Gruyter.

Hickey, R. (2007). *Irish English: History and Present-Day Forms.* Cambridge: Cambridge University Press.

Hillenbrand, J., Getty, L. A., Clark, M. J., and Wheeler, K. (1995). Acoustic characteristics of American English vowels. *Journal of the Acoustical Society of America*, 97(5), 3099–3111.

Hirst, D. and Di Cristo, A. (1998). *Intonation Systems: A Survey of Twenty Languages.* Cambridge: Cambridge University Press.

Hoffman, M. F. and Walker, J. A. (2010). Ethnolects and the city: ethnic orientation and linguistic variation in Toronto English. *Language Variation and Change*, 22(1), 37–67.

Hollien, H., Moore, P., Wendahl, R. W., and Michel, J. W. (1966). On the nature of vocal fry. *Journal of Speech and Hearing Research*, 9, 245–7.

Honoring Nations (2006). The Cherokee language revitalization projects: https://hpaied.org/publications/cherokee-language-revitalization-project.

Hornibrook, J., Ormond, T., and Maclagan, M. (2018). Creaky voice or extreme vocal fry in young women. *New Zealand Medical Journal*, 131(1486), 36–40.

Horvath, B. M. (2004). Australian English: phonology. In B. Kortmann, E. W. Schneider, K. Burridge, R. Meshtrie, and C. Upton (eds.), *A Handbook of Varieties of English 1: Phonology* (pp. 625–44). Berlin: Mouton de Gruyter.

Howard-Hill, T. H. (2006). Early modern printers and the standardization of English spelling. *Modern Language Review*, 101, 16–29.

Hughes, A. and Trudgill, P. (1996). *English Accents and Dialects: An Introduction to Social and Regional Varieties of English in the British Isles.* London: Arnold.

Hung, T. T. N. (2012). Hong Kong English. In E. L. Low and A. Hashim (eds.), *English in Southeast Asia: Features, Policy and Language in Use* (pp. 113–33). Amsterdam: John Benjamins.

Hyman, L. M. (2009). How (not) to do phonological theory: the case of pitch-accent. *Language Sciences*, 31, 213–38.

International Phonetic Association (1999). *Handbook of the International Phonetic Association: A Guide to the Use of the International Phonetic Alphabet*. Cambridge: Cambridge University Press.

International Phonetic Association (2015). Full IPA chart: www .internationalphoneticassociation .org/content/ipa-chart.

Internet World Statistics (2020). Internet world users by language: www.internetworldstats.com/stats7 .htm.

Jansen, S. (2014). Salience effects in the North-West of England. *Linguistik Online*, 66, 91–110.

Jenkins, J. (2009). *World Englishes: A Resource Book for Students* (2nd ed.). London: Routledge.

Jenkins, J. (2017). ELF and WE: competing or complementing paradigms. In E. L. Low and A. Pakir (eds.), *World Englishes: Rethinking Paradigms* (pp. 12–28). London: Routledge.

Jespersen, A. B. (2015). Intonational rises and interactional structure in Sydney Aboriginal English. Paper presented at the International Congress of Phonetic Sciences, Glasgow.

Jian, H.-L. (2004). On the syllable timing in Taiwan English. Paper presented at Speech Prosody 2004, Nara, Japan.

Johnson, W. and Britain, D. J. (2007). L-vocalisation as a natural phenomenon: explorations in sociophonology. *Language Sciences*, 29(2–3), 294–315.

Kachru, B. B. (1985). Standards, codification and sociolinguistic realism: English language in the outer circle. In R. Q. H. Widowson (ed.), *English in the World: Teaching and Learning the Language and Literatures* (pp. 11–36). Cambridge: Cambridge University Press.

Kachru, B. B., Kachru, Y., and Nelson, C. L. (2009). Introduction: the world of World Englishes. In B. B. Kachru, Y. Kachru, and C. L. Nelson (eds.), *The Handbook of World Englishes* (pp. 1–16). Malden, MA: Wiley-Blackwell.

Kadenge, M. (2009). African Englishes: the indigenization of English vowels by Zimbabwean native Shona speakers. *Journal of Pan African Studies*, 3(1), 156–73.

Kastovsky, D. (2006). Vocabulary. In D. Denison and R. Hogg (eds.), *A History of the English Language* (pp. 199–270). Cambridge: Cambridge University Press.

Keating, P., Garellek, M., and Kreiman, J. (2015). Acoustic properties of different kinds of creaky voice. Paper presented at the International Congress of Phonetic Sciences 2015, Glasgow.

Kerswill, P., Torgersen, E. N., and Fox, S. (2008). Reversing 'drift': innovation and diffusion in the London diphthong system. *Language Variation and Change*, 20, 451–91.

Khatiwada, R. (2009). Nepali. *Journal of the International Phonetic Association*, 39(3), 373–80.

King, B. (2015). Top five rappers who rhyme words with themselves. *Medium*: https://medium.com/@anygiventues/top-five-rappers-who-rhyme-a-word-with-itself-bbc1ee500ece.

Kirkpatrick, A. (2007). *World Englishes: Implications for International Communication and English Language Teaching.* Cambridge: Cambridge University Press.

Koffi, E. (2019). An acoustic phonetic analysis of the intelligibility of Nepali-accented English vowels. *Linguistic Portfolios*, 8, 93–112.

Korbey, H. (2016). How hip-hop can bring Shakespeare to life. *KQED*: www.kqed.org/mindshift/46215/how-hip-hop-can-bring-shakespeare-to-life.

Kretzschmar, W. A., Jr (2004). Standard American English pronunciation. In B. Kortmann, E. W. Schneider, K. Burridge, R. Meshtrie, and C. Upton (eds.), *A Handbook of Varieties of English 1: Phonology* (pp. 257–69). Berlin: Mouton de Gruyter.

Labov, W. (2010). *Principles of Linguistic Change: Cognitive and Cultural Factors.* Oxford: Wiley-Blackwell.

Labov, W., Ash, S., and Boberg, C. (2006). *The Atlas of North American English: Phonetics, Phonology, and Sound Change.* Berlin: Mouton de Gruyter.

Ladd, D. R. (2008). *Intonational Phonology* (2nd ed.). Cambridge: Cambridge University Press.

Ladefoged, P. and Johnson, K. (2014). *A Course in Phonetics* (7th ed.). Boston, MA: Wadsworth Cengage Learning.

Lai, L. and van Hell, J. (2020). Intonation and voice quality of Northern Appalachian English: a first look. Paper presented at Speech Prosody 2020, Tokyo.

Lane, J. (2019). The 10 most spoken languages in the world: www.babbel.com/en/magazine/the-10-most-spoken-languages-in-the-world.

Lass, R. (1999). *The Cambridge History of the English Language 1476–1776.* Cambridge: Cambridge University Press.

Lass, R. (2006). Phonology and morphology. In D. Denison and R. Hogg (eds.), *A History of the English Language* (pp. 43–108). Cambridge: Cambridge University Press.

Laver, J. (1980). *The Phonetic Description of Voice Quality.* Cambridge: Cambridge University Press.

Lee-Kim, S.-I., Davidson, L., and Hwang, S. (2013). Morphological effects on the darkness of English intervocalic /l/. *Laboratory Phonology*, 4(2), 475–511.

Levis, J. W. A. and Wichman, A. (2015). English intonation – form and meaning. In M. Reed and J. M. Levis (eds.), *The Handbook of English Pronunciation* (pp. 139–56). Malden, MA: John Wiley & Sons Ltd.

Levon, E. (2016). Gender, interaction and intonational meaning: the discourse function of High Rising Terminals in London. *Journal of Sociolinguistics*, 20, 133–63.

Levon, E. (2020). Same difference: the phonetic shape of High Rise

Terminals in London. *English Language and Linguistics*, 24(1), 49–73.

Levon, E. and Fox, S. (2014). Social salience and the sociolinguistic monitor: a case study of ING and TH-fronting in Britain. *Journal of English Linguistics*, 42(3), 185–217.

Lim, L. (2009). Revisiting English prosody: (some) New Englishes as tone languages? *English World-Wide*, 30(2), 218–39.

Lim, L. and Gisborne, N. (2009). The typology of Asian Englishes: setting the agenda. *English World-Wide*, 30(2), 123–32.

Lippi-Green, R. (2012). *English with an Accent: Language, Ideology, and Discrimination in the United States* (2nd ed.). Abingdon: Routledge.

Lisker, L. and Abramson, A. S. (1964). A cross-language study of voicing in initial stops: acoustical measurements. *Word*, 20(3), 384–422.

Low, E. L. (2012). Singapore English. In E. Low and A. Hashim (eds.), *English in Southeast Asia: Features, Policy, and Language in Use* (pp. 35–53). Amsterdam: John Benjamins.

Low, E. L. and Brown, A. (2005). *English in Singapore: An Introduction*. Singapore: McGraw Hill.

Low, E. L. and Grabe, E. (1995). Prosodic patterns in Singapore English. Paper presented at the XIIIth International Congress of Phonetic Sciences, Stockholm.

Low, E. L., Grabe, E., and Nolan, F. (2000). Quantitative characterizations of speech rhythm: syllable-timing in Singapore English. *Language and Speech*, 43(4), 377–401.

Maddieson, I. (1984). UCLA Phonological Segment Inventory Database (UPSID) (web page): http://phonetics.linguistics.ucla .edu/sales/software.htm#upsid.

Maddieson, I. (2013a). Consonant inventories. In M. S. Dryer and M. Haspelmath (eds.), *The World Atlas of Language Structures Online*. Leipzig: Max Planck Institute for Evolutionary Anthropology.

Maddieson, I. (2013b). Syllable structure. In M. S. Dryer and M. Haspelmath (eds.), *The World Atlas of Language Structures Online*. Leipzig: Max Planck Institute for Evolutionary Anthropology.

Maddieson, I. (2013c). Tone. In M. S. Dryer and M. Haspelmath (eds.), *The World Atlas of Language Structures Online*. Leipzig: Max Planck Institute for Evolutionary Anthropology.

Mahboob, A. and Ahmar, N. H. (2004). Pakistani English: phonology. In B. Kortmann and E. W. Schneider (eds.), *A Handbook of Varieties of English* (pp. 1003–16). Berlin: Mouton de Gruyter.

Malarski, K. and Jekiel, M. (2018). Cross-dialectal analysis of English pitch range in male voices and its influence on aesthetic judgments of speech. *Poznan Studies in Contemporary Linguistics*, 54(2), 255–80.

Malcolm, I. G. (2004). Australian creoles and Aboriginal English:

phonetics and phonology. In B. Kortmann, E. W. Schneider, K. Burridge, R. Meshtrie, and C. Upton (eds.), *A Handbook of Varieties of English 1: Phonology* (pp. 656–70). Berlin: Mouton de Gruyter.

Marsden, S. (2017). Are New Zealanders 'rhotic'? The dynamics of rhoticity in New Zealand's small towns. *English World-Wide*, 38(3), 275–304.

Mastin, L. (2011). The history of English: www.thehistoryofenglish.com.

Mendis, D. and Rambukwella, H. (2010). Sri Lankan Englishes. In A. Kirkpatrick (ed.), *The Routledge Handbook of World Englishes* (pp. 181–96). Abingdon: Routledge.

Meyler, M. (2012). Sri Lankan English. In B. Kortmann and K. Lunkenheimer (eds.), *The Mouton Atlas of Variation in English* (pp. 540–7). Berlin: Mouton de Gruyter.

Mok, P. and Dellwo, V. (2008). Comparing native and non-native speech rhythm using acoustic rhythm measures: Cantonese, Beijing Mandarin, and English. Paper presented at the Speech Prosody, Brazil.

Moseley, C. E. (2010). Atlas of the world's languages in danger (3rd ed.): www.unesco.org/culture/en/endangeredlanguages/atlas.

Mtallo, G. and Mwanbula, H. A. (2018). The phonological influence of ethnic community languages in learning Kiswahili, a case of Kinyakyusa in Mbeya, Tanzania. *Journal of Language Teaching and Research*, 9(4), 702–14.

Mutonya, M. (2008). African Englishes: acoustic analysis of vowels. *World Englishes*, 27(3/4), 434–49.

Nagy, N. and Irwin, P. (2010). Boston (r): neighbo(r)s nea(r) and far(r). *Language Variation and Change*, 22(2), 241–78.

Nagy, N. and Roberts, J. (2004). New England: phonology. In B. Kortmann, E. W. Schneider, K. Burridge, R. Meshtrie, and C. Upton (eds.), *A Handbook of Varieties of English 1: Phonology* (pp. 270–81). Berlin: Mouton de Gruyter.

Nayan, N. M. and Setter, J. (2016). Malay English intonation: the Cooperative Rise. *English World-Wide*, 37(3), 293–322.

Nevalainen, T. and Tieken-Boon van Ostade, I. (2006). Standardisation. In D. Denison and R. Hogg (eds.), *A History of the English Language* (pp. 271–311). Cambridge: Cambridge University Press.

Newmark, K., Walker, N., and Stanford, J. (2016). 'The rez accent knows no borders': Native American ethnic identity expressed through English prosody. *Language in Society*, 45, 633–64.

Noah Webster House (2021). Noah Webster history: https://noahwebsterhouse.org.

Obias, R. (2017, 9 January). 12 fictional film and TV languages you can actually learn. *Mental Floss*: www.mentalfloss.com/article/84993/12-fictional-film-and-tv-languages-you-can-actually-learn.

Oxford University Museum of Natural History (n.d.). Settlers: genetics, geography and the peopling of Britain: www.oum.ox.ac.uk/settlers.

Pandey, P. (2015). Indian English pronunciation. In M. Reed and J. M. Levis (eds.), *The Handbook of English Pronunciation* (pp. 301–19). Chichester: Wiley Blackwell.

Pandey, S. B. (2020). English in Nepal. *World Englishes*, 39(4), 500–13.

Parker, S. (2011). Sonority. In M. van Oostendorp, C. J. Ewen, E. Hume, and K. Rice (eds.), *The Blackwell Companion to Phonology* (Vol. II, pp. 1–25). Malden, MA: Wiley-Blackwell.

Penhallurick, R. (2004). Welsh English: phonology. In B. Kortmann, E. W. Schneider, K. Burridge, R. Meshtrie, and C. Upton (eds.), *A Handbook of Varieties of English 1: Phonology* (pp. 98–112). Berlin: Mouton de Gruyter.

Penney, J., Cox, F., and Szakay, A. (2021). Glottalisation of word-final stops in Australian English unstressed syllables. *Journal of the International Phonetic Association*, 51(2), 229–60.

Pernet, C. R. and Belin, P. (2012). The role of pitch and timbre in voice gender categorization. *Frontiers in Psychology*, 3(23), 1–11.

Peterson, G. E. and Barney, H. L. (1952). Control methods used in a study of the vowels. *Journal of the Acoustical Society of America*, 24(2).

Pickering, L. and Wiltshire, C. (2000). Pitch accent in Indian-English teaching discourse. *World Englishes*, 19(2), 173–83.

Piercy, C. (2012). A transatlantic cross-dialectal comparison of non-prevocalic /r/. *University of Pennsylvania Working Papers in Linguistics*, 18(2), 77–86.

Pierrehumbert, J. (1990). *The Phonology and Phonetics of the Intonation of English*. New York: Garland.

Pierrehumbert, J. B. and Hirschberg, J. (1990). The meaning of intonational contours in the interpretation of discourse. In P. Cohen, J. Morgan, and M. Pollack (eds.), *Intentions in Communication* (pp. 271–311). Cambridge, MA: MIT Press.

Pike, K. L. (1946). *The Intonation of American English*. Ann Arbor, MI: University of Michigan Press.

Poedjosoedarmo, G. (2000). The media as a model and source of innovation in the development of Singapore Standard English. In A. Brown, D. Deterding, and L. E. Ling (eds.), *The English Language in Singapore: Research on Pronunciation* (pp. 112–20). Singapore: Singapore Association for Applied Linguistics.

Port, R. (1999). ToBI intonation transcription summary: https://legacy.cs.indiana.edu/~port/teach/306/tobi.summary.html.

Prechtel, C. and Clopper, C. G. (2016). Uptalk in Midwestern American English. Paper presented at Speech Prosody 2016, Boston.

Pressley, J. M. and the Shakespeare Resource Center (2021): www.bardweb.net/language.html.

Rajadurai, J. (2006). Pronunciation issues in non-native contexts: a

Malaysian case study. *Malaysian Journal of ELT Research*, 2, 42–59.

Ritchart, A. and Arvaniti, A. (2014). The form and use of uptalk in Southern Californian English. Paper presented at Speech Prosody 2014, Dublin, Ireland.

Roach, P. (2009). *English Phonetics and Phonology: A Practical Course* (4th ed.). Cambridge: Cambridge University Press.

Romaine, S. (1978). Postvocalic /r/ in Scottish English: sound change in progress? In P. Trudgill (ed.), *Sociolinguistic Patterns in British English* (pp. 144–57). London: Edward Arnold.

Rosenfelder, I. (2009). Rhoticity in Jamaican English: an analysis of the spoken component of ICE-Jamaica. In T. Hoffmann and L. Siebers (eds.). *World Englishes – Problems, Properties and Prospects: Selected Papers from the 13th IAWE Conference* (pp. 61–82). Amsterdam: John Benjamins.

Santa Ana, O. and Bayley, R. (2004). Chicano English: phonology. In B. Kortmann, E. W. Schneider, K. Burridge, R. Meshtrie, and C. Upton (eds.), *A Handbook of Varieties of English 1: Phonology* (pp. 417–34). Berlin: Mouton de Gruyter.

Schachter, P. and Otanes, F. T. (1972). *Tagalog Reference Grammar*. Berkeley: University of California.

Schleef, E., Meyerhoff, M., and Clark, L. (2012). Teenagers' acquisition of variation: a comparison of locally-born and migrant teens' realisation of English (ing) in Edinburgh and London. *English World-Wide*, 32(2), 206–36.

Schmied, J. (2004). East African English (Kenya, Uganda, Tanzania): phonology. In B. Kortmann, E. W. Schneider, K. Burridge, R. Meshtrie, and C. Upton (eds.), *A Handbook of Varieties of English 1: Phonology* (pp. 918–30). Berlin: Mouton de Gruyter.

Schneider, E. W. (2007). *Postcolonial English: Varieties Around the World*. Cambridge: Cambridge University Press.

Schoux Casey, C. (2016). Ya hear me? Rhoticity in post-Katrina New Orleans English. *American Speech*, 91(2), 166–99.

Shakespeare, W. (2000). *Romeo and Juliet*, ed. J. Levenson. Oxford: Oxford University Press.

Shakespeare Birthplace Trust (2021). Shakespeare's phrases: www .shakespeare.org.uk/explore-shakespeare/shakespedia/ shakespeares-phrases.

Shokeir, V. (2008). Evidence for the stable use of uptalk in South Ontario English. *University of Pennsylvania Working Papers in Linguistics*, 14(2), 15–24.

Shousterman, C. (2014). Speaking English in Spanish Harlem: the role of rhythm. *University of Pennsylvania Working Papers in Linguistics*, 20(2), 159–68.

Simpson, A. (2001). Dynamic consequences of differences in male and female vocal tract dimensions. *Journal of the Acoustical Society of America*, 109(5), 2153–64.

Skoog Waller, S., Eriksson, M., and Sörqvist, P. (2015). Can you hear my age? Influences of speech rate and speech spontaneity on estimation of speaker age. *Frontiers in Psychology*, 6(978), 1–11.

Smith, J., Durham, M., and Fortune, L. (2009). Universal and dialect-specific pathways of acquisition: caregivers, children, and t/d deletion. *Language Variation and Change*, 21(1), 69–95.

Starks, D., Christie, J., and Thompson, L. (2007). Niuean English: initial insights into an emerging variety. *English World-Wide*, 28(2), 133–46.

Starks, D., Gibson, A., and Bell, A. (2015). Pasifika Englishes in New Zealand. In J. P. Williams, E. W. Schneider, P. Trudgill, and D. Schreier (eds.), *Further Studies in Lesser-Known Varieties of English* (pp. 288–304). Cambridge: Cambridge University Press.

Starks, D. and Reffell, H. (2006). Reading 'TH': vernacular variants in Pasifika Englishes in South Auckland. *Journal of Sociolinguistics*, 10(3), 382–92.

Steriade, D. (2002). The syllable. In W. Bright (ed.), *The Oxford Encyclopedia of Linguistics* (pp. 1–15). Oxford: Oxford University Press.

Stuart-Smith, J. (2004). Scottish English: phonology. In B. Kortmann and C. Upton (eds.), *Varieties of English: The British Isles* (pp. 48–70). Berlin: Mouton de Gruyter.

Stuart-Smith, J., Sonderegger, M., Rathcke, T., and Macdonald, R. (2015). The private life of

stops: VOT in a real-time corpus of spontaneous Glaswegian. *Laboratory Phonology*, 6(3–4), 505–49.

Stuart-Smith, J., Timmins, C., and Tweedie, F. (2007). 'Talkin' Jockney'? Variation and change in Glaswegian accent. *Journal of Sociolinguistics*, 11(2), 221–60.

Sudbury, A. and Hay, J. (2002). The fall and rise of /r/: rhoticity and /r/-sandhi in early New Zealand English. *University of Pennsylvania Working Papers in Linguistics: Selected Papers from NWAV 30*, 8(3), 281–95.

Sutton, P. (1989). Postvocalic R in an Australian English dialect. *Australian Journal of Linguistics*, 9(1), 161–3.

Szakay, A. (2006). Rhythm and pitch as markers of ethnicity in New Zealand English. Paper presented at the 11th Australian International Conference on Speech Science & Technology, University of Auckland, New Zealand.

Szakay, A. (2012). Voice quality as a marker of ethnicity in New Zealand: from acoustics to perception. *Journal of Sociolinguistics*, 16(3), 382–97.

Szakay, A. and Torgersen, E. (2016). An acoustic analysis of voice quality in London English: the effect of gender, ethnicity and F0. Paper presented at the International Congress of Phonetic Sciences 2015, Glasgow.

Tagliamonte, S. (2006). *Analyzing Sociolinguistic Variation*.

Cambridge: Cambridge University Press.

Tagliamonte, S. and Temple, R. (2005). New perspectives on an ol' variable: (t,d) in British English. *Language Variation and Change*, 17(3), 281–302.

Tan, R. S. K. and Low, E. L. (2014). Rhythmic patterning in Malaysian and Singapore English. *Language and Speech*, 57(2), 196–214.

Tan, Y.-Y. (2012). To *r* or not to *r*: social correlates of /ɹ/ in Singapore English. *International Journal of the Sociology of Language*, 218, 1–24.

Tan, Y.-Y. (2016). The Americanization of the phonology of Asian Englishes: evidence from Singapore. In G. Leitzner, A. Hashim, and H. G. Wolf (eds.), *Communicating with Asia*, pp. 120–34. Cambridge: Cambridge University Press.

Tayao, M. L. G. (2004). Philippine English: phonology. In B. Kortmann, E. W. Schneider, K. Burridge, R. Meshtrie, and C. Upton (eds.), *A Handbook of Varieties of English 1: Phonology* (pp. 1047–59). Berlin: Mouton de Gruyter.

Tent, J. (2001). Yod deletion in Fiji English: phonological shibboleth or L2 English. *Language Variation and Change*, 13, 161–91.

Tent, J. and Mugler, F. (2004). Fiji English: phonology. In B. Kortmann, E. W. Schneider, K. Burridge, R. Meshtrie, and C. Upton (eds.), *A Handbook of Varieties of English 1: Phonology* (pp. 750–79). Berlin: Mouton de Gruyter.

Thomas, E. R. (2004). Rural Southern white accents. In B. Kortmann, E. W. Schneider, K. Burridge, R. Meshtrie, and C. Upton (eds.), *A Handbook of Varieties of English 1: Phonology* (pp. 300–24). Berlin: Mouton de Gruyter.

Thomas, E. R. (2007). Phonological and phonetic characteristics of African American Vernacular English. *Language and Linguistics Compass*, 1(5), 450–75.

Thomas, E. R. (2010). *Sociophonetics: An Introduction*. Basingstoke: Palgrave Macmillan.

Thomas, E. R. and Carter, P. M. (2006). Prosodic rhythm and African American English. *English World-Wide*, 27(3), 331–55.

Thomas, E. R. and Reaser, J. (2004). Delimiting perceptual cues used for the ethnic labeling of African American and European American voices. *Journal of Sociolinguistics*, 8(1), 54–87.

Toefy, T. (2017). Revisiting the KIT-split in Coloured South African English. *English World-Wide*, 38(3), 336–63.

Tolkien, J. R. R. and Gordon, E. V. (1967). *Sir Gawain and the Green Knight*. Oxford: Oxford University Press.

Torgersen, E. and Szakay, A. (2011). A study of rhythm in London: is syllable-timing a feature of Multicultural London English? *University of Pennsylvania Working Papers in Linguistics*, 17(2), 165–74.

Trudgill, P. (2004). *New Dialect Formation: The Inevitability of*

Colonial Englishes. Edinburgh: Edinburgh University Press.

Trudgill, P. and Gordon, E. (2006). Predicting the past: dialect archaeology and Australian English rhoticity. *English World-Wide,* 27(3), 235–46.

UNESCO (2011). *UNESCO Project: Atlas of the World's Languages in Danger.* Paris: United Nations Educational, Scientific and Cultural Organization.

Upton, C. (2015). British English. In J. Levis and M. Reed (eds.), *The Handbook of English Pronunciation* (pp. 251–4). Chichester: Wiley Blackwell.

van der Hulst, H. and Smith, N. (1988). The variety of pitch-accent systems. In H. van der Hulst and N. Smith (eds.), *Autosegmental Studies on Pitch Accent* (pp. i–xiv). Dordrecht: Foris.

van Rooy, B. (2004). Black South African English: phonology. In B. Kortmann, E. W. Schneider, K. Burridge, R. Meshtrie, and C. Upton (eds.), *A Handbook of Varieties of English 1: Phonology* (pp. 943–52). Berlin: Mouton de Gruyter.

van Rooy, B. (2014). English in South Africa. In M. Filppula, J. Klemola, and D. Sharma (eds.), *The Oxford Handbook of World Englishes* (pp. 1–25). Oxford: Oxford University Press.

Warren, P. (2015). *Uptalk: The Phenomenon of Rising Intonation.* Cambridge: Cambridge University Press.

Warren, P. and Bauer, L. (2004). Maori English: phonology. In B. Kortmann, E. W. Schneider, K. Burridge, R. Meshtrie, and C. Upton (eds.), *A Handbook of Varieties of English 1: Phonology* (pp. 614–24). Berlin: Mouton de Gruyter.

Warren, P. and Britain, D. (2000). Intonation and prosody in New Zealand English. In A. Bell and K. Kuiper (eds.), *New Zealand English* (pp. 11–22). Amsterdam: John Benjamins.

Wee, L. (2004). Singapore English: phonology. In B. Kortmann, E. W. Schneider, K. Burridge, R. Meshtrie, and C. Upton (eds.), *A Handbook of Varieties of English 1: Phonology* (pp. 1017–33). Berlin: Mouton de Gruyter.

Wee, L.-H. (2016). Tone assignment in Hong Kong English. *Language,* 92(2), 67–87.

Wells, J. (1982). *Accents of English.* Cambridge: Cambridge University Press.

Wells, J. (2008). *Longman Pronunciation Dictionary* (3rd ed.). Harlow: Pearson Longman.

Wells, S. and Taylor, G. (eds.) (1986). *William Shakespeare. The Complete Works: Original-Spelling Edition.* Oxford: Clarendon Press.

Widyalankara, R. C. (2015). Acoustic characteristics of three vowels of Standard Sri Lankan English. *International Journal of Science and Research,* 4(8), 235–42.

Wiltshire, C. and Harnsberger, J. (2006). The influence of Gujarati and Tamil L1s on Indian English: a preliminary study. *World Englishes*, 25, 91–104.

Wiltshire, C. and Moon, R. (2003). Phonetic stress in Indian English vs. American English. *World Englishes*, 22(3), 291–303.

Wolf, H.-G. (2010). East and West African Englishes: differences and commonalities. In A. Kirkpatrick (ed.), *The Routledge Handbook of World Englishes* (pp. 197–201). Abingdon: Routledge.

Wolfram, W. and Dannenberg, C. (1999). Dialect identity in a tri-ethnic context: the case of Lumbee American Indian English. *English World-Wide*, 20, 179–216.

Wolk, L., Abdelli-Beruh, N. B., and Slavin, D. (2012). Habitual use of vocal fry in young adult female speakers. *Journal of Voice*, 26(3), e111–e116.

Wood, E. (2003). TH-fronting: the substitution of f/v for θ/ð in New Zealand English. *New Zealand English Journal*, 2003, 50–6.

Wood, J. (2015). Top languages of the Internet, today and tomorrow: https://unbabel.com/blog/top-languages-of-the-internet.

Woodman, S. (2017, 3 November). 11 pop songs in Indigenous languages you need to listen to. *Culture Trip*: https://theculturetrip.com/south-america/articles/11-pop-songs-in-indigenous-languages-you-need-to-listen-to.

Yuasa, I. P. (2010). Creaky voice: a new feminine voice quality for young urban-oriented mobile American women. *American Speech*, 85(3), 315–37.

Zerbian, S. (2013). Prosodic marking of narrow focus across varieties of South African English. *English World-Wide*, 34, 26–47.

Zwicker, E. and Terhardt, E. (1980). Analytical expressions for critical-band rate and critical bandwidth as a function of frequency. *Journal of the Acoustical Society of America*, 68, 1523–4.

Index